Lecture Notes in Artificial Intelligence 12058

Subseries of Lecture Notes in Computer Science

Series Editors

Randy Goebel
University of Alberta, Edmonton, Canada
Yuzuru Tanaka
Hokkaido University, Sapporo, Japan
Wolfgang Wahlster
DFKI and Saarland University, Saarbrücken, Germany

Founding Editor

Jörg Siekmann
DFKI and Saarland University, Saarbrücken, Germany

More information about this series at http://www.springer.com/series/1244

Louise A. Dennis · Rafael H. Bordini ·
Yves Lespérance (Eds.)

Engineering
Multi-Agent Systems

7th International Workshop, EMAS 2019
Montreal, QC, Canada, May 13–14, 2019
Revised Selected Papers

 Springer

Editors
Louise A. Dennis (iD)
University of Liverpool
Liverpool, UK

Yves Lespérance
University of York
Toronto, ON, Canada

Rafael H. Bordini (iD)
Pontifical Catholic University of Rio Grande
do Sul
Porto Alegre, Brazil

ISSN 0302-9743   ISSN 1611-3349 (electronic)
Lecture Notes in Artificial Intelligence
ISBN 978-3-030-51416-7   ISBN 978-3-030-51417-4 (eBook)
https://doi.org/10.1007/978-3-030-51417-4

LNCS Sublibrary: SL7 – Artificial Intelligence

This Springer imprint is published by the registered company Springer Nature Switzerland AG
The registered company address is: Gewerbestrasse 11, 6330 Cham, Switzerland

Preface

The International Workshop on Engineering Multi-Agent Systems (EMAS) is intended as a venue for the presentation of results and discussion about the theory and practice of engineering intelligent agents: theories, architectures, languages, platforms, methodologies for designing, implementing, and running intelligent agents.

Despite a substantial existing body of knowledge about the design and development of multi-agent systems (MAS), the systematic development of large-scale and open MAS still poses many challenges. Even though various languages, models, techniques, and methodologies have been proposed in the literature, researchers and developers are still faced with fundamental questions pertaining to their engineering.

The overall purpose of the workshop is to facilitate the cross-fertilization of ideas and experiences from various fields in order to:

- Enhance our knowledge and expertise in MAS engineering and improve the state of the art
- Define new directions for MAS engineering that are useful to practitioners, arising from results and recommendations from different research areas
- Investigate how practitioners can use, or need to adapt, established methodologies for the engineering of large-scale and open MAS
- Encourage masters and PhD students to become involved in and contribute to the area

Like previous editions, the 7th edition of the workshop was co-located with AAMAS (International Conference on Autonomous Agents and Multiagent Systems) which in 2019 took place in Montreal, Canada. The previous editions were held in Stockholm (LNAI 11375), Sao Paulo (LNAI 10738), St. Paul (LNAI 8245), Paris (LNAI 8758), Istanbul (LNAI 9318), and Singapore (LNAI 10093).

In 2019, the EMAS workshop was held as a two-day event. In total, 20 papers were submitted to the workshop and after a double review process, 13 papers were selected for inclusion in this volume. All the contributions were revised by taking into account the comments received and the discussions at the workshop.

Finally, we would like to thank the members of the Program Committee for their work during the reviewing phase, as well as the members of the EMAS Steering Committee for their valuable suggestions and support. We also acknowledge the EasyChair conference management system for its support in the workshop organization process.

March 2020

Louise A. Dennis
Rafael H. Bordini
Yves Lespérance

Organization

Organizing Committee

Rafael H. Bordini	PUCRS, Brazil
Louise A. Dennis	The University of Liverpool, UK
Yves Lespérance	York University, Canada

Program Committee

Natasha Alechina	Universiteit Utrecht, The Netherlands
Matteo Baldoni	Università degli Studi di Torino, Italy
Bita Banihashemi	York University, Canada
Luciano Baresi	Politecnico di Milano, Italy
Cristina Baroglio	Università degli Studi di Torino, Italy
Clara Benac Earle	Universidad Politécnica de Madrid, Spain
Olivier Boissier	École Nationale Supérieure des Mines de Saint-Étienne, France
Daniela Briola	Università degli Studi di Torino, Italy
Moharram Challenger	Universiteit Antwerpen, The Netherlands
Andrei Ciortea	University of St. Gallen, Switzerland
Stefania Costantini	Università degli Studi dell'Aquila, Italy
Fabiano Dalpiaz	Universiteit Utrecht, The Netherlands
Mehdi Dastani	Universiteit Utrecht, The Netherlands
Lavindra de Silva	University of Cambridge, UK
Jürgen Dix	Technische Universität Clausthal, Germany
Angelo Ferrando	The University of Liverpool, UK
Lars-Åke Fredlund	Universidad Politécnica de Madrid, Spain
Maíra Gatti de Bayser	IBM Research, Brazil
Adriana Giret	Universidad Politécnica de Valencia, Spain
Jorge J. Gómez-Sanz	Universidad Complutense de Madrid, Spain
Zahia Guessoum	Université de Reims Champagne-Ardenne, France
James Harland	RMIT University, Australia
Vincent Hilaire	Université Bourgogne Franche-Comté, France
Koen Hindriks	Vrije Universiteit, The Netherlands
Benjamin Hirsch	Degussa Bank, Germany
Tom Holvoet	Katholieke Universiteit Leuven, Belgium
Jomi Fred Hübner	Universidade Federal de Santa Catarina, Brazil
Nadin Kokciyan	University of Edinburgh, UK
João Leite	Universidade Nova de Lisboa, Portugal
Brian Logan	University of Nottingham, UK
Viviana Mascardi	Università degli Studi di Genova, Italy
Phlippe Mathieu	Université de Lille, France

John-Jules Meyer	Universiteit Utrecht, The Netherlands
Frédéric Migeon	Université Paul Sabatier Toulouse, France
Jörg P. Müller	Technische Universität Clausthal, Germany
Enrico Pontelli	New Mexico State University, USA
Alessandro Ricci	Università di Bologna, Italy
Valieria Seidita	Università delgi Studi di Palermo, Italy
Jaime Sichman	Universidade deo São Paulo, Brazil
Viviane Silva	Universidade Federal Fluminente, Brazil
Wamberto Vasconcelos	University of Aberdeen, UK
Jørgen Villadsen	Danmarks Tekniske Universitet, Denmark
Gerhard Weiss	Maastricht University, The Netherlands
Rym Zalila Wenkstern	The University of Texas at Dallas, USA
Michael Winikoff	Victoria University of Wellington, New Zealand
Neil Yorke-Smith	Technische Universiteit Delft, The Netherlands

Steering Committee

Matteo Baldoni	Università degli Studi di Torino, Italy
Rafael Bordini	PUCRS, Brazil
Mehdi Dastani	Universiteit Utrecht, The Netherlands
Jurgen Dix	Technische Universität Clausthal, Germany
Amal El Fallah-Seghrouchni	Sorbonne Université, France
Brian Logan	University of Nottingham, UK
Jörg P. Müller	Technische Universität Clausthal, Germany
Alessandro Ricci	Università di Bologna, Italy
M. Birna van Riemsdijk	Universiteit Twente, The Netherlands
Danny Weyns	Katholieke Universiteit Leuven, Belgium
Michael Winikoff	Victoria University of Wellington, New Zealand
Rym Zalila-Wenkstern	The University of Texas at Dallas, USA

Additional Reviewers

Bita Banihashemi
Davide Dell'Anna
Ben Wright

Contents

Multi-agent Interaction and Organization

Accountability and Responsibility in Multiagent Organizations for Engineering Business Processes

Matteo Baldoni[1] , Cristina Baroglio[1] (✉) , Olivier Boissier[2] ,
Roberto Micalizio[1] , and Stefano Tedeschi[1]

[1] Dipartimento di Informatica, Università degli Studi di Torino, Turin, Italy
{matteo.baldoni,cristina.baroglio,
roberto.micalizio,stefano.tedeschi}@unito.it
[2] Laboratoire Hubert Curien UMR CNRS 5516, Institut Henri Fayol,
MINES Saint-Etienne, Saint-Etienne, France
Olivier.Boissier@emse.fr

Abstract. Business processes realize a business goal by coordinating the tasks undertaken by multiple interacting parties. Given such a distributed nature, Multiagent Organizations (MAO) are a promising paradigm for conceptualizing and implementing business processes. Yet, MAO still lack of a systematic method for reporting to the right agents feedback about success or failure of a task. We claim that an explicit representation of accountability and responsibility assumptions provides the right abstractions to engineer MAO for supporting the execution of business processes. Basing our programming approach on MAO, we present two accountability patterns for developing accountable agents. To illustrate this approach we use the JaCaMo multi-agent programming platform.

1 Introduction

Weske [37] defines a business process as "a set of activities that are performed in coordination in an organizational and technical environment. These activities jointly realize a business goal." In general, a business goal is achieved by breaking it up into sub-goals, which are distributed to a number of actors. Each actor carries out part of the process, and depends on the collaboration of others to perform its task. One limit of business processes is that they integrate, at the same abstraction level, both the business logic and the interaction logic (message passing). This makes their reuse problematic; whenever different coordination schemas are to be enacted the business process must be revised. Moreover, since message exchanges lie at the level of data, it is difficult to assess the correctness of individual processes in isolation.

Multiagent Systems (MAS), and in particular models for multi-agent organizations (MAO), are promising candidates to supply the right abstractions to

L. A. Dennis et al. (Eds.): EMAS 2019, LNAI 12058, pp. 3–24, 2020.
https://doi.org/10.1007/978-3-030-51417-4_1

keep processes linked together in a way that allows reasoning about the correctness of the overall system in terms of goals rather than of messages. In order to provide the right support to BPs, however, MAO need to be enriched with a systematic way to properly handle feedback about the execution, that can be provided by the agents as explanation of goal achievement or non-achievement. Such feedback will generally be of interest to (and should be handled by) some agent which is not the one that can produce it. Consequently, for connecting agents in the right way, an appropriate "infrastructure" needs to be devised. A significant special case of feedback provision and management is exception handling. In this case, the availability of means for reporting the produced feedback (the exception) to an agent that is capable of tackling it, would increase system robustness. Approaches for modeling exceptions in a multiagent setting have been proposed in the literature (see, e.g., [26,30,34]) but no consensus has been reached yet on how accommodating the usual exception handling semantics with the peculiar properties of agents, such as autonomy, openness, heterogeneity, and encapsulation.

In this paper we argue that the notions of *accountability* and *responsibility* are useful both to the general purpose of enriching MAOs with a feedback infrastructure, and to the specific purpose of accommodating exception handling.

In [2] a proposal was made to use accountability and responsibility relationships to state the rights and duties of agents in the organization, given the specification of a normative structures. From this understanding, we define what it means for an agent to be accountable when taking on responsibilities in the execution of part of a business process. That is, we address the notion of accountability from a computational perspective and study its role as a design property [5].

In the following we use these concepts as tools to systematize and guide the design and development of the agents. We, then, exemplify how such concepts can be introduced in multi-agent systems realized in JaCaMo, where agents will execute under a normative organization expressing a business process as accountability and responsibility relationships among agents. We use, as a reference example, a revisited version of the Incident Management case from the BPMN examples by the OMG [29]. The implementation is available at https://di.unito.it/incident.

2   Enhancing MAOs to Better Support BPs

The Incident Management case [29] (Fig. 1), that we use as a running example, models the interaction between a customer and a company for the management of a problem that was reported by the customer. It involves several actors. The Customer reports the problem to a Key Account Manager who, based on her experience, can either solve the problem directly or ask for the intervention of First-level Support. The problem can, then, be recursively treated by different support levels until, in the worst case, it is reported to the software developer.

Goal distribution over a group of processes bears strong similarities with proposals from research on MAO. In the Incident Management example, the business aim of the process (to solve the reported problem) is decomposed and distributed over up to five BPMN processes, whose execution requires interaction and coordination–realized in this case through message exchange. Noticeably, as always with business processes, the way in which goals are achieved matters, so the agents that will participate into the organization are expected not only to fulfill their assigned goals but also to respect the business process. Indeed, from an organizational perspective, the "goal" is that the process takes place [1]. As Fig. 1 shows, the case includes treatment of anomalous situations, in terms of message passing. For instance, an issue at the level of Software Developer Support is propagated upwards towards the Customer causing certain activities to occur.

One common limitation of the kind of modularity implemented both by BPs and by MAOs is that the overall process structure of the goal is intended mainly as a way for constraining the agents' autonomy, and not as information provided to support the agents in their work. In particular, MAOs (see, e.g., [11,15]) allow structuring complex organizational goals by functional decomposition, assigning subgoals to the agents. The coordinated execution of subgoals is often supported by a normative specification, with which the organization issues obligations towards the agents (e.g., [9,13,14,18]). However, by focusing merely on the achievement of the assigned sub-goals, agents loose sight of the overall process, and ignore the place their achievement has within the organization. Moreover, agents may have the capability of achieving the assigned goals but in ways that do not fit into the process specification and, importantly, in presence of anomalous situations, the organization has no explicit mechanism for sorting out what occurred, for a redress. On the other hand, in BPMN the relationships between the actors are just *loosely* modeled via message exchange, there is no explicit representation of the legitimate expectations each actor has about the others, and there is no notion of responsibility.

So, even if MAOs solve part of the limits of BPMN, what is actually missing is the agents' awareness of their part in the organization, not only in terms of the goals assigned to them, but also (and equally important) in terms of the relationships they have with the others, of their mutual dependencies, and, more broadly, of the dependence of the organization on its members for what concerns the *realization of the business process*. We claim that the notions of *responsibility* and *accountability* serve this purpose in an intuitive, yet effective way. A first conceptualization of how these notions can be used in the context of distributed processes is discussed in [7], here we discuss more practical, programming aspects.

Responsibility and Accountability

According to Dubnick [16], accountability "emerges as a primary characteristic of governance where there is a sense of agreement and certainty about the legitimacy of expectations between the community members." So, within an institutional frame, accountability manifests as rules, through which authority

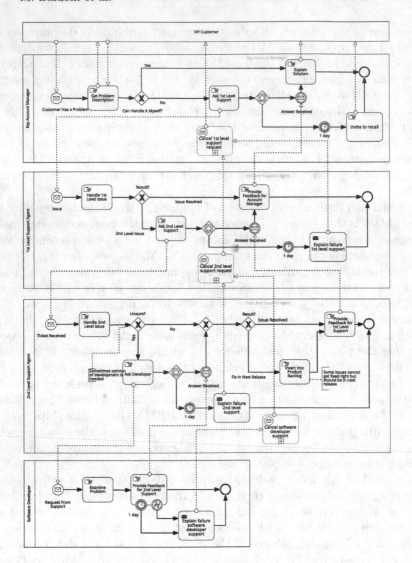

Fig. 1. The incident management BPMN diagram enriched with exception management.

is "controlled" so that it is exercised in appropriate ways. In human organizations, it amounts to the enactment of mechanisms for dealing with expectations/uncertainty. In complex task environments where multiple, diverse and conflicting expectations arise, it is a means for managing an otherwise chaotic situation. Further on this line [20], accountability implies that some actors have the right to hold other actors to a set of standards, to judge whether they have fulfilled their responsibilities in light of these standards, and to impose sanctions if they determine that these responsibilities have not been met. They explain that accountability presupposes a relationship between power-wielders and those holding them accountable, where there is a general recognition of the legitimacy of (1) the operative standards for accountability and (2) the authority of the parties to the relationship (one to exercise particular powers and the other to hold them to account).

Concerning responsibility, [36] proposes an ontology relating six different responsibility concepts (capacity, causal, role, outcome, virtue, and liability), that capture: doing the right thing, having duties, an outcome being ascribable to someone, a condition that produced something, the capacity to understand and decide what to do, something being legally attributable. In the context of Information Systems (in particular, access rights models and rights engineering methods), the meta-model ReMMO [17] represents responsibility as a unique charge assigned to an agent, and in the cited literature most of the authors acknowledge that responsibility aims at conferring one or more obligation(s) to an actor (the responsibility owner). As a consequence, this causes a moral or formal duty, in the mind of the responsibility owner, to justify the performance of the obligation to someone else, by virtue of its accountability.

Business processes show all the characteristics of accountability settings: they represent an agreed behavior, they involve tasks the interacting parties should take care of, they introduce expectations on how they will act, and require some kind of governance in order for the process to be enacted. However, the lack of an adequate representation of the involved relationships obfuscates the accountability [28] (that results hidden into some kind of collective responsibility), possibly compromising the functioning of the system as a whole or its governance. As Thompson [35] explains, typically adopted solutions, like applying hierarchical or collective forms of responsibility, are wanting, and personal responsibility approaches, based on some weak causal connection between individuals and events, should be preferred.

It is worth noting that accountability and responsibility are not primitive concepts. Rather, they are properties that emerge in carefully designed software systems. This means that when we use accountability/responsibility for system engineering, we actually constrain the ways in which software is designed and developed.

3   Engineering MAO with Accountability/Responsibility

Since the proposal is set into the JaCaMo framework [9] (whose organization model is briefly introduced below), the coordinated execution of the agents is regulated by obligations, that are issued by the organization. In [2], it is proposed to improve the specification of an organization by complementing the functional decomposition of the organizational goal with a set of accountability and responsibility specifications. As in that proposal, we denote by $R(x, q)$ and $A(x, y, r, u)$ responsibility and accountability relationships, respectively. $R(x, q)$ expresses an expectation on any agent playing role x on pursuing condition q (x is in position of being considered to control q). Instead, $A(x, y, r, u)$ expresses that x, the account-giver (a-giver), is accountable towards y, the account-taker (a-taker), for the condition u when the condition r (*context*) holds. We see u in the context of r as an agreed standard which brings about expectations inside the organization. Accountability relationships can be collected in a set **A**, called an *accountability specification*. The organization designer will generally specify a set of accountability specifications which is denoted by $\mathbb{A}$.

In the following, besides introducing JaCaMo organizational model, we discuss a programming pattern for accountable agents, that is, for programming agents that provide an account of their conduct both when they succeed in achieving their goals, and when, for some reason, they fail in the attempt. We will also describe a full implementation of JaCaMo with accountabilities.

JaCaMo Organisation Model

JaCaMo [9] is a conceptual model and programming platform that integrates agents, environments and organizations. A MAS in JaCaMo consists of an agent organization, realized through MOISE [24], involving Jason [10] autonomous agents, working in a shared, artifact-based environment, programmed in CArtAgO [32]. A Jason agent consists of a set of plans, each having the structure *triggering_event* : ⟨*context*⟩ ← ⟨*body*⟩. On occurrence of *triggering_event* (belief/goal addition or deletion), under the circumstances given by *context*, the course of action *body* should be taken.

MOISE includes an organization modeling language and an organization management infrastructure [23]. The specification of an organization is decomposed into three dimensions. The *structural* dimension specifies roles, groups and links between roles in the organization. The *functional* dimension is composed of one (or more) scheme capturing how the global organizational goal is decomposed into subgoals, and how subgoals are grouped in sets, called missions, to be distributed to the agents. The *normative* dimension binds the two previous dimensions by specifying roles' permissions and obligations for missions.

JaCaMo provides various kinds of organizational artifacts that allow encoding the state and behavior of the organization, in terms of groups, schemes and normative states. Obligations are issued on the basis of a normative program, written in NOPL [22]. Norms have the form $id : \phi \rightarrow \psi$, where id is a unique identifier of the norm; ϕ is a formula that determines the activation condition for the norm; and ψ is the consequence of the activation of the norm (either a failure or the generation of an obligation). Obligations, thus, have a well-defined lifecycle. Once created, an obligation is *active*. It becomes *fulfilled* when the agent, to which the obligation is directed, brings about the state of the world specified by the obligation before a given deadline. An obligation is *unfulfilled* when the agent does not bring it about before the deadline. When the condition ϕ does not hold anymore, the state of the obligation becomes *inactive*.

Accountability/Responsibility Specifications in the JaCaMo Organisation Model

To specify the execution conditions that are object of accountability and responsibility, we use the event-based linear logic called *precedence logic* [33]. Such a language allows modeling complex expressions, under the responsibility of many agents, whose execution needs to be coordinated. The interpretation deals with occurrences of events along runs (i.e., sequence of instanced events). Event occurrences are assumed non-repeating and persistent: once an event has occurred, it has occurred forever. The logic has three primary operators: '$\vee$' (choice), '$\wedge$' (concurrence), and '·' (before). The *before* operator constrains the order with which two events must occur: $a \cdot b$ means that a must occur before b, but not necessarily one immediately after the other. If e be an event, $\overline{e}$ (the complement of e) is also an event. Initially, neither e nor $\overline{e}$ hold. On any run, either of the two may occur, not both. Complementary events allow specifying situations in which an expected event e does not occur, either because of the occurrence of an opposite event, or because of the expiration of a time deadline.

  Residuation, inspired by [27,33], allows tracking the progression of temporal logic expressions, hopefully arriving to completion of their execution. The *residual* of a temporal expression q with respect to an event e, denoted as q/e, is the remainder temporal expression that would be left over when e occurs, and whose satisfaction would guarantee the satisfaction of the original temporal expression q. Residual can be calculated by means of a set of rewrite rules. The following equations are due to Singh [27,33]. Here, r is a sequence expression, and e is an event or $\top$. Below, Γ_u is the set of literals and their complements mentioned in u. Thus, for instance, $\Gamma_e = \{e, \overline{e}\} = \Gamma_{\overline{e}}$ and $\Gamma_{e \cdot f} = \{e, \overline{e}, f, \overline{f}\}$. We have that:

$$
\begin{aligned}
0/e &\doteq 0 & \top/e &\doteq \top \\
(r \wedge u)/e &\doteq ((r/e) \wedge (u/e)) & (r \vee u)/e &\doteq ((r/e) \vee (u/c)) \\
(e \cdot r)/e &\doteq r, \text{ if } e \notin \Gamma_r & (e' \cdot r)/e &\doteq 0, \text{ if } e \in \Gamma_r \\
r/e &\doteq r, \text{ if } e \notin \Gamma_r & (\overline{e} \cdot r)/e &\doteq 0
\end{aligned}
$$

Using the terminology in [2], we say that an event e is *relevant* to a temporal expression p if that event is involved in p, i.e. $p/e \not\equiv p$. Let us denote by e a sequence $e_1, e_2, \ldots, e_n$ of events. We extend the notion of residual of a temporal expression q to a sequence of events e as follows: $q/e = (\ldots ((q/e_1)/e_2)/\ldots)/e_n$. If $q/e \equiv \top$ and all events in e are relevant to q, we say that the sequence e is an *actualization* of the temporal expression q (denoted by $\widehat{q}$).

Agent Programming Patterns

In general, given a set of accountability specifications $\mathbb{A}$, and a set of responsibility assumptions $\mathbf{R}$ (responsibility distribution), the organization is properly specified when the *accountability fitting* "$\mathbf{R}$ *fits* $\mathbb{A}$" (denoted by $\mathbf{R} \rightsquigarrow \mathbb{A}$) holds [2]. This happens if $\exists \, \mathbf{A} \in \mathbb{A}$ such that $\forall \, A(x, y, r, u) \in \mathbf{A}$, $\exists \, R(x, q) \in \mathbf{R}$ such that, for some actualization $\widehat{q}$, $(u/r)/\widehat{q} \equiv \top$. Fitting has a relevant impact on *organization design*: When $\mathbf{R} \rightsquigarrow \mathbb{A}$ holds, any set of agents playing roles into the organization (consistently with $\mathbf{R}$ and one accountability specification $\mathbf{A} \in \mathbb{A}$) can actually accomplish the organizational goal. Thus, fitting also provides a guide for developing agents that are *accountable by design*, because it expresses (1) what each agent is engaged to achieve, by fulfilling its responsibilities, and (2), through accountability, how this achievement is related to that process which is the goal of the organization.

In other words, $\mathbf{R} \rightsquigarrow \mathbb{A}$ provides a specification the agents must explicitly conform to, when enacting organizational roles. When an agent enacts some role in an organization, it declares to be aware of all the responsibilities that come with that role, and by accepting them it declares to adhere to the fitting exposed by the organization itself. That is, the accountability fitting exposed by an organization specifies the requirements that agents, willing to play roles in that organization, must satisfy.

When an agent accepts a responsibility it accepts to *account for* the achievement, or failure, of some state of interest. In our metaphor, thus, an agent acts with the aim of preparing the account it should provide. In this way, we reify the cited "sense of agreement and certainty about the legitimacy of expectations between the community members" which otherwise remains implicit both in business processes and in MAO. Leveraging these concepts for developing agents provides interesting advantages from a software engineering point of view.

As a tool for realizing the accountability fitting that specifies an organization, we are about to introduce a *programming pattern* that allows realizing accountable agents, but before we need to identify the portion of fitting involving each single individual.

Definition 1. *Given the fitting $\mathbf{R} \rightsquigarrow \mathbb{A}$, and a role x in its scope, the projection of the fitting over role x is defined as $\mathbf{R}_x \rightsquigarrow \mathbb{A}_x$ where $\mathbf{R}_x \equiv \{R(x,q)|R(x,q) \in \mathbf{R}\}$, and $\mathbf{A}_x \equiv \{A(x,y,r,u)|A(x,y,r,u) \in \mathbf{A}\}$, and where for every $A(x,y,r,u) \in \mathbf{A}_x$, there is $R(x,q) \in \mathbf{R}_x$, such that $(u/r)/\widehat{q} \equiv \top$ holds for some actualization $\widehat{q}$ of q.*

Thanks to a proper programming pattern, for all agents playing role x, the fitting projection over role x can be mapped into a number of Jason plans that will be part of the actual agent program. We provide such a pattern in a way that suits JaCaMo (i.e. the setting of this work) by exploiting the obligations implied by accountabilities and responsibilities [20]. The pattern is expressed in AgentSpeak(ER) [31] because it allows encapsulating a set of plans into a same context that, in our case, depends on x player being accountable towards another agent y about some condition q, and will be adopted until for some reason it drops its responsibility inside the organization (e.g. the agent leaves the organization). More in details, AgentSpeak(ER) extends Jason by introducing two types of plans: *g-plans* and *e-plans*. G-plans encapsulate the strategy for achieving a goal and can be further structured into sub-plans. Besides triggering events and contexts, g-plans include a goal condition, specifying until when the agent should keep pursuing the goal. E-plans are defined in the scope of a g-plan, and embody the reactive behavior to adopt while pursuing the g-plan's goal.

Definition 2 (Pattern Specification). *The fitting relationship represented by each pair* $\langle R(x,q),\ A(x,y,\ r,u)\rangle$ *in* $\boldsymbol{R}_x \leadsto \boldsymbol{A}_x$, *is mapped into an AgentS-peak(ER) g-plan according to the following pattern:*

$+!be\_accountable(x,\ y,\ q) <: drop\_fitting(x,\ y,\ q)$ {

    $+obligation(x,\ q)\ :\ r \wedge c$ **Well-Doing e-plan**

    $<- body_q.$

    $+oblUnfulfilled(x,\ q)\ :\ r \wedge c'$ **Wrong-Doing e-plan**

    $<- body_f.$

}

Such that: (1) $body_q$ *satisfies the* fitting-adherence *condition (see below); (2)* $body_f$ *includes the sending of an explanation for the failure from x to y.*

The agent will perceive certain events as events it should tackle, by means of some behavior of its own, thanks to the part of its identity that is provided by the organizational role it plays. The agent will also be aware of its social position both (1) by knowing which other agents will have the right, under certain conditions, to ask for an account and (2) by including specific behavior for building such an account. The two e-plans encode the proactive behavior of an agent assuming a responsibility. From that moment on, and until the responsibility is not dropped, the agent starts reacting to obligations in accordance to the accountability relationship specified in the fitting.

Well-Doing e-Plan. The first e-plan is triggered when the specified obligation is issued by the normative organization. That will be the usual obligation a Jason agent receives from the $\mathcal{M}$OISE organization when it is time to pursue a particular goal. The context expression, $r \wedge c$, is satisfied when condition r activating the agent accountability holds together with some possibly empty condition c: a local condition that encodes the possibility for the agent to have multiple well-doing e-plans to react to the same obligation, i.e. multiple ways to achieve a same result in different (local) circumstances (e.g., a 1st Level Support Agent could decide to handle a task directly or ask to 2nd Level Support). Condition c allows the developer to discriminate between these alternatives, if any. It's worth noting that if multiple alternative e-plans with different c are present, the developer must take care of defining such conditions so that for each obligation issued, at least one e-plan is always triggered. Due to the accountability fitting the agent has accepted, the body of the plan(s) ($body_q$) must, then, be such to satisfy the responsibility assumption represented by the pair $\langle R(x,q), A(x,y,r,u)\rangle$. That is, the plan body has to satisfy the following *fitting-adherence* condition.

Definition 3 *(Fitting-adherence). Let* $[body_q]_u$ *denote the set of sequences of events generated by the execution of* $body_q$, *restricted to the events that are relevant for the progression of* u. $body_q$ *satisfies the* fitting-adherence *condition if:* $\exists$ *sequence* $s \in [body_q]_u$ *such that* $s \equiv \hat{q}$ *and* $(u/r)/\hat{q} \equiv \top$.

Note that fitting adherence requires the agent to be just able to activate at least one actualization s of q, not all of them. In other words, the agent needs to be able to perform at least one of the possibly many ways for carrying out q. The rationale is that any actualization of q generates a sequence of events that brings the condition u/r to $\top$; hence, it is sufficient for an agent to implement one actualization in order to meet its responsibility. As we have discussed above, an accountable agent provides an account of its conduct. Sometimes, the account of an agent that behaved as expected will be evident to the interested agents from the way in which it operated in the environment [19]. In this case, the obligation to give an account for the satisfaction of an obligation is implicitly resolved by satisfying the very same obligation, and there is no need to explicitly capture the obligation to provide an account. When, however, it is not possible to see the agent's operations as a proof, an explicit account should be provided also for the well-doing case. This, for instance, happens when there is the need of reporting facts that occur in one context, but are meaningful also in others where they are not directly observable by the involved parties, see e.g., [4]. It is also the case in which an agent's behavior requires some certification for having been performed up to some standard.

Wrong-Doing e-Plan. The second pattern allows agents to provide accounts also in the case they did not complete a task, for some reason. The triggering event, *oblUnfulfilled*, is generated by the MOISE organization when a previously issued obligation has been left unsatisfied. The context of the pattern is again a condition that is true when the accountability is activated (i.e., r holds), and when some local condition c' is satisfied. $body_f$, this time, has to produce an account about the failure. We can think of such an account as an explanation that the agent produces so that another agent, possibly the a-taker y, can use it to resume the execution, thus managing the exception. The correct use of the pattern guarantees, by design, that exceptional events, when occurring, are reported to the agents who can handle them properly. Accountability fulfills this purpose because, by nature, it brings about an obligation on the a-giver to give an account of what it does. The account, then, can be used by the a-taker to recover, when possible, from the exceptional situation. Under this respect, the account should be provided in terms that can be understood by all the interested agents in the organization. This aspect, however, is strongly domain dependent. As well as in the positive pattern, the agent will produce an account by modifying its environment in a way that is meaningful for the agents that have to capture and interpret it. Along this line, a promising approach to the synthesis of an account is discussed in [12].

4   Shaping Business Processes as Accountable Agents in JaCaMo

In JaCaMo [9] the state of an organization is encoded in terms of group instances, that map agents to the roles they play, and scheme instances, that allow tracing which goals have been achieved and which are ready for pursue. By exploiting these instances, the organization issues proper obligations to the agents. Due to the declarative nature of scheme instances, agents can autonomously decide how to satisfy their obligations. They are, however, held to notify the organization about the completion of their tasks by means the special directive *goalAchieved*.

When implementing a business process as a JaCaMo organization, one has to be aware of a substantial difference between the two underlying paradigms. A business process describes an activity flow where choices, upon alternative execution branches, depend on the *data* produced by the activities performed that far. Instead, in JaCaMo each organization generally has a complex goal, whose structure is provided as a functional decomposition into subgoals, *overlooking the data dimension*. The functional decomposition is used to track and guide the execution, understanding when a sub-goal is to be pursued and emitting the correspondant obligation.

The implementation of business processes through JaCaMo organizations, thus, requires some special treatment, especially for what concerns the BPMN gateways, where choices upon data are taken. Specifically, we capture these gateways and their alternative branches as *special goals* within the functional decomposition. Considering a choice, the goals amounting to the various alternatives are mutually exclusive: the achievement of one of such alternative goals determines a specific execution path that constrains the evolution of the remainder of the social scheme. This stratagem allows incorporating, at least in part, within a functional decomposition the execution flow based on data. A dedicated *manager* agent will be in charge of satisfying the obligations issued upon such special goals.

Having this in mind, the following steps provide a guideline to map a number of interacting business processes into a JaCaMo organization.

1. For each process, a corresponding *manager* role in the organization is defined. The agent(s) playing this role will have to decide on the alternative branches to choose in the process execution;
2. For all the activities in a process, suitable *worker* roles in the organization are defined. These roles will be played by the agents in charge of executing the activities;
3. For each process:
   - A group collecting the manager and all the workers involved in the process is defined;
   - A social scheme is created to organize the activities as a goal decomposition tree[1]. Corresponding missions are defined, to be assigned to roles of the group in charge of the process by defining corresponding norms;
4. For each set of activities to be executed in sequence, the corresponding goals are added to the social scheme by means of the "sequence" operator;

---

[1] Here, we restrict our attention to processes that do not include loops; otherwise it would not be possible to express them as decomposition trees.

5. For each set of activities to be executed without strict ordering, the corresponding goals are added to the social scheme by means of the "parallel" operator;

6. If a choice is present inside a process, a corresponding goal is added to the social scheme by means of the "choice" operator. Each subgoal represents a possible course of action (alternative branch). Every alternative in the choice should include a goal, encoding the chosen path to be assigned to the process manager. Depending on which goal will be achieved by the manager, the execution will follow a branch or another;

7. If a process sends a message that makes another process start, the message should be sent to the process manager, which, as a consequence, will instantiate the social scheme corresponding to the process;

8. If a process includes waiting for a message from another process to proceed, a corresponding goal is added to the social scheme and assigned to the manager; such goal is to be set as achieved only after the message is received. The introduction of this goal is necessary to ensure the coordination, and synchronization during the execution, of the social schemes corresponding to the two processes.

Example 1 (Incident Management as a JaCaMo Organization). Let us now explain how the Incident Management scenario can be mapped into a JaCaMo organization by applying these steps. For the sake of simplicity, we will just consider the Key Account Manager process. First, we introduce a manager role *am* and, for each activity in the process, we define a corresponding worker. aw_1, for instance, will be in charge of *get-description*, aw_2 will be in charge of *explain-solution*, and so on. As a further step we define a Key Account group collecting *am* and all of its workers. At the beginning of the execution, the customer agent *c* will send a message to *am* reporting the problem. As a consequence the agent playing role *am* will instantiate a scheme that will be assigned to this group and will encompass the overall Key Account Manager process. The root goal of such scheme will be assigned to *am* that, in order to satisfy it, will have to manage the successful execution of the social scheme.

Figure 2 shows the scheme available for instantiation to *am* that represents the possible courses of actions during the execution of the Key Account Manager process. Subgoals in a sequence are anticipated by a number denoting the position of the goal in the sequence. Goals including a choice are underlined. The picture also shows how goals are grouped together into missions and which agents such missions are assigned to (through norms). The scheme is to be instantiated as soon as a problem to be solved is reported. Indeed, we map the scheme instantiation to *report-problem*. As a consequence, the obligation to achieve *get-description* will be issued to the corresponding worker aw_1. After the successful achievement of *get-description*, two obligations under a choice will be issued towards *am*: the former related to the *can-handle* goal and the latter to *cannot-handle*. Depending on the result of the previous activity (i.e., whether the problem requires further support or can be handled at that level), *am* will decide to achieve either one of the two goals, the choice made by *am* thus con-

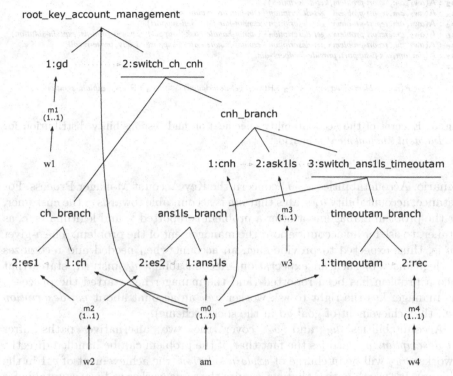

Fig. 2. Social scheme realizing the Key Account Manager process.

strains the subsequent obligations that will be generated. In the former case, the normative system will simply issue the obligation to *explain-solution*, while in the latter it will issue the obligation to ask support to the first level. In the second case, after a request for support has been made, again two options are available to the manager. If an answer is received from the first level support, the solution has to be explained; in this case *am* will achieve *answer-from-fls*. On the contrary, if a feedback is not received after one day, causing a timeout in the BPMN diagram, an invitation to recall will be sent to the customer. ∎

4.1 Adding Accountabilities and Responsibilities

The approach described above is applied to the three remaining processes in the example, whose translation in JaCaMo is not discussed here for the sake of simplicity. The organization specification we obtain can, then, be enriched with an accountability specification that allows us to capture BPMN exceptions.

Example 2 (Incident Management with Accountabilities). Figure 3 shows an excerpt of an accountability specification $\mathbf{A}_{incident}$ for the incident management

a_1 : A($am, c, report\text{-}problem, problem\text{-}management$)
a_2 : A($aw_1, am, report\text{-}problem, get\text{-}description$)
a_3 : A($aw_2, am, report\text{-}problem \cdot get\text{-}description \cdot can\text{-}handle, explain\text{-}solution$)
a_4 : A($aw_3, am, report\text{-}problem \cdot get\text{-}description \cdot cannot\text{-}handle, ask\text{-}fl\text{-}support$)
a_5 : A($aw_2, am, report\text{-}problem \cdot get\text{-}description \cdot cannot\text{-}handle \cdot ask\text{-}fl\text{-}support \cdot answer\text{-}from\text{-}fls, explain\text{-}solution$)
a_6 : A($aw_4, am, report\text{-}problem \cdot get\text{-}description \cdot cannot\text{-}handle \cdot ask\text{-}fl\text{-}support \cdot 1\text{-}day, invite\text{-}recall$)
a_7 : A($flm, am, ask\text{-}fl\text{-}support, provide\text{-}feedback\text{-}am_{fls}$)
...

r_1 : R($am, problem\text{-}management$) r_2 : R($aw_1, get\text{-}description$) r_3 : R($aw_2, explain\text{-}solution$)
...

Fig. 3. Excerpt of the accountability specification and responsibility distribution for the *Incident Management* scenario.

scenario. Accountabilities a_1–a_6 concern the Key Account Manager Process. For instance, accountability a_1 states that am is accountable towards c, the customer, for the problem management after a problem is reported [2], and legitimates c, as a-taker, to ask for an account about the management of the problem. The a-giver am is, thus, expected to provide such an account when needed and recognizes the legitimacy of such an expectation. Accountability a_2, instead, states that once a problem has been reported (and the manager has started the process), the manager has the right to ask worker aw_1 an account about *get-description* (i.e., the achievement of goal gd in the social scheme).

Accountabilities a_3 and a_4 cover the two alternative paths after *get-description*. a_3 encodes the fact that, if the problem can be handled directly, a worker aw_2 will be in charge of *explain-solution* (the achievement of es1 in the scheme). It's worth noting that we require the same worker to be accountable for that activity also in another context, as stated by a_5. This accountability states that the same worker should account for *explain-solution* if the problem cannot be handled directly, too, but in case support has been requested to the first level support and an answer provided (see es2 in the social scheme). Accountability a_4, conversely, states that another worker aw_3 is accountable for asking further support if the problem cannot be handled. Accountability a_4, finally, is related to the *invite-recall* condition. Should an answer not be received within one day from the first level, a worker aw_4 would be accountable for the *invite-recall* (rec in the social scheme) activity. These accountabilities, together, completely characterize the Key Account Manager process[3]. Accountability a_7, in turn, involves the manager of the first level of support. It states that such agent is accountable towards am for providing a feedback, once a request for support has been made. In this case, too, such accountability will be supported by further accountabil-

[2] Event *problem-management* corresponds to the achievement of *root_key_account_management*, the root goal of the social scheme in Fig. 2.

[3] It's worth noting that we do not define any accountability relationship w.r.t. *can-handle, cannot-handle, answer-from-fls* and *1-day*. Such goals are the ones whom the manager is in charge of and would encompass the manager both as a-giver and a-taker.

ity relationships, not reported here, built upon the First Level Support process'
decomposition tree.   ■

Accountabilities capture only a part of the organization specification. A business process captures an activity flow, that is, it involves activities that are meant
to be executed. It is, thus, necessary to identify those agents which are in position of being capable of carrying out the various activities. This is captured by
responsibilities. For instance, in the case at issue, due to r_1, am is responsible
of *problem-management*.

In order for the organization to execute the business process so that a full
account can be provided, it is necessary to bind accountabilities with responsibility assumptions. This is done by the accountability fitting, that, by exploiting
the pattern described in the previous section, enables the implementation of
exception handling mechanisms. With the accountability specification $\mathbf{A}_{incident}$
as a basis, the designer can identify a suitable responsibility distribution which
fits it. An excerpt of an acceptable one is reported in Fig. 3. It is easy to verify
that for each $a_i \in \mathbf{A}_{am}$ there is a $r_j \in \mathbf{R}_{am}$ which fits it. For instance, if we
consider a_1 and r_1, we have that:

$$problem\text{-}management/report\text{-}problem/problem\text{-}management \equiv \top$$

We now briefly explain how, by relying on an accountability specification
and on the programming patterns described above, it is possible to implement
an agent playing role am whose behavior is accountable for a given set of relevant
events.

Example 3 (Key Account Manager with Exceptions). First of all, an agent playing role am has to instantiate the scheme for the Key Account Manager (see
Fig. 2) process as soon as it receives a request from a customer. This behavior is
realized through the following plan:

```
1 +problem
2     : group(g1,key_account_management_group,GrArtId)
3     <- createScheme(am_sch, scheme_key_account_management, SchArtId);
4        addScheme(am_sch)[artifact_id(GrArtId)].
```

Let us now show how to apply the programming pattern based on the
accountability specification discussed above. For instance, let us consider the
fitting $r_1 \rightsquigarrow a_1$: the agent being developed must be in control of responsibility r_1 (i.e., *problem-management*), and assume an accountable behavior towards
the customer for *problem-management*, when condition *report-problem* holds. We
recall that we map *problem-management* to the achievement of the root goal of
the scheme in Fig. 2, and *report-problem* to the instantiation of such scheme.
Following the pattern described in the previous section, the programmer should
define in the agent body a g-plan containing *well-doing* and *wrong-doing* e-
plans. However, the actual framework we use for implementation is JaCaMo,
where Jason still implements AgentSpeak(L) rather than AgentSpeak(ER), and
hence it is not possible to define nested e-plans. The *well-doing* and *wrong-doing*
e-plans are therefore rendered by means of two plain Jason plans. The fitting
involving $r_1 \rightsquigarrow a_1$ is implemented by the following plans:

```
1  account_to(ATaker,root_key_account_management)  :- play(ATaker,customer,g1).
2
3  +obligation(Ag,_,What,_)
4     :  .my_name(Ag) &
5        done(am_sch,root_key_account_management,Ag)=What &
6        scheme(am_sch,_,SchId)
7     <- goalAchieved(root_key_account_management)[artifact_id(SchId)].
8
9  +oblUnfulfilled(O)
10    :  .my_name(Ag) &  obligation(Ag,_,What,_) = O &
11       done(am_sch,root_key_account_management,Ag)=What &
12       scheme(am_sch,_,SchId) &
13       account_to(ATaker,root_key_account_management)
14    <- .send(ATaker, tell, reason_for_failure).
```

The first plan, in particular, realizes the *well-doing* part of the pattern. Recalling Definition 2, the plan is triggered as soon as an obligation concerning the scheme root is issued (Line 3). The obligation object (*What*) is the satisfaction of the organizational goal root_key_account_management –corresponding to the *problem-management* condition in Fig. 3. Indeed, in JaCaMo, the achievement of an organizational goal fulfills the corresponding obligation. Then, as requested by the pattern, the contexts of both plans must include the conditions specified in a_1. In JaCaMo we represent this condition (*report-problem*) in terms of scheme being instantiated (see Line 6). Considering the fitting-adherence condition, we have that r is *report-problem*, and u is *problem-management*. Thus $q \equiv u/r$ is just *problem-management*. The plan for *well-doing* needs to include some actions that amount to such an event. In this setting we consider the event to be occurred as soon as the corresponding organizational goal is set as achieved. This is trivially true in the example (see Line 7). The second plan, at Line 9, instead, deals with the *wrong-doing* part of the pattern. Should, for any reason, the obligation be unfulfilled, the agent, by virtue of its accountability, must provide a motivation about the unsatisfaction of the obligation. In this case, a proper message encoding the explanation for the failure is sent to the account-taker agent (see Line 14). Note that the agent could be equipped with multiple plans covering the wrong-doing part to take care of several causes of failures each with its own specific explanation to be sent to a precise a-taker. These two plans ensure that, no matter how the scheme execution evolves, c will always receive an account from *am*, consisting either of a notification about the achievement of *problem-management*, or of an explanation for the failure. ∎

The implementation of an agent playing the *am* role must also take into account that the agent is the manager of the Key Account Manager process. Therefore the agent should also be provided with plans for *controlling the execution flow*, that is, for deciding which goals amount to choices it needs to satisfy.

Example 4 (Controlling Alternatives). In our case there are two alternative goals ch and cnh, whose achievement corresponds to *can-handle* and *cannot-handle*), respectively. Specifically, after goal *get-description* gets accomplished, the organizational infrastructure will issue two obligations at the same time, directed to *am*, one for ch and one for cnh. The agent will then decide to achieve either one of the two goals depending on data that are not captured by the functional decomposition, but that may be accessible to the agent by means of artifacts. The two plans below realize this behavior:

```
1   +obligation(Ag,_,What,_)
2      : .my_name(Ag) &
3        done(am_sch,ch,Ag)=What &
4        description(easy_problem) &
5        scheme(am_sch,_,SchId)
6      <- goalAchieved(ch)[artifact_id(SchId)].
7
8   +obligation(Ag,_,What,_)
9      : .my_name(Ag) &
10       done(am_sch,cnh,Ag)=What &
11       description(hard_problem) &
12       scheme(am_sch,_,SchId)
13     <- goalAchieved(cnh)[artifact_id(SchId)].
```

If the problem is directly solvable, the agent will fulfill the first obligation, otherwise it will satisfy the second one. The choice of which obligation is actually fulfilled obviously affects the subsequent activities. In the second case, in fact, a new sub-process needs to be activated, that is, a new functional scheme needs to be instantiated.   ∎

Worker agents for the Key Account Manager process are developed in a similar way, following the pattern. For instance, let's consider the agent playing the aw_1 role. The agent is involved in $r_2 \rightsquigarrow a_2$. The well-doing and wrong-doing plans are defined as follows:

```
1   account_to(ATaker,gd) :- play(ATaker,key_account_manager,g1).
2
3   +obligation(Ag,_,What,_)
4      : .my_name(Ag) &
5        done(am_sch,gd,Ag)=What &
6        play(C,customer,g1)
7      <- .send(C,tell,ask_description).
8
9   +description(D)
10     : account_to(AccountTaker,gd) &
11       scheme(am_sch,_,SchId)
12     <- .send(AccountTaker,tell,description(D));
13       goalAchieved(gd)[artifact_id(SchId)].
14
15  +oblUnfulfilled(O)
16     : .my_name(Ag) & obligation(Ag,_,What,_) = O &
17       done(am_sch,gd,Ag)=What &
18       scheme(am_sch,_,SchId) &
19       not description(D) &
20       account_to(ATaker,root_key_account_management)
21     <- .send(ATaker, tell, no_description_from_customer).
```

The first two plans, together, realize the well-doing part of the pattern. The first plan (Line 3), in particular, is triggered as soon as the obligation to achieve gd is issued. As a result, the agent will send a message to the customer asking for a description. To successfully complete the activity and achieve its goal, however, the agent has to wait for an answer. The second plan, at Line 9, is triggered as soon as a description is received from the customer and finally leads to the achievement of the organizational goal (Line 13). Before that, nonetheless, the worker forwards the description to his manager (Line 12), which will then use it to decide how to proceed, as explained above. The plan at Line 15 realizes the wrong-doing part of the pattern. In this case, should the obligation become unfulfilled because of a missing response from the customer (see Line 19), the account sent to the a-taker would be `no_description_from_customer` (see Line 21).

The *am* agent, in turn, being account-taker in several accountability relationships, can include also some plans to handle the accounts provided by its account-givers, both in positive and negative circumstances. Let's consider again a_2. As explained above, in case of failure, aw_1 would send a precise message to *am*. The very same message can be used as triggering event in a recovery plan, as follows:

```
1 no_description_from_customer
2    : play(C,customer,g1) &
3      scheme(am_sch,_,SchId)
4 <- .send(C,tell,please_answer);
5    resetGoal(gd)[artifact_id(SchId)].
```

A possible way to deal with the failure could be to send a further message to the customer and reset the failed goal. In general considerations related to how to handle a failure are strictly domain dependent.

Notably, considering the accountability specification as a requirement, the actual implementation of the system results robust. The accountable *am* for instance, to satisfy the requirement of being accountable, must be capable, on the one side, of capturing exceptions from other agents, and on the other side, of providing an account to its a-taker (i.e., the customer).

5   Conclusions

We have discussed how the agent technology can be exploited for the implementation of business processes modeled as BPMN schema. To be effective, however, agent system needs to take care of some peculiarities of business processes, as for instance, the handling of exceptional events, that possibly interrupt the execution of a process. Approaches for modeling exceptions in a multi-agent setting have been proposed (see, e.g., [26,30,34]), but these proposal fall short in addressing the typical properties of MAS, such as autonomy, openness, heterogeneity, and encapsulation.

In this paper we have coped with BPMN exceptions by relying on the notions of accountability and responsibility as elements for the specification of an agent organization. In addition, we have proposed a programming pattern for developing agents that adhere to such a specification. The pattern, when applied systematically, brings along positive consequences. First of all, an accountability/responsibility specification provides a programmer with all the relevant information for developing an agent that is aware of the process as characterization of the goal (see [1]). In fact, while a responsibility distribution is a coverage of the functional decomposition, an accountability specification conveys how the agents contribute to the process. Hence, the accountabilities provide the programmer with a behavioral specification agents must satisfy.

Our approach is specular to [38], whose aim is to determine whether a group of agents can be attributed the responsibility for a given goal. Once the responsibility can be attributed to the agents, their accountability is implicitly modeled in the inferred plan. Here, instead, we aim at developing agents that, by construction, satisfy the organization specification. Indeed, an interesting evolution of the present work goes in the direction of an agent-oriented type checking (see e.g., [3]). Having an explicit model of the organization in terms of accountabilities and responsibilities, it would be possible to mechanize a type checking system that verifies whether, at role enacting time, an agent possesses all the necessary plans for role playing.

The proposal moves MAOs closer to other paradigms where exceptions are handled. In the actor model (e.g., [21]), for instance, when an actor cannot handle an exception, it usually reports the exception to its parent actor, which in turns decides to either handle the exception or report it further. In an agent-based system such a scheme is not directly applicable since agents are independent entities, and rarely are related to each other by a parent-child relationship. Accountabilities can fill in this gap: when an obligation is not satisfied, it is reasonable to report the exception to the a-taker. This is achieved quite naturally with the *Wrong-Doing Pattern*, that allows an agent to provide an account for an unsatisfied obligation. Interestingly, the choice "on-the-fly" of which branch to follow, performed by the manager, can be seen as a form of *planning autonomy*: "This type of autonomy dictates if an agent is able (or unable) to create, choose or modify plans to achieve a specific goal" [25]. The integration of this type of autonomy into an organizational model (i.e., $\mathcal{MOISE}$) discussed in [25] opens interesting perspectives in the modeling of BPMN processes for our accountable agents.

Commitment-based protocols (e.g., [39]), as well as standard NorMAS [8], provide alternatives for modeling coordination. Roughly speaking, a commitment is a promise that a debtor does in favor to a creditor that in case some antecedent condition is satisfied, the debtor will bring about a consequent condition. When the antecedent holds, the commitment is detached, and amounts to an obligation on the debtor to bring about the consequent. When the consequent is no longer achievable, the commitment is violated. In such a case, the creditor has the right to complain against the debtor, the creditor cannot hold the debtor to provide an explanation. This lack of information hampers both the understanding of what has occurred, and any attempt of recovery from the failure. However, commitments have the power of enforcing accountability when properly used. For instance, the ADOPT protocol [6] establishes an accountability relationship, expressed via a commitment-based protocol, between an organization and its agents.

References

1. Adamo, G., Borgo, S., Di Francescomarino, C., Ghidini, C., Guarino, N.: On the notion of goal in business process models. In: Ghidini, C., Magnini, B., Passerini, A., Traverso, P. (eds.) AI*IA 2018. LNCS (LNAI), vol. 11298, pp. 139–151. Springer, Cham (2018). https://doi.org/10.1007/978-3-030-03840-3_11
2. Baldoni, M., Baroglio, C., Boissier, O., May, K.M., Micalizio, R., Tedeschi, S.: Accountability and responsibility in agent organizations. In: Miller, T., Oren, N., Sakurai, Y., Noda, I., Savarimuthu, B.T.R., Cao Son, T. (eds.) PRIMA 2018. LNCS (LNAI), vol. 11224, pp. 261–278. Springer, Cham (2018). https://doi.org/10.1007/978-3-030-03098-8_16
3. Baldoni, M., Baroglio, C., Capuzzimati, F., Micalizio, R.: Type checking for protocol role enactments via commitments. J. Auton. Agents Multi-Agent Syst. **32**(3), 349–386 (2018). https://doi.org/10.1007/s10458-018-9382-3
4. Baldoni, M., Baroglio, C., Chopra, A.K., Singh, M.P.: Composing and verifying commitment-based multiagent protocols. In: Wooldridge, M., Yang, Q. (eds.) Proceedings of 24th International Joint Conference on Artificial Intelligence, IJCAI 2015, Buenos Aires, Argentina, 25th July–31th 2015 (2015). http://ijcai-15.org/
5. Baldoni, M., Baroglio, C., May, K.M., Micalizio, R., Tedeschi, S.: Computational accountability. In: Chesani, F., Mello, P., Milano, M. (eds.) Deep Understanding and Reasoning: A Challenge for Next-Generation Intelligent Agents, URANIA 2016, vol. 1802, pp. 56–62. CEUR Workshop Proceedings, Genoa, December 2016. http://ceur-ws.org/Vol-1802/paper8.pdf
6. Baldoni, M., Baroglio, C., May, K.M., Micalizio, R., Tedeschi, S.: Computational accountability in MAS organizations with ADOPT. Appl. Sci. **8**(4), 489 (2018)
7. Baldoni, M., Baroglio, C., Micalizio, R.: Goal distribution in business process models. In: Ghidini, C., Magnini, B., Passerini, A., Traverso, P. (eds.) AI*IA 2018. LNCS (LNAI), vol. 11298, pp. 252–265. Springer, Cham (2018). https://doi.org/10.1007/978-3-030-03840-3_19
8. Boella, G., van der Torre, L.W.N., Verhagen, H.: Introduction to normative multi-agent systems. In: Normative Multi-Agent Systems. Dagstuhl Seminar Proceedings, vol. 07122 (2007)
9. Boissier, O., Bordini, R.H., Hübner, J.F., Ricci, A., Santi, A.: Multi-agent oriented programming with JaCaMo. Sci. Comput. Program. **78**(6), 747–761 (2013). https://doi.org/10.1016/j.scico.2011.10.004
10. Bordini, R.H., Hübner, J.F., Wooldridge, M.: Programming Multi-Agent Systems in AgentSpeak Using Jason. Wiley, Chichester (2007)
11. Corkill, D.D., Lesser, V.R.: The use of meta-level control for coordination in distributed problem solving network. In: Bundy, A. (ed.) Proceedings of the 8th International Joint Conference on Artificial Intelligence (IJCAI 1983), pp. 748–756. William Kaufmann, Los Altos (1983)
12. Cranefield, S., Oren, N., Vasconcelos, W.W.: Accountability for practical reasoning agents. In: Lujak, M. (ed.) AT 2018. LNCS (LNAI), vol. 11327, pp. 33–48. Springer, Cham (2019). https://doi.org/10.1007/978-3-030-17294-7_3
13. Dastani, M., Tinnemeier, N.A., Meyer, J.J.C.: A programming language for normative multi-agent systems. In: Handbook of Research on Multi-Agent Systems: Semantics and Dynamics of Organizational Models, pp. 397–417. IGI Global (2009)
14. Dignum, V.: A model for organizational interaction: based on agents, founded in logic. Ph.D. thesis, Utrecht University (2004). Published by SIKS

15. Dignum, V.: Handbook of Research on Multi-Agent Systems: Semantics and Dynamics of Organizational Models (2009)
16. Dubnick, M.J., Justice, J.B.: Accounting for accountability. Annual Meeting of the American Political Science Association, September 2004. https://pdfs.semanticscholar.org/b204/36ed2c186568612f99cb8383711c554e7c70.pdf
17. Feltus, C.: Aligning access rights to governance needs with the responsability Meta-Model (ReMMo) in the frame of enterprise architecture. Ph.D. thesis, University of Namur, Belgium (2014)
18. Fornara, N., Viganò, F., Verdicchio, M., Colombetti, M.: Artificial institutions: a model of institutional reality for open multiagent systems. Artif. Intell. Law **16**(1), 89–105 (2008). https://doi.org/10.1007/s10506-007-9055-z
19. Garfinkel, H.: Studies in Ethnomethodology. Prentice-Hall Inc., Englewood Cliffs (1967)
20. Grant, R.W., Keohane, R.O.: Accountability and abuses of power in world politics. Am. Polit. Sci. Rev. **99**(1), 29–43 (2005)
21. Haller, P., Sommers, F.: Actors in scala - concurrent programming for the multi-core era. Artima (2011)
22. Hübner, J.F., Boissier, O., Bordini, R.H.: A normative organisation programming language for organisation management infrastructures. In: Padget, J., et al. (eds.) COIN -2009. LNCS (LNAI), vol. 6069, pp. 114–129. Springer, Heidelberg (2010). https://doi.org/10.1007/978-3-642-14962-7_8
23. Hübner, J.F., Boissier, O., Kitio, R., Ricci, A.: Instrumenting multi-agent organisations with organisational artifacts and agents. Auton. Agents Multi-Agent Syst. **20**(3), 369–400 (2010). https://doi.org/10.1007/s10458-009-9084-y
24. Hübner, J.F., Sichman, J.S., Boissier, O.: Developing organised multiagent systems using the MOISE+ model: programming issues at the system and agent levels. Int. J. Agent-Oriented Softw. Eng. **1**(3/4), 370–395 (2007)
25. Maia, A., Sichman, J.S.: Explicit representation of planning autonomy in MOISE organizational model. In: 7th Brazilian Conference on Intelligent Systems, BRACIS 2018, São Paulo, Brazil, 22–25 October 2018, pp. 384–389 (2018)
26. Mallya, A.U., Singh, M.P.: Modeling exceptions via commitment protocols. In: Proceedings of the Fourth International Joint Conference on Autonomous Agents and Multiagent Systems, AAMAS 2005, pp. 122–129. ACM (2005)
27. Marengo, E., Baldoni, M., Baroglio, C., Chopra, A., Patti, V., Singh, M.: Commitments with regulations: reasoning about safety and control in REGULA. In: Proceedings of the 10th International Conference on Autonomous Agents and Multiagent Systems (AAMAS), vol. 2, pp. 467–474 (2011)
28. Nissenbaum, H.: Accountability in a computerized society. Sci. Eng. Ethics **2**(1), 25–42 (1996). https://doi.org/10.1007/BF02639315
29. Object Management Group: BPMN specification - business process model and notation (2018). http://www.bpmn.org/. Accessed 08 Nov 2018
30. Platon, E., Sabouret, N., Honiden, S.: An architecture for exception management in multiagent systems. Int. J. Agent-Oriented Softw. Eng. **2**(3), 267–289 (2008)
31. Ricci, A., Bordini, R.H., Hübner, J.F., Collier, R.: AgentSpeak(ER): an extension of AgentSpeak(L) improving encapsulation and reasoning about goals. In: AAMAS, pp. 2054–2056. International Foundation for Autonomous Agents and Multiagent Systems, Richland/ACM (2018)
32. Ricci, A., Piunti, M., Viroli, M., Omicini, A.: Environment programming in CArtAgO. In: El Fallah Seghrouchni, A., Dix, J., Dastani, M., Bordini, R.H. (eds.) Multi-Agent Programming, pp. 259–288. Springer, Boston, MA (2009). https://doi.org/10.1007/978-0-387-89299-3_8

33. Singh, M.P.: Distributed enactment of multiagent workflows: temporal logic for web service composition. In: Proceedings of the Second International Joint Conference on Autonomous Agents & Multiagent Systems, AAMAS 2003, Melbourne, Victoria, Australia, 14–18 July 2003, pp. 907–914. ACM (2003)
34. Souchon, F., Dony, C., Urtado, C., Vauttier, S.: Improving exception handling in multi-agent systems. In: Lucena, C., Garcia, A., Romanovsky, A., Castro, J., Alencar, P.S.C. (eds.) SELMAS 2003. LNCS, vol. 2940, pp. 167–188. Springer, Heidelberg (2004). https://doi.org/10.1007/978-3-540-24625-1_10
35. Thomson, J.J.: Remarks on causation and liability. Philos. Public Aff. **13**(2), 101–133 (1984)
36. Vincent, N.A.: A structured taxonomy of responsibility concepts. In: Vincent, N., van de Poel, I., van den Hoven, J. (eds.) Moral Responsibility. LOET, vol. 27, pp. 15–35. Springer, Dordrecht (2011). https://doi.org/10.1007/978-94-007-1878-4_2
37. Weske, M.: Business Process Management: Concepts, Languages, Architectures. Springer, Heidelberg (2007). https://doi.org/10.1007/978-3-540-73522-9
38. Yazdanpanah, V., Dastani, M.: Distant group responsibility in multi-agent systems. In: Baldoni, M., Chopra, A.K., Son, T.C., Hirayama, K., Torroni, P. (eds.) PRIMA 2016. LNCS (LNAI), vol. 9862, pp. 261–278. Springer, Cham (2016). https://doi.org/10.1007/978-3-319-44832-9_16
39. Yolum, P., Singh, M.P.: Commitment machines. In: Meyer, J.-J.C., Tambe, M. (eds.) ATAL 2001. LNCS (LNAI), vol. 2333, pp. 235–247. Springer, Heidelberg (2002). https://doi.org/10.1007/3-540-45448-9_17

From Goals to Organisations: Automated Organisation Generator for MAS

Cleber Jorge Amaral[1,2]([⊠])(iD) and Jomi Fred Hübner[2]([⊠])(iD)

[1] Federal Institute of Santa Catarina (IFSC), São José, SC, Brazil
cleber.amaral@ifsc.edu.br
[2] Federal University of Santa Catarina (UFSC), Florianópolis, SC, Brazil
jomi.hubner@ufsc.br
http://www.ifsc.edu.br/, http://pgeas.ufsc.br/en/

Abstract. An explicit organisational structure helps entrants in open multi-agent systems (MAS) to reason about their positions in the organisation for cooperating to achieve mutual goals. In spite of its importance, there are few studies on automatic organisation generators that create explicit organisational structures. This paper introduces *GoOrg*, a proposal for automatic design of organisations. Our approach considers as inputs a goal decomposition tree (*gdt*) and user preferences. From the *gdt* with annotations such as necessary skills to achieve organisational goals, predicted workload and throughput, *GoOrg* creates roles in the form of an organisational chart. The main challenge is to define strategies to search the space of all organisational structures for those that can achieve the goals respecting constraints and taking into account user preferences. We can, for instance, prefer a *flatter* or a *taller* structure, more specialist or more *generalist* roles, and we can accept *matrix connections* or not.

Keywords: Automated organisation design · Organisational chart · Organisational structure · Open Multi-Agent Systems

1 Introduction

The organisational structure is an instrument used to split, organise and coordinate activities of Multi-Agent System (MAS) organisations. It reflects authority relations and responsibility for goals, providing a typical way to assign tasks to agents [15]. An explicit organisational structure helps agents to know where they fit relatively to others and which are their responsibilities [9,13,21,30].

Currently, there are a few studies on the automatic design of organisations that generates explicit organisational structures [10,17,23,26]. Although seminal, there is still space for improvements, for instance, automating the roles creation process. This paper presents an ongoing work in the context of a PhD thesis that proposes *GoOrg*, an automated organisation generator which takes a

---

Supported by Petrobras project AG-BR, IFSC and UFSC.

L. A. Dennis et al. (Eds.): EMAS 2019, LNAI 12058, pp. 25–42, 2020.
https://doi.org/10.1007/978-3-030-51417-4_2

goal decomposition tree (*gdt*) and produces as output an organisational chart, i.e., an explicit organisational structure, according to user preferences. The main novelty of our method is its capability of creating roles from the inputs. In this sense, our method may produce a larger range of possible organisational charts.

To discuss the problem and to describe the proposed generator, Sect. 2 presents the concept of automatic organisation design and the state of art of this research area. Section 3 describes the problem, i.e., the challenge we want to overcome. Section 4 presents our organisation generator *GoOrg*. Section 5 describes the research method we are applying in, the status of this research and planned evaluation. Finally, Sect. 6 presents related works and Sect. 7 presents our conclusions.

2   Organisation Design

Pattinson et al. [22] define organisation design as "the problem of choosing the best organisation class - from a set of class descriptions - given knowledge about the organisation's purpose (goal, task, and constraints on the goal) and the environment in which the organisation is to operate". Given necessary input, an organisation generator can give as output organisational aspects, such as, structure, goals definitions, strategy, how leadership will work, which reward system will be used, among others [2]. We have identified three classes of organisation generators in the MAS domain [1].

The first class is the *automated organisation design by task planning*. These generators usually create *problem-driven* organisations, for specific and generally short term purposes [8]. The organisational structure is typically not explicit being an unintended result of a task allocation process. Such generators are focused on solving a given problem by decomposing tasks, allocating them on the available agents [4]. Agents are previously known, and usually, roles are not necessary. The agents generally cooperate by fulfilling their tasks which, when combined, implies in the achievement of global goals.

The second class uses *self-organisation* approaches. In this class, the organisations usually emerge by agents common interest and interactions [13]. Resulting organisations are dynamic, may operate continuously, have overlapping tasks, have no external or central control, and hierarchy and information flow in many directions [32]. The organisational structure is an informal implicit outcome of this bottom-up process. The target of this method is to solve some problem and not precisely to carefully design an organisation [26,28].

Finally, the third class is the *automated explicit organisation generators*. It is focused "on a specification of desired outcomes and the course of actions for achieving them, analysis of the organisational environment and available resources, allocation of those resources and development of organisational structures and control system" [15]. It considers inputs such as organisational goals, available agents, resources and performance targets, producing explicit organisation definitions, which may include roles, constraints, assignments of responsibilities, hierarchy and other relations.

The first class can provide a very efficient way to allocate tasks among agents when the MAS is solving a previously known problem, usually in deterministic environments. However, it may lack the ability to deal with entrants in case of open systems, because it is supposed to know at planning time the available agents. In this sense, a new agent would not know what to do and how to cooperate unless a *replanning* is triggered, which can be computationally heavy.

Whether dealing with uncertainty and dynamic environments, the second class has advantages over other classes, which cannot deal with unpredictable situations [13]. However, in some cases, an entrant of an open system would need to negotiate with other agents his participation what may be slow to accommodate due to message exchanging.

Alternatively, the latter class cares on designing explicit structures which foster entrances and exits [11]. When adopting a role, an entrant receives its responsibilities, starting to cooperate with other organisational members. In many cases, an entrance does not require any extra designing effort since the roles already have assigned tasks. An exit works in the same way. A role, as an abstract description of a position in the system, is a fundamental concept in this class [23].

3   Organisation Design Problem

This research proposes to develop an *automated explicit organisational generator*. We hypothesise that it is possible to create roles from a *gdt* automatically. A *gdt* is a plan to achieve the main goal of the system, which includes operators that ensure that the decomposition satisfaction is equivalent to the main goal satisfaction [24].

In short, our proposal assigns goals to roles in a structured organisational chart taking into consideration some characteristics of the goals such as the ones that have the same parent goal, require the same skills to be performed, have a low predicted workload, etc. Additionally, design preferences can also determine whether to gather goals into a role or not, e.g., whether it is preferred a *flatter* or *taller* organisation; more *specialist* or *generalist* roles, if *matrix relations* are allowed or not, maximum *workload* per agent, etc. Moreover, the predicted throughput associated with a goal may indicate the need for the creation of new hierarchy levels and a *performer index* may imply that the same agent must, or must not, perform some goals.

For example, in a *gdt* for Printed Circuit Board (PCB) production, shown in Fig. 1a, the main goal is decomposed into two sub-goals: *Buy Supplies* and *PCB Assembly*. *Buy Supplies* also has two sub-goals: *Buy Components* and *Buy Other Supplies*. For these sub-goals, the skill *Purchase* is associated, which means that the agent(s) that will perform both *buy* sub-goals must be able to purchase items. The goal *PCB Assembly* has three sub-goals: *Apply Paste*, *Place Components* and *Soldering Components*. The first is associated with the skill *Print*, the second with the skill *Pick and Place* and the latter with the skill *Heat*.

Figure 1b shows a possible organisational chart based on the given *gdt* configured to be more *generalist*. In this example, the sub-goals *Buy Components* and

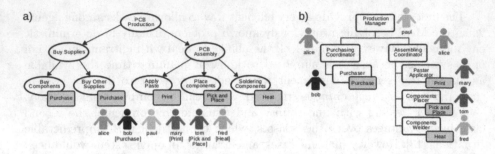

Fig. 1. Automated design for PCB Production. a) Inputs: goals tree and necessary skills. b) Output: organisational chart with the more generalist roles considering inputs.

Buy Other Supplies are assigned to the same role. In this sense, the same agent will perform both *Components* and *Other Supplies* purchases. This created role was placed below the *Purchasing Coordinator* role, as a subordinate.

However, one may ask: "is that solution the best one to choose?". Still, there is no sufficient information to tell whether that structure is suitable or not. For instance, how many PCB's are being produced per hour? How many different models are being produced? Are there other available resources? Any privacy requirement? These questions regard to varying situations in which the chosen structure depends on.

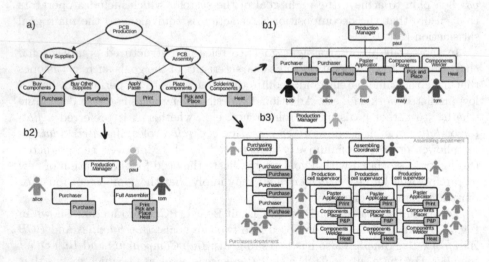

Fig. 2. Which organisational structure should be chosen?

Figure 2 illustrates how diverse can the results be for the same given *gdt*. There is a solution in which only three roles were created in a very generalist and flat organisational structure. Another solution goes in the opposite direction, being very tall (hierarchical) and specialised. In fact, many aspects can influence organisational structures outcomes such as the chained sub-goals, agents' limited skills and goals fulfilment capacity, agents' communication capabilities and privacy needs, and so on [20]. Our proposal intends to address this problem by adding annotations to the goals to generate and choose a suitable organisational structure.

4   Proposed Method

We investigate the use of search algorithms to address the problem of creating and choosing an organisational structure. In this sense, the search space O is composed of all possible organisational charts $o \in O$. Each state o is composed of: (i) a set of role identifiers used in the organisational chart; (ii) the function gr for addressing the set of goals assigned to each role; (iii) the function pr for addressing the parent of each role which represent its immediate superior in the organisational chart where ϵ represents "no parent", so that the root role r has $pr(r) = \epsilon$; and (iv) the function sr for mapping the set of skills in S which are associated with each role[1].

$$o = \langle R, gr, pr, sr \rangle$$
$$gr : R \to 2^G$$
$$pr : R \to R \cup \{\epsilon\}$$
$$sr : R \to 2^S$$

We can thus state that GoOrg searches for an organisational chart $o \in O$ that is suitable for a particular gdt. A gdt is composed of: (i) a set of goal identifiers G; (ii) the function pg that returns the parent of each goal of the tree where ϵ represents "no parent", so that the root goal g has $pg(g) = \epsilon$; and (iii) the function sg that addresses the set of necessary skills to achieve a given goal.

$$gdt = \langle G, pg, sg \rangle$$
$$pg : G \to G \cup \{\epsilon\}$$
$$sg : G \to 2^S$$

The difference of G and the set of goals assigned to roles is the set of not allocated goals nag, where:

$$nag(gdt, o) = gdt.G \smallsetminus \bigcup_{r \in o.R} gr(r)$$

---

[1] In a future work we will add other properties of goals and inputs for *GoOrg*.

4.1   State Transformations

All possible organisations populate the search space. To help the search for organisational charts, we define a transformation relation between two states. Figure 3
represents each of the currently supported transformations in a respective area.
Top and bottom of each area show respectively previous and final states. On
each area, the graph on the left side is a *gdt* with three goals. Grey goals are
the ones that were already assigned, and the black one is the goal that is being
assigned. The graph on the right represents the roles of the organisational chart
that is being created. The information between brackets describes the assigned
goals, and eventually below it has the necessary skills to perform the respective
role. Grey roles already exist, and the black one represents the role which is
being explored for applying transformations.

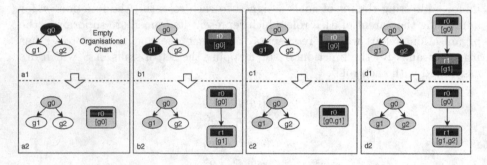

Fig. 3. Supported transformations.

In this illustration, we have: (a) the root goal generates the *root role*; (b)
a sub-goal is assigned to a role to be subordinate of the role that contains its
parent goal; (c) a sub-goal is vertically brought joining to the role that includes
its parent; and (d) the sub-goal is horizontally carried joining to the role
that contains its sibling sub-goal. For instance, the first transformation is illustrated on the area *a*, i.e., Fig. 3a shows the transformation of *a1* into *a2*. In this
case, the root goal $g0$ is going to be assigned and the organisational chart is
empty as represented on part *a1*. After this transformation the chart has the
role r0 as represented by part *a2*. Considering the given input as $pg(g) = \epsilon$, the
transformation for adding the root role is as follows:

$$o = \langle \{\}, \{\}, \{\}, \{\} \rangle$$

$addRootRole(g)$ _____

$$o' = \langle \{\mathbf{r}\}, \{\mathbf{r} \mapsto \{g\}\}, \{\mathbf{r} \mapsto \epsilon\}, \{\mathbf{r} \mapsto sg(g)\} \rangle$$

On the area *b* of Fig. 3 the goal $g1$ was assigned to a new role r1 added as a
subordinate of r0. This transformation is a possible process after the transformation displayed on area *a*. For this case, to add the role r as subordinate of r'

and allocate goal g to r, we require that g is a sub-goal of g' $(pg(g) = g')$ and g' is already allocated to r' $(g' \in gr(r'))$ and have the following transformation:

$$o = \langle R, gr, pr, sr \rangle$$

$$addSubordinate(g, r') \overline{}$$
$$o' = \langle R \cup \{\mathbf{r}\}, gr \cup \{\mathbf{r} \mapsto \{g\}\}, pr \cup \{\mathbf{r} \mapsto \mathbf{r'}\}, sr \cup \{\mathbf{r} \mapsto sg(g)\} \rangle$$

On area c the goal $g1$ was assigned to the existing role $\mathbf{r0}$ joining with the previously assigned goal $g0$. Again it can be illustrated from the state displayed on area a. In this case, there is no new role, the goal to be assigned is joined with a previously assigned goal $g0$. Formally, let the input be $pg(g) = g'$, and considering that $\{r' \mapsto g'\} \in gr$, the transformation for joining a subordinate is as follows:

$$o = \langle R, gr, pr, sr \rangle$$

$$joinASubordinate(g, r') \overline{}$$
$$o' = \langle R, gr \cup \{\mathbf{r'} \mapsto \{g\}\}, pr, sr \cup \{\mathbf{r'} \mapsto sg(g) \rangle$$

Finally, on area d the goal $g2$ was assigned to the existing role $\mathbf{r1}$ joining with the previously assigned goal $g1$. This transformation can be applied from the state illustrated on area b. In this case, let the input be $pg(g) = g''$, there is a goal g' which parent is same, i.e., $pg(g') = g''$, and considering that $\{r'' \mapsto g''\} \in gr$ and $\{r' \mapsto g'\} \in gr$. In this sense, the transformation for joining a pair is as follows:

$$o = \langle R, gr, pr, sr \rangle$$

$$joinAPair(g, r') \overline{}$$
$$o' = \langle R, gr \cup \{\mathbf{r'} \mapsto \{g\}, pr, sr \cup \{\mathbf{r'} \mapsto sg(g)\} \rangle$$

In fact, a goal can be assigned into a role in many ways. Currently, besides the parent relation of assigned goal(s), the associated necessary skills are also being taking into account. The parent is the way the algorithm use to assume relations among goals. A goal that is parent or a sibling of another potentially can be joined in the same role or it can be created as a close role, being a subordinate, according to the relation. The decision to join or not depends on the skills. The role skills must be compatible to be joined, which means, the role must already have the necessary skills of a goal candidate to be joined.

4.2 The Search Tree

To illustrate how the algorithm performs the search, Fig. 4 shows a gdt with three goals. There is a parent goal ($g0$) and two sub-goals ($g1$ and $g2$). To be fulfilled, $g1$ requires the skill $s1$. In the given gdt, two goals have no annotation. In case of $g1$, since it requires the skill $s1$, a role able to perform $s1$ can be assigned to other goals that also requires $s1$ or does not require anything. Of course, a role that has no skills associated cannot perform the goal $g1$.

Fig. 4. Example of a simple goal decomposition tree (*gdt*).

The algorithm creates and visits states, as illustrated in Fig. 5. The transformation of making the *root goal* be the *root role* of the organisational chart generates the first state. As expected, the first transformation has removed the element $g0$ from the list of *to assign* goals, assigning it to the just created role called $r0$. The three possible successors of this state, is to add a role to assign $g1$ as a subordinate of $r0$, add a role for $g2$ as a subordinate of $r0$ or even, bring up $g2$ assigning it to $r0$, joining with other assigned goal(s) since their skills match.

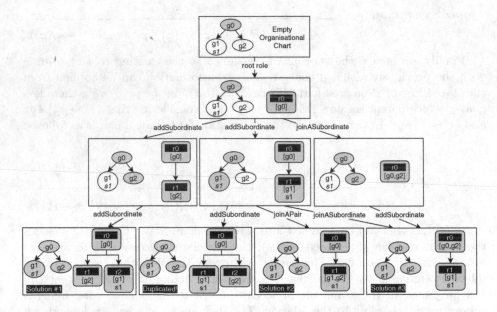

Fig. 5. Step by step of state search with all possible solutions for the given *gdt*.

Applying the transformations in the just created state on the left, where the goal $g2$ was assigned to the role $r1$, it creates a role $r2$ to assign $g1$ putting it as a subordinate of $r0$. This is a target state since all goals were assigned successfully. This state is represented by the area with the label "Solution #1". The next area on the right is a duplicated solution. Indeed, our method ignores the role name, using only assigned goals and parent relation to check redundancy, which is the case of solutions #1 and #2. Still, there are other solutions, as indicated by the other two areas.

Table 1 shows the referred solutions, or target states, generated by this method. The "Solution #1" is the most obvious chart, which is the generation of a role for each goal. The "Solution #2" is the result of joining horizontally the goals $g1$ and $g2$. It is possible because these goals are siblings and also the skills are compatible. The "Solution #3" is the result of joining vertically the goals $g0$ and $g2$. It was possible because the skills are compatible; in this case, both goals have no necessary skills. The arrows represent parent relations among goals.

Table 1. Organisational charts for a simple goals tree having a goal with an annotation

Solution	Chart	Description
#1	r0 [g0] → r1 [g1] s1, r2 [g2]	Organisational chart from adding two subordinates (r1 and r2) to the role r0. The same result would be achieved adding either r1 or r2 as subordinate of r0 and later add the other as a pair. This is the most specialised solution for the given goals tree.
#2	r0 [g0] ↓ r1 [g1,g2] s1	Organisational chart from adding r1 as subordinate of r0 and then joining the goals $g1$ and $g2$ into the role r1. It is possible because before assigning $g2$ the role r1 already had the skills needed by $g2$, which is actually nothing. The other way round would not be possible ($g2$ has not $s1$). It is one of the more generalist solutions for the given goals tree.
#3	r0 [g0,g2] ↓ r1 [g1] s1	Organisational chart from joining $g0$ and $g2$, since $g0$ has all the necessary skills needed by $g2$. Later r1 was added as a subordinate of r0. This solution is the more generalised and one of the more generalist solutions for the given goals tree.

In terms of hierarchy, i.e., the number of levels, all three solutions have the same height. In this case, it is not applicable any preference to choose a *flatter* or *taller* hierarchy. In terms of specialisation, "Solution #1" has more specialist roles, and the other solutions have more generalist roles for the given *gdt*.

Regarding the "Solution #2", one may ask: why $g2$ joined with $g1$ and not the other way round? The reason is that a role created to perform $g2$ does not have any skills associated, and $g1$ needs the skill $s1$ to be performed. Since there is a sub-goal which has a skill associated, it was not possible to assign all the goals into a unique role. It would be the chart with more *generalist* roles and also the *flattest* solution since it would have assigned $g0$, $g1$ and $g2$ into an unique role.

4.3 The Search Algorithm

The proposed method for creating and choosing an organisational structure uses uninformed search also called blind search. We are using the well-known depth

---

Algorithm 1: Depth-limited Search

Data: Organisation o_0
Result: Organisation
Stack n
begin
    $n.push(o_0)$
    while $n \neq \varnothing$ **do**
        $o \leftarrow n.pop()$
        if $nag(gdt, o) = \varnothing$ **then**
            return o
        end
        $n.push(successors(gdt, o))$
    end
    return $null$ // `failed on finding a goal state!`
end

---

state-space search algorithm to illustrate how *GoOrg* is being implemented. As presented in Algorithm 1, it starts adding to a stack the given first state $o_0 \in O$.

It represents the organisation that only has the *root role* created in the organisational chart R. The procedure, over and over, checks if the visiting state is a target state. When the tested state is not a target, the algorithm opens its successors to visit them later. The search ended when all the goals were assigned, i.e., $nag(gdt, o)$ is empty. The limit of this search, regarding the maximum depth of the tree, is G size, in this example it has three levels.

The function to get successors is illustrated in Algorithm 2. It is responsible for generating all possibilities for assigning a goal to roles. Indeed, as illustrated, the algorithm tries to place the goal to be assigned on each existing role applying the supported transformations. The $gr(r)$ function refers to the assigned goals for the specific role r, the same for the functions pr and sr.

The algorithms for transformations are roughly similar. The parent is eventually unknown because joining process may assign multiple goals into a unique role. For this reason, the algorithm tries to find the parent goal of the sub-goal to be allocated into the existing roles. Then $nag(gdt, o)$ is almost a copy, just skipping the current goal. Later the R is copied and also is updated with the just created role. Finally, this new or modified role is considered a possible successor state for further searches.

In the previous example, as illustrated in Fig. 5, all the possible solutions are being shown. However, the algorithm stops after finding the first solution, which remarks on the importance of ordering. The solutions are sorted by *cost* functions which are related to the user preferences. For instance, if a more *generalist* structure is preferred so "pair roles" creation is costly, and joining pairs is cheaper. It makes preferable a chart with fewer pairs as possible.

Algorithm 2: successors

Data: List $\langle G, pg, sg \rangle$ gdt, Organisation o
Result: List (Organisation)
begin
   List suc
   foreach Goal g of $nag(gdt, o)$ **do**
      foreach Role r of $o.R$ **do**
         if $gr(r)$ **contains** $pg(g)$ **then**
            $addSubordinate(r, suc, g)$ // Add as a child role
            if $sg(g) \in sr(r)$ **then**
               | $joinASubordinate(r, suc, g)$ // Join g into *this* role
            end
         else if $pg(g) \in gr(pr(r))$ **and** $sg(g) \in sr(r)$ **then**
            | $joinAPair(r, suc, g)$ // Join goal g into *this* role
         end
      end
   end
   return suc
end

---

5 Future Work

For the next step of our research, the designing process is being split into two phases: the *organisation design* and the *resource allocation* process. With this separation, it is expected that *GoOrg* becomes more suitable to deal with asynchronous changes on the system's resources availability and redesign requests.

On the next step, still on designing process, we will add new inputs such as *predicted workload, necessary resources, performer index, communication topics*, and *predicted throughput*. The *predicted workload* can be used to know how many agents should take the same role or if the same agent can perform more than one role. The *performer index* indicates that the same agent must perform some goals and, contrarily, can tell that two goals cannot be performed by the same agent, for instance in a process in which something is made and must be verified by another agent. With *communication topics* and *predicted throughput*, the hierarchy levels and departmentalisation can be set. These data may also allow enhancing the algorithm to decide when a coordination role can be subtracted, maintained or even new ones created. Other state-space search algorithm and cost functions will be experienced for optimisation purpose and to give more possibilities in terms of structures.

In the sequence, we plan to develop the second process, i.e., *resources allocation*. This process will bind resources and roles. The inputs are *available agents* and *skills, available artefacts* and organisation design *preferences*. This allocation process aims to guarantee that the created structure is viable, i.e., can be well-formed when it runs with the given resources. Finally, the output is an organisational chart with artefacts allocated and agents assigned to roles.

The allocation process can solve some challenges that do not require a redesign. To illustrate it, back to *PCB Production* example, consider that *Buy Components* sub-goal also needs *Electronics Knowledge* skill and the chart has created different roles for purchasing, they can be called *Components Purchaser* and *Other Inputs Purchaser*. Consider that *agent A* and *agent B* play, respectively, the referred roles having all the necessary skills to play both. Consider now that *agent A* left the system and *agent C* has joined it, but this agent has no *Electronics Knowledge* skill. The resource allocation process can move *agent B* to *Components Purchaser* role, assigning *agent C* to *Other Inputs Purchaser* role.

It is also expected to make *GoOrg* suitable to deal with asynchronous changes on the system's resources availability and redesign requests. For instance, with simple changes in the availability of resources, the process can be lighter. However, with more significant changes, for example, on the *gdt*, a complete redesign process may be necessary, a function that can be triggered by the allocation phase. In this solution, as illustrated in Fig. 6b1, the goals were centralised in a unique role which is more *generalist* to achieve more goals with sometimes different associated skills.

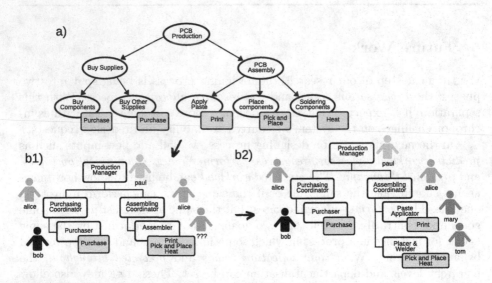

Fig. 6. More generalist organisation chart for the given goals and available agents.

However, the illustration also exemplifies a situation where there is no available agent with all necessary skills to perform the role *Assembler* since it is gathering the skills *Print, Pick and Place* and *Heat*. Figure 6b2 shows a possible solution assuming that an agent *mary* is able to perform *Print* and an agent *tom* can perform *Pick and Place* and *Heat*. In this case, the more *generalist* well-formed organisation is represented by this last chart.

We also expect to create other organisational aspects as outputs, i.e., *Organisational Scheme* and *Organisational Norms*. The former refers to sets of goals allocated to different roles that should be performed by the same agent in a specific sequence. The latter regards especially to general obligations, such as, when adopting a role created by the method *GoOrg* the agent is obligated to perform the missions associated with the referred role.

Finally, we will evaluate our solution using existing domains [3,17,26]. We will first assess the number of input parameters needed by *GoOrg*. With these inputs, we will evaluate the ability of *GoOrg* to design organisations properly. We will vary aspects of the simulated domains presenting them as more static or dynamic, with shorter or longer goals, with more chained or independent goals, etc. These domains will be used to experiment with different user preference parameters.

From a literature perspective, we can select an organisational structure by its features as the potentially better solution for the given problem and scenario. Besides testing this candidate, other organisational structures will be created for comparison purposes. It is expected to fulfil all the goals in less time with the best candidate. The results of the simulations should give us insights to discuss literature perspectives, the adhesion of our method and simulation with literature and potentially *GoOrg* application as a *testbed* for organisational structures.

Among the assumptions we want to evaluate, we have: how the span of control affects the effectiveness of the organisation [13] varying the height of the hierarchy to check the impact on agents communication and coordination [14,30]. In this sense, we can check whether a few number of levels really can lead to faster decisions and lower overhead costs [14,30] and if highly structured organisations are best for repetitive operations [13].

6   Related Work

In the administration area, there are many studies about organisation design, including some frameworks that may help companies and other organisations to design their structures [2,7]. In multi-agent systems, we usually have *manual organisational generators*, i.e., approaches that allow a human to design organisations in a wide variety of structures and other aspects as norms, roles, relations, organisational goals and ontologies, e.g., Moise+ [18], THOMAS [5], STEAM [31] and AALADIN [12].

In spite of having many studies about organisation design, there are still many gaps regarding the full range of disciplines and high complexity of organisations. Considering only automatic organisation generators, the focus of this research, there are few studies.

Automated planning is a research area that has produced many contributions to MAS design. When developing planners for multiple agents, the organisation design is an intrinsic outcome. Some examples of planners able to generate organisations are TÆMS [8] which provides a way to quantitatively describe individual tasks which are performed in shared environments, DOMAP [3] which is a decentralised MAS task planning and Sleight's agent-driven planner [27] using a decentralised Markov Decision Process Model.

Considering bottom-up approaches So [29] did one of the earlier researches on Multi-Agent Systems organisation design. This study over the characterisation of different organisation designs, including self-organised ones and the reconfiguration process for stable organisations. There are several studies over self-organised swarms which use very computationally limited agents [19], and there is no complex coordination mechanism among agents [32].

In the class we have positioned our research, we found only a few works: SADDE [23] and ODML [17], which are algorithms that use as input mathematical models to predict efforts and create an organisational structure; MaSE-e [10] which is a method for creating organisation structures extending the engineering method MaSE; and KB-ORG [25, 26] that takes goals and roles to bind agents and create coordination levels. Although seminal, we think the methods have challenges to overcome, especially regarding inputs in which we are proposing a method to produce *roles* in a way to make inputs easier to handle.

Table 2 gives an overview of *explicit organisation generators* we have found[2]. We are comparing a few features related to inputs, intrinsic features and outputs. The first columns refer to inputs. We start checking whether *goals are inputs* since it gives an idea of the start point of each approach. The *no need roles as inputs* indicates if the generator needs this input. The column *Bound Agents are inputs* represents the capability of the generator to receive as inputs a structure earlier created with bound resources.

Table 2. Comparison among organisation generation methods.

Organisation Generator	Goals are inputs	No need roles as inputs	Bound Ag. are inputs	Has quantitative analysis	Organisations are explicit	Is domain-independent	Creates Roles	Creates Coord. Levels	Creates viable org.	Synthesise Org. Norms	Bind agents and roles	Creates departments	Represents roles in a chart	Does state reorganisation	Does structure reorg.
GoOrg	Y	Y	Y	Y	Y	Y	Y	Y	Y	R	Y	R	Y	R	R
SADDE	Y	-	-	Y	Y	Y	-	-	Y	-	Y	-	-	-	-
MaSE-e	Y	-	Y	Y	Y	Y	-	-	Y	-	Y	-	*2	Y	R
KB-ORG	Y	-	-	Y	Y	Y	-	Y	Y	-	Y	-	Y	-	-
ODML	Y	-	-	Y	Y	Y	-	-	Y	-	Y	-	*1	-	-

---

[2] Legend: (Y)es, (-)No, On (R)oadmap and (*) comments. Table comments: *1 The output is a nodes tree, not exactly an organisational chart. *2 There is no hierarchy.

The next columns represent features of the generators. The column *has quantitative analysis* describes the capability of the generator the assess the goals creating structures that take into account quantitative parameters such as goal expected needed effort to be performed. *Organisations are explicit* refers to methods that use explicit organisation representations. *Is domain-independent* relates to methods that are suitable for any problem domain.

The next columns are related to the main outputs of the generators. *Creates roles* refers to the ability to automatically create roles, combined with *roles are inputs* says whether the approach uses or not the concept of roles. The *creates coordination levels* column represents the ability of the method to create coordination roles according to coordination needs automatically. *Create viable organisations* represents the ability of the generator to check available resources to create organisations that can be fulfilled when running. *synthesise organisational norms* inform whether generators are automatically creating organisational norms. *Bind agents and roles* tells whether the method is doing agents allocation job or not.

The next columns regard to byproducts of the generators. *Creates departments* refers to the specific ability of the generator to create organisational departments automatically. *Represents roles in a chart* relates to methods that represent organisations as usual organisational charts.

The following columns are related to the capability of the generators to deal with reorganisations. *Does state reorganisation* refers to the ability to move agents from some responsibility to another without needing to trigger a restructuring process. *Does structure reorganisation* refers to the ability to create new structures based on an old one.

Finally, as we agree with many authors that there is no single type of organisation suitable for all situations [16], we also recognise that there is no individual approach ideal for creating all organisations [6]. In both cases, each offers some advantages that the others may lack, especially regarding different organisation generator classes. In the presented comparison, we tried to show an overview of those organisation generators based on the assumption that explicit organisational structures can provide advantages on designing open systems.

7   Conclusion

This paper has presented a proposal for an automated generator of explicit organisations based on goals and annotations as inputs. The current status of this research shows that it is feasible to draw an organisational chart using as input organisational goals with some annotations such as necessary skills to perform each goal. It is intended to enhance the current version of our method adding new inputs to bring necessary information to produce useful organisational charts, taking advantage of opportunities to join goals on the same roles, adding or removing coordination levels. According to performance issues, we can add heuristics to improve the search algorithm.

We have also presented our classification regarding related research of automated organisation generators: (i) *automated organisation design by task planning*; (ii) *self-organisation* approaches; and (iii) *automated explicit organisation generators*. It shows that different strategies address the challenge of *organisation design*. The approaches have advantages and drawbacks being more suitable according to the system's purpose and environment conditions. Besides, we think that each class gives some contribution and a combination of them can lead to a comprehensive MAS design.

Besides the organisational chart creation itself, an extra outcome of *GoOrg* is a proposition of a model that identifies different designing phases done by various methods which potentially can be used together to design a whole MAS. Indeed, when splitting *GoOrg* to fit this model, we could identify that our method is actuating on two processes: organisation design and resources allocation. The allocation of resources done before the execution is a guarantee that when running the created organisational chart can be filled by the available resources, i.e., can be a well-formed organisation.

About evaluation criteria, it is intended to apply the model in known domains testing if it can build suitable structures. These organisations will be simulated in a variety of conditions and checked if goals were fulfilled. By tuning preferences, it is expected to create better arrangements for our testing domains. We also intend to compare the results in terms of time to accomplish the goals between the best candidate and other organisational structures.

References

1. Amaral, C.J., Hübner, J.F.: Goorg: automated organisational chart design for open multi-agent systems. In: De La Prieta, F., et al. (eds.) PAAMS, vol. 1047, pp. 318–321. Springer, Cham (2019). https://doi.org/10.1007/978-3-030-24299-2_28
2. Burton, R.M., Obel, B., Desanctis, G.: Organizational Design: A Step-by-Step Approach. Cambridge University Press, Cambridge (2011)
3. Cardoso, R.C., Bordini, R.H.: A modular framework for decentralised multi-agent planning. In: Proceedings of the 16th Conference on Autonomous Agents and MultiAgent Systems, São Paulo, Brazil, pp. 1487–1489 (2017)
4. Cardoso, R.C., Bordini, R.H.: Decentralised Planning for Multi-Agent Programming Platforms (AAMAS), pp. 799–807 (2019)
5. Criado, N., Argente, E., Botti, V.: THOMAS: an agent platform for supporting normative multi-agent systems. J. Logic Comput. **23**(2), 309–333 (2013)
6. Daft, R.L.: Organization Theory and Design, 10th edn. South-Western College Pub, Centage Learning (2009)
7. De Pinho Rebouças De Oliveira, D.: Estrutura Organizacional: Uma Abordagem Para Resultados e Competitividade. ATLAS EDITORA (2006)
8. Decker, K.S.: Environment centered analysis and design of coordination mechanisms. Ph.D. thesis, University of Massachusets, May 1995
9. DeLoach, S.A.: Modeling organizational rules in the multi-agent systems engineering methodology. In: Cohen, R., Spencer, B. (eds.) Advances in Artificial Intelligence, pp. 1–15. Springer, Heidelberg (2002). https://doi.org/10.1007/3-540-47922-8_1

10. DeLoach, S.A., Matson, E.: An organizational model for designing adaptive multiagent systems. In: The AAAI-04 Workshop on Agent Organizations: Theory and Practice (AOTP 2004), pp. 66–73 (2004)
11. Deloach, S.A., Oyenan, W.H., Matson, E.T.: A capabilities-based model for adaptive organizations. Auton. Agents Multi-Agent Syst. **16**, 13–56 (2008)
12. Ferber, J., Gutknecht, O.: A meta-model for the analysis and design of organizations in multi-agent systems. In: Proceedings - International Conference on Multi Agent Systems, ICMAS 1998, pp. 128–135 (1998)
13. Fink, S., Jenks, R., Willits, R.: Designing and Managing Organizations. Irwin Series in Financial Planning and Insurance, R.D. Irwin (1983)
14. Galbraith, J.R.: Designing Organizations: An Executive Briefing on Strategy, Structure, and Process. Jossey-Bass Publishers, San Francisco (1995)
15. Hatch, M.: Organization Theory: Modern, Symbolic, and Postmodern Perspectives. Oxford University Press, Oxford (1997)
16. Horling, B., Lesser, V.: A survey of multi-agent organizational paradigms. Knowl. Eng. Rev. **19**(4), 281–316 (2004)
17. Horling, B., Lesser, V.: Using quantitative models to search for appropriate organizational designs. Auton. Agents Multi-Agent Syst. **16**(2), 95–149 (2008)
18. Hübner, J.F., Sichman, J.S.: Organização de sistemas multiagentes. III Jornada de MiniCursos de Inteligência Artificial JAIA03 **8**, 247–296 (2003)
19. Labella, T.H., Dorigo, M., Deneubourg, J.L.: Division of labor in a group of robots inspired by ants' foraging behavior. ACM Trans. Auton. Adapt. Syst. **1**(1), 4–25 (2007)
20. Leitão, P., Karnouskos, S., Ribeiro, L., Lee, J., Strasser, T., Colombo, A.W.: Smart agents in industrial cyber physical systems. In: Proceedings of the IEEE (2016)
21. Mintzberg, H.: The design school: reconsidering the basic premisses of strategic management. Strateg. Manag. J. **11**(May 1989), 171–195 (1990)
22. Pattison, H.E., Corkill, D.D., Lesser, V.R.: Chapter 3 - instantiating descriptions of organizational structures. In: Huhns, M.N. (ed.) Distributed Artificial Intelligence, pp. 59–96 (1987)
23. Sierra, C., Sabater, J., Augusti, J., Garcia, P.: SADDE: Social Agents Design Driven by Equations. In: Methodologies and Software Engineering for Agent Systems, pp. 1–24. Kluwer Academic Publishers (2004)
24. Simon, G., Mermet, B., Fournier, D.: Goal decomposition tree: an agent model to generate a validated agent behaviour. In: Baldoni, M., Endriss, U., Omicini, A., Torroni, P. (eds.) Declarative Agent Languages and Technologies III, vol. 3904, pp. 124–140. Springer, Heidelberg (2006). https://doi.org/10.1007/11691792_8
25. Sims, M., Corkill, D., Lesser, V.: Knowledgeable automated organization design for multi-agent systems. Challenge 1–42 (2007)
26. Sims, M., Corkill, D., Lesser, V.: Automated organization design for multi-agent systems. Auton. Agents Multi-Agent Syst. **16**(2) (2008)
27. Sleight, J., Durfee, E.H.: Organizational design principles and techniques for decision-theoretic agents. In: Proceedings of the 2013 International Conference on Autonomous Agents and Multi-agent Systems, AAMAS 2013, pp. 463–470. International Foundation for Autonomous Agents and Multiagent Systems, Richland, SC (2013)
28. Sleight, J.L., Durfee, E.H., Baveja, S.S., Cohn, A.A.E.M., Lesser, E.V.R.: Agent-Driven Representations, Algorithms, and Metrics for Automated Organizational Design (2015)
29. So, Y.P., Durfee, E.H.: Chapter X. Designing Organizations for Computational Agents (1996)

30. Stoner, J., Freeman, R.: Management. Prentice-Hall, Upper Saddle River (1992)
31. Tambe, M.: Towards flexible teamwork. J. Artif. Intell. Res. **7**, 83–124 (1997)
32. Ye, D., Zhang, M., Vasilakos, A.V.: A survey of self-organisation mechanisms in multi-agent systems. IEEE Trans. SMC: Syst. **47**(3) (2016)

On Enactability of Agent Interaction Protocols: Towards a Unified Approach

Angelo Ferrando[1], Michael Winikoff[2(✉)], Stephen Cranefield[3],
Frank Dignum[4,5,6], and Viviana Mascardi[7]

[1] Liverpool University, Liverpool, UK
angelo.ferrando@liverpool.ac.uk
[2] Victoria University of Wellington, Wellington, New Zealand
michael.winikoff@vuw.ac.nz
[3] University of Otago, Dunedin, New Zealand
stephen.cranefield@otago.ac.nz
[4] Umeå University, Umeå, Sweden
frank.dignum@umu.se
[5] Utrecht University, Utrecht, The Netherlands
[6] CVUT Prague, Prague, Czech Republic
[7] Genova University, Genova, Italy
viviana.mascardi@unige.it

Abstract. Interactions between agents are usually designed from a global viewpoint. However, the implementation of a multi-agent interaction is distributed. It is well known that this difference between the specification and the implementation levels can introduce problems, allowing designers to specify protocols from a global viewpoint that cannot be implemented as a collection of individual agents. This leads naturally to the question of whether a given (global) protocol is *enactable*, namely, whether it can be implemented in a distributed way. We consider this question in the powerful setting of trace expressions, considering a range of message ordering interpretations (specifying what it means to say that an interaction step occurs before another), and a range of possible constraints on the semantics of message delivery, corresponding to different properties of the underlying communication middleware. We provide a definition of enactability, along with an implementation of the definition that is applied to a number of example protocols.

Keywords: Agent interaction protocols · Enactability ·
Enforceability · Implementability · Realizability · Projectability · Trace
Expressions

Michael was at the University of Otago when this work was carried out.
A. Ferrando—Work supported by EPSRC as part of the ORCA [EP/R026173] and
RAIN [EP/R026084] Robotics and AI Hubs.

L. A. Dennis et al. (Eds.): EMAS 2019, LNAI 12058, pp. 43–64, 2020.
https://doi.org/10.1007/978-3-030-51417-4_3

1   Introduction

Alice's country's laws forbid students to be enrolled in two different courses of studies at the university level at the same time. Alice knows this rule and its serious consequences: a fine may be issued for not respecting the law and, in the worst case, a degree obtained at University A while being also enrolled in University B may be invalidated[1].

When Alice decides to give up her studies in University A and move to University B, she informs University A that she wishes to unenroll by posting a letter a few days before enrolling in University B.

This situation can be represented by the following global Agent Interaction Protocol:

$$changeUni = Alice \stackrel{Unenroll}{\Longrightarrow} UniA \cdot Alice \stackrel{Enroll}{\Longrightarrow} UniB$$

where $a1 \stackrel{M}{\Longrightarrow} a2$ models the interaction between $a1$ and $a2$ to exchange message M[2] and "·" models interaction concatenation. Alice believes that the above protocol correctly meets her country's regulations, but she is fined anyway: UniB received Alice's enrollment request before UniA received the unenrollment communication, and for a few days Alice turned out to be enrolled in both of them. What went wrong is the *interpretation* of "before". To Alice, it meant that she should send *Unenroll* before she sent *Enroll*, while for her country's regulations it (also) meant that UniA should receive *Unenroll* before UniB received *Enroll*. This ambiguity would have had no impact on Alice if the physical *communication model* guaranteed that between the sending and receiving stages of an interaction, nothing could happen. Although Alice waited for a couple of days before sending the *Enroll* communication, the *Unenroll* one was delivered after. While it is evident that the postal service cannot guarantee that the order of posting is the same as the order of delivery, such guarantees cannot even be easily ensured by software communication platforms. This issue has important implications that we explore in this paper: Alice's story shows that enacting the intent of a global protocol without clear semantics of the meaning of "before", without guarantees from the platform implementation on message delivery order, and without hidden communications between the participants ("covert channels"), may not be possible. Many other real situations are similar to this one: for example, a citizen must wait for the bank to have received (and processed) the request to add some money to a new empty account, before sending a request to move that money to another account, otherwise he can go into overdraft.

---

[1] This is a real example: in Italy, a law dating back to 1933 prevents students from being enrolled in more than one Italian course at university level at the same time; the only – recent – exception is being enrolled in a conservatory and in a university. The ambiguities in the law article are many, and appeals to the courts are in the thousands.

[2] This notation has been used in the most recent papers on Trace Expressions [3,5]; although not being standard, it is consistent with the background theory.

This kind of issue is not new in the field and various authors use different terms for global protocols that can be enforced by distributed participants: conformant [23], enforceable [6,13], enactable [14], implementable [27], projectable [10,20], and realizable [25,28]. The concept behind these names is however the same: by executing the localised versions of the protocol implemented by each participant, the global protocol behaviour is obtained, with no additional communication. We will use the term *enactability* to denote this property. However, despite the large amount of work on enactability, there is no existing work that considers both the intended *message ordering* and the *communication model* of the infrastructure in which the agents will be implemented, that recognises the need to use a *decision structure* to enforce consistent choices, and that provides an implementation for checking protocol enactability. Together, these are the innovative and original features of our contribution.

Although it might be argued that it is desirable to have robust protocol specifications that are independent of the underlying platform implementation, we observe that robustness can make the protocol more complex, and hence harder to maintain. For example, considering again the protocol $changeUni = Alice \stackrel{Unenroll}{\Longrightarrow} UniA \cdot Alice \stackrel{Enroll}{\Longrightarrow} UniB$ we observe that, depending on which interpretation we choose, we can have different conclusions on what to expect from the protocol implementation. This can be avoided if we add additional acknowledgement messages, which gives a more message-intensive protocol such as $changeUni = Alice \stackrel{Unenroll}{\Longrightarrow} UniA \cdot UniA \stackrel{AckUnenroll}{\Longrightarrow} Alice \cdot Alice \stackrel{Enroll}{\Longrightarrow} UniB$, in which *Alice* would not have been fined. However, adding additional acknowledgement messages increases the complexity of the protocol and reduces opportunities for concurrency. We therefore prefer to take into account what the underlying implementation guarantees with respect to communication, so that we can relax our specifications, and use as simple a protocol as possible. Additionally, a protocol that is not enactable in some platform may be enactable in some other platform. Our work is therefore relevant to both platform designers and protocol designers.

The paper is structured as follows. Section 2 introduces the Trace Expressions formalism, a taxonomy of standard communication models, and some possible message orderings taken into account by the literature, which together provide the background of our work. Section 3 generalises and formalises the notion of Message Order Interpretation (MOI), introduces the communication models semantics, and faces the main objective of the paper by showing – also by means of examples – when an interaction protocol is strongly (or weakly) enactable, given an MOI semantics and a communication model. Section 4 discusses related work and future plans.

2   Background

Trace Expressions. Trace expressions [4] are a compact and expressive formalism inspired by global types [1] and then extended and exploited in different application domains [2,15,16]. Initially devised for runtime verification of multi-agent systems, trace expressions are expressive, and can define context-sensitive languages.

A trace expression τ denotes a set of possibly infinite event traces, and is defined on top of the following operators:[3]

- ϵ (empty trace), denoting the singleton set $\{\langle\rangle\}$ containing the empty event trace $\langle\rangle$.
- M (event), denoting a singleton set $\{\langle M\rangle\}$ containing the event trace $\langle M\rangle$.
- $\tau_1 \cdot \tau_2$ (concatenation), denoting the set of all traces obtained by concatenating the traces of τ_1 with those of τ_2.
- $\tau_1 \wedge \tau_2$ (intersection), denoting the intersection of the traces of τ_1 and τ_2.
- $\tau_1 \vee \tau_2$ (union), denoting the union of the traces of τ_1 and τ_2.
- $\tau_1 | \tau_2$ (shuffle), denoting the union of the sets obtained by shuffling each trace of τ_1 with each trace of τ_2 (see [9] for a more precise definition).

Trace expressions are cyclic terms, thus they can support recursion without introducing an explicit construct.

As is customary, the operational semantics of trace expressions is specified by a transition relation $\delta \subseteq \mathcal{T} \times \mathcal{E} \times \mathcal{T}$, where $\mathcal{T}$ and $\mathcal{E}$ denote the sets of trace expressions and of events, respectively [4]. We do not present all the transition rules for space constraints. They are standard ones (see e.g. [4]) that state, for example, that $\delta(ev \cdot \tau, ev, \tau)$, meaning that the protocol whose state is modelled by $ev \cdot \tau$ can move to state τ if ev occurs, and that $\delta(\tau_1 \vee \tau_2, ev, \tau)$ if $\delta(\tau_1, ev, \tau)$, meaning that if the protocol whose state is modelled by τ_1 can move to state τ if ev occurs, then also the protocol whose state is modelled by $\tau_1 \vee \tau_2$ can. The denotational semantics is defined as follows, where $t_1 \bowtie t_2$ is the set of all interleavings of t_1 and t_2, and $\circ$ is concatenation over sequences:

$$
\begin{aligned}
\llbracket \epsilon \rrbracket &= \{\langle\rangle\} \\
\llbracket M \rrbracket &= \{\langle M\rangle\} \\
\llbracket \tau_1 \cdot \tau_2 \rrbracket &= \{t_1 \circ t_2 \mid t_1 \in \llbracket \tau_1 \rrbracket \wedge t_2 \in \llbracket \tau_2 \rrbracket\} \\
\llbracket \tau_1 \wedge \tau_2 \rrbracket &= \llbracket \tau_1 \rrbracket \cap \llbracket \tau_2 \rrbracket \\
\llbracket \tau_1 \vee \tau_2 \rrbracket &= \llbracket \tau_1 \rrbracket \cup \llbracket \tau_2 \rrbracket \\
\llbracket \tau_1 | \tau_2 \rrbracket &= \{z \mid t_1 \in \llbracket \tau_1 \rrbracket \wedge t_2 \in \llbracket \tau_2 \rrbracket \wedge z \in t_1 \bowtie t_2\}
\end{aligned}
$$

Events can be, in principle, of any kind. In this paper, we will limit ourselves to consider *interaction* and *message* events.

An interaction has the form $a \xrightarrow{M} b$ and gives information on the protocol from the global perspective, collapsing sending and receiving into a single event. We say that τ is an *interaction protocol* if all the events therein are interactions. Interaction protocols take other names in other communities, such as Interaction

---

[3] Binary operators associate from left, and are listed in decreasing order of precedence; that is, the first operator has the highest precedence. The operators "$\vee$" and "$\wedge$" are the standard notation for trace expressions.

Oriented Choreography [23] in the service-oriented computing community, and global type in the community working on process calculi and types [11].

Message events have the form $aM!$ (a sends M) and $bM?$ (b receives M). They model actions that one agent can execute, hence taking a local perspective. A trace expression where all events are messages will be named a *message protocol* throughout the paper. Message protocols have different names in different communities, such as Process Oriented Choreography [23] and local type or session type in the global types community [19, 30].

Communication Models. As our proposal explicitly takes the communication model supported by the MAS infrastructure into account, we provide a summary of some communication models based on [12]. We use CM0 to CM6 to identify them in a compact way.

CM0: Synchronous Communication. Sending and receiving are synchronised: the sender cannot send if the receiver is not ready to receive.

CM1: Realisable with Synchronous Communication (RSC). After a communication transition consisting of a send event of a message, the only possible communication transition is the receive event of this message. This asynchronous model is the closest one to synchronous communication and can be implemented with a 1-slot unique buffer shared by all agents.

CM2: FIFO n-n Communication. Messages are globally ordered and are delivered in their emission order: if sending of M_1 takes place before sending of M_2, then reception of M_1 must take place before reception of M_2. This model can be implemented by means of a shared centralised object, such as a queue.

CM3: FIFO 1-n Communication. Messages from the same sender are delivered in the order in which they were sent. It can be implemented by giving each agent a separate queue where it puts its outgoing messages, with peers fetching messages from this queue.

CM4: FIFO n-1 Communication. A send event is implicitly and globally ordered with regard to all other sending actions toward the same agent. This means that if agent b receives M_1 (sent by agent a) and later it receives M_2 (sent by agent c), b knows that the sending of M_1 occurred before the sending of M_2 in the global execution order, even if there is no causal path between the two sending actions. The implementation of this model can, similarly to FIFO 1-n, be done by providing each agent with a queue: messages are sent by putting them into the queue of the recipient agent. Implementing this model is expensive as it requires a shared real-time clock or a global agreement on event order.

CM5: Causal. Messages are delivered according to the causality of their emissions [22]: if a message M_1 is causally sent before a message M_2 then an agent cannot get M_2 before M_1. Implementing this model requires sharing the causality relation.

CM6: Fully Asynchronous. No order on message delivery is imposed. Messages can overtake others or be arbitrarily delayed. The implementation can be modelled by a bag.

Other communication models exist, such as the one named FIFO 1-1 communication in [12], where messages between any two peers are delivered in their send order. Messages from/to different peers are independently delivered. This is the model supported by Erlang[4].

Message Ordering. The statement "one interaction comes before another" is ambiguous, as exemplified in Sect. 1. This ambiguity has been recognised by some authors who suggested how to interpret message ordering when moving from the interaction (global) level to the message (local) level. In this section we summarise and compare the proposals by Lanese *et al.* [23] and Desai and Singh [14].

To identify the interpretations, we will use the acronyms used in [14] when available, and our own acronyms otherwise. The starting point for interpreting message ordering is the interaction protocol $\tau = a \xrightarrow{M_1} b \cdot c \xrightarrow{M_2} d$. For the sake of clarity, we denote $aM_1!$ with $s1$, $bM_1?$ with $r1$, $cM_2!$ with $s2$, and $dM_2?$ with $r2$; we characterise the message ordering interpretations by the traces of message events that respect them.

RS: Under this message ordering interpretation the meaning of "interaction event M_1 occurs before M_2" is that M_1 is received before M_2 is sent. The set of traces that respect this model is $\{\langle s1, r1, s2, r2 \rangle\}$. This interpretation is named *RS (receive before send)* in [14] and *disjoint semantics* in [23].

SS: M_1 is sent before M_2 is sent, and there are no constraints on the delivery order. The set of traces that respect this model is $\{\langle s1, r1, s2, r2 \rangle, \langle s1, s2, r1, r2 \rangle, \langle s1, s2, r2, r1 \rangle\}$. This interpretation is named *SS (send before send)* in [14] and *sender semantics* in [23].

RR: M_1 is received before M_2 is received, and there are no constraints on the sending order. The set of traces that respect this model is $\{\langle s1, r1, s2, r2 \rangle, \langle s1, s2, r1, r2 \rangle, \langle s2, s1, r1, r2 \rangle\}$. This interpretation is named *RR (receive before receive)* in [14] and *receiver semantics* in [23].

RR & SS: this combines the requirements of **RR** and of **SS:** M_1 is sent before M_2 is sent and also M_1 is received before M_2 is received. The set of traces that respect this model is $\{\langle s1, r1, s2, r2 \rangle, \langle s1, s2, r1, r2 \rangle\}$: both $s1$ comes before $s2$ ("coming before" according to the senders), and $r1$ comes before $r2$ ("coming before" according to the receivers). This interpretation is named *sender-receiver semantics* in [23].

SR: M_1 is sent before M_2 is received. The set of traces that respect this model is $\{\langle s1, r1, s2, r2 \rangle, \langle s1, s2, r1, r2 \rangle, \langle s1, s2, r2, r1 \rangle, \langle s2, s1, r1, r2 \rangle, \langle s2, s1, r2, r1 \rangle\}$. This interpretation is named *SR (send before receive)* in [14].

---

[4] http://erlang.org/doc/apps/erts/communication.html, Section 2.1, accessed on September 2019.

It is easy to see that the following inclusions among asynchronous models hold: **RS** $\subset$ **RR** & **SS** $\subseteq$ **SS** $\subset$ **SR** and **RS** $\subset$ **RR** & **SS** $\subset$ **RR** $\subset$ **SR**. The **SS** and **RR** interpretations are not comparable. In the remainder of this paper we consider only the four interpretations defined by Desai & Singh, i.e. we do not consider "RR & SS".

3 Defining Enactability Using a Semantic Approach

Basic Notation. In the following, let $ComModel = \{CM1, CM2, CM3, CM4, CM5, CM6\}$ be the set of possible (asynchronous) communication models, and $MOISet = \{SS, SR, RS, RR\}$ the set of possible message order interpretations that can be imposed. We also define $\mathcal{A} = \{a, b, c, d, a_1, a_2, \ldots, a_n\}$ to be the set of agents involved in the interaction protocol.

Recall that we consider both interaction and message protocols. When we say that τ is an *interaction* protocol, we mean that the protocol represents sequences of *interaction events*. The set of traces recognized is obtained following the semantics defined in Sect. 2, and for an interaction protocol τ we define $\mathcal{I}(\tau)$ to be the set of interactions involved in the interaction protocol: $\mathcal{I}(\tau) = \{i \mid \exists I : I \in [\![\tau]\!] \land i \in I\}^5$. We define $\mathcal{I}$ to be the set of all possible interaction events. Similarly, when τ is a *message* protocol, it represents sequences of send and receive events of the form $aM!$ (send event) and $bM?$ (receive event), and given a particular set of possible interactions $\mathcal{I}$, we define $\mathcal{E}_{\mathcal{I}}$ to be the corresponding set of events: $\mathcal{E}_{\mathcal{I}} = \{aM! \mid \exists_{b \in \mathcal{A}} . a \xrightarrow{M} b \in \mathcal{I}\} \cup \{bM? \mid \exists_{a \in \mathcal{A}} . a \xrightarrow{M} b \in \mathcal{I}\}$. In a message protocol τ we have that $E \in [\![\tau]\!] \implies \forall_{e \in E} . e \in \mathcal{E}_{\mathcal{I}(\tau)}$. Given a message protocol τ we also define $\mathcal{E}(\tau)$ to be the set of message events that occur in the protocol.

Next, we define the language of traces (i.e. of *sequences* of events) for interaction protocols and message protocols. For interaction protocols, the set of all possible traces is defined to be^6: $\mathcal{L}_{\mathcal{I}} = \mathcal{I}^* \cup \mathcal{I}^\omega$. For message protocols, the definition is somewhat more complex, since there is a relationship between a send and a receive event. Specifically, the set of all possible traces of events is constrained so that a message being received must be preceded by that message having been sent. We also constrain the set so that each message can be sent at most once, and received at most once (i.e. message names are unique). The assumption is made by most authors, see [12] for example, and is considered harmless, since we can integrate many elements to the notion of "message name", such as content, protocol ID and conversation ID, to discriminate between messages at design time. We define $\mathcal{L}_{\mathcal{E}_{\mathcal{I}}}$ as follows, where we treat a sequence E as a function from indices to elements, and $dom(E)$ is the domain of this function:

---

^{5} We extend the operator "$\in$" to denote membership of an item in a sequence.
^{6} The superscripts $*$ and ω are standard notations for (respectively) all finite (all infinite) sequences built from a given set.

$$\mathcal{L}_{\mathcal{E}_{\mathcal{I}}} = \{E \in \mathcal{E}_{\mathcal{I}}^* \cup \mathcal{E}_{\mathcal{I}}^\omega \mid$$
$$(\forall_{i,j \in dom(E)} . E[i] = aM! \wedge E[j] = aM! \implies i = j) \wedge$$
$$(\forall_{i,j \in dom(E)} . E[i] = bM? \wedge E[j] = bM? \implies i = j) \wedge$$
$$(\forall_{i \in dom(E)} . E[i] = bM? \implies (\exists_{j \in dom(E)} . E[j] = aM! \wedge j < i))$$

Message Order Interpretation (MOI). As discussed earlier, we follow prior work in considering four message ordering interpretations (*SS*, *SR*, *RS*, and *RR*). We formalise this by defining a variant semantics that takes an *interaction* protocol τ and returns its semantics in terms of *events* rather than interactions. The possible sequences of events are constrained: given a situation where τ specifies that M_1 must occur before M_2, we constrain the possible sequence of events with the appropriate constraint on events corresponding to the selected MOI.

Definition 1 (Order on interactions in a trace). *Let $I \in \mathcal{L}_{\mathcal{I}}$ be a trace of interaction events, $E \in \mathcal{L}_{\mathcal{E}_{\mathcal{I}}}$ be a trace of send and receive events, moi $\in$ MOISet a message ordering interpretation, and a $\overset{M_1}{\Longrightarrow} b \in \mathcal{I}$, $c \overset{M_2}{\Longrightarrow} d \in \mathcal{I}$ two interactions. Abbreviating $a \overset{M_1}{\Longrightarrow} b$ as I_1 and $c \overset{M_2}{\Longrightarrow} d$ as I_2, we define the message ordering interpretation constraint, denoted $I_1 \prec_{moi}^E I_2$, as follows:*

$$I_1 \prec_{SS}^E I_2 \text{ iff } aM_1! \prec_E cM_2! \qquad\qquad I_1 \prec_{SR}^E I_2 \text{ iff } aM_1! \prec_E dM_2?$$
$$I_1 \prec_{RS}^E I_2 \text{ iff } bM_1? \prec_E cM_2! \qquad\qquad I_1 \prec_{RR}^E I_2 \text{ iff } bM_1? \prec_E dM_2?$$

where $e_1 \prec_E e_2$ iff $\exists_{i,j \in dom(E)} . E[i] = e_1 \wedge E[j] = e_2 \wedge i < j$ is the constraint that in event trace E the event e_1 occurs before e_2.

Formalising the MOI is not as simple as it might seem. An obvious approach that does not work is to compute the semantics of the interaction protocol τ, and then map each sequence $I \in [\![\tau]\!]$ to a set of message event traces. This does not work because the trace is linear, and therefore a total order, whereas a protocol can specify a partial order[7] (and indeed, in the case of the SR MOI, the ordering may not even be partial, since SR is not transitive). Instead, we define a variant semantics, denoted $[\![\tau]\!]_{moi}$, which is compositional. The semantics follow the standard semantics (Sect. 2) with a few exceptions. Firstly, the semantics of an interaction I is given as the sequence of sending the message, followed by receiving it (denoted $s(I)$ and $r(I)$, respectively). Secondly, the semantics for a

---

[7] An illustrative example is $\tau = (M_1 \cdot M_2) \mid M_3$. This simple protocol has three sequences of interactions: $\{\langle M_1, M_2, M_3 \rangle, \langle M_1, M_3, M_2 \rangle, \langle M_3, M_1, M_2 \rangle\}$. Assuming an RS message ordering interpretation, then each of the message sequences corresponds to exactly one sequence of events, giving (where we abbreviate sending and receiving M as respectively $M!$ and $M?$): $\{\langle M_1!, M_1?, M_2!, M_2?, M_3!, M_3? \rangle, \langle M_1!, M_1?, M_3!, M_3?, M_2!, M_2? \rangle, \langle M_3!, M_3?, M_1!, M_1?, M_2!, M_2? \rangle\}$. However, the protocol does not specify any constraint on M_3, so should also allow other interpretations where the occurrences of $M_3!$ and $M_3?$ are not constrained relative to the other events, for example $\langle M_1!, M_1?, M_3!, M_2!, M_2?, M_3? \rangle$.

sequence $\tau_1 \cdot \tau_2$ is given in terms of the semantics of τ_1 and τ_2. These are then combined by interleaving them (rather than simply concatenating them), but with the constraint that the result must satisfy the appropriate MOI constraint $(I_1 \prec_{moi}^E I_2)$ for all possible final messages of τ_1 (I_1) and all possible initial messages of τ_2 (I_2). Determining initial and final messages is itself somewhat complex, and is done using partially ordered sets.

A partially ordered set (poset) is a pair $(E, <)$ where E is the set of elements (in this case interactions) and $<$ is a transitive binary relation on E. We define the union operator to act piecewise on posets, and to take the transitive closure of the resulting relation, i.e. $(E_1, <_1) \cup (E_2, <_2) = (E_1 \cup E_2, (<_1 \cup <_2)^*)$. The sets of minimal and maximal elements of a poset P are denoted $\min(P)$ and $\max(P)$, respectively.

We can then define the poset of an interaction protocol as follows:

$$\text{poset}(\epsilon) = (\varnothing, \varnothing)$$
$$\text{poset}(I) = (\{I\}, \varnothing)$$
$$\text{poset}(\tau_1 \wedge \tau_2) = \text{poset}(\tau_1) \cup \text{poset}(\tau_2)$$
$$\text{poset}(\tau_1 \mid \tau_2) = \text{poset}(\tau_1) \cup \text{poset}(\tau_2)$$
$$\text{poset}(\tau_1 \vee \tau_2) = \text{poset}(\tau_1) \cup \text{poset}(\tau_2)$$
$$\text{poset}(\tau_1 \cdot \tau_2) = \text{poset}(\tau_1) \cdot \text{poset}(\tau_2)$$
$$(E_1, <_1) \cdot (E_2, <_2) = (E_1 \cup E_2, <_1 \cup <_2 \cup E_1 \times E_2)$$

where we define a sequence of two posets $(E_1, <_1) \cdot (E_2, <_2)$ by collecting the orderings of each of E_1 and E_2, and adding additional ordering constraints between every element of E_1 and every element of E_2. We can now proceed to define the variant compositional semantics $[\![\tau]\!]_{moi}$.

$$[\![\epsilon]\!]_{moi} = \{\epsilon\}$$
$$[\![I]\!]_{moi} = \{\langle s(I), r(I)\rangle\}$$
$$[\![\tau_1 \vee \tau_2]\!]_{moi} = [\![\tau_1]\!]_{moi} \cup [\![\tau_1]\!]_{moi}$$
$$[\![\tau_1 \wedge \tau_2]\!]_{moi} = [\![\tau_1]\!]_{moi} \cap [\![\tau_1]\!]_{moi}$$
$$[\![\tau_1 \cdot \tau_2]\!]_{moi} = \{t \mid t_1 \in [\![\tau_1]\!]_{moi} \wedge t_2 \in [\![\tau_2]\!]_{moi} \wedge t \in t_1 \bowtie t_2 \wedge$$
$$\forall I_1 \in \max(\text{poset}(\tau_1)), \forall I_2 \in \min(\text{poset}(\tau_2)).$$
$$I_1 \in t \wedge I_2 \in t \Rightarrow I_1 \prec_{moi}^t I_2\}$$
$$[\![\tau_1 \mid \tau_2]\!]_{moi} = \{z \mid t_1 \in [\![\tau_1]\!]_{moi} \wedge t_2 \in [\![\tau_2]\!]_{moi} \wedge z \in t_1 \bowtie t_2\}$$

Where $t_1 \bowtie t_2$ is the set of all interleavings of t_1 and t_2; and $(A \xRightarrow{M} B) \in t$ iff $AM! \in t$.

Communication Model Semantics. We formalise the defined communication model semantics by defining, for each communication model CMi, a corresponding language of event traces that incorporates the appropriate restriction, ruling out event sequences that violate the communication model. For example, for $CM1$ the constraint is that immediately after each sending event in u we have its corresponding receiving event, with nothing in the middle; etc. Note that each $\mathcal{L}_{CMi}^{\mathcal{E}_{\mathcal{I}}}$ takes as a parameter the set of message events $\mathcal{E}_{\mathcal{I}}$.

$$\mathcal{L}_{CM1}^{\mathcal{E}_{\mathcal{I}}} = \{E \in \mathcal{L}_{\mathcal{E}_{\mathcal{I}}} | \forall_{a \xrightarrow{M_1} b \in \mathcal{I}} . \forall_{k \in dom(E)} . aM_1! = E[k-1] \implies bM_1? = E[k]\}$$

$$\mathcal{L}_{CM2}^{\mathcal{E}_{\mathcal{I}}} = \{E \in \mathcal{L}_{\mathcal{E}_{\mathcal{I}}} | \forall_{a \xrightarrow{M_1} b \in \mathcal{I}} . \forall_{c \xrightarrow{M_2} d \in \mathcal{I}} . \forall_{i,j,k,l \in dom(E)} . (bM_1? = E[i] \wedge$$
$$dM_2? = E[j] \wedge aM_1! = E[k] \wedge cM_2! = E[l] \wedge k < l) \implies i < j\}$$

$$\mathcal{L}_{CM3}^{\mathcal{E}_{\mathcal{I}}} = \{E \in \mathcal{L}_{\mathcal{E}_{\mathcal{I}}} | \forall_{a \xrightarrow{M_1} b \in \mathcal{I}} . \forall_{a \xrightarrow{M_2} d \in \mathcal{I}} . \forall_{i,j,k,l \in dom(E)} . (bM_1? = E[i] \wedge$$
$$dM_2? = E[j] \wedge aM_1! = E[k] \wedge aM_2! = E[l] \wedge k < l) \implies i < j\}$$

$$\mathcal{L}_{CM4}^{\mathcal{E}_{\mathcal{I}}} = \{E \in \mathcal{L}_{\mathcal{E}_{\mathcal{I}}} | \forall_{a \xrightarrow{M_1} b \in \mathcal{I}} . \forall_{c \xrightarrow{M_2} b \in \mathcal{I}} . \forall_{i,j,k,l \in dom(E)} . (bM_1? = E[i] \wedge$$
$$bM_2? = E[j] \wedge aM_1! = E[k] \wedge cM_2! = E[l] \wedge k < l) \implies i < j\}$$

$$\mathcal{L}_{CM5}^{\mathcal{E}_{\mathcal{I}}} = \{E \in \mathcal{L}_{\mathcal{E}_{\mathcal{I}}} | \forall_{a \xrightarrow{M_1} b \in \mathcal{I}} . \forall_{a \xrightarrow{M_2} b \in \mathcal{I}} . \forall_{i,j,k,l \in dom(E)} . (bM_1? = E[i] \wedge$$
$$bM_2? = E[j] \wedge aM_1! \prec_{Causal}^{E} aM_2!) \implies i < j\}$$
$$\text{where } aM_1! \prec_{Causal}^{u} bM_2! \iff$$
$$((a = b \vee M_1 = M_2) \wedge$$
$$\exists_{i,j \in dom(u)} . (u[i] = aM_1! \wedge bM_2! = u[j] \wedge i < j))$$
$$\vee (\exists_{ev \in E} . aM_1! \prec_{Causal}^{u} ev \wedge ev \prec_{Causal}^{u} bM_2!)$$

$$\mathcal{L}_{CM6}^{\mathcal{E}_{\mathcal{I}}} = \mathcal{L}_{\mathcal{E}_{\mathcal{I}}}$$

We can then apply a particular communication model to an *interaction* protocol τ_i using $[\![\tau_i]\!]_{moi}^{CM}$, and to a *message* protocol τ_m using $[\![\tau_m]\!]^{CM}$, which are defined as follows[8].

$$[\![\tau_i]\!]_{moi}^{CM} = [\![\tau_i]\!]_{moi} \cap \mathcal{L}_{CM}^{\mathcal{E}_{\mathcal{I}(\tau)}}$$
$$[\![\tau_m]\!]^{CM} = [\![\tau_m]\!] \cap \mathcal{L}_{CM}^{\mathcal{E}(\tau)}$$

Projection. Projection is defined, intuitively, as focusing on the aspects of the protocol that are relevant for a given role. It is defined as follows, where we write τ^A to denote projecting trace τ for role A.

---

[8] Note that in the first line we have an *interaction* protocol τ_i, and so the set of message events is given by determining the set of interaction events $\mathcal{I}(\tau)$, and then determining the set of message events $\mathcal{E}_{\mathcal{I}(\tau)}$. By contrast, in the second line, τ_m is a *message* protocol, so we just determine the set of message events directly ($\mathcal{E}(\tau)$).

$$(\epsilon)^A = \epsilon$$

$$(a \xrightarrow{M} b)^A = \begin{cases} aM!, \text{if } a = A \\ bM?, \text{if } b = A \\ \epsilon, \text{otherwise} \end{cases}$$

$$(aM!)^A = \begin{cases} aM!, \text{ if } a = A \\ \epsilon, \text{otherwise} \end{cases}$$

$$(aM?)^A = \begin{cases} aM?, \text{ if } a = A \\ \epsilon, \text{otherwise} \end{cases}$$

$$(\tau_1 \otimes \tau_2)^A = (\tau_1)^A \otimes (\tau_2)^A \text{ (where } \otimes \text{ is any operator)}$$

We then define the *distribution* of τ, denoted $\ulcorner \tau \urcorner$, where τ involves roles $a_1 \ldots a_n$ as[9]:

$$\ulcorner \tau \urcorner = \tau^{a_1} \| \cdots \| \tau^{a_n}$$

To give an example, let us consider again the scenario proposed in Sect. 1. In order to move to University B, Alice needs to book an apartment close to her new university. At the beginning, Alice reserves the apartment owned by Bob. When Alice discovers that Carol rents a cheaper and larger apartment, she decides to cancel the reservation of Bob's apartment and book Carol's one. This situation can be represented by

$$modifyRes = Alice \xrightarrow{Canc} Bob \cdot Alice \xrightarrow{Res} Carol$$

We point out that *modifyRes* suffers from the same problem as *changeUni*: Bob might receive the cancellation request after Carol receives the booking, and this might cause Alice to have some nights booked (and to pay) in both apartments.

To complete the reservation, Carol needs some information from Alice. This information can be wrong or incomplete, in which case Carol gives Alice an opportunity to amend the information, and in either case the interaction then concludes with Carol confirming the booking. This can be represented as the following specification:

$$reqInfo = Alice \xrightarrow{Info} Carol \cdot$$

$$(Carol \xrightarrow{Wrong} Alice \cdot Alice \xrightarrow{Info'} Carol \vee \epsilon) \cdot$$

$$Carol \xrightarrow{Booked} Alice$$

---

[9] We use $\|$ to distinguish between parallel composition of different agents, and parallel composition within a protocol.

Let us consider *main* as the sequential combination of the two protocols: $main = modifyRes \cdot reqInfo$. Then the projection of *main* on each single agent gives the following distribution.

$$\ulcorner main \urcorner = main^{Alice} \parallel main^{Bob} \parallel main^{Carol}$$
$$main^{Alice} = modifyRes^{Alice} \cdot reqInfo^{Alice}$$
$$modifyRes^{Alice} = AliceCanc! \cdot AliceRes!$$
$$reqInfo^{Alice} = AliceInfo! \cdot (AliceWrong? \cdot AliceInfo'! \vee \epsilon) \cdot$$
$$AliceBooked?$$
$$main^{Bob} = modifyRes^{Bob} \cdot reqInfo^{Bob} = BobCanc? \cdot \epsilon$$
$$main^{Carol} = modifyRes^{Carol} \cdot reqInfo^{Carol}$$
$$modifyRes^{Carol} = CarolRes?$$
$$reqInfo^{Carol} = CarolInfo? \cdot (CarolWrong! \cdot CarolInfo'? \vee \epsilon) \cdot$$
$$CarolBooked!$$

In order to define the semantics of a projected protocol we need to first define what we term a *decision structure*. This is needed in the semantics in order to deal correctly with projected protocols. Specifically, the intuition for enactability (see Sect. 3) is that an interaction protocol τ involving, say, three roles a, b and c is enactable iff there exist three protocols τ^a, τ^b and τ^c such that their concurrent interleaving results in the same behaviour as the original protocol. However, when a protocol contains choices ($\vee$) we need to ensure that the occurrences of $\vee$ in each of τ^a, τ^b and τ^c arising from the same $\vee$ in τ are treated consistently. For example, consider the protocol $\tau = a \xrightarrow{M_1} b \vee a \xrightarrow{M_2} c$. This protocol is simple: it specifies that agent a can either send a message M_1 to b, or it can send a different message M_2 ($M_2 \neq M_1$) to agent c. When we distribute the protocol by projecting it (see Sect. 3) and forming $\tau^a \parallel \tau^b \parallel \tau^c$, we obtain the distributed protocol $(aM_1! \vee aM_2!) \parallel (bM_1? \vee \varepsilon) \parallel (\varepsilon \vee cM_2?)$. However, if we interpret each $\vee$ independently (as the semantics would naturally do) then we can have *inconsistent* choices. For example, we could have $(aM_1!) \parallel (\varepsilon) \parallel (\varepsilon)$ where the message is sent by a, but b does not elect to receive it. So what we need to do is ensure that each of the three occurrences of "$\vee$" represent the *same* choice, and that the choice should be made consistently.

The heart of the issue is that the trace expression notation offers a choice operator ($\vee$), which is adequate for global protocols. However, for local protocols it is important to be able to distinguish between a choice that represents a free (local) choice, and a choice that is forced by earlier choices. In this example, a can freely choose whether to send M_1 or M_2. However, the choice of b whether to receive M_1 or not is not a free choice, but is forced by a's earlier choice.

Our semantics handles this by defining a *decision structure* that is used to enforce consistent choices. Formally, given a protocol τ, we define $d(\tau)$ as a set of *decision structures*. A decision structure is a syntactic structure that mirrors the structure of τ, except that each $\vee$ is annotated with a decision (e.g. L or R). We define three operations on a decision structure: to get the sub-decision structure corresponding to the left part (denoted $d.L$), to get the right part $(d.R)$ and to get the decision (L or R) associated with the current $\vee$ node (denoted $d.D$). We define $d(\tau)$ to create a set of decision structures, each of which corresponds to the structure of τ, but where all possible assignments of decisions are made. Observe that If τ contains N occurrences of $\vee$ then the set $d(\tau)$ contains 2^N elements.

For example, given $\tau = a \overset{M_1}{\Longrightarrow} b \vee a \overset{M_2}{\Longrightarrow} b$ we have that $d(\tau) = \{\_ \overset{L}{\vee} \_, \_ \overset{R}{\vee} \_\}$ where we use $\_$ to indicate an irrelevant part of a decision structure, and $\overset{L}{\vee}$ to denote a node tagged with a decision L.

In addition to decisions of L and R, the definition of $d(\tau_1 \vee \tau_2)$ has a second case $(\ldots \cup \{t_1 \overset{LR}{\vee} t_2 \mid \ldots\})$. The reason is that it is only possible to enforce consistent choice if the choice is made by a single agent. If this is not the case, then we annotate with "LR" to indicate that a mixed choice is possible. For example, given $\tau = b \overset{M_1}{\Longrightarrow} a \vee a \overset{M_2}{\Longrightarrow} b$ we have that $d(\tau) = \{\_ \overset{LR}{\vee} \_\}$ because the agents associated with the set of possible initial messages in each branch are different $(ag(\tau_1) = \{b\} \neq ag(\tau_2) = \{a\})$.

$$d(\varepsilon) = \{\varepsilon\} \qquad\qquad d(I) = \{I\}$$

$$d(\tau_1 \vee \tau_2) = \{t_1 \overset{x}{\vee} t_2 \mid t_1 \in d(\tau_1) \wedge t_2 \in d(\tau_2)$$
$$\wedge\, x \in \{R, L\} \wedge |ag(\tau_1) \cup ag(\tau_2)| = 1\}$$
$$\cup \{t_1 \overset{LR}{\vee} t_2 \mid t_1 \in d(\tau_1) \wedge t_2 \in d(\tau_2) \wedge |ag(\tau_1) \cup ag(\tau_2)| \neq 1\}$$
$$\text{where } ag(\tau) = \{p \mid p \overset{M}{\Longrightarrow} r \in \min(\text{poset}(\tau))\}$$
$$d(\tau_1 \oplus \tau_2) = \{t_1 \oplus t_2 \mid t_1 \in d(\tau_1) \wedge t_2 \in d(\tau_2)\}$$

$$(\tau_L \otimes \tau_R).L = \tau_L \qquad (\tau_L \otimes \tau_R).R = \tau_R \qquad (\tau_L \overset{X}{\vee} \tau_R).D = X$$

Where $\otimes$ is any operator, and $\oplus$ is any operator other than $\vee$.

We now specify the semantics of a distributed protocol, denoted $[\![\tau]\!]_{\text{dist}}$. The semantics is defined in terms of a union over possible decision structures (first line). The remaining equations for the semantics carry along the decision structure, and follow it in recursive calls, and for the semantics of $\vee$ it enacts the decision specified in the structure, rather than considering both sub-protocols. Note that projection is defined using $\|$ rather than the usual $|$. The difference in the semantics below is that $\|$ passes the *same* decision structure to both arguments. This ensures consistency between agents, but not within agents.

$$[\![\tau]\!]_{\text{dist}} = \bigcup_{dt \in d(\tau)} [\![\tau^{a_1} \| \ldots \| \tau^{a_n}]\!]^{dt}$$

$$[\![M]\!]^{dt} = \{\langle M \rangle\}$$

$$[\![\varepsilon]\!]^{dt} = \{\langle \rangle\}$$

$$[\![\tau_1 \cdot \tau_2]\!]^{dt} = \{t_1 \circ t_2 \mid t_1 \in [\![\tau_1]\!]^{dt.L} \wedge t_2 \in [\![\tau_2]\!]^{dt.R}\}$$

$$[\![\tau_1 \wedge \tau_2]\!]^{dt} = [\![\tau_1]\!]^{dt.L} \cap [\![\tau_2]\!]^{dt.R}$$

$$[\![\tau_1 \vee \tau_2]\!]^{dt} = \text{if } dt.D = R \text{ then } [\![\tau_2]\!]^{dt.R} \text{ else if } dt.D = L \text{ then } [\![\tau_1]\!]^{dt.L}$$
$$\text{else } [\![\tau_2]\!]^{dt.R} \cup [\![\tau_1]\!]^{dt.L}$$

$$[\![\tau_1 | \tau_2]\!]^{dt} = \{z \mid t_1 \in [\![\tau_1]\!]^{dt.L} \wedge t_2 \in [\![\tau_2]\!]^{dt.R} \wedge z \in t_1 \bowtie t_2\}$$

$$[\![\tau_1 \| \tau_2]\!]^{dt} = \{z \mid t_1 \in [\![\tau_1]\!]^{dt} \wedge t_2 \in [\![\tau_2]\!]^{dt} \wedge z \in t_1 \bowtie t_2\}$$

Note that if τ does not contain any occurrences of $\vee$ then the semantics above reduce to the standard semantics.

Finally, we define $[\![\tau_i]\!]_{\text{dist}}^{CM}$, which computes the semantics of an interaction protocol τ_i by distributing it, and also applies a particular communication model CM.

$$[\![\tau_i]\!]_{\text{dist}}^{CM} = [\![\tau_i]\!]_{\text{dist}} \cap \mathcal{L}_{CM}^{\mathcal{E}_{\mathcal{I}(\tau)}}$$

Enactability. We are now finally in a position to define enactability. The intuition is that an interaction protocol τ is enactable iff the semantics of τ, with respect to a selected message ordering interpretation and communication model, can be realised by a distributed version of the protocol. In other words, if there exists for each role r a corresponding message protocol τ_r such that the combination of these protocols realises the same behaviour as τ. However, instead of considering whether there exists some τ_r, we let $\tau_r = \tau^r$, i.e. we take for each role the projected protocol as its protocol.

We also consider a notion of *weak* enactability. This applies in a situation where the distributed enactment is able to avoid violating the behaviour specified by τ, but is not able to recreate all of the behaviours that τ specifies. In other words, if a protocol is weakly enactable, the interleaving of the corresponding local protocols generates a subset of its traces (with a fixed *moi* and communication model). This means that a distributed implementation of the protocol can be sound (generates only valid traces), but cannot be complete (not all the traces are generated). This situation can arise with weaker message ordering interpretations (see below for examples). Weak enactability can also arise in situations where two ordered messages have two overlapping roles (e.g. $\tau = a \xRightarrow{M_1} b \cdot b \xRightarrow{M_2} a$). In this situation the projection operator is too strict: it has $\tau^b = r(M_1) \cdot s(M_2)$, which requires that M_1 is received before M_2 is sent. However, if we adopt an SR message ordering interpretation, then we do not need to ensure that M_2 is sent after M_1 is received, only that M_1 is sent before M_2 is received, which role a can ensure on its own.

Definition 2 (Strongly/Weakly Enactable). *Let τ be an interaction protocol, $\{a_1, a_2, ..., a_n\}$ the set of agents involved in τ, moi $\in$ MOISet a message order interpretation and $CM \in$ ComModel a communication model. We say that, τ is strongly (weakly) enactable, for moi semantics in CM model iff the decomposition of τ through projection on its agents $\{a_1, a_2, ..., a_n\}$ recognizes the same (a subset of) traces recognized by τ. Formally:*

$$enact(\tau)^{CM}_{moi} \quad iff \quad [\![\tau]\!]^{CM}_{dist} = [\![\tau]\!]^{CM}_{moi}$$
$$weak\_enact(\tau)^{CM}_{moi} \quad iff \quad [\![\tau]\!]^{CM}_{dist} \subseteq [\![\tau]\!]^{CM}_{moi}$$

$a \xrightarrow{M_1} b \cdot b \xrightarrow{M_5} c$

CM	RS	RR	SS	SR
CM1	✔	✔	✔	✔
CM2	✔	(✔)	(✔)	(✔)
CM3	✔	(✔)	(✔)	(✔)
CM4	✔	(✔)	(✔)	(✔)
CM5	✔	(✔)	(✔)	(✔)
CM6	✔	(✔)	(✔)	(✔)

$a \xrightarrow{M_1} b \cdot a \xrightarrow{M_2} c$

CM	RS	RR	SS	SR
CM1	✔	✔	✔	✔
CM2	✗	✔	✔	(✔)
CM3	✗	✔	✔	(✔)
CM4	✗	✗	✔	(✔)
CM5	✗	✗	✗	(✔)
CM6	✗	✗	✔	(✔)

$a \xrightarrow{M_1} b \cdot c \xrightarrow{M_6} b$

CM	RS	RR	SS	SR
CM1	✔	✔	✔	✔
CM2	✗	✔	✔	(✔)
CM3	✗	✔	✗	(✔)
CM4	✗	✔	✔	(✔)
CM5	✗	✔	✗	(✔)
CM6	✗	✔	✗	(✔)

$a \xrightarrow{M_1} b \cdot c \xrightarrow{M_4} a$

CM	RS	RR	SS	SR
CM1	✔	✔	✔	✔
CM2	✗	✗	✗	✔
CM3	✗	✗	✗	✔
CM4	✗	✗	✗	✔
CM5	✗	✗	✗	✔
CM6	✗	✗	✗	✔

$a \xrightarrow{M_1} b \cdot a \xrightarrow{M_2} b$

CM	RS	RR	SS	SR
CM1	✔	✔	✔	✔
CM2	✗	✔	✔	(✔)
CM3	✗	✔	✔	(✔)
CM4	✗	✔	✔	(✔)
CM5	✗	✔	✔	(✔)
CM6	✗	(✔)	(✔)	(✔)

$a \xrightarrow{M_1} b \cdot b \xrightarrow{M_3} a$

CM	RS	RR	SS	SR
CM1	✔	✔	✔	✔
CM2	✔	(✔)	(✔)	(✔)
CM3	✔	(✔)	(✔)	(✔)
CM4	✔	(✔)	(✔)	(✔)
CM5	✔	(✔)	(✔)	(✔)
CM6	✔	(✔)	(✔)	(✔)

$a \xrightarrow{M_1} b \lor a \xrightarrow{M_2} c$

CM	RS	RR	SS	SR
CM1	✔	✔	✔	✔
CM2	✔	✔	✔	✔
CM3	✔	✔	✔	✔
CM4	✔	✔	✔	✔
CM5	✔	✔	✔	✔
CM6	✔	✔	✔	✔

$a \xrightarrow{M_1} b \lor b \xrightarrow{M_3} a$

CM	RS	RR	SS	SR
CM1	✔	✔	✔	✔
CM2	✗	✗	✗	✗
CM3	✗	✗	✗	✗
CM4	✗	✗	✗	✗
CM5	✗	✗	✗	✗
CM6	✗	✗	✗	✗

Fig. 1. Automatically generated analyses of enactability.

Figure 1 show the results of applying this definition to a number of cases, with different message ordering interpretation, and different communication models. These tables were all generated by the Haskell implementation of the definitions in this paper, in which ✔ and (✔) denote *strongly* and *weakly* enactable, respectively. The prototype has around 300 LOC. It implements the trace expression standard semantics, message order interpretation, communication model semantics and enactability check[10].

Looking at the tables in Fig. 1, we make the following observations.

Firstly, CM1 is quite strict: all the cases considered are enactable under CM1, regardless of the selected message ordering interpretation. This is expected: we know that CM1 is quite strong.

Secondly, for many examples there is not a difference in enactability with the different communication models (other than CM1). The exception is where the communication model corresponds to the combination of MOI and the pattern in the protocol. For example, in the top row, second table from the right, the simple protocol is enactable given the SS message ordering interpretation only with

---

[10] The code is available at http://enactability.altervista.org/.

CM2 and CM4 (and, of course, CM1). This is because, for this protocol, both messages are received by the same agent but sent by different agents, and, given an RR MOI, the desired constraint that agent B receives the first message before the second, can only be enforced using a communication model that guarantees delivery of messages to the same recipient in the order in which messages were sent. Both CM2 and CM4 provide this guarantee (in fact CM4 provides exactly this, and CM2 is stronger).

Thirdly, RS appears to be a good choice for message ordering interpretation, since it is the only MOI where protocols are never weakly enactable. For the other message ordering interpretations, there are protocols that are only weakly enactable (for communication models other than CM1). A protocol being weakly enactable indicates that the desired behaviour specified by the MOI is too loose: it permits behaviours that the distributed realisation cannot realise. On the other hand, in the case of the left-most table on the bottom row (protocol $a \stackrel{M_1}{\Longrightarrow} b \cdot a \stackrel{M_2}{\Longrightarrow} b$), the protocol is not enactable under RS (except for CM1), but is enactable under SS and under RR. Turning to SR, we observe that it seems to be too weak: almost all the protocols in the figure are enactable (although in most cases only weakly enactable).

We now return to the example from the introduction:

$$changeUni = Alice \stackrel{Unenroll}{\Longrightarrow} UniA \cdot Alice \stackrel{Enroll}{\Longrightarrow} UniB$$

This corresponds to the second table from the left in the top row of Fig. 1, which shows that, if one desires an RR MOI, then the underlying message communication must be $CM1$, $CM2$ or $CM3$ in order for the protocol to be enactable.

Two further examples are discussed in the sequel.

Booking Protocol. The *Booking* protocol is a very simple two party protocol presented in [32]. It starts with the user U requesting the system S to book a ticket, followed by the system asking the user to pay for the ticket. Upon the reception of the user payment message, the protocol ends with the booking system sending a confirmation back to the user.

The *Booking* protocol is described by the following trace expression:

$$booking = U \stackrel{Book}{\Longrightarrow} S \cdot S \stackrel{Pay}{\Longrightarrow} U \cdot U \stackrel{Payment}{\Longrightarrow} S \cdot S \stackrel{Confirm}{\Longrightarrow} U$$

Figure 2 shows the results obtained by running the Haskell prototype on it. As we expected, the protocol turns out to always be at least weakly enactable. Since each pair of sequential messages always shares Receiver and Sender, the *Booking* protocol is strongly enactable only when the RS MOI is considered, whatever the selected CM. The motivation for this result resides in the definition of enactability and in the set of traces generated by the corresponding global and distributed protocols: U and S have the power to enforce each reception to be consumed before each sending.

Considering the other MOIs, the protocol is always weakly enactable except for the RSC model (CM1) when the asynchronous messages cannot be interleaved. This result is also a consequence of the power of U and S. We explain it

CM	RS	RR	SS	SR
CM1	✔	✔	✔	✔
CM2	✔	(✔)	(✔)	(✔)
CM3	✔	(✔)	(✔)	(✔)
CM4	✔	(✔)	(✔)	(✔)
CM5	✔	(✔)	(✔)	(✔)
CM6	✔	(✔)	(✔)	(✔)

Fig. 2. Automatically generated analysis for the *Booking* protocol.

for RR; the same explanation holds for the other MOIs. Since the enactability test returns (✔), we know that all the traces generated by the distributed protocol $\ulcorner booking \urcorner$ are also recognised by the global protocol, but there must be at least one which is only recognised by the global one. Always considering RR, and the first pair of sequential messages $U \overset{Book}{\Longrightarrow} S \cdot S \overset{Pay}{\Longrightarrow} U$, the global protocol, through $[\![booking]\!]_{RR}$, contains the trace $t = \langle s(Pay), s(Book), r(Book), r(Pay) \rangle$ where the reception of *Book* takes place before the reception of *Pay*, but the sending of *Book* takes place after the sending of *Pay* (the two messages are received in the opposite order they have been sent). This is a suitable trace which respects the global protocol constraints, since the RR MOI constrains the reception order only.

The distributed version of the *Booking* protocol, $\ulcorner booking \urcorner$, is the following:

$$\ulcorner booking \urcorner = booking^U \parallel booking^S$$
$$booking^U = UBook! \cdot UPay? \cdot UPayment! \cdot UConfirm?$$
$$booking^S = SBook? \cdot SPay! \cdot SPayment? \cdot SConfirm!$$

With respect to the first pair of sequential messages, we note that S locally enforces the reception of the *Book* message before enabling the sending of *Pay*. Consequently, we cannot observe the trace generated by the global protocol execution, where messages reception is in the correct order, but sending is not. For this reason the protocol is only weakly enactable.

Play Date Protocol. The *Play Date* protocol[11] has been chosen as an example of a non-enactable protocol. It is a two party protocol and, like the *Booking* one, it involves a user U and the system S.

The protocol starts with the user asking the system to organise a Play Date event, *ReqPD*. After this request more information can be either required by the system (*Req*), or given spontaneously by the user (*GiveInfo*). The user may also asking the system to forget something that he had previously communicated (*Forget*). This choice is followed by a further choice between the system confirming the event (*ConfirmPD*) or the user cancelling it (*CancelPD*).

---

[11] We present a simplified version of the play date protocol introduced in [32], where we replaced a loop involving a choice among *Req*, *GiveInfo*, or *Forget*, with a single iteration only.

The *Play Date* protocol can be described by the following trace expression:

$$playdate = U \xRightarrow{ReqPD} S\cdot$$
$$(S \xRightarrow{Req} U \vee U \xRightarrow{GiveInfo} S \vee U \xRightarrow{Forget} S)\cdot$$
$$(S \xRightarrow{ConfirmPD} U \vee U \xRightarrow{CancelPD} S)$$

As Fig. 3 shows, this is not enactable with any choice of CM and MOI. The reason is that the protocol is extremely flexible, and, in particular, it allows the user or the system to take the initiative, which allows for a race condition.

CM	RS	RR	SS	SR
CM1	✗	✗	✗	✗
CM2	✗	✗	✗	✗
CM3	✗	✗	✗	✗
CM4	✗	✗	✗	✗
CM5	✗	✗	✗	✗
CM6	✗	✗	✗	✗

Fig. 3. Automatically generated analysis for the *Play Date* protocol.

4 Related Work and Discussion

Global protocols may be modelled using many different formalisms including global types [11], Petri Nets [24], WS-CDL [31], AUML [21], Statecharts [18], and causal logic [17]. In each of these formalisms the enactability problem has been addressed in some ad hoc way. Despite their diversity, most of these formalisms do not support protocol concatenation which is needed to achieve a high expressivity, and very few approaches consider how message ordering and decision structures affect its definition. Also, very few come with an implemented prototype, and none considers the issues raised by the communication model.

Taking all these features into account in a unified semantic-driven way, and demonstrating the potential of the approach on a highly expressive protocol language, are the innovative and original features of this contribution.

Desai and Singh [14] limit their investigation to the RS message ordering interpretation, which they consider the standard of correctness. Hence, despite the introduction they provide to other message orderings and to the problems they might raise, the definition of enactability they provide is not parametric in the MOI.

Lanese *et al.* [23] move a step further, but the generality of their approach is still limited. They define three different notions of enactability, which they name conformance: sender conformance, receiver conformance, and disjoint conformance. That approach is more flexible than the one by Desai and Singh, but less general than ours, where the definition of enactability is parametric in the MOI and does not require different cases. Also, they only consider how sequence and choice are affected by MOIs, leaving the study of other operators for the future. Moreover, when discussing interaction protocols whose most external operator is a choice, they put a very strong constraint for enactability, namely that the agents involved in the two branches of the choice (excluding the agents involved in the choice itself) are the same. We added decision structures to overcome this restriction, and provide a notion of enactability that can succeed even when that constraint is not met.

Neither Desai and Singh, nor Lanese *et al.* use formalisms for protocol representation as expressive as trace expressions, and neither of them present experiments obtained from a working prototype, as we do.

With respect to the introduction of decision structures to remove unnecessary restrictions on enactability of protocols when choice is involved, our proposal is similar to that by Qiu *et al.* [27]. However, as for the other works we have discussed in this section, we implemented our enactability checker, whereas their work only provides definitions. Additionally, our approach is simpler in that we do not need to label the choice operator with agents as they do, and, finally, they do not consider as general a setting (with a range of message ordering interpretations and communication semantics).

In the future, we will address both theoretical and practical issues. On the theoretical side, we plan to take more communication models into account including the FIFO 1-1, and to carry out a systematic analysis of the relationships between the communication model and the message ordering interpretation, to identify those combinations that provide some guarantees by design. We will also explore the relationship between enactability and distributed monitorability [16], since the two notions are related.

On the practical side, we plan to improve our working prototype to provide a tool to assess protocols for enactability. Apart from providing a user-friendly interface, a key issue to address will be to provide a way to isolate the part of a non-enactable protocol that makes it non-enactable. Also, trace expressions are interpreted in a coinductive way [29] to represent infinite traces of events. Since Haskell does not support coinduction, the existing prototype can be only used on acyclic message and interaction protocols. Haskell has been chosen because the implementation mimics the semantics, which makes it easy to check that the Haskell implementation correctly implements the formal definitions. In order to fully implement the proposed features we are planning to develop the enactability check using SWI-Prolog[12], which natively supports coinduction. We also will explore alternative approaches to dealing with cyclic trace expressions, including the possibility of translating them to (e.g.) Büchi automata. Additionally, to stress-test the prototype and assess its performance from a qualitative and quantitative viewpoint we plan to create a library of interaction protocols known to be "problematic" with respect to enactability, and perform systematic experiments.

---

[12] http://www.swi-prolog.org.

Finally, this work highlighted the need to characterise existing agent infrastructures such as JADE [7], Jason [8] and Jadex [26] in terms of the communication models they support. We asked the developers of the three frameworks, and all agreed that they support the CM4 model, which was the answer we expected. Nevertheless, this answer was far from being trivial to identify for the developers themselves. As an example, Lars Braubach pointed out that Jadex uses service interaction on top of messages, i.e. communication is fully asynchronous but based on interfaces and method calls from a user perspective, which makes answering the question more subtle than it might seem. Both Jomi Fred Hübner (Jason) and Agostino Poggi (JADE) recognized that they had to spend some time on the issue, also because the classification CM0-CM6 based on [12] requires time to be read and understood. This suggests two further directions of work. On the one hand, we might run experiments on the three platforms above, to confirm their CM and try to check if other models are (unexpectedly) supported. On the other hand, the EMAS community[13] might devise a standard taxonomy for CMs, such as the as one in [12], and provide each platform with a set of agreed upon "platform standard metadata" (how many agents can run concurrently without experiencing problems; learning curve for different types of professionals; known practical applications; etc.). These metadata should include CM as well. This piece of information, along with the approach we have proposed in this paper, would allow the developers to determine whether a protocol is enactable on a given infrastructure.

Acknowledgements. We thank Lars Braubach, Jomi Fred Hübner, and Agostino Poggi for their support in understanding the communication model supported by Jadex, Jason, and JADE.

References

1. Ancona, D., Drossopoulou, S., Mascardi, V.: Automatic generation of self-monitoring MASs from multiparty global session types in jason. In: Baldoni, M., Dennis, L., Mascardi, V., Vasconcelos, W. (eds.) DALT 2012. LNCS (LNAI), vol. 7784, pp. 76–95. Springer, Heidelberg (2013). https://doi.org/10.1007/978-3-642-37890-4_5

2. Ancona, D., Ferrando, A., Franceschini, L., Mascardi, V.: Parametric trace expressions for runtime verification of Java-like programs. In: FTfJP@ECOOP, pp. 10:1–10:6. ACM (2017)

3. Ancona, D., Ferrando, A., Franceschini, L., Mascardi, V.: Coping with bad agent interaction protocols when monitoring partially observable multiagent systems. In: Demazeau, Y., An, B., Bajo, J., Fernández-Caballero, A. (eds.) PAAMS 2018. LNCS (LNAI), vol. 10978, pp. 59–71. Springer, Cham (2018). https://doi.org/10.1007/978-3-319-94580-4_5

4. Ancona, D., Ferrando, A., Mascardi, V.: Comparing trace expressions and linear temporal logic for runtime verification. In: Ábrahám, E., Bonsangue, M., Johnsen, E.B. (eds.) Theory and Practice of Formal Methods. LNCS, vol. 9660, pp. 47–64. Springer, Cham (2016). https://doi.org/10.1007/978-3-319-30734-3_6

---

[13] http://emas.in.tu-clausthal.de/.

5. Ancona, D., Ferrando, A., Mascardi, V.: Agents interoperability via conformance modulo mapping. In: Cossentino, M., Sabatucci, L., Seidita, V. (eds.) Proceedings of the 19th Workshop "From Objects to Agents", CEUR Workshop Proceedings, Palermo, Italy, 28–29 June 2018, vol. 2215, pp. 109–115. CEUR-WS.org (2018). http://ceur-ws.org/Vol-2215/paper_18.pdf
6. Autili, M., Tivoli, M.: Distributed enforcement of service choreographies. In: Cámara, J., Proença, J. (eds.) 13th International Workshop on Foundations of Coordination Languages and Self-Adaptive Systems (FOCLASA). Electronic Proceedings in Theoretical Computer Science (EPTCS), vol. 175, pp. 18–35 (2014). https://doi.org/10.4204/EPTCS.175.2
7. Bellifemine, F.L., Caire, G., Greenwood, D.: Developing Multi-Agent Systems with JADE. Wiley, Hoboken (2007)
8. Bordini, R.H., Hübner, J.F., Wooldridge, M.: Programming Multi-Agent Systems in AgentSpeak Using Jason. Wiley Series in Agent Technology. Wiley, Hoboken (2007)
9. Broda, S., Machiavelo, A., Moreira, N., Reis, R.: Automata for regular expressions with shuffle. Inf. Comput. **259**(2), 162–173 (2018)
10. Carbone, M., Honda, K., Yoshida, N.: Structured communication-centred programming for web services. In: De Nicola, R. (ed.) ESOP 2007. LNCS, vol. 4421, pp. 2–17. Springer, Heidelberg (2007). https://doi.org/10.1007/978-3-540-71316-6_2
11. Castagna, G., Dezani-Ciancaglini, M., Padovani, L.: On global types and multi-party sessions. In: Bruni, R., Dingel, J. (eds.) FMOODS/FORTE -2011. LNCS, vol. 6722, pp. 1–28. Springer, Heidelberg (2011). https://doi.org/10.1007/978-3-642-21461-5_1
12. Chevrou, F., Hurault, A., Quéinnec, P.: On the diversity of asynchronous communication. Form. Aspects Comput. **28**(5), 847–879 (2016). https://doi.org/10.1007/s00165-016-0379-x
13. Decker, G., Weske, M.: Local enforceability in interaction petri nets. In: Alonso, G., Dadam, P., Rosemann, M. (eds.) BPM 2007. LNCS, vol. 4714, pp. 305–319. Springer, Heidelberg (2007). https://doi.org/10.1007/978-3-540-75183-0_22
14. Desai, N., Singh, M.P.: On the enactability of business protocols. In: Fox, D., Gomes, C.P. (eds.) Twenty-Third AAAI Conference on Artificial Intelligence, pp. 1126–1131. AAAI Press (2008). http://www.aaai.org/Library/AAAI/2008/aaai08-178.php
15. Ferrando, A., Ancona, D., Mascardi, V.: Monitoring patients with hypoglycemia using self-adaptive protocol-driven agents: a case study. In: Baldoni, M., Müller, J.P., Nunes, I., Zalila-Wenkstern, R. (eds.) EMAS 2016. LNCS (LNAI), vol. 10093, pp. 39–58. Springer, Cham (2016). https://doi.org/10.1007/978-3-319-50983-9_3
16. Ferrando, A., Ancona, D., Mascardi, V.: Decentralizing MAS monitoring with DecAMon. In: Larson, K., Winikoff, M., Das, S., Durfee, E.H. (eds.) Proceedings of the 16th Conference on Autonomous Agents and MultiAgent Systems, AAMAS 2017, São Paulo, Brazil, 8–12 May 2017, pp. 239–248. ACM (2017). http://dl.acm.org/citation.cfm?id=3091164
17. Giunchiglia, E., Lee, J., Lifschitz, V., McCain, N., Turner, H.: Nonmonotonic causal theories. Artif. Intell. **153**(1–2), 49–104 (2004). https://doi.org/10.1016/j.artint.2002.12.001
18. Harel, D.: Statecharts: a visual formalism for complex systems. Sci. Comput. Program. **8**(3), 231–274 (1987). https://doi.org/10.1016/0167-6423(87)90035-9
19. Honda, K., Vasconcelos, V.T., Kubo, M.: Language primitives and type discipline for structured communication-based programming. In: Hankin, C. (ed.) ESOP

1998. LNCS, vol. 1381, pp. 122–138. Springer, Heidelberg (1998). https://doi.org/10.1007/BFb0053567

20. Honda, K., Yoshida, N., Carbone, M.: Multiparty asynchronous session types. In: Necula, G.C., Wadler, P. (eds.) 35th ACM SIGPLAN-SIGACT Symposium on Principles of Programming Languages (POPL), pp. 273–284. ACM (2008). https://doi.org/10.1145/1328438.1328472

21. Huget, M.-P., Odell, J.: Representing agent interaction protocols with agent UML. In: Odell, J., Giorgini, P., Müller, J.P. (eds.) AOSE 2004. LNCS, vol. 3382, pp. 16–30. Springer, Heidelberg (2005). https://doi.org/10.1007/978-3-540-30578-1_2

22. Lamport, L.: Time, clocks, and the ordering of events in a distributed system. Commun. ACM **21**(7), 558–565 (1978). https://doi.org/10.1145/359545.359563

23. Lanese, I., Guidi, C., Montesi, F., Zavattaro, G.: Bridging the gap between interaction- and process-oriented choreographies. In: Cerone, A., Gruner, S. (eds.) Sixth IEEE International Conference on Software Engineering and Formal Methods (SEFM), pp. 323–332. IEEE Computer Society (2008). https://doi.org/10.1109/SEFM.2008.11

24. Peterson, J.L.: Petri nets. ACM Comput. Surv. **9**(3), 223–252 (1977). https://doi.org/10.1145/356698.356702

25. Poizat, P., Salaün, G.: Checking the realizability of BPMN 2.0 choreographies. In: 27th Annual ACM Symposium on Applied Computing (SAC), pp. 1927–1934. ACM (2012). https://doi.org/10.1145/2245276.2232095

26. Pokahr, A., Braubach, L., Lamersdorf, W.: Jadex: a BDI reasoning engine. In: Bordini, R.H., Dastani, M., Dix, J., El Fallah Seghrouchni, A. (eds.) Multi-Agent Programming. MSASSO, vol. 15, pp. 149–174. Springer, Boston (2005). https://doi.org/10.1007/0-387-26350-0_6

27. Qiu, Z., Zhao, X., Cai, C., Yang, H.: Towards the theoretical foundation of choreography. In: Williamson, C.L., Zurko, M.E., Patel-Schneider, P.F., Shenoy, P.J. (eds.) 16th International World Wide Web Conference (WWW), pp. 973–982. ACM (2007). https://doi.org/10.1145/1242572.1242704

28. Salaün, G., Bultan, T., Roohi, N.: Realizability of choreographies using process algebra encodings. IEEE Trans. Serv. Comput. **5**(3), 290–304 (2012). https://doi.org/10.1109/TSC.2011.9

29. Sangiorgi, D.: On the origins of bisimulation and coinduction. ACM Trans. Program. Lang. Syst. **31**(4), 15:1–15:41 (2009). https://doi.org/10.1145/1516507.1516510

30. Takeuchi, K., Honda, K., Kubo, M.: An interaction-based language and its typing system. In: Halatsis, C., Maritsas, D., Philokyprou, G., Theodoridis, S. (eds.) PARLE 1994. LNCS, vol. 817, pp. 398–413. Springer, Heidelberg (1994). https://doi.org/10.1007/3-540-58184-7_118

31. W3C: Web Services Choreography Description Language Version 1.0 (2005). https://www.w3.org/TR/ws-cdl-10/

32. Winikoff, M., Yadav, N., Padgham, L.: A new hierarchical agent protocol notation. Auton. Agents Multi-Agent Syst. **32**(1), 59–133 (2017). https://doi.org/10.1007/s10458-017-9373-9

Simulation

An Architecture for Integrating BDI Agents with a Simulation Environment

Alan Davoust[1,2(✉)], Patrick Gavigan[1], Cristina Ruiz-Martin[1],
Guillermo Trabes[1,3], Babak Esfandiari[1], Gabriel Wainer[1], and Jeremy James[4]

[1] Carleton University, Ottawa, Canada
{patrickgavigan,cristinaruizmartin,guillermotrabes,babak,
gwainer}@sce.carleton.ca
[2] Université du Québec en Outaouais, Gatineau, Canada
alan.davoust@uqo.ca
[3] Universidad Nacional de San Luis, San Luis, Argentina
[4] Cohort Systems, Ottawa, Canada
jjames@cohortsys.com

Abstract. We present Simulated Autonomous Vehicle Infrastructure
(SAVI), an open source architecture for integrating Belief-Desire-
Intention (BDI) agents with a simulation platform. This allows for separation of concerns between the development of complex multi-agent
behaviours and simulated environments to test them in.

We identify and address the *impedance mismatch* between modelling
and simulation, where time is explicitly modelled and differs from "wall
clock" time, and BDI systems, where time is not explicitly managed. Our
approach avoids linking the environment's simulation time step to the
agents' reasoning cycles, relying instead on real time simulation where
possible, and ensuring that the reasoning module does not get ahead of
the simulation. This contributes to a realistic approximation of a real
environment for the simulated BDI agents.

This is accomplished by running the simulation cycles and the agent
reasoning cycles each in their own threads of execution, and managing
a single point of contact between these threads. Finally, we illustrate
the use of our architecture with a case study involving the simulation of
Unmanned Aerial Vehicles (UAVs) following birds.

Keywords: Belief-Desire-Intention (BDI) · Modeling and simulation ·
Architecture · Jason · AgentSpeak Language (ASL)

1 Introduction

Multi-agent systems are often designed to be embedded in highly dynamic environments. In these environments, the wide range of possible input signals may
produce complex group-level behaviours which are difficult to accurately predict or to produce by design. During the development process, the behaviour
of the agents must therefore be thoroughly tested in a controlled yet realistic

© Springer Nature Switzerland AG 2020
L. A. Dennis et al. (Eds.): EMAS 2019, LNAI 12058, pp. 67–84, 2020.
https://doi.org/10.1007/978-3-030-51417-4_4

environment before the system can be deployed. In this research, we are concerned with the development of agents using the Belief-Desire-Intention (BDI) paradigm [25], and of an appropriate simulated environment to test the agent system. The main challenge in this task is the lack of frameworks to appropriately handle both the development of complex cognitive agents and of a realistic simulated environment [2,29].

Existing BDI frameworks, such as Jason [11,15] and lightJason [5,19], include simple environments that can be reused and extended, but these environments lack the sophistication and graphical capabilities of proper simulation platforms. Conversely, the field of Modelling and Simulation provides a set methodologies with their own simulation tools. These formalisms include the Discrete Event System Specification (DEVS) formalism [37] with simulators such as CD++ [35] and PyDEVS [30], and the methodology of Agent Based Modelling (ABM) with tools including Repast [23] or NetLogo [36]). There are also domain-specific simulation platforms for communication networks (e.g. OMNET++ [34]), traffic simulation (e.g. MITSIMLab [8], Microscopic Traffic Simulator [18]), and other domains. However, these are poorly suited for modelling complex cognitive processes [2]; in particular, they do not provide any support for techniques such as BDI.

As a result, the main approaches to integrating these two pieces involve either writing custom simulation code in a BDI framework, or custom BDI support in a simulation platform, or finally integrating two separate, mature frameworks from the two areas, with a considerable *impedance mismatch* problem [29]. By this term we refer to the conceptual and technical issues faced when integrating components defined using different methodologies, formalisms or tools.

Our work follows the third approach, and aims to integrate BDI agents with a simulated environment. Our main contribution is Simulated Autonomous Vehicle Infrastructure (SAVI), an architecture that seamlessly connects the Jason BDI framework [11,15] with a simulation environment developed using Processing [14], addressing several key elements of the impedance mismatch problem.

In particular, our architecture decouples the agents from the simulation environment, making it easy to develop them independently, and allowing them to run as separate processes interacting in an asynchronous manner. This avoids linking the environment's simulation advances to the agent's responses: if the agent is for some reason slow (e.g. due to expensive computation), the simulation will continue unaffected, making the transition to a natural environment more realistic.

The rest of the paper is organized as follows: in Sect. 2 we provide a summary of background followed by related work in Sect. 3. This is followed by a definition of the proposed SAVI architecture is in Sect. 4. In Sect. 5 we describe a case study applying our architecture. Finally, we conclude in Sect. 6 followed by a brief section on future work.

2   Background

In this section we present the BDI paradigm for developing multi-agent systems and discuss different approaches to develop a BDI agent system in a simulated environment.

2.1   Belief-Desire-Intention Architecture

The BDI architecture was introduced by Bratman and others in the 1980s [12] as a way to develop complex intelligent and autonomous agents. In this method, agents have a set of beliefs, stored in a *belief base* about their state as well as the state of their environment. They can perceive their environment to update these beliefs. These agents also have goals, or *desires*, that they need to achieve. The agents also have a set of plans that they can execute, stored in a *plan base*. The plans can involve updates to the belief base, or actions that the agent can apply to the environment. When an agent reasons about its *beliefs* and desires and selects an appropriate plan to execute, this plan becomes an *intention*. As the agent executes these plans, the agent can drop intentions based on changes in their beliefs if they are no longer achievable due to some change in the environment. The execution cycle for a BDI agent, from perception to action, is called the *reasoning cycle*.

BDI architectures have become especially relevant with the development of autonomous vehicles, in particular, self-driving cars (see [27] for example). However, as testing the vehicles' decision-making in a real-life setting is challenging, it is crucial that they can be developed in a realistic simulated environment.

2.2   Simulation Requirements for Multi-agent Systems

A multi-agent system is situated in an environment (real or simulated) which the agents can perceive through different types of sensors (e.g. a camera or lidar sensor), and modify through actuators (e.g. moving to a new location, picking up an object).

An important property of the environment is whether it is *static* or *dynamic* [28]: a static environment contains only static objects that remain fixed and unchanging (the agents change only their internal state); a simple dynamic environment changes over time, but only due to the agents' actions; and finally a complex dynamic environment changes over time, due to the agents' actions but also due to other external factors, including natural phenomena, and agents outside of the considered agent system (e.g. humans).

The actions performed by the agents and the changes to the environment, either in response to the agents' actions or due to external factors, update the state of the system over time. There are several ways to model time in a simulation. One approach, Discrete-Event Modelling [6], updates the model's state variables every time an event occurs, and allows the model (or each sub-model of a composite model) to schedule its next state change, at any time. This allows arbitrarily fine-grained precision along the time axis. In an alternative approach,

Discrete Time Modelling, the state of the simulation is updated at discrete points in time. The difference between a point in time and the next one is called the *time step*. This approach is well suited for applications where the system state changes very quickly or many events happen in a short period of time.

3   Related Work: Simulated Environments for BDI Systems

There are three main approaches to simulate the environment of a BDI agent system [29]: the simulation can be built into the BDI engine, or else an existing simulation platform can be extended to support BDI, or finally a simulation platform can be connected to a BDI engine.

3.1   Simulation Within MAS Development Platforms

Several agent development platforms have basic built-in simulation capabilities; this includes BDI platforms such as Jason.

In [10], the authors provide their own custom simulation environment for BDI agents. Another such custom simulation is [33], which includes *heavyweight agents* (i.e. agents with very advanced reasoning) combined with *lightweight agents* (i.e. agents that only reacts to their environment). However, if we compare these custom environments to other simulator platforms such as Repast, their features and capabilities are very limited. Typically, they are meant to support simple dynamic environments (which only change according to the agents' actions), and do not explicitly model time.

3.2   Modelling Cognitive Processes in Simulation Platforms

The second approach is to model the cognitive capabilities of agents (BDI, in our case) on standard simulation platforms.

Established ABM modeling tools (such as Netlogo or Repast) are not meant to directly model complex agent behaviours or realistic physical systems: their strength is rather in modelling the behaviour of complex systems as the emergent result of very simple interacting agent models. Similarly, general-purpose simulation systems (e.g. Mason [20]) and formalisms (e.g. DEVS) do not have built-in capabilities to model cognitive processes (such as the basic machinery of the BDI paradigm). However, there have been several attempts to build models of cognitive processes using modelling and simulation formalisms, in particular the DEVS formalism.

Several projects have implemented BDI reasoning with the DEVS formalism [2,31,32,38].

JAMES [31,32] is a Java based agent modeling environment for simulation, to be used as test beds for multi-agent systems. It allows the execution of agents in distributed environments. In JAMES, an agent is represented as a DEVS atomic model, where its autonomous behaviour is represented by the internal function and the perceptions are represented through the external function. The actions of the agent in the environment are represented as the output function. In JAMES, the BDI architecture is incorporated in the internal state of the atomic model. Because in ABM, new agents are usually created and destroyed during the simulation, the authors also introduced Dynamic DEVS (DynDEVS).

The proposals of Akplogan et al. [2] and Zhang et al. [38] are very similar to the JAMES approach. The former uses the classic dynamic DEVS (DS-DEVS) introduced by Barros [7] on a platform targeted at the simulation of agriculture called RECORD [9], whereas the latter implements PRS [16], a BDI-based reasoning architecture, on the D-SOL simulation platform [17]. Another model of cognitive processes, ACT-R, has also been modelled with DEVS [21].

DIVAs [4] is a simulation platform for dynamic and open environments that includes some machinery for agents' cognitive processes, including base classes to implement agent knowledge, tasks and plans. However, it is unclear whether this system uses an established simulation formalism or an established cognitive reasoning model.

3.3 Connecting Simulation Platforms and Cognitive Reasoning Engines

A third approach, the one presented in this paper, aims to couple a mature platform for developing cognitive agents with an existing simulation platform. This can provide an improved modeling capability for simulations that involve complex agent behaviors. The main existing work in this direction [24, 29] is an integration of the commercial JACK platform [3] (for BDI agents) with the Repast agent based simulation software [22]. This is then generalized to an architecture that can accommodate wider range of ABM platforms and a wider range of platforms for modelling cognitive agents.

Our approach is similar, although we have chosen Processing [14] as a simulation environment rather than an ABM tool. In our experience – shared by others [1, 26] – ABM modelling tools (such as Netlogo or Repast) are poorly suited to model complex dynamic environments. The agent-based modelling approach tends to model the entire system of interest (including physical systems deprived of any agency) as a system of (numerous) interacting agents. When the environment includes a small number of complex cognitive agents and a small number of (potentially complex) physical systems, other modelling methodologies appear more appropriate.

Our choice of Processing is motivated by its powerful built-in visualization capabilities, its built-in synchronization with real time (further discussed below and in Sect. 4.2) and the option of using discrete-event simulation (although at this point our simulations are all discrete-time). A powerful graphical interface is useful for the demonstration of real scenarios to a non-technical audience. This is specially important for our use case, a military application where we need to test the resilience of the BDI agents.

A key difference with our approach is the way time is synchronized between the two environments. In the approach of [24] and [29], the discrete-time simulation steps are synchronized with the reasoning cycles of the cognitive agents. This implies that each reasoning cycle of the agent takes a fixed (simulated) time, and is probably appropriate for very simple cognitive tasks of predictable or negligible duration (with respect to the simulation time frame). In the context of an autonomous agent travelling at potentially high speed in a physical world, delays and variations in reasoning may have major impacts, including for example collisions that could happen while the agent is attempting to decide how to avoid the obstacle. Our approach aims instead to synchronize simulated time with real time (which is to some extent handled by Processing, unlike many traditional simulation platforms), and considers that the BDI agent also reasons in "'real time", i.e. at the same speed in simulation as in its future deployment. This approach is further discussed in Sect. 4.2, along with its assumptions and limitations.

4   SAVI Architecture

This section details the proposed SAVI architecture for integrating BDI agents with a simulated environment. Specifically, we will focus on solving the problems resulting from the impedance mismatch between BDI and simulation systems. First, we introduce our framework setup, and briefly discuss the impedance mismatch problems. Then we introduce the open source SAVI architecture [13] and explain how these problems are addressed.

4.1   Setup

Our overarching problem is to connect an agent system built with a BDI framework to a model of the environment, designed using a framework appropriate for simulation. In our case, the BDI framework is Jason [11,15], and our simulation runs in Processing [14]. Both are Java applications, which makes the integration manageable through direct method invocations, but the same approach would be feasible with any frameworks that expose the appropriate information via an external Application Programming Interface (API).

Our assumption is that the BDI agents are simply the reasoning engine (the *brain*) for agents with a physical presence in the simulated environment (e.g., drones or unmanned vehicles). In our case (see case study in Sect. 5), these agent models are drones.

In order to connect the two "worlds" (i.e. simulation and BDI agents), the agent brains must receive perceptions of the world from the simulated agents, and send actions for the agent models to execute in the simulated world. Eventually, these agent brains will be connected to physical agents transmitting the same information as their simulated counterparts, and the goal is for the simulated behaviour to carry over into the real world.

4.2   Decoupling Simulation and Reasoning

In this context, one approach (adopted for example by Singh et al. [29]) is to use the discrete-time simulation process as a driver for the agents' reasoning: at each time-tick, update each simulated model, and invoke one reasoning cycle from the agent brains. This has the advantage of simplifying the integration of the two platforms, but it arguably comes at a significant cost in terms of a realistic simulation. In particular, it implies that changing the simulation time step (simply to change the granularity of the simulation), would directly affect the agents' *reasoning clock*: the agent reasoning will not be simulated more or less precisely, it will instead directly increase or decrease the agent's relative computational power, by allowing unbounded time for each decision. Pushed to the extreme, we might imagine for example an agent getting *lost in thought* while computing intractable plans, and the world would then *wait* for the agent. Of course, this cannot happen in a *real world* environment: if an agent is lost in thought, the environment will continue to update while the agent performs its reasoning.

More generally, a key component of the "impedance mismatch" problem is the lack of explicit time management (modelling) in existing BDI engines, where there is no notion of *simulation time*. Unlike typical simulation settings, the BDI agent is not a *model* that can be executed at an arbitrary speed: it is essentially the *real* process that will be deployed, and the speed it will run at only depends on the hardware on which it will be deployed. This implies that if we attempt to speed up the simulation beyond real-time, we may force the agent to make decisions faster than it could in a real deployment, and therefore reduce the fidelity of the simulation. We can increase the rate of discrete-time "ticks", but these ticks must represent shorter increments of the simulation time. The only factor that may allow the simulation to run faster than real-time would be a significant difference in hardware capability, meaning that we could simulate the real robot's reasoning faster than it would happen once deployed. This would, however, require precise models of the deployment hardware.

Our approach addresses this problem by running the simulation in real time, which is the only speed available to the BDI engine (excluding the hardware acceleration possibility discussed above). In order to remove the synchronization between the simulation time-step and the BDI reasoning cycles, we allow the agents' brains to run as their own processes (threads, more specifically), while the simulation will update on its own schedule. The two sides must now interact asynchronously, which brings several challenges (generically described above as the impedance mismatch between the two frameworks).

For one thing, actions may be initiated by the agent asynchronously, whereas the simulation system constrains changes to happen at fixed time steps. This is connected to a thread-safety issue, if both an agent process and the simulation process attempt to concurrently modify the environment.

Another challenge is the constraint of running a real-time simulation. This is not always possible: if we attempt to shorten the time-step too much, then the simulator may not be able to keep up with real time. As we can see in our experiments (Sect. 5), Processing will not run *faster* than real-time, but if the simulation gets too computationally intensive, it will run slower than real time.

There is therefore a delicate balance to maintain between the simulation speed and the agents' reasoning speed. On one hand, if the agent reasons too fast, then it might repeatedly perceive an outdated state of the world and misinterpret the consequences of its latest action, which the simulation engine has not yet computed. The problem here is that this would not happen in the real world: there cannot be any delay between an action being initiated by the an agent in the real world, and this action initiating its effect on the environment. On the other hand, if the agent is slow and the perceptions from the environment come as messages, the agents might accrue a backlog of these messages, and again be attempting to act on an outdated perception of reality. In this case an agent being too slow to keep up with its environment is perfectly possible. However, the environment would not be sending overwhelming numbers of updates in the form of messages[1].

4.3   The SAVI Architecture

In order to address these challenges, we designed the SAVI architecture shown in Fig. 1.

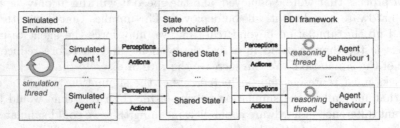

Fig. 1. Simulation and agent behaviour architecture.

This architecture uses three main modules for implementing the interface between the BDI agents and the simulation infrastructure. These include the *Simulated Environment* module, the *State Synchronization* module, and the *Agent Behaviour* module. To ensure that the simulation time step is independent of the agent reasoning cycle rate of each of the agents, the simulation engine and each individual agent's behavioural model run in separate threads of execution.

The Simulated Environment module is responsible for providing the simulated environment as well as a simulated model of the agents' physical presence in that environment. This includes all movements and interactions of the agents. In our case, this module also provides a visualization of the environment for monitoring the simulation.

---

[1] Of course, the perception infrastructure may do so, and again using the present architecture to implement that interface could solve the problem.

Individual agents perceive this simulated environment as well as their own properties, and perform actions. These interactions are mediated by the State Synchronization module. This module is responsible for ensuring mutual exclusion of the different execution processes over perception, messages, and actions being passed between the environment and agent objects in the Agent Behaviour module. This mutual exclusion is managed by ensuring that the variables representing the agent's perception are always calculated and set by the simulation side and only read by the behavioural models. Mutual exclusion of data between the simulation and agent threads is ensured using thread safe variables, and happens separately for each agent, meaning that there is no centralized bottleneck.

The agent behaviour module provides the implementation of the BDI based behaviour model. It receives environmental perceptions and messages from other agents via the State Synchronization module and responds by sending actions and messages back. These responses are determined using the BDI reasoning cycle, which runs as a separate thread of execution for each agent. This enables the updates to the environment to be decoupled from the execution time of the individual reasoning cycles of each agent. In addition, since the perceptions are represented as state variables to be read, as opposed to messages, there is never a backlog of perceptions waiting for the agent, even if the reasoning is slow.

Finally, in the case where the agent reasons faster than the simulation can update the environment variables, we ensure that the agent waits for new perceptions by implementing a *producer-consumer* pattern: if the simulation clock has not advanced since the previous reasoning cycle, the agent waits. For this purpose, the simulation engine timestamps every update of the state variables.

The effects of this speed coordination are illustrated by measurements of the simulation update speed and the reasoning speed, discussed in Sect. 5.4.

5 Case Study

In this section, we describe our implementation of the SAVI architecture. We demonstrate the separation of the simulation from the implementation of the agent behaviours in BDI. We also show that we have overcome the impedance mismatch between these two techniques. Our case study scenario involves an airport safety patrol made up of Unmanned Aerial Vehicles (UAVs) chasing migratory birds away from the airport. The implementation of SAVI, including this case study, are available as an open-source project [13].

5.1 Scenario

In this scenario, UAVs are controlled by BDI agents in order to chase migratory birds away from the airport property. The simulation environment represents the Ottawa airport area, the UAVs, and the different threats (migratory birds) that can appear in that area. Because the objective of the case study is to show our simulation architecture, and not necessarily to demonstrate the performance of complex behaviours, we use a simplified version of the problem where the UAVs' mission is simply to follow the different threats near the airport.

Each UAV perceives the environment through four sensors:

1. A Global Positioning System (GPS) receiver that provides the position of the UAV,
2. A velocity sensor that indicates the UAV's speed and direction of travel,
3. A camera that can see nearby threats and other UAVs up to a maximum range,
4. A clock.

Each UAV also has a set of simple actions related to moving in the environment. These include:

1. Turning to the left,
2. Turning to the right,
3. Activating a thruster to move forward,
4. Deactivating a thruster to stop moving.

The behavior of the UAVs in this simulation is defined in AgentSpeak Language (ASL) as follows:

- When the UAV does not perceive any threats, the UAV stops and keep turning until a threat is perceived.
- When the UAV perceives threats, it turns to face the nearest one and then follows it.

5.2   Implementation

The simulation is built using Processing [14], which handles the set-up and discrete-time simulation as well as visualisation. The agent behaviour to be deployed in the UAVs is defined using the BDI paradigm, with behaviours written in the ASL and interpreted using Jason [11,15]. These two components are integrated as described above, using our SAVI architecture. The threat behaviour is directly implemented in Java: each threat sets a random destination and then travels in a straight line from its actual position. Once they arrive, they choose a new random destination.

5.3   Testing

Our case study consists of two scenarios, which can be easily set up in the simulation environment's configuration file. In the first scenario, shown in Fig. 2, we simulated the Ottawa airport area with 10 bird threats. The area is patrolled by three UAVs which have a limited camera perception range, as shown in the figure by a semicircle. Objects that are visible to a UAV are shown with circles around them. In the figure we can see that all the UAVs have a threat within

Fig. 2. Scenario 1: Test bed with 3 UAVs with short perception distance and 10 threats.

their camera range; however, there is a large area that is not observed by the UAVs.

In the second scenario, shown in Fig. 3, we simulated the Ottawa airport area with 15 threats. The area was patrolled by 10 UAVs with longer-range cameras, also represented by a semicircle in the figure. In the figure we can see that all the threats are perceived at least by one UAV. Likewise, all the UAVs are perceived by at least another UAV, however some areas are not covered.

5.4 Results

The key objectives of the SAVI architecture were to connect BDI agents to a simulation platform and resolve the challenges of synchronizing time between the two components. Our simulations are run as discrete time simulations, and can be run with different time step values. Processing allows us to set a *frame rate*, which specifies the number of execution cycles to be run per (real) second, and by setting the timestep to the inverse of this frequency we obtain real-time simulation, provided the computation can run quickly enough. As we request higher frame rates the simulation cannot keep up and we lose the "real time" property.

Our simulations were successfully run at several different frame rates, and the agents were able to carry out their task, largely unaffected by these variations. This demonstrates the suitability of our SAVI architecture to integrate a BDI framework with a simulation platform.

Fig. 3. Scenario 2: Test bed with 10 UAVs with large perception distance and 15 threats.

As noted earlier, we wanted to ensure that the agents' reasoning cycle and the simulation cycles were decoupled, and that we could manage their relative speeds. In effect, we needed to be certain that the simulation environment does not wait for the agent reasoning cycle to complete prior to computing the next simulation step. Furthermore, it was also of concern to ensure that the agent cannot reason faster than the simulation rate.

In order to demonstrate the effects of our safeguards on the speed coordination, we ran the test scenarios discussed in this case study under various frame rates and measured the effective simulation and reasoning cycle periods. The results for this test are shown in Fig. 4. The frame rate used as a reference along the X axis is the *requested* simulation speed, which may not be achievable in a computationally intensive simulation. We therefore plot the effective simulation speed (measured by the effective period between two frames) and the effective duration of the agents' reasoning cycles.

The plot shows that the reasoning cycle and the simulation time step follow an identical time step for lower frame rates, below approximately 65 frames per second. At these slower simulation speeds, the agent must synchronize its speed to only reason on up-to-date environment perceptions. The decreasing simulation time step also shows that the simulator is able to achieve the requested frame rate.

As the simulation frame rate increases, the simulation time step and the reasoning cycle period decrease but begin to diverge, and then they approximately

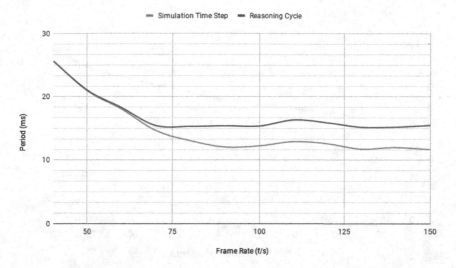

Fig. 4. Difference in simulation time step and reasoning cycle periods at different frame rates.

stabilize at the highest speed that the simulator is able to achieve for this scenario. At a frame rate of approximately 75 frames per second we can clearly see the reasoning cycle period lag behind the simulation time step. This means that the agent is reasoning more slowly than the simulation updates proceed. The simulated environment is not delayed by a slow agent's reasoning cycle, and the agent does not develop a backlog of messages (which would affect the agents' performance and possibly the reasoning speed).

In addition to showing that the reasoning cycle and simulation rates were decoupled, we also sought to demonstrate the scalability of SAVI. To test this property we recorded the change in performance of the simulation with an increasing number of agents and objects. These scenarios were performed using a desktop computer with an Intel i5 9400 processor and 16 GB of RAM. We performed two test scenarios: a test of the simulation refresh rate relative to the number of agents in the simulation, and a second test where we varied the number of other objects present, in this case the number of threats.

In Fig. 5 we show the increase in simulation refresh time as we increase the number of agents in the simulation. This test was not possible with more than 80 agents as the simulation cannot be performed in real time. In a similar way, in Fig. 6, we compare the simulation refresh time against the number of threat objects in the environment. In this scenario, the number of agents was fixed as two agents. We found that the number of objects in the environment had less of an impact on performance as it required more than 2000 objects to be included in the simulation in order for the simulation to refresh below the frame rate needed to be used on a real time scenario. Note that these results are hardware dependant, a more powerful computer would be expected to yield more favourable results. Additionally, because the number of objects has less

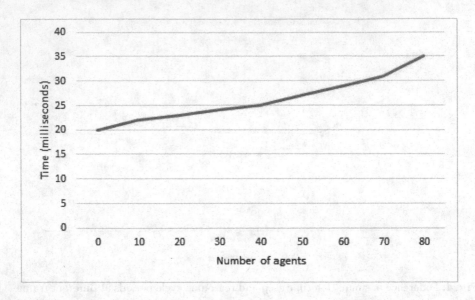

Fig. 5. Simulation refresh time vs. number of agents.

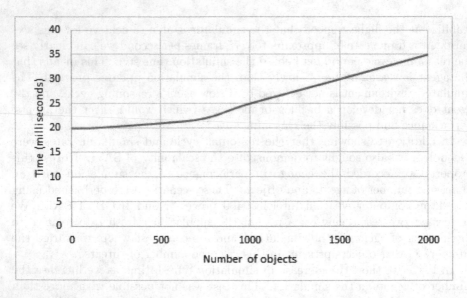

Fig. 6. Simulation refresh time vs. number of threats.

impact than the number of agents, we anticipate that the reasoning complexity of the agent and the agent's interactions are important factors. As future work, we will analyze the factors affecting the scalability such as the complexity of the agents, the agent-platform and the agent interactions among others.

6   Conclusion

We have presented the SAVI architecture to integrate multi-agent systems developed using the BDI paradigm with a simulation platform. Our architecture decouples the execution of a time stepped simulation from the agent's reasoning processes, allowing them to run as separate processes interacting in an asynchronous manner. This contributes to a more realistic simulation by allowing the simulation of environment to proceed regardless of the agents' decision-making speed. However, we are nonetheless able to prevent the reasoning cycle from executing faster than the simulation rate. This should not be possible in an environment that is meant to approximate dynamic environments in continuous time. These benefits of our architecture should make the transition to a natural environment more realistic. In addition, the decoupling of the two component frameworks makes it easy to develop them independently, and has allowed our team to successfully separate these two unrelated concerns during the development process. We have made our reference implementation available to the community as an open-source project [13].

Future Work

As the SAVI project is under active development, there are several developments planned as ongoing and future work.

One direction is to strengthen the validity of the simulation side, by using other modelling and simulation methodologies (discrete-time approaches, in particular), and by setting the reasoning speed to match the expected performance of real embedded reasoning systems.

A second direction is to enrich the architecture to bring it closer to a real environment. This includes connecting a human interface for providing command and control for the agent activities as well as a means for the agents to inform users of the state of the environment and as their state. This could also mean connecting SAVI to agents that are loaded on real world hardware, where SAVI would stand in for a real world environment so that real world hardware can be tested in a controlled setting. Related to the goal of connecting to real world hardware, the SAVI project currently does not use any analogue sensing of the environment. Development is required in order to support the use agents with simulated analogue sensors which are connected to agents using BDI for higher level reasoning as part of a broader agent architecture.

Acknowledgement. We acknowledge the support of Cohort Systems, Ottawa, Ontario, Canada.

The work has been partially funded by Department of National Defence (DND) Contract Number: W7714-196749/001/SV.

We acknowledge the support of the Natural Sciences and Engineering Research Council of Canada (NSERC), [funding reference number 518212].

Cette recherche a été financée par le Conseil de recherches en sciences naturelles et en génie du Canada (CRSNG), [numéro de référence 518212].

References

1. Abar, S., Theodoropoulos, G.K., Lemarinier, P., O'Hare, G.M.: Agent based modelling and simulation tools: a review of the state-of-art software. Comput. Sci. Rev. **24**, 13–33 (2017)
2. Akplogan, M., Quesnel, G., Garcia, F., Joannon, A., Martin-Clouaire, R.: Towards a deliberative agent system based on DEVS formalism for application in agriculture. In: Proceedings of the 2010 Summer Computer Simulation Conference, SCSC 2010, pp. 250–257. Society for Computer Simulation International, San Diego (2010). http://dl.acm.org/citation.cfm?id=1999416.1999447
3. AOSGroup: Jack. http://www.aosgrp.com/products/jack/. Accessed 04 Feb 2019
4. Araujo, F., Valente, J., Al-Zinati, M., Kuiper, D., Zalila-Wenkstern, R.: DIVAs 4.0: a framework for the development of situated multi-agent based simulation systems. In: Proceedings of the 2013 International Conference on Autonomous Agents and Multi-Agent Systems, pp. 1351–1352. International Foundation for Autonomous Agents and Multiagent Systems (2013)
5. Aschermann, M., Kraus, P., Müller, J.P.: LightJason: a BDI framework inspired by Jason. In: Criado Pacheco, N., Carrascosa, C., Osman, N., Julián Inglada, V. (eds.) EUMAS/AT 2016. LNCS (LNAI), vol. 10207, pp. 58–66. Springer, Cham (2017). https://doi.org/10.1007/978-3-319-59294-7_6
6. Banks, J., Carson, J., Nelson, B., Nicol, D.: Discrete-Event System Simulation, 5th edn. Prentice Hall, Upper Saddle River (2010)
7. Barros, F.J.: Dynamic structure discrete event system specification: a new formalism for dynamic structure modeling and simulation. In: Proceedings of the 27th Conference on Winter Simulation, WSC 1995, pp. 781–785. IEEE Computer Society, Washington, DC (1995). https://doi.org/10.1145/224401.224731
8. Ben-Akiva, M., et al.: Traffic simulation with MITSIMLab. In: Barceló, J. (ed.) Fundamentals of Traffic Simulation. ISOR, vol. 145, pp. 233–268. Springer, New York (2010). https://doi.org/10.1007/978-1-4419-6142-6_6
9. Bergez, J.E., et al.: RECORD: a new software platform to model and simulate cropping systems. Farming System Design, Monterey, CA (2009)
10. Bordini, R.H., Hübner, J.F.: BDI agent programming in agentspeak using *Jason*. In: Toni, F., Torroni, P. (eds.) CLIMA 2005. LNCS (LNAI), vol. 3900, pp. 143–164. Springer, Heidelberg (2006). https://doi.org/10.1007/11750734_9
11. Bordini, R.H., Hübner, J.F., Wooldridge, M.: Programming Multi-Agent Systems in AgentSpeak Using Jason (Wiley Series in Agent Technology). Wiley, Hoboken (2007)
12. Bratman, M.: Intention, Plans, and Practical Reason, vol. 10. Harvard University Press, Cambridge (1987)
13. Davoust, A., et al.: Simulated autonomous vehicle infrastructure. https://github.com/NMAI-lab/SAVI. Accessed 19 Feb 2019
14. Fry, B., Reas, C.: Processing. https://processing.org/. Accessed 16 Feb 2019
15. Hübner, J.F., Bordini, R.H.: Jason: a Java-based interpreter for an extended version of AgentSpeak. http://jason.sourceforge.net. Accessed 16 Feb 2019
16. Ingrand, F.F., Georgeff, M.P., Rao, A.S.: An architecture for real-time reasoning and system control. IEEE Expert **7**(6), 34–44 (1992)
17. Jacobs, P.H., Lang, N.A., Verbraeck, A.: D-SOL; a distributed Java based discrete event simulation architecture. In: Proceedings of the Winter Simulation Conference, vol. 1, pp. 793–800. IEEE (2002)

18. Jaworski, P., Edwards, T., Burnham, K.J., Haas, O.C.L.: Microscopic traffic simulation tool for intelligent transportation systems. In: 2012 15th International IEEE Conference on Intelligent Transportation Systems, pp. 552–557 (2012)
19. Kuper, C., Müller, J.P., Spitzer, M., Tatasadi, E.: LightJason. https://lightjason.org/. Accessed 15 Mar 2019
20. Luke, S., Cioffi-Revilla, C., Panait, L., Sullivan, K., Balan, G.: Mason: a multiagent simulation environment. Simulation **81**(7), 517–527 (2005)
21. Mittal, S., Douglass, S.A.: Net-centric ACT-R-based cognitive architecture with DEVS unified process. In: Proceedings of the 2011 Symposium on Theory of Modeling & Simulation: DEVS Integrative M&S Symposium, TMS-DEVS 2011, pp. 34–44. Society for Computer Simulation International, San Diego (2011). http://dl.acm.org/citation.cfm?id=2048476.2048480
22. North, M.J., Howe, T.R., Collier, N.T., Vos, J.R.: A declarative model assembly infrastructure for verification and validation. In: Takahashi, S., Sallach, D., Rouchier, J. (eds.) Advancing Social Simulation: The First World Congress, pp. 129–140. Springer, Tokyo (2007). https://doi.org/10.1007/978-4-431-73167-2_13
23. North, M.J., et al.: Complex adaptive systems modeling with Repast Simphony. Complex Adapt. Syst. Model. **1**(1), 3 (2013). https://doi.org/10.1186/2194-3206-1-3
24. Padgham, L., Scerri, D., Jayatilleke, G., Hickmott, S.: Integrating BDI reasoning into agent based modeling and simulation. In: Proceedings of the Winter Simulation Conference, WSC 2011, pp. 345–356. Winter Simulation Conference (2011). http://dl.acm.org/citation.cfm?id=2431518.2431555
25. Rao, A.S., George, M.P.: BDI agents: from theory to practice. In: Proceedings of the First International Conference on Multi-Agent Systems, ICMAS 1995, pp. 312–319 (1995). http://www.agent.ai/doc/upload/200302/rao95.pdf
26. Robertson, D.: Agent-based modeling toolkits NetLogo, RePast, and Swarm. Acad. Manag. Learn. Educ. **4**, 524–527 (2005). https://doi.org/10.5465/AMLE.2005.19086798
27. Rüb, I., Dunin-Kęplicz, B.: BDI model of connected and autonomous vehicles. In: 6th International Workshop on Engineering Multi-Agent Systems, EMAS 2018 (2018). http://emas2018.dibris.unige.it/images/papers/EMAS18-16.pdf
28. Russell, S., Norvig, P.: Artificial Intelligence: A Modern Approach, 3rd edn. Prentice Hall Press, Upper Saddle River (2009)
29. Singh, D., Padgham, L., Logan, B.: Integrating BDI agents with agent-based simulation platforms. Auton. Agents Multi-Agent Syst. **30**(6), 1050–1071 (2016). https://doi.org/10.1007/s10458-016-9332-x
30. Tendeloo, Y.V., Vangheluwe, H.: An evaluation of DEVS simulation tools. Simulation **93**(2), 103–121 (2017). https://doi.org/10.1177/0037549716678330
31. Uhrmacher, A.M.: A system theoretic approach to constructing test beds for multi-agent systems. In: Sarjoughian, H.S., Cellier, F.E. (eds.) Discrete Event Modeling and Simulation Technologies: A Tapestry of Systems and AI-Based Theories and Methodologies, pp. 315–339. Springer, New York (2001). https://doi.org/10.1007/978-1-4757-3554-3_15
32. Uhrmacher, A.M., Kullick, B.G.: "Plug and test" - software agents in virtual environments. In: 2000 Winter Simulation Conference Proceedings (Cat. No. 00CH37165), vol. 2, pp. 1722–1729, December 2000. https://doi.org/10.1109/WSC.2000.899162
33. Van Dyke Parunak, H., Nielsen, P., Brueckner, S., Alonso, R.: Hybrid multi-agent systems: integrating swarming and BDI agents. In: Brueckner, S.A., Hassas, S.,

Jelasity, M., Yamins, D. (eds.) ESOA 2006. LNCS (LNAI), vol. 4335, pp. 1–14. Springer, Heidelberg (2007). https://doi.org/10.1007/978-3-540-69868-5_1

34. Varga, A., Hornig, R.: An overview of the OMNeT++ simulation environment. In: Proceedings of the 1st International Conference on Simulation Tools and Techniques for Communications, Networks and Systems & Workshops, Simutools 2008, pp. 60:1–60:10. ICST (Institute for Computer Sciences, Social-Informatics and Telecommunications Engineering), ICST, Brussels (2008). http://dl.acm.org/citation.cfm?id=1416222.1416290

35. Wainer, G.: CD++: a toolkit to develop DEVS models. Softw.: Pract. Exp. **32**(13), 1261–1306 (2002). https://doi.org/10.1002/spe.482

36. Wilensky, U.: NetLogo. Center for Connected Learning and Computer-Based Modeling, Northwestern University, Evanston, IL (1999). http://ccl.northwestern.edu/netlogo/

37. Zeigler, B.P., Praehofer, H., Kim, T.: Theory of Modelling and Simulation: Integrating Discrete Event and Continuous Complex Dynamic Systems, 2nd edn. Academic Press, San Diego (2000)

38. Zhang, M., Verbraeck, A.: A composable PRS-based agent meta-model for multi-agent simulation using the DEVS framework. In: Proceedings of the 2014 Symposium on Agent Directed Simulation, ADS 2014, pp. 1:1–1:8. Society for Computer Simulation International, San Diego (2014). http://dl.acm.org/citation.cfm?id=2665049.2665050

Using MATSim as a Component in Dynamic Agent-Based Micro-Simulations

Dhirendra Singh[1,3]([✉]) [iD], Lin Padgham[1] [iD], and Kai Nagel[2] [iD]

[1] RMIT University, Melbourne, Australia
{dhirendra.singh,lin.padgham}@rmit.edu.au
[2] Technical University, Berlin, Germany
kai.nagel@tu-berlin.de
[3] CSIRO Data61, Melbourne, Australia
dhirendra.singh@data61.csiro.au

Abstract. This paper discusses use of the widely used transport simulator, MATSim, as one component in a large complex agent based microsimulation where dynamic changes in the environment require the agents to be reactive as well as goal directed. We describe a number of refinements to MATSim that have been made to facilitate its use within our deployed wildfire evacuation applications, as well as some tools that have been developed which complement MATSim. All code is freely available under open source licenses. As applications increasingly require complex microsimulations, with many aspects, it is important to use existing software where possible. However most simulation systems, like MATSim, have been developed as standalone systems. We identify ways that MATSim has needed to be extended or modified in order for it to be used as a component in a larger whole. The paper provides details that will be useful for anyone wanting to use MATSim within their specific application.

Keywords: MATSim · Belief-Desire-Intention · BDI · Agent-based simulation

1 Introduction

It is often necessary to couple simulation systems long after they were designed and implemented. Reasons for this include that most groups neither have the resources for a start from scratch, nor a sufficiently broad expertise in all domains that may be needed. In consequence, both for cutting-edge research applications as well as for cost-effective real-world applications, the coupling of existing systems is of interest. This paper focusses on the use of the MATSim (Multi-Agent Transport Simulation) [13] traffic simulator as a component in large scale agent based micro-simulations, where, as is increasingly relevant, it is often important to make use of detailed real world data (e.g. [7,29]). The unifying aspect of our contributions was their need in a family of applications in the evacuation

© Springer Nature Switzerland AG 2020
L. A. Dennis et al. (Eds.): EMAS 2019, LNAI 12058, pp. 85–105, 2020.
https://doi.org/10.1007/978-3-030-51417-4_5

domain [24], although they are also more widely applicable. The work described here is currently being used in decision support tools within the emergency services in Australia.[1]

Originally MATSim was developed for finding traffic equilibrium as individual agents adapt their travel behaviour to a specified transport infrastructure, based on their individual activity patterns. The system is initialised with a set of agents, having various attributes, each having an "activity plan" which specifies the location and duration of various activities throughout the day. The system then determines the best route between activities at suitable times, embellishing the plans with specific detailed routes for each trip.[2] The execution simply steps through these plans. The executed plans are scored, taking into account congestion and other, possibly unexpected, occurences during plans execution. At the end of each one day simulation, plans are reviewed and some poorly rated ones are modified using an evolutionary algorithm, until eventually after some number of iterations a stable state is reached.

This approach is successful for assessing the impact of proposed new infrastructure in situations where behavior is repetitive from one day to the next. However it is not suitable for applications where decisions need to be made reactively, based directly on a dynamic situation. Two examples of such situations are evacuation simulations and simulations involving taxis which must respond to the evolving environment. In recent years there has been a focus on modifying the *mobsim* component of MATSim to accommodate this, using what is called *within-day replanning* or *en-route replanning* [5,9]. It is this aspect of MATSim which is considered in the current paper, using only a single iteration of the agents over a simulated day.

The BDI-MATSim system [17] is one approach to supporting the ability of MATSim agents to be reactive to a dynamic situation. It builds on an infrastructure developed for integrating any existing cognitive system (as long as it relies on percepts and actions) with any agent-based model that fills certain requirements [25]. The integration facilitates within-day replanning in MATSim by allowing agents to proactively make decisions to change their original plan, depending on both environmental situations and agent goals. Conceptually, the "brain" of a MATSim agent is modelled in the BDI system (as a BDI agent) while the "body" remains inside MATSim. The communication between these agent counterparts is defined based on standard agent concepts, *percepts* and *actions*. A MATSim agent sends percepts to the BDI counterpart, which conducts high-level reasoning and issues a (BDI) *action* for the MATSim agent to execute. *Percepts* from the MATSim counterpart agent can be either information about its own state (e.g. location), or an observation from the MATSim environment. Basically, a BDI action modifies the travel plan of a MATSim agent using low-level MATSim functions. The evacuation applications which have motivated

---

[1] The code for these models is accessible from https://github.com/agentsoz/ees.

[2] A *plan* encompasses *activities*, *trips* which contain the (possibly multi-modal) movement between activities, and *routes* which are the detailed road/path segments to be traversed by a vehicle/person.

and used the extensions and tools described in this paper have all used the BDI-MATSim system.

In developing large and complex simulations it is essential to be able to incorporate components which are themselves large and complex pieces of software. These must all work together – and preferably continue to work together as components are further modified and developed.

Our own experiences in this direction are mixed. There are several issues: The coupling of simulation systems written in different programming languages often resorts to writing to and reading from file. The data exchange can be made somewhat typesafe by using a format such as XML (eXtensible Markup Language, [27]) which allows to certify a grammar via DTD or XSD files. This, however, needs a lot of effort. Also data exchange via files is inefficient. See [16] for an example in the domain considered here. An alternative might be to use message passing, e.g. MPI [15]. This is an established approach for mathematical objects such as vectors or arrays, but does not support object oriented structures such as variable-length lists or maps. One could instead use XML again, but send it via messages. The implementation effort remains large, and the conversion from binary numbers to strings and back is inefficient. See [11] for an example. The fairly recent emergence of Google protocol buffers [20] and similar approaches confirms that there has been a lack of tools that allow to exchange objects between different programming languages. These newer approaches address problems of type safety and efficiency, but require significant effort since both the prototypes and the adapter classes need to be written.

However, even when staying within the same programming language, challenges remain. One of them is to find the right level of abstraction for the interchange between the pre-existing codes. This was the main problem after our initial prototype [18]: Although MATSim in principle provided the necessary functionality, in practice it was very difficult to use by the BDI group because it was at a too low level.

We are not aware of any other effort that combines dynamic behavior, large scale, dealing with real-world scenarios, and being in the transport domain. Clearly, when taking a step back, then our work has many connections into a variety of different communities. *En-route replanning* was mentioned above and is common in the transport domain, albeit other approaches do not use the flexibility of a (BDI or other) framework. *Multi-agent systems* (e.g. [30]) are related, but concentrate on the *systems* rather than the *simulation* aspect. Artificial intelligence (e.g. [22]) is related, but concentrates more on individual agents rather than their emergent properties, and also is more interested in "rational" agents rather than the spontaneous, rule-based reactions that are considered in our study. Agent-based social simulation (e.g. [10]) shares the aspect of emergence, but is typically less strongly connected to real-world data than our studies. Urban planning has consistently used agent-based approaches (e.g. [4,26]) and has been discussing simular issues of model coupling [28], but it does not have the same spontaneous real-time aspect as our work.

The contributions of this paper are a result of our learnings and refinements of the BDI-MATSim coupling from extensive use over the years. Figure 1 shows the two components in detail, highlighting the original MATSim and Jill BDI artifacts, the pre-existing extensions which we build on, and the new additions that are described in this paper. More generally our contributions reduce the practical effort in maintaining a sustainable coupling between the two independently developed systems: the MATSim traffic model and the Jill BDI cognition model. Specifically they:

1. standardise the mechanism of data passing and control through a high-level controller where MATSim is a slave component among others, as opposed to being the master as in [18] (Sect. 2.1).
2. simplify the process of programming the behaviours of the MATSim agents through cognitive reasoning that is coded in the BDI system (Sects. 2.2, 2.3, 2.4 and 3);
3. unify the description of the individuals of the agent population with respect to their BDI behaviour attributes and their MATSim activities through a common schema (being MATSim's population scheme), as well as their construction through support tools for population synthesis (Sects. 4); and
4. facilitate cleaner cognitive agent designs (Sect. 5).

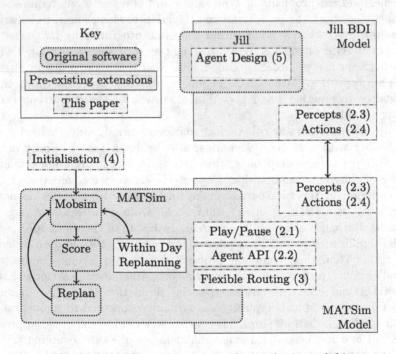

Fig. 1. The BDI-MATSim sub-system and contributions of this paper

The complete model consists of the BDI-MATSim components amongst others as shown in Fig. 2, where a controller pauses and continues the execution of components as well as providing a mechanism for data sharing. The setup is conceptually similar to that prescribed by HLA [8] standard, although, unlike HLA, multiple models can represent aspects of the same conceptual agents at the same time, as long as aspects are managed to ensure consistency, as they are in the BDI-ABM integrated framework described in [25]. We support models that run on different size timesteps as well as variable time steps such as discrete event models. Data exchange is based on a publish/subcribe scheme whereby a model is called on one of two events: to handle incoming data from other models that it is subscribed to, or to publish its own data at a frequency (fixed or variable) under its full control. If there is a producer consumer relationship with respect to data produced and used within the same simulation time step, then the controller must sequence the component executions appropriately. The model cannot deal with circular relationships between components within a single timestep, only with pipeline relationships. The issues of shared resource management as handled by frameworks like OpenSim [23] that were built for integrating existing models do not apply here.

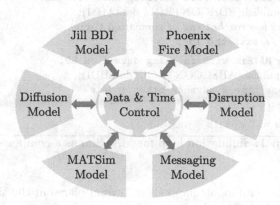

Fig. 2. High level view of the component based simulation

2   MATSim as a Component

For MATSim to operate as a component within this framework, rather than as a standalone application, it is necessary to allow stopping and starting from an external controller (unlike [17] where all control was with MATSim), as well as options for MATSim to receive and provide data. To support additional functionality likely to be needed for new applications it is also desirable to have a principled API providing access to internal MATSim functionality. These aspects are discussed in the subsections of this section.

2.1   External Control of MATSim Steps

Algorithm 1 shows the high level simulation loop where MATSim is a component. Each model is first initialised (line 1), and registers with the central controller of Fig. 2 all data types it wishes to publish or subscribe to (line 2). We do this upfront, but models are free to register types also during the simulation conditional on some event. Then on every simulation loop iteration (line 3), the BDI model is called first (line 4) followed by MATSim so that new or dropped BDI actions passed via container `dataBDI` are handled by MATSim immediately in the same time step (line 7). BDI actions status' and percepts coming back from MATSim in `datABM` are handled by the BDI model in the next iteration of the loop. Other models are called as needed (line 8) and the entire simulation terminates (lines 5–6) when MATSim itself reaches the end of its own simulation.

Result: Simulation completed
1   `// initialise all models`
2   `// register ordered models with controller`
3 **while** *true* **do**
     `// invoke BDI model with incoming data from ABM`
4   controller.publish(BDI_CONTROL, dataABM);
5   **if** *MATSim has reached end of simulation* **then**
6   break; `// exit the loop`
     `// invoke MATSim with incoming data from BDI`
7   controller.publish(ABM_CONTROL, dataBDI);
     `// progress time & advance other models`
8   controller.stepTime();
9   `// terminate all models`

Algorithm 1: Simulation loop for MATSim as a component

Data flow between models happens in several places in the simulation loop. Direct data passing from publisher models to subscriber models occurs in the controller's `stepTime()` function (line 8). We use this to directly feed, for instance, time-stamped fire shape data from the Phoenix Fire Model into MATSim to dynamically increase link penalties on road segments impacted by fire. Data flow between the BDI-MATSim coupling is managed more precisely by the controller as mentioned already, by routing the data from the models (`dataBDI` and `dataABM`) through the controller.

A new facility called `PlayPauseSimulationControl` was implemented in MATSim to provide a `doStep(time)` function to continue the MATSim simulation forward up until `time` and return. This new play/pause API also ensures that the simulation clock of the controller is not tied to MATSim's simulation clock. The approach consists of starting MATSim in a separate thread, and inserting a so-called `MobsimAfterSimStepListener` into the mobsim, which stops the thread when control is to be returned to the central controller. This is one of the cases where the functionality would already have been available previously, albeit at a too low level.

2.2 API to Modify MATSim Agent Behaviour

Previously, while it was possible to modify MATSim agent behaviour in all sorts of ways, this involved editing into the internals of MATSim in functions that even if they were public, possibly should not have been, and were in danger of changing as MATSim developed. There are now three clearly specified classes allowing for editing of plans (`EditPlans`), routes (`EditRoutes`) and trips (`EditTrips`).[3] These classes provide a clean interface for programming functions to change agent behaviour, as well as for querying MATSim regarding aspects of an agent's current plan. Plans are the highest level of abstraction and consist of a sequence of activities at specific locations, interleaved with trips between locations. A trip may consist of several legs, which may have a variety of different modes, including car, public transport, and walking. A route is the specific set of links to be traversed within a leg. Table 1 shows the API functions for plan editing. Trip and route editing follow a similar pattern. Basically these are the typical insert/add/remove/modify methods that one knows from the Java List class, plus some helper methods that have to do with the data model.

Table 1. High level API for plan editing.

```
addActivityAtEnd (agent, activity, routingMode)
createFinalActivity (type, newLinkID)
findIndexOfRealActAfter (agent, index)
findRealActAfter (agent, index)
findRealActBefore (agent, index)
flushEverythingBeyondCurrent (agent)
getModeOfCurrentOrNextTrip (agent)
insertActivity (agent, index, activity)
isAtRealActivity (agent)
isRealActivity (agent, planElement)
removeActivity (agent, index, mode)
replaceActivity (agent, index, newAct)
rescheduleActivityEndtime (agent, index, newEndTime)
```

---

[3] http://matsim.org/javadoc → matsim main → `EditPlans`, `EditRoutes`, `Edit-Trips`.

2.3   Adding BDI Actions to MATSim

When a BDI action is sent to MATSim, it performs the necessary changes to the agent's plan elements using suitable API functions (of Sect. 2.2). In particular there must always be some event(s) which indicate that the action has terminated – normally successfully, but possibly that it has failed. Information which needs to be provided to the BDI agent is then packaged up for transmission to the relevant BDI agent as a percept, along with information that the BDI action has succeeded or failed (see Sect. 2.4).

An example reusable BDI action is `drive-to(args)` for which we provide a default action handler on the MATSim side (in `MATSimModel`), which on reception of the BDI action (i) inserts a new activity immediately following the agent's current activity/leg, on the network link nearest to the coordinates given in `args`; (ii) optionally sets the end time of the current activity, if the agent is currently performing an activity, to some future time given in `args`; and (iii) registers an event handler for the MATSim `PersonArrivalEvent` event, which when triggered on the link of the newly inserted activity indicates the end of the `drive-to` action.

A particular application may introduce both new BDI actions and new percepts to be used by the BDI agents in their reasoning. This necessitates new application code to be added to MATSim to implement the percept handlers (see Sect. 2.4), and also to implement the MATSim realisation of the BDI action. The latter is done by registering an application specific action handler in `MATSimModel` at initialisation. The syntax approximately is

`agent.registerBDIAction( actionType, actionHandler ) ;`

This means that when the BDI system wants to execute the action `actionType`, then `actionHandler` is called. The action handler itself has the following structure:

```
... handleAction( String agentID, ..., Object[] args ) {
    // modify plan of MATSim agent
    ...
}
```

The notification about the completion of the action contains the status, i.e., `PASSED`, `FAILED`, or `DROPPED`, and is composed in the relevant MATSim event handler as explained in Sect. 2.4.

2.4   Generating BDI Percepts from MATSim

MATSim's mobility simulation, or mobsim, that is responsible for moving the agents around according to their plans, generates a stream of events that capture the movement of people between activities. This stream gives MATSim extensions a mechanism to plug in and listen to events of interest and perform their own computations as needed. In our case, this mechanism is used to perform the necessary computations to construct a BDI percept that can be sent back to the BDI agent.

It is also possible to add custom MATSim events based on the application's requirements. For the evacuation application, we defined two new events that are both relevant when the agent is engaged in a `drive-to` BDI-action. The event `AgentInCongestionEvent` flags the condition that the vehicle is stuck in traffic congestion, while the event `NextLinkBlockedEvent` is triggered if the vehicle is about to enter a link that is blocked, due to a road closure for instance. Corresponding custom handlers generate the appropriate BDI percept information for passing back to the BDI agent as well as deciding if the BDI-action should potentially be deemed failed.[4]

From a BDI programming viewpoint, the agent code registers to perceive the kinds of events it cares about, such as the event of arriving at a road blockage, as shown in the sequence diagram of Fig. 3. `MATSimModel` then monitors MATSim's event stream for the `NextLinkBlockedEvent` event, and for every such event that is generated for the MATSim agent counterpart, it adds the `BLOCKED` percept to the global data container. The percept is eventually received by the BDI agent via the `handlePercept` call. For some percepts, such as `BLOCKED`, the percept handler code in `MATSimModel` will also check if the agent in question has an active `drive-to` action, and if found, will also add a `drive-to` action update with status `FAILED`. In this case the BDI agent will additionally be notified via

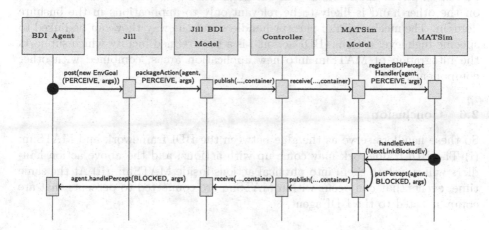

Fig. 3. Sequence diagram for percept registration (from BDI) and generation (from MATSim)

---

[4] The custom `AgentInCongestionEvent` is triggered on `LinkLeaveEvent` if $(t_{k,i} - t_{k,i}^*)/t_{k,i}^* > w$, where k is some traversed link, i is the current link, time $t_{k,i}$ is the recorded travel time for the route taken from k to i, and $t_{k,i}^*$ is the expected travel time if travelling at freespeed on that route. The constant w is the congestion tolerance threshold. Practically, we set a time period T for congestion evaluation and take the maximum permissible $t_{k,i}$ such that $t_{k,i} \leq T$. For instance, $T = 300, w = 0.4$ means that an agent will consider itself to be stuck in congestion if over the last 5 min, the time delay in travelling the route from k to i was greater than 40% of the expected travel time for that route. – The `nextLinkBlocked` event is generated when the following link has freespeed close to zero as the intent is to prevent the agent from entering a blocked link where it might get stuck forever.

the `updateAction` call that its current driving action has failed (evidently due to the road block as indicated by the accompanying `BLOCKED` percept).

2.5   Generating Additional BDI Percepts Based on External Model

The architecture of Fig. 2 supports data flow directly between models, as described in Sect. 2.1. Such incoming "data events" can therefore be used by the MATSim model to generate BDI percepts. For instance, on reception of updated fire(smoke) shape information from the Phoenix Fire model, `MATSimModel` first queries MATSim for a list of all agents that are within the polygon shape (plus some configurable buffer around the shape) at that timestep, generates `fire(smoke)-visual` BDI percepts for all those agents, and packages these inside a data container that is received by `JillBDIModel`.

As different applications are developed with MATSim as one component, it is anticipated that a range of application specific percepts and percept handlers will be developed, some of which will be reusable across multiple applications. The `in-congestion` percept is one such addition which could be expected to be reused across applications. The smoke and fire percept and percept handler on the other hand is likely to be relevant only to applications in the bushfire domain. The mechansim of percept handlers and the way they can be linked to specific high level actions (BDI-actions) is a new/refined facility which supports the integration of MATSim into new application areas, combined with other components.

2.6   Conclusion

So these handlers serve as the glue between the BDI framework and MATSim: (i) The BDI framework may come up with actions, and the above action handlers will translate them into physical actions inside MATSim. (ii) At the same time, events that can occur within MATSim are connected to percepts that are communicated to the BDI agent.

3   Flexible Route Planning

The activity of driving is made up of a hierarchy of decisions such as accelerating/braking, changing lanes, taking turns at intersections (= routing), or the decision to arrive (= destination choice). It needs to be decided at which level external code can interact with the travel model. In the original MATSim design for external mental models, accelerating/braking as well as changing lanes were treated within MATSim, while routing and destination choice were assumed to be treated in the external mental model.

During the practical work with the evacuation application, it turned out that having the routing inside the mental model is too heavyweight. For example, it means that the mental model needs a copy of the road network, and routers of its own. It was thus decided to rather use the pre-existing routing infrastructure of MATSim.

Here, however, one is confronted with the inverse problem: There are mental concepts that now need to be included into the router, for example if the agent is assumed to have global knowledge (e.g. about congestion or blockage) or not, or if the routing is for an emergency vehicle, which should be allowed to drive towards the danger, or for an evacuee, which should accept such routing only if unavoidable.

An additional challenge is that there are dynamic elements both outside the mental and outside the travel model that may influence either one. For example, a fallen tree may block a road, but will also influence the global knowledge routing. Smoke may influence the routing.

Our resulting design decision was to use the travel model to provide the routers, but have several such routers corresponding to several mental models, and to flexibly allow to add such routers. The remainder of this section will explain this in more detail.

3.1   Route Planning in MATSim

Whenever an agent needs to plan its route between destinations it calls a router. The router uses a Djikstra-like algorithm to find a close to optimal path to the destination, based on the cost of the links. Link cost is based on a function of link attributes such as link travel time, link length, monetary toll, etc. Link travel times are typically based on traffic conditions.

3.2   The Evacuation System Routers

For a given vehicle type/mode, the standard router in MATSim is always the same. In the evacuation application we needed to use different route planning in different situations, for the same vehicle type: sometimes a car would require using a free speed router, sometimes a router based on global knowledge, and emergency vehicles required different link costs again. The refinement to MATSim that was introduced was to allow a specific router to be specified dynamically as a parameter, together with the destination node for a trip.

3.3   Fire Avoidance

One issue with evacuation routing is how danger avoidance is included. A possible approach [12, 14] is to label nodes by their distance to the danger, and accept danger-increasing moves only when no other moves are possible. For the fire evacuation, links within the danger zone (the fire area) are given high penalties, so that vehicles take the fastest way out. Links in a buffer around the fire area are given penalties only when leading towards the fire, with the penalty related to the risk increase. The travel time can either be maximum link speed, or actual (congested) current link speed. This successfully controls the behaviour of the agents such that they do not "mindlessly" drive into the fire, but if they have a goal to reach a destination within the danger zone (such as rescuing family members), then they are not prevented from doing so.

```
<population>
 <person id="">
  <attributes>...</attributes
  <plan selected="yes">
   <activity type="home" x="" y="" end_time="" />
   <leg mode="car" />
   ...
  </plan>
 </person>
 ...
</population>
```

Fig. 4. Structure of MATSim's input population XML file

We currently have three different routers for our evacuation applications: carFreespeed, carGlobalInformation and emergencyVehicle, with the ability to switch between them depending on context. The emergencyVehicle router is similar to the carGlobalInformation router but imposes lower penalties for coming close to the fire – it allows taking of greater risks.

Within our system the road link penalties used by the routers are updated periodically based on information from the fire model. This information is also used to provide percepts to the (BDI) agents to be potentially used in their reasoning process. The sequence of execution is as follows: (i) updated smoke and fire shape information is published by the Phoenix Fire model; (ii) the MATSim model has subscribed to this information and therefore receives it immediately; (iii) at the next MATSim step MATSim places penalties on links and also produces smoke/fire percepts for relevant agents in the areas (as explained in Sect. 2.4); and (iv) at the next BDI step the smoke percepts are passed to the specified BDI agents where it affects their decision making.

The ability to dynamically choose which router to use, combined with the ability to set penalties dynamically based on a changing situation provides great flexibility which can be relatively easily extended and modified for different application needs.

4   Initialisation of MATSim

Like most microsimulations MATSim typically includes data from real environments, and creates agents with attributes and activities taken from data. The easiest way to create a road network is to use OpenStreetMap[5] and then convert to MATSim representation using the MATSim utility class OsmNetworkReader. The population of agents is given by an input file in XML format as shown in Fig. 4.

---

[5] https://www.openstreetmap.org/.

4.1   Creating the Agent Population

It is relatively straightforward to create a set of individuals that match census data with regard to attributes such as gender, age, etc. These attributes can be directly encoded as attributes of a person in the MATSim population using the `attributes` set as shown in Fig. 4. Grouping individuals into family and household structures that also match census data is more complex. Various approaches have been used in the literature, and for Australian census data there is software available that can create a population, assigned to households with address coordinates.[6]

The `attributes` are also used to specify for each agent a `BDIAgentType`, which defines, by a fully qualified Java class name, the BDI behaviors for that agent.

4.2   Creating the Activities

For the bushfire applications we have a user requirement to simulate the agents going about their daily business, prior to the evacuation request. There are a number of approaches that have been used for creating the activity schedules of the agents. These include activity based demand generation models (e.g. [21]), smart card or mobile phone data (e.g. [1,6]), hourly origin destination matrices [3], or commuting matrices [2]. One can additionally calibrate against emergent properties such as traffic counts (e.g. [31]). The challenge is to combine the data that is locally available, and which is typically different in each location, to come up with a good approximation.

For the evacuation application in the Australian context, we have developed the following approach:

1. Since the census data includes information on whether individuals work, where they work (at a suitably fine geographical granularity), and mode of transport to work, then reasonable initial activity schedules for work travel can be created by assigning travel to and from a work activity of appropriate length, for a suitable number of people in each geographical area. Work locations can be assigned randomly within the relevant geographical area, or probabilistically according to knowledge of centres of activity. Timings must also be assigned based on some assumptions (or data) about usual length and time of work activities. Code is available which allocates these work activity schedules to the population described in Sect. 4.1, based on census data of individuals and households.
2. In order to simulate other activity we have developed a tool that allows us to use expert knowledge about the approximate proportions of different agent types doing various activities at certain times of day, in order to generate representative activity schedules. The tool takes as input, for each population subgroup, a table of activities distributions for the day, a list of GIS shapes associated with each activity signifying places where those activities

---

[6] Software is available at https://github.com/agentsoz/synthetic-population.

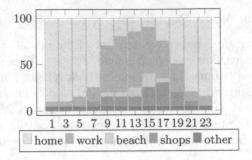

Fig. 5. Example input weekday activities for `Resident`s.

can be performed, and the number of persons of the subgroup to generate. For instance, given the example activities distributions for the `Resident` subgroup in Fig. 5 – that tells us what activities the subgroup is doing at different times of the day and in what proportion – the algorithm constructs a population whose activities taken together resemble these distributions.[7,8]

The output is a MATSim population file in GZipped-XML (`.xml.gz`) format.

5   Designing Agents and Their Behaviours

Designing the agents and their behaviours in a complex simulation involving multiple components will typically involve some level of interaction between these components. Decisions must be made about which components receive, and are affected by, which information. In some cases agents may be represented in different components to take advantage of specialised representations and modelling. This is the case in BDI-ABM integration as described in [25], where the cognitive reasoning of the agents is in a different component than the interaction of the agent with the environment. This raises questions regarding the design of the agents and what aspects should be in which component. This will always depend on the particular application and the specifics of the components.

The principle with BDI-ABM agents has always been that reasoning decisions should be made by the cognitive system, with actions carried out by the ABM. In practice however this is a fuzzy boundary. As already discussed in Sec. 3, route planning is a cognitive process, but it is tightly coupled with the representation

---

[7] This software can be accessed at https://github.com/agentsoz/ees-synthetic-population/tree/master/plan-algorithm.

[8] The aim is not to build calibrated populations, but instead build representative populations that capture sufficient richness of activities while being relatively easy for domain experts to specify. However this tool is potentially suitable only for relatively small geographical areas in its current state, as with large scale scenarios, a random destination choice with a uniform distribution leads to distances that are too large (in the average half the scenario diameter). Nevertheless it has been useful for the current applications and is an area of ongoing work.

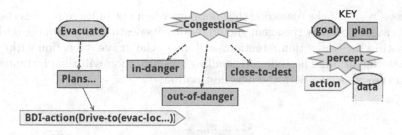

Fig. 6. Basic design of handling of congestion percept

of the road network. Given that MATSim has route planning as an integral part of the system it would be a lot of additional work to reproduce this in the BDI system. It is also the case that as it is MATSim which has detailed location information regarding agents, it is sometimes MATSim that must receive information and then channel it to the relevant (BDI) agents. In consequence, an active design decision needs to be made at which level of abstraction the BDI model operates. For our present applications, we assume that the BDI model knows about certain fixed location coordinates (e.g. activity locations), but not about the road network, or dynamic co-ordinates such as agent location.

When a BDI-action is sent to MATSim, then the BDI goal of which it is a part is suspended until MATSim returns from that action with completion status like PASSED or FAILED. We note that failing a BDI action is not the same as failing a BDI plan, as an action is a plan step (similar to a sub-goal), and therefore should, like a sub-goal, raise a consideration of alternative options for achieving success for that action, rather than automatic failure, leading to failure of the containing plan. We have developed a mechanism to specify (possibly with some analysis or query regarding the current situation) together with an action, what should be done if it fails.

Sometimes a percept relevant to a BDI-action may be better provided to the BDI system as a trigger for reasoning, rather than associated with immediate success or failure of the BDI-action. This allows the BDI system to reason about the situation using standard goals and plans with context conditions, in order to determine what should be done. The BDI action can then be aborted/replaced if that is considered appropriate.

A simplified example of this situation is shown in Fig. 6 using the detailed design diagram of the Prometheus agent system design methodology [19]. This figure shows an evacuate goal which through some series of plans and subgoals has led to a BDI-action to drive to the evacuation destination. The design specifies that if a congestion percept arrives (which will happen only while the agent is engaged in some drive-to), then an appropriate plan is chosen to assess the situation. Here we show 3 different plans depending on whether the agent is 1. still in the danger zone, 2. out of the danger zone but far from the destination, 3. close to the destination.

If as a result of the reasoning that happens when one of these plans is chosen, there is a decision that the agent should modify its destination, then the decision code within the congestion intention[9] will abort the `drive-to` action within the Evacuate intention. The code for handling this situation will then instantiate a new `drive-to` action with the new destination.

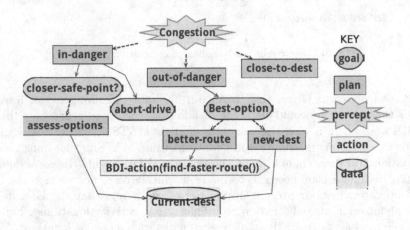

Fig. 7. Detailed design of handling of congestion percept

There may be a number of subgoals and further plans associated with the plans for handling the congestion percept. Figure 7 shows a possible design. Plan in-danger results in the agent querying MATSim to find a location outside the danger zone to which there is a faster route (given congestion) than the point outside the danger zone on the current route. If such exists the agent will register the new destination and abort the current `drive-to` action allowing it to be replaced with a new `drive-to` action. The new destination will be accessed and provided as a parameter to the new `drive-to`. MATSim will then add the route in standard fashion. The code for failing/aborting the `drive-to` action for this case will, in addition to instantiating a new `drive-to`, need to ensure this is followed by a choice of final destination once out of the danger zone.

If the out-of-danger plan is chosen the agent may consider either looking for a new route to the current evacuation destination, or looking for an alternative destination which is faster to get to, given congestion. Let us assume that the agent first looks for a better route, by choosing the better-route plan, resulting in instantiating a new BDI-action to "find-faster-route". If this has been properly set up in MATSim as described in Sect. 2.4, then the action will be generated in MATSim to replace the current route with a faster one if such exists and return PASSED. At this point the intention triggered by the congestion percept would complete. If no faster route was found then a FAIL would be returned, in which case the plan can just be allowed to fail and the standard BDI execution will

---

[9] An intention is simply the code stack resulting from a top-level instantiated goal.

lead to the plan new-dest which can consider alternative evacuation destinations. Depending on the outcome of that reasoning, either a new destination may be chosen or it may be determined that there is nothing better and no change is made. The former will result in aborting the current `drive-to` and instantiating a `drive-to` with new destination (as in case (1)), while the latter would simply terminate with no change. Case (3) may simply be a no-op where the agent does no further reasoning, as they are anyway close to the destination.

The key aspects that we have identified for design are: (i) percepts should always be handled by a new separate intention. This may simply alter a belief that affects a current intention, it may generate a substantial reasoning process regarding what to do with regards to a current intention, or it may generate new behaviour unrelated to other current intentions. (ii) any reasoning, other than that specifically related to route planning or simple locational reasoning, should be done by the BDI system. (iii) action failures must be handled differently to plan failures - they are more like goal failures. (Future work should investigate infrastructure support for high level specification and management of such, in the same style as is done for goal failure with a search for alternative plans based on context). (iv) there is a need for aborting an action, which arises from BDI reasoning, as well as failing an action which arises from the environment. (v) querying of MATSim may be needed in order to do the BDI reasoning. This is supported by the BDI-ABM infrastructure of [25].

Agent intentions may also be triggered by messages from another agent. This happens in the evacuation domain when a policeman "sees" (via a percept from MATSim) an approaching agent, and directs them to take a particular turn. A similar approach to that shown with the congestion percept is appropriate. First generate an intention that reasons about the message, and any effect on current intention(s). Then modify current intentions as needed.

6   Evaluation

All required functionality as described in Sect. 1 was successfully implemented. At the same time, the combined system became more streamlined, e.g. by clarifying the interaction between the BDI system and MATSim, mediated via the Controller (Sect. 2).

Figure 8 shows a view of the Surf Coast Shire bushfire evacuation simulation[10] which was built in collaboration with the emergency services. The simulation contains 10,000 agents to whom a range of daily activities were assigned based on expert knowledge (as per Sect. 4). The scenario models a bushfire that starts at 12pm (red shape is fire, blue shape is smoke) and moves in a south-easterly direction eventually engulfing the township of Anglesea along the Great Ocean Road. Vehicles can be seen moving about the region (green are travelling at freespeed, red are slowed by congestion). BDI reasoning causes agents to perform within-day re-routing in MATSim for a range of reasons including driving to the

---

[10] https://github.com/agentsoz/ees/tree/master/scenarios/surf-coast-shire/population-subgroups.

location of dependants, driving to chosen evacuation points, and re-planning to find alternative routes or evacuation locations when delayed in congestion.

Fig. 8. Surf Coast Shire bushfire simulation with 10,000 agents.

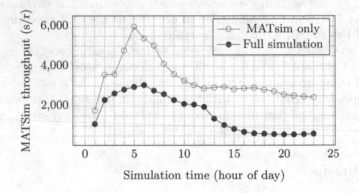

Fig. 9. Comparison of MATSim throughput for the Surf Coast Shire bushfire simulation when run in the combined simulation and directly in MATSim.

The work conducted since [17,18,25] and presented here has significantly improved the runtime for large scenarios. We have made significant improvements that impact performance–such as thread-safety of data structures used–in all aspects of the BDI-MATSim integration, however these are more difficult to discuss in the paper. As an example, the Surf Coast Shire simulation of Fig. 8 that contains all the components shown in Fig. 2 runs on a recent-day laptop[11] within 3 min. Figure 9 shows the relative performance[12] of the combined simulation of Fig. 2 against MATSim alone, for the Surf Coast Shire scenario with

---

[11] Macbook Pro 15,2 with 4 i7 cores (2.7 GHz) and 16 GB RAM.

[12] The reported metric is the simulation to real time ratio (s/r), i.e. how much faster than reality the simulation is.

10,000 agents. The MATSim-only run was produced by running the simulation configuration directly in MATSim (since the configuration files are compatible with MATSim, see Sect. 4). The main difference is that of course in MATSim there is no bushfire and the population just goes about its day, whereas in the combined simulation the bushfire commences at 12pm, following which the BDI agents start to respond by choosing destinations and re-routing as necessary. We can see that prior to 12pm, the combined simulation is slow by a factor of about 1.5-2x, and post-12pm by about 5–6x. The majority of slowdown post commencement of the bushfire at 12pm can be attributed to the extra path planning that occurs in MATSim due to the BDI agents rerouting.

7   Discussion and Conclusion

In this paper we have described some of the important aspects of MATSim which facilitate its use as a component in large complex simulations, including some new extensions and some supporting tools. MATSim is itself a large and complex system. However, where transport simulation is an important aspect of a larger micro-simulation it does not make sense to implement a simpler (and likely less efficient and accurate) alternative. Rather effort should be made to facilitate the re-use and incorporation of this existing and highly flexible software. The work described here contributes to this effort.

A number of the aspects described have been motivated by our use of MAT-Sim as a component in evacuation applications and in an urban planning application. We believe that this description will assist others in using MATSim in similar ways. The key aspects we have described are: (i) Architecture that enables external control of multiple simulation components. Components must be able to be started and paused externally. (ii) A well specified API to support addition of new percepts and actions, as well as the structure within which to do this. (iii) An ability to modify the environment dynamically, in this case using dynamic penalties and flexible routers. (iv) Tools to assist in creating a suitable representative initial scenario for the simulation. (v) Design of cognitive agents within the BDI-MATSim system.

We also gave examples of how we have used these facilities within evacuation applications, where requirements were user driven. One of these applications is currently deployed and the other is expected to be deployed within coming months.

References

1. Anda, C., Erath, A., Fourie, P.J.: Transport modelling in the age of big data. Int. J. Urban Sci. **21**(sup1), 19–42 (2017). https://doi.org/10.1080/12265934.2017. 1281150
2. Balmer, M., Axhausen, K., Nagel, K.: A demand generation framework for large scale micro simulations. Transp. Res. Rec. **1985**, 125–134 (2006). https://doi.org/ 10.3141/1985-14

3. Balmer, M., Rieser, M., Vogel, A., Axhausen, K., Nagel, K.: Generating day plans using hourly origin-destination matrices. In: Bieger, T., Laesser, C., Maggi, R. (eds.) Jahrbuch 2004/05 Schweizerische Verkehrswirtschaft, pp. 5–36, Schweizer Verkehrswissenschaftliche Gesellschaft (2005)
4. Batty, M.: Fifty years of urban modeling: macro-statics to micro-dynamics. In: The Dynamics of Complex Urban Systems: An Interdisciplinary Approach, Ascona/Ticino, Switzerland, 4–6 November 2004, p. 27 (2004)
5. Bazzan, A., Amarante, M.D.B.D., Sommer, T., Benavides, A.J.: ITSUMO: an agent-based simulator for ITS applications. In: Rossetti, R., Liu, H., Tang, S. (eds.) Proceedings of the 4th Workshop on Artificial Transportation Systems and Simulation. IEEE, September 2010
6. Bouman, P., Lovric, M.: Rotterdam: revenue management in public transportation with smart-card data enabled agent-based simulations. In: Horni, A., Nagel, K., Axhausen, K.W. (eds.) The Multi-Agent Transport Simulation MATSim, chap. 81. Ubiquity, London (2016). https://doi.org/10.5334/baw
7. Bruch, E., Atwell, J.: Agent-based models in empirical social research. Sociol. Methods Res. **44**(2), 186–221 (2015)
8. Dahmann, J.S., Kuhl, F., Weatherly, R.: Standards for simulation: as simple as possible but not simpler: the high level architecture for simulation. Simulation **71**(6), 378–387 (1998)
9. Dobler, C., Nagel, K.: Within-day replanning. In: Horni, A., Nagel, K., Axhausen, K.W. (eds.) The Multi-Agent Transport Simulation MATSim, chap. 30, pp. 187–200. Ubiquity Press, London (2016)
10. Epstein, J., Axtell, R.: Growing Artificial Societies. MIT Press, Cambridge (1996)
11. Gloor, C., Cavens, D., Nagel, K.: A message-based framework for real-world mobility simulations. In: Klügl, F., Bazzan, A., Ossowski, S. (eds.) Applications of Agent Technology in Traffic and Transportation, Whitestein Series in Software Agent Technologies and Autonomic Computing, pp. 193–209. Birkhäuser, Basel (2005). https://doi.org/10.1007/3-7643-7363-6_13
12. Hamacher, H., Tjandra, S.: Mathematical modelling of evacuation problems: a state of art. Technical report, Fraunhofer ITWM (2001)
13. Horni, A., Nagel, K., Axhausen, K.W. (eds.): The Multi-Agent Transport Simulation MATSim. Ubiquity, London (2016). https://doi.org/10.5334/baw
14. Lämmel, G., Klüpfel, H., Nagel, K.: Risk minimizing evacuation strategies under uncertainty. In: Peacock, R., Kuligowski, E., Averill, J. (eds.) Pedestrian and Evacuation Dynamics, pp. 287–296. Springer, Berlin (2011). https://doi.org/10.1007/978-1-4419-9725-8_26
15. Message Passing Interface (MPI) web page. https://www.mpi-forum.org. Accessed 2019
16. Nicolai, T.W., Nagel, K.: Coupling MATSim and UrbanSim: software design issues. SustainCity Working Paper 6.1, also VSP WP 10–13 (2010). http://www.vsp.tu-berlin.de/publications
17. Padgham, L., Nagel, K., Singh, D., Chen, Q.: Integrating BDI agents into a MATSim simulation. In: ECAI 2014, pp. 681–686. IOS Press, Prague (2014)
18. Padgham, L., Singh, D.: Making MATSim agents smarter with the Belief-Desire-Intention framework. In: Horni, A., Nagel, K., Axhausen, K.W. (eds.) The Multi-Agent Transport Simulation MATSim, chap. 31, pp. 201–210. Ubiquity Press, London (2016)
19. Padgham, L., Winikoff, M.: Developing Intelligent Agent Systems: A practical guide. Wiley Series in Agent Technology. Wiley, Hoboken (2004)

20. Protocol Buffers Web. https://developers.google.com/protocol-buffers/. Accessed 2015
21. Rieser, M., Nagel, K., Beuck, U., Balmer, M., Rümenapp, J.: Truly agent-oriented coupling of an activity-based demand generation with a multi-agent traffic simulation. Transp. Res. Rec. **2021**, 10–17 (2007). https://doi.org/10.3141/2021-02
22. Russel, S.J., Norvig, P.: Artificial Intelligence - A Modern Approach, 3rd edn. Pearson Education, Upper Saddle River (2010)
23. Singh, D., Padgham, L.: OpenSim: a framework for integrating agent-based models and simulation components. In: ECAI 2014, pp. 837–842. IOS Press, Prague (2014)
24. Singh, D., Padgham, L.: Emergency Evacuation Simulator (EES) - a tool for planning community evacuations in Australia. In: Proceedings of the Twenty-Sixth International Joint Conference on Artificial Intelligence Organization, pp. 5249–5251, Melbourne, August 2017. https://doi.org/10.24963/ijcai.2017/780
25. Singh, D., Padgham, L., Logan, B.: Integrating BDI agents with agent-based simulation platforms. Auton. Agent. Multi-Agent Syst. **30**(6), 1050–1071 (2016). https://doi.org/10.1007/s10458-016-9332-x
26. Strauch, D., et al.: Linking Transport and Land Use Planning: The Microscopic Dynamic Simulation Model ILUMASS, chap. 20, pp. 295–311. CRC Press, Boca Raton (2005)
27. W3C: eXtensible Markup Language (XML). World Wide Web Consortium (W3C) (2008). www.w3.org/XML
28. Waddell, P., Ševčíková, H., Socha, D., Miller, E., Nagel, K.: OPUS: an open platform for urban simulation. In: 9th Conference on Computers in Urban Planning and Urban Management (CUPUM), vol. 428, University College London, UK (2005). http://128.40.111.250/cupum/searchpapers/detail.asp?pID=428
29. Waddell, P., Borning, A., Noth, M., Freier, N., Becke, M., Ulfarsson, G.: Microsimulation of urban development and location choices: design and implementation of urbansim. Netw. Spat. Econ. **3**(1), 43–67 (2003)
30. Weiss, G. (ed.): Multiagent Systems. A Modern Approach to Distributed Artificial Intelligence. The MIT Press (1999)
31. Zilske, M., Nagel, K.: A simulation-based approach for constructing all-day travel chains from mobile phone data. Procedia Comput. Sci. **52**, 468–475 (2015). https://doi.org/10.1016/j.procs.2015.05.017

Social Awareness and Explainability

Incorporating Social Practices in BDI Agent Systems

Stephen Cranefield[1]([⊠]) [iD] and Frank Dignum[2,3,4] [iD]

[1] University of Otago, Dunedin, New Zealand
stephen.cranefield@otago.ac.nz
[2] Umeå University, Umeå, Sweden
frank.dignum@umu.se
[3] Czech University of Technology in Prague, Prague, Czech Republic
frank.dignum@aic.fel.cvut.cz
[4] Utrecht University, Utrecht, The Netherlands
f.p.m.dignum@uu.nl

Abstract. When agents interact with humans, either through embodied agents or because they are embedded in a robot, it would be easy if they could use fixed interaction protocols as they do with other agents. However, people do not keep fixed protocols in their day-to-day interactions and the social environment is often dynamic, making it impossible to use fixed protocols. Deliberating about interactions from fundamentals is not very scalable either, because in that case all possible reactions of a human have to be considered in the agent's plans. In this paper we argue that social practices can be used as an inspiration for designing flexible and scalable interaction mechanisms that are also robust. However, using social practices requires extending the traditional BDI deliberation cycle to monitor landmark states and perform expected actions by leveraging existing plans. We define and implement this mechanism in Jason using a periodically run meta-deliberation plan, supported by a metainterpreter, and illustrate its use in a realistic scenario.

1 Introduction

Imagine the scenario where a disabled person, living alone, is assisted by a care robot. The robot makes sure that the person gets up every morning and that he drinks some coffee and takes his morning pills (if needed). Then they read the newspaper together, which means that the person looks at the pictures in the paper and the robot reads the articles out loud for the person to hear.

When agents in the role of this type of personal assistant or care robot have to interact with humans over a longer time period and in a dynamic environment (that is not controlled by the agent), the interaction management becomes very difficult. When fixed protocols are used for the interaction they are often not appropriate in all situations and cause breakdowns and consequent loss of trust in the system. However, to have real-time deliberation about the best response during the interaction is not very scalable, because in real life the contexts are dynamic and complex and thus the agent would need to take many parameters into consideration at each step. Thus we need something

© Springer Nature Switzerland AG 2020
L. A. Dennis et al. (Eds.): EMAS 2019, LNAI 12058, pp. 109–126, 2020.
https://doi.org/10.1007/978-3-030-51417-4_6

in between a completely scripted interaction that is too brittle and a completely open interaction that is not scalable.

As we have done before in the agent community, we take inspiration from human interactions and the way they are managed by individuals. Humans classify situations into standard contexts in which a certain *social practice* can be applied. Social science has studied this phenomenon in social practice theory. Social practice theory comes forth from a variety of different sub-disciplines of social science. It started from philosophical sociology with proponents like Bourdieu [3] and Giddens [8]. Later on Reckwitz [16] and Shove [18] have expanded on these ideas, and also Schatzki [17] made some valuable contributions.

These authors all claim that important features of human life should be understood in terms of organized constellations of interacting persons, which together constitute social practices. People are not just creating these practices, but our deliberations are also based on the fact that most of our life is shaped by social practices. Thus, we use social practices to categorize situations and decide upon ways of behaviour based on social practices. The main intuition behind this is that our life is quite cyclic, in that many activities come back with a certain regularity. We have meals every day, go to work on Monday until Friday, go to the supermarket once a week, etc. These so-called Patterns of Life [7] can be exploited to create standard situations and expectations. It makes sense to categorize recurrent situations as social practices with a kind of standard behaviour for each of them.

Unfortunately social practice theory has not been widely used in computer science or in HCI and thus there are no ready-to-use tools in order to incorporate them in agents. It is clear from the above description that social practices are more than just a protocol or a frame to be used by the agent in its deliberation. Therefore, in this paper we make the following contributions. We propose a mechanism for BDI agents to maintain awareness about active social practices, and to leverage their existing plans to act in accordance with these practices. We focus on these aspects of social practices (discussed in more detail in Sect. 2): (a) they are relevant in specific contexts, defined in terms of the actors, resources and places involved; and (b) they are modelled as plan patterns, structured as a set of partially ordered landmarks, each with an associated purpose (a goal) and a sequence of actions that is a partial prescription for reaching the landmark.

Our mechanism is presented as a meta-deliberation plan that can be directly executed by Jason agents, or treated as a specification for an optimised implementation in an extended agent platform. This plan has been deployed in the (simulated) care robot scenario, to confirm that awareness of and adherence to a social practice enables the robot to have a more successful interaction with the patient over a longer period of time. As some of the features needed to implement this scenario, and to support our meta-deliberation plan, are not available in Jason[1], we also present a Jason metainterpreter, which provides this extended functionality, but can also be used independently to support other research on extensions to BDI practical reasoning.

---

[1] These features are finding a plan for a goal that ensures a given action is performed, and support for durative and joint actions.

In the next section, we give an introduction to the purpose and structure of social practices. Section 3 elaborates on the care robot scenario and how we have modelled it in Jason. Section 4 describes the role of social practices in this scenario, and discusses the requirements this imposes for a BDI agent. Section 5 presents our mechanism for extending Jason to leverage social practices, and the metainterpreter needed to support this. We finish the paper with some conclusions and suggestions for future work.

2   Social Practices

Social practices are defined as accepted ways of doing things, contextual and materially mediated, that are shared between actors and routinized over time [16]. They can be seen as patterns that can be filled in by a multitude of single and often unique actions. Through (joint) performance, the patterns provided by the practice are filled out and reproduced.

According to Reckwitz [16] and Shove et al. [18], a social practice consists of three parts:

- Material: covers all physical aspects of the performance of a practice, including the human body and objects that are available (relates to physical aspects of a context).
- Competence: refers to skills and knowledge that are required to perform the practice (relates to the notion of deliberation about a situation).
- Meaning: refers to the issues which are considered to be relevant with respect to that material, i.e. understandings, beliefs and emotions (relates to social aspects of a situation).

Let us consider these three parts of a social practice in the scenario of the care robot scenario introduced in Sect. 1. Material refers to the room where the robot serves morning coffee for the disabled person. It includes the materials that are needed to make coffee (such as coffee and a coffee maker) and serve it (such as a cup and tray). However, it also includes the table and other furniture in the room, the newspaper (if present), the TV, radio, computer, tablet, and the robot and person (and possible other people that may be present).

Competence describes the activities every party can perform and expectations about what they will actually do. For example, the robot is capable of making coffee and serving it. The person can drink his coffee by himself. They can jointly read the newspaper or watch TV. The expectation is that the robot wakes the person if he is not awake yet, makes the coffee and gives it to the person. After that they will read the newspaper together to provide mental stimulation. Note, these are expectations, not a protocol. So, parties can deviate from it and they can also fill the parts in, in ways they see fit best.

Meaning has to do with all the social interpretations that come with the social practice, e.g. drinking coffee in the morning might give the person a sense of well-being that he can use to face the challenges of the rest of the day. When the coffee is cold or weak the person might interpret it as disinterest on the part of the robot in his well-being. The goal of reading the newspaper might also be not just to get the information from it, but a form of entertainment and feeling related to the robot, because the human and robot are doing something together.

From the above description it can already be seen that social practices are more encompassing than conventions and norms. Conventions focus on the strategic advantage that an individual gets by conforming to the convention. The reason to follow a convention is that if all parties involved comply, a kind of optimal coordination is reached, i.e. if we all drive on the left side of the road, traffic will be smoother than when everyone chooses the side to drive on freely. Thus, conventions focus on the actual actions being performed and how they optimize the coordination. Social practices focus on common expectations and ways to achieve them. For example, if we go to a presentation, we sit down as soon as we see chairs standing in rows in the room. However, we could also keep standing (as is often done outside).

Social practices are also different from norms. Norms usually dictate a very specific behaviour rather than creating a set of loosely coupled expectations as is the case for social practices. For example, if the norm states that a car has to stop for a red light, it gives a very specific directive. If a norm is more abstract (like "drive carefully") then we need to translate this into concrete norms for specific situations.

One framework that seems very close to social practices is the notion of *scripts*. However, social practices are not just mere scripts in the sense of Minsky [14]. Practices are more flexible than the classical frames defined by scripts, in that they can be extended and changed by learning, and the "slots" only need to be filled in as far as they are needed to determine a course of action. Using these structures changes planning in many common situations to pattern recognition and filling in parameters. They support, rather than restrict, deliberation about behaviour. For example, the social practice of "going to work" incorporates usual means of transport that can be used, timing constraints, weather and traffic conditions, etc. Normally you take a car to work, but if the weather is exceptionally bad, the social practice does not force the default action, but rather gives input for deliberation about a new plan in this situation, such as taking a bus or train (or even staying home). Thus, social practices can be seen as a kind of flexible script. Moreover, scripts do not incorporate any social meaning for the activities performed in them as social practices do.

Social practices have been used in applications in a variety of ways. In [12, 15] they have been used as part of social simulations. In those applications, social practices are used as a standard package of actions with a special status. Thus individuals can use them with a certain probability given the circumstances are right. However, these applications do not use the internal structure of social practices for the planning of the individuals. Social practices have been used for applications in natural language and dialogue management in [1, 9]. Here, the social practices are used to guide the planning process, but are geared towards a particular dialogue rather than as part of a more general interaction. In [13] it is shown how social practices can be used by a traditional epistemic multi-agent planner to provide efficient and robust plans in cooperative settings. However, in this case the planner was not part of a BDI agent with its own goals and plans, but completely dedicated to finding a plan for the situation at hand. In [6] a first structure of social practices was presented that is more amenable for the use by agents. The paper is only conceptual and no implementation was made yet. In this paper we will follow the structure described in [6]. However, we mainly concentrate on the plan patterns that are a core part of the social practices and show how they work with BDI agents in the Jason platform.

The complete structure for social practices (based on [6]) is as follows:

Context

- *Roles* describe the competencies and expectations about a certain type of actor. Thus the robot is expected to be able to make a cup of coffee.
- *Actors* are all people and autonomous systems involved, that have capability to reason and (inter)act. This indicates the agents that are expected to fulfil a part in the practice. In our scenario, these are the robot and the person.
- *Resources* are objects that are used by the actions in the practice, such as cups, coffee, trays, curtains, and chairs. So, they are assumed to be available both for standard actions and for the planning within the practice.
- *Affordances* are the properties of the context that permit social actions and depend on the match between context conditions and actor characteristics. For example, the bed might be used as a chair, or a mug as a cup.
- *Places* indicates where all objects and actors are usually located relative to each other, in space or time: the cups are in the cupboard in the kitchen, the person is in the chair (or in bed), etc.

Meaning

- *Purpose* determines the social interpretation of actions and of certain physical situations. For example, the purpose of reading the newspaper is to get information about current affairs and to entertain the person.
- *Promotes* indicates the values that are promoted (or demoted, by promoting the opposite) by the social practice. Giving coffee to the person will promote the value of "caring".
- *Counts-as* are rules of the type "X counts as Y in C" linking brute facts (X) and institutional facts (Y) in the context (C). For example, reading the newspaper with the person counts as entertaining the person.

Expectations

- *Plan patterns* describe usual patterns of actions defined by the *landmarks* that are expected to occur (states of affairs around which the inter-agent coordination is structured). For example, the care robot first checks if the person is awake then makes sure there is coffee served. Landmarks are usually very naturally given by the people involved. They describe a social practice in terms of the phases of which it consists and use the landmarks to denote fixed points that have to be reached before the next phase can start.
- *Norms* describe the rules of (expected) behaviour within the practice. For example, the robot should ask the person if he wants coffee, before starting to make it.
- *Strategies* indicate condition-action pairs that can occur at any time during the practice. For example, if the person drops the coffee, the robot will clean it up. If the robot notices the person is asleep (again) it will try to wake him.

- A *Start condition*, or trigger, indicates how the social practice starts, e.g. the practice of having morning coffee starts at 8 am.
- A *Duration*, or *End condition*, indicates how the social practice ends, e.g., the morning routine takes around 45 min and ends when the newspaper is read and the coffee is finished.

Activities

- *Possible actions* describe the expected actions of actors in the social practice, e.g. making coffee, reading the newspaper, and opening curtains.
- *Requirements* indicate the type of capabilities or competences that the agent is expected to have in order to perform the activities within this practice. For example, the robot is expected to know how to make coffee and read the newspaper.

In [5] there is a first formalization of all these aspects based on dynamic logic. Due to space limitations we will not include this formalization here, but just discuss a few points that are important for the current implementation of social practices in Jason.

The core element of the social practice for an agent is the plan pattern, which gives it handles to plan its behaviour. Plan patterns are parallel, choice or sequential combinations of plan parts expressed as $\gamma\phi$. These plan parts stand for all possible sequences of actions γ that contain actions contributing towards the achievement of ϕ (starting from a particular situation). ϕ is the *purpose* of that part of the practice. There can be more effects, but they are not all specified. So, in our morning routine practice, the plan pattern can be defined as $\gamma_1\phi_1; (\gamma_2\phi_2 \& \gamma_3\phi_3); \gamma_4\phi_4$, where ϕ_1 denotes the person being awake, ϕ_2 denotes the coffee being served, ϕ_3 denotes the pills being taken, and ϕ_4 denotes the person being mentally stimulated.

Thus, the purpose of the first part of the morning routine is that the person is awake. This might be done by opening the curtains, making a loud noise, or otherwise. If the purpose is achieved by opening the curtains, not only is the person awake, but the curtains are also open. The latter is merely a side effect of achieving the purpose.

Two more things should be noted about these patterns. One is that the overall pattern is supposed to achieve the overall purpose of the social practice. This is a formal constraint, but we only treat this implicitly. The other is that after a part of the plan pattern is finished, it automatically triggers the start of the next part of the pattern. In the full formalism this is assured, but is not explicit from only this fragment. In the same way, a social practice is started when the start condition becomes true. It then becomes available for execution and can be used by any agent present in the situation.

Finally, the formalism of social practices also guarantees that there is a common belief in the elements of the social practice and if actions are taken everyone has at least a common belief about the effects in as far as they are important for the social practice. Thus it guarantees a common situation awareness.

3   The Care Robot Scenario

In this section we elaborate on the care robot scenario outlined in the introduction, and describe how we have modelled and implemented it using Jason.

We assume the high-level operation of the robot is based on a BDI interpreter, and that it comes equipped with goals and plans to trigger and enact its care activities (most likely with some customisation of key parameters possible). In this section, we consider only a small subset of the robot's duties: to wake the patient at a certain time in the morning, to provide coffee as required, and to provide mental stimulation. We do not specify any goals of the robot outside the practice here, but normally the care robot would also have its own goals such as powering its battery, cleaning a room and taking care of the health of the patient.

Social practices provide patterns of coordination for multiple agents in terms of landmark states rather than explicit sequences of actions. Therefore they do not make limiting assumptions about the temporal aspects of actions and their effects leading up to a landmark. Only the landmarks themselves are explicitly temporally ordered. Monitoring of landmark states is necessarily decoupled from the performance of actions, as reaching a landmark may depend on another agent or agents, or may be the result of a delayed effect of an action. To provide a non-trivial test case, we include some temporal complexity in the scenario by including durative actions (i.e. those that take place across an interval of time), an action with a delayed effect, and a joint durative action, which has its desired effect only if two participants perform it during overlapping time intervals. Durative and joint actions are implemented using a Jason metainterpreter[2] that is described in Sect. 5. To simulate the passing of time, we use a "ticker" agent with a recursive plan that periodically performs a tick action to update the time recorded in the environment. We use Jason's synchronous execution mode, so the robot, patient and ticker agents perform a single reasoning cycle in every step of the simulation.

Listing 1 shows the robot's initial beliefs, rules and plans. The plans in lines 22–41 have declarative goals (i.e. their triggering goals express desired states) and use Jason preprocessing directives to transform them according to a predefined declarative achievement goal pattern [2].

The first set of plans (lines 22–26) is for achieving a state where the patient is awake, with alternative plans for talking to the patient, shaking him, and opening the curtains and waiting for the light to wake him. The *exclusive backtracking declarative goal* ("ebdg") pattern specifies that additional failure-handling logic should be added to ensure that all the plans will be tried (once each) until the goal is achieved, or all plans fail. Opening the curtains has a delayed effect: it will eventually wake the patient[3].

The second set of plans (lines 28–33) handles the goal of having the patient mentally simulated, and also uses the ebdg pattern. The first plan waits for the patient to be awake, and then fails so that the other plans will be tried. The other two alternatives involve playing the music of Mozart to the patient, and initiating the joint action of reading the newspaper with the patient. As joint actions are not directly supported by Jason, line 32 calls this action via a solve goal that is handled by our metainterpreter.

---

[2] A metainterpreter is a programming language interpreter written in the same, or a similar, language to the one being interpreted. It can be used to prototype extensions to the base language.

[3] Actions are implemented in Jason by defining an *execute* method in a Java class modelling the environment. The delay is currently hard-coded in this class.

```
1  /* Initial beliefs and rules */
2  durative(makePodCoffee).
3  durative(readNewspaper).
4  joint(readNewspaper).
5  durative_action_continuation_pred(readNewspaper, continueReadingNewspaper).
6  durative_action_continuation_pred(makePodCoffee, continueMakingPodCoffee).
7  durative_action_cleanup_goal(readNewspaper, cleanupReadNewspaper).
8  continueReadingNewspaper :-
9      started(readNewspaper, T1) &
10     not started_durative_action(readNewspaper, patient, _) &
11     time(T2) &
12     T2 <= T1 + 20.
13 continueReadingNewspaper :-
14     started_durative_action(readNewspaper, patient, _) &
15     not stopped_durative_action(readNewspaper, patient, _).
16
17 continueMakingPodCoffee :- state(coffee, not_made).
18
19 wake_up_phrase("Good morning sleepyhead!").
20
21 /* Plans */
22 {begin ebdg(state(patient,awake))}
23 +!state(patient,awake) : wake_up_phrase(P) <- talkToPatient(P).
24 +!state(patient,awake) <- shakePatient.
25 +!state(patient,awake) <- openCurtains; .wait(state(patient, awake), 30000).
26 {end}
27
28 {begin ebdg(state(patient,mentally_stimulated))}
29 +!state(patient, mentally_stimulated) <- .wait(state(patient, awake)); .fail.
30 +!state(patient, mentally_stimulated) <- play_mozart.
31 +!state(patient, mentally_stimulated) <-
32     !solve({ readNewspaper[participants([patient,robot])] }).
33 {end}
34
35 +!state(coffee, served) <- !state(coffee, made); serveCoffee.
36
37 {begin ebdg(state(coffee,made))}
38 +!state(coffee, made) : resource(coffee_pods) & resource(coffee_pod_machine) <-
39     makePodCoffee; .wait(state(coffee, made), 10000).
40 +!state(coffee, made) : resource(instant_coffee) <- makeInstantCoffee.
41 {end}
42
43 +performing_durative_action(Act, Agent, Time) :
44         not started_durative_action(Act, Agent, _) <-
45     // Cache percept as a belief
46     +started_durative_action(Act, Agent, Time).
47
48 +stopped_durative_action(Act, StoppedParticipant, Time)[source(percept)] <-
49     // Cache percept as a belief
50     +stopped_durative_action(Act, StoppedParticipant, Time);
51     -started_durative_action(Act, StoppedParticipant, Time).
52
53 +!cleanupReadNewspaper <-
54     -stopped_durative_action(readNewspaper, _, _)[source(self)].
55
56 { include("metainterpreter.asl") }
```

Listing 1. Plans for the care robot domain

These plans are followed by a single plan for serving coffee. This has the subgoal of having the coffee made, and then the action of serving the coffee is performed.

The fourth set of plans (lines 37–41) is triggered by the goal of reaching a state in which the coffee is made. The options are to use a coffee pod machine and wait for it to finish, or to make instant coffee.

The environment sends a percept to all participants of a joint action when any other participant performs the action for the first time or performs a stop action with the joint action as an argument. The remaining three plans handle receipt of these percepts, and a belief 'clean-up' goal that is created by the metainterpreter (if the agent declares that it has one—see line 7) when the agent stops performing a joint action.

The initial segment of the listing contains initial beliefs and rules related to the processing of durative actions: declarations of which actions are declarative and/or joint, and of predicates and associated rules defining the circumstances in which the robot will continue performing the durative actions.

In a real scenario, the patient will be a human, not a BDI agent, but we simulate the patient using a Jason agent. "He" (the patient agent) has a plan to take his pills once he is awake. He also has a plan that will respond to the robot beginning the joint newspaper reading action by also beginning that action. He will continue reading the newspaper for 40 time units if he is in a good mood, but only 20 if he is in a bad mood. Being woken by daylight (after the curtains are opened) leaves him in a good mood; being shaken awake leaves him in a bad mood, and talking will not wake him up. Thus, if the robot begins with goals to have the patient awake and mentally stimulated, the patient will be left in a bad mood by being shaken awake and the newspaper reading will be shorter (and less stimulating) than if he were in a good mood.

4 A Care Robot with Social Practices

Section 3 introduced the care robot scenario. In this section, we consider how the robot could be enhanced using social practices. We focus on the robot's awareness of a social practice's context, and its temporal structure as a partially ordered set of landmarks, each described in terms of a purpose and a sequence of actions to be performed[4].

As noted previously, it is assumed that the robot comes equipped with appropriate goals and plans, and that it is possible to customise certain parameters such as the time the user likes to wake up, and the time and style of coffee that he likes to have. However, customising each plan in isolation will not easily provide the coordination between activities and dynamic adaptability to different contexts that can be provided by social practices. To perform most effectively, the robot should choose, for a given context, the plans for each goal that will achieve the best outcomes for the patient, and furthermore, consider constraints on goal orderings that arise from preferences and habit. For example, if the patient prefers to be woken at a certain time in a given context (e.g. when his family is due to visit) and/or in a certain way (e.g. by the curtains being opened), his mood is likely to be adversely affected if he is woken at a different time, and his engagement with subsequent activities (such as reading the newspaper together) may be reduced. In this section we describe how this type of contextual information can be addressed by the use of a social practice.

In Sect. 3, we described the various plans and actions available to the robot. We now assume that the following "morning routine" social practice has emerged[5]. We present this as a set of beliefs in the form used by our social practice reasoning plans that will be

---

[4] Currently we only handle a single action for each landmark.

[5] It is beyond the scope of this paper to consider how social practices might be learned.

discussed in Sect. 5. Note that we only illustrate a small subset of what would be likely to be a real morning routine for a patient and his/her care robot, but this is sufficient to highlight the nature of social practices and their relation to BDI agents.

```
social_practice(morningRoutine,
    [state(location, home), resource(coffee_pods), resource(coffee_pod_machine),
     resource(pills), resource(newspaper_subscription),
     (time(T) & T < 1200)]).

landmark(morningRoutine, pa, [],
    [action(robot, openCurtains)], state(patient, awake)).

landmark(morningRoutine, pt, [pa],
    [action(patient, takePills)], state(pills, taken)).

landmark(morningRoutine, cs, [pa],
    [action(robot, makePodCoffee)], state(coffee, served)).

landmark(morningRoutine, ms, [pt,cs],
    [action([robot,patient], readNewspaper)], state(patient, mentally_stimulated)).
```

The first belief above encodes the name of the social practice and a list of conditions that must all hold for it to become active: there are constraints on the location, the resources available, and the time (here, the number 1200 is a proxy for some real-world time that ends the morning routine period).

The other four beliefs model the landmarks, specifying the social practice they are part of, an identifier for the landmark, a list of landmarks that must have been reached previously, a list of actions and their actors that are associated with the landmark, and finally, a goal that is the purpose of the landmark. The landmarks are: (1) to have the patient awake due to the robot opening the curtains, (2) for the patient to have taken his pills, (3) to have the coffee served, which should involve the robot making pod coffee, and (4) for the patient to be mentally stimulated due to the newspaper being read jointly. These landmarks are partially ordered with 1 before 2 and 3, which both precede 4.

Comparing this social practice to the robot plans shown in Listing 1, it can be seen that it avoids an ineffective attempt to wake the patient by talking to him, and prevents him from being left in a bad mood after being shaken awake. It agrees with the first-ordered plan for making coffee (by making pod coffee), and avoids an ill-fated attempt by the robot to provide mental stimulation by playing Mozart. Furthermore, it specifies an ordering on these activities that is not intrinsic to the plans themselves. Note also, that the social practice does not provide complete information on how to reach the landmark of having coffee served: it indicates that the robot should make pod coffee, but doesn't specify the action of serving the coffee. While a planning system could deduce the missing action using a model of actions and their effects [13], a BDI agent does not have this capability. Instead, a BDI agent using social practices must reason about how its existing plans could be used to satisfy landmarks given potentially incomplete information about the actions it must perform.

Furthermore, the robot may already have goals to wake the patient, provide mental stimulation, etc., and the activation of a social practice should not create independent instances of those goals. Thus, the activation of a social practice should override the agent's normal behaviour (for the relevant goals) during the period of activation.

As social practices are structured in terms of ordered landmarks, which model expected states to be reached in a pattern of inter-agent coordination, it is necessary for the agent to monitor the status of landmarks once their prior landmarks have been achieved, and to actively work towards the fulfilment of the current landmarks for which it has associated actions. In the next section, we present a meta-deliberation cycle for Jason agents that addresses this and the other issues outlined above, and which enables the successful execution of our care robot enhanced with social practices.

5 Implementation

5.1 Meta-level Reasoning About Social Practices

Maintaining awareness of social practices (SPs), and contributing to them in an appropriate way, requires agents to detect when each known social practice becomes active or inactive, to monitor the state of the landmarks in an active social practice, and to trigger the appropriate activity if an active SP has an action for the agent associated with the current landmark. This is a type of meta-level reasoning that the agent should perform periodically, and it may override the performance of any standard BDI processing of goals, which is not informed by social practices. We note that, on an abstract level, the same was done in [1] where the plan pattern was translated into a global pattern in Drools (Java based expert system) and the specific interactions within each phase were programmed in a chatbot.

The question then arises of how best to implement such a meta-level reasoner in a BDI architecture. The best performance can, no doubt, be achieved by extending a BDI platform using its underlying implementation language. However, it would require a change of the basic deliberation cycle to include not only reasoning about goals, plans and intentions, but also taking into account the social practice context. Thus, this approach requires significant knowledge of the implementation and requires using an imperative coding style that is not best suited to reasoning about goals [10] and for rapid prototyping and dissemination of new reasoning techniques. Therefore, in this work we define the meta-level reasoner as a plan for a `metadeliberate` goal that reasons about social practices, sleeps and then calls itself recursively. This, and some other plans it triggers, are shown in Listing 2. The plans make use of some extensions to Jason, handled by a metainterpreter that is described in the following subsection[6].

The social practice reasoner runs in response to the goal `metadeliberate` (line 10 in Listing 2). Lines 13 to 31 show the plan for this goal. The `atomic` annotation on the plan label ensures that steps of this plan are not interleaved with steps of other plans. The plan begins by (re)considering which social practice (if any) should be active. It uses the rules in lines 3 to 7 to find social practices that are relevant (i.e. all their requirements hold), and to select one (currently, the first option is always selected). If none are relevant (lines 17–20), any existing belief about the currently selected social practice is retracted. Otherwise (lines 21–29), if the selection has changed, the belief about the selection is updated. Any monitored landmarks are then checked to see if their purpose has been fulfilled (lines 26–28). If so, a belief about their completion is added. The plan then sleeps for a period, before triggering itself to be re-run in a new intention (lines 30–31). The new intention is needed for the recursive call because the plan is atomic, and the agent's other plans must be allowed to run.

---

[6] See https://github.com/scranefield/jason-social-practices for source code.

```
1  /* Rules */
2  // Omitted: has_plan_generating_action/3 and for_all/1
3  relevant_sp(SP) :-
4      social_practice(SP, Requirements) & forall(Requirements).
5  sp_selection(Options, CurrentSP) :-
6      selected_sp(CurrentSP) & .member(CurrentSP, Options).
7  sp_selection([SP|_], SP).
8
9  /* Initial goal */
10 !metadeliberate.
11
12 /* Plans */
13 @metaplan[atomic]
14 +!metadeliberate <-
15     .findall(SP, ( relevant_sp(SP) & not completed_sp(SP) ),
16             RelevantSPs);
17     if (RelevantSPs == []) {
18         if (selected_sp(CurrentlySelectedSP)) {
19             -selected_sp(CurrentlySelectedSP)
20         }
21     } else {
22         if ( sp_selection(RelevantSPs, SelectedSP) &
23              not selected_sp(SelectedSP) ) {
24             -+selected_sp(SelectedSP)
25         }
26         for (monitored(Purpose, SP, ID)) {
27             if (Purpose) { +completed_landmark(SP, ID, Purpose) }
28         }
29     }
30     .wait(500);
31     !!metadeliberate.
32
33 +selected_sp(SP) <-
34     for (landmark(SP, ID, _, _, Purpose)) {
35         PurposeNoAnnots[dummy] = Purpose[dummy];
36         if (.intend(PurposeNoAnnots)) {
37             .suspend(PurposeNoAnnots);
38             +suspended_intention(SP, ID, PurposeNoAnnots)
39         }
40         .add_plan({@suspend_purpose(SP,ID)
41                 +!PurposeNoAnnots <- .suspend(PurposeNoAnnots)},
42                 landmark(SP,ID), begin)
43     }
44     for (landmark(SP, ID, [], Actions, Purpose)) {
45         !activate_landmark(SP, ID, Actions, Purpose)
46     }.
47
48 @activate_landmark[atomic]
49 +!activate_landmark(SP, ID, Actions, Purpose) <-
50     PurposeNoAnnots[dummy] = Purpose[dummy];
51     +monitored(PurposeNoAnnots, SP, ID)
52     if (Actions = [action(Actors, Act)] &
53         (Actors = Me | (.list(Actors) & .member(Me, Actors)))) {
54         if (has_plan_generating_action({+!Purpose}, Act, Path)) {
55             !!solve({ !Purpose }, Path)
56         } elif (joint(Act)) {
57             !!solve({ Act[participants(Actors)] })
58         } elif (durative(Act)) {
59             !!solve({ Act })
60         } else { Act }
61     } else { .print("Multiple actions are not yet supported"); }.
62
```

Listing 2. Rules and plans for social practice reasoning

```
63  @completed_landmark[atomic]
64  +completed_landmark(SP, ID, Purpose) <-
65     .succeed_goal(Purpose);
66     -monitored(Purpose, SP, ID);
67     .remove_plan(suspend_purpose(SP,ID));
68     for ( landmark(SP, ID2, PrecedingLMs, Actions, Purpose2) &
69           not completed_landmark(SP, ID2, _) &
70           .findall(PrecID, (.member(PrecID, PrecedingLMs) &
71                             completed_landmark(SP, PrecID, _)),
72                    CompletedPrecIDs) &
73           .difference(PrecedingLMs, CompletedPrecIDs, []) ) {
74        !activate_landmark(SP, ID2, Actions, Purpose2)
75     }
76     .findall(ID2, ( landmark(SP, ID2, _, _,_) &
77                     not completed_landmark(SP, ID2, _) ),
78              PendingLandmarks);
79     if (PendingLandmarks == []) { +completed_sp(SP) }.
```

Listing 2. Rules and plans for social practice reasoning (continued)

A new belief about a selected social practice is handled by the plan in lines 33–46. This loops through the landmarks to check if the agent already has intentions to achieve any of their purposes[7]. If so, these intentions are suspended, and this is recorded in a belief so the intentions can be later marked as successful if the landmark is completed (see line 67). A plan is also temporarily added (lines 40–42) to ensure that if some other active plan of the agent separately creates this intention, it will be immediately suspended (the new plan is placed before any existing plans for that goal). For each landmark in the social practice that has no prior landmarks, a goal is created to activate it (lines 44–46).

Landmark activations are handled by the plan in lines 48–61. A belief recording that the landmark's purpose should be monitored is added, then the action associated with the landmark is processed (only a single action is supported currently). If the action is to be performed by the agent, three options are considered. First (line 54), a query is made to find a solution for achieving the landmark's purpose that involves performing the specified action. A set of rules (not shown) handle this query by searching for the action recursively (up to a prespecified depth bound) through the plans that achieve the purpose, and the subgoals in those plans, and so on[8]. Context conditions are checked for the top level plans (those for the landmark's purpose), but not for the recursive calls, as, in general, it cannot be known how the state of the world will change as these plans are executed. If such a solution is found, it is recorded as a goal-plan tree "path" (see Sect. 5.2) and passed to our Jason metainterpreter via a `solve` goal (line 55). If no such solution is found, and the action is joint, or durative but not joint, the metainterpreter is called to handle this (lines 57 and 59). Otherwise, the action is performed directly (line 60). Note that this plan is declared to be executed atomically (line 48). This prevents steps of the agent's other plans from being interleaved with this one, and thus ensures the landmark is activated promptly. To ensure that other plans can run again once the correct course of action has been identified by this plan, the calls to the metainterpreter are created as a separate intention (using "! !").

---

[7] The unifications in lines 35 and 50 instantiate the variable on the left with the value of the variable on the right, but with any Jason annotations removed.

[8] At present we assume that the plan body will contain only one achievement subgoal.

```
1  // Solve plan body, with optional path through the goal-plan tree
2  // Example goal: !solve({action; ?test(X); !g})
3  +!solve(PlanBody) <- !solve(PlanBody, no_path).
4
5  +!solve({}, _).
6  +!solve({BodyTerm;BodyTerms}, Path) <-
7      !solve_bt(BodyTerm, Path);
8      !solve(BodyTerms, no_path). // Path is applied to first body term only
9
10 // Solve body term
11 +!solve_bt(G, _)
12   : .member(G, [test(_), addBel(_), delBel(_), internalAction(_)]) <- G.
13 +!solve_bt(achieve(solve(PB)), Path) <- !solve(PB, Path).
14 +!solve_bt(achieve(G), Path) <-
15     .relevant_plans({+!G}, RPlans);
16     if (.list(Path) & Path = [N|PathTail]
17                      & .nth(N, RPlans, plan(Label,_,Context,PlanBody))
18                      & Context                                        ) {
19         !solve(PlanBody, PathTail);
20     } else {
21         !applicable_plans(RPlans, [plan(Label,_,_,PlanBody)|_]);
22         !solve(PlanBody, Path);
23     }.
24 // Handle durative action
25 +!solve_bt(BT, _) :
26     BT = action(A) & NoAnnotsA[dummy] = A[dummy] & durative(NoAnnotsA) <-
27     ?durative_action_continuation_pred(NoAnnotsA, Query);
28     if (durative_action_cleanup_goal(NoAnnotsA, CleanupGoal)) {
29         CUGoal = CleanupGoal;
30     } else {
31         CUGoal = true;
32     }
33     if (joint(NoAnnotsA) & NoAnnotsA[participants(P)] = A) {
34         ParticipantsAnnot = [participants(P)];
35     } else {
36         ParticipantsAnnot = [];
37     }
38     AnnotatedA = NoAnnotsA[durative|ParticipantsAnnot];
39     .term2string(AnnotatedA, S);
40     .concat("{", S, "}", BodyTermString);
41     .term2string(AnnotatedBT, BodyTermString);
42     AnnotatedBT;
43     ?time(T); // Must be supplied as a percept from the environment
44     -+started(NoAnnotsA, T)[source(meta)];
45     !solve_durative(Query, AnnotatedBT, NoAnnotsA, ParticipantsAnnot, CUGoal).
46 // Handle non-durative action
47 +!solve_bt(ActionGoal, _) : ActionGoal = action(_) <- ActionGoal.
48
49 +!solve_durative(Query, ActionBT, Action, ParticipantsAnnot, CleanupGoal) <-
50     if (Query) {
51         ActionBT;
52         !solve_durative(Query, ActionBT, Action, ParticipantsAnnot, CleanupGoal);
53     } else {
54         stop(Action)[durative|ParticipantsAnnot];
55         if (CleanupGoal \== true) { !CleanupGoal; }
56     }.
57 -!solve_durative(_, _, Action, _, _) <- -started(Action, _).
58
59 @applicable_plans[atomic]
60 +!applicable_plans([], []).
61 +!applicable_plans([P|T], [P|T2]) : P = plan(_,_,C,_) & C <-
62     !applicable_plans(T, T2).
63 +!applicable_plans([P|T], T2) : P = plan(_,_,C,_) & not C <-
64     !applicable_plans(T, T2).
```

Listing 3. A Jason metainterpreter

Finally, the plan in lines 63–79 handles completed landmarks—those for which the purpose has been achieved. Any suspended intentions for the purpose are succeeded, the belief stating that the landmark should be monitored is retracted, and the temporary plan added in lines 40–42 is removed. The plan then checks for subsequent landmarks that should now be activated (if all their prior landmarks are completed), and finally adds a belief that the social practice has completed if all its landmarks are completed. Another plan (not shown) is needed to handle social practices that become inactive when their relevance conditions cease to hold. In this case, any active landmarks should be abandoned, and original intentions to achieve their purposes can be resumed.

5.2 A Jason Metainterpreter

Listing 3 shows our Jason metainterpreter[9], which extends the AgentSpeak metainterpreter defined by Winikoff [19], and specialises it for use with Jason. The metainterpreter is initiated by calling a solve goal with a Jason plan body $\{g_1, \cdots, g_n\}$ as an argument, where the g_i may be of the various types of goals and actions that Jason supports, such as test goals (queries to the belief base), belief additions and deletions, achievement goals that trigger plans, and actions that may be internal (built-in or user-defined) or external (defined by the environment). An additional Path argument, explained below, may also be supplied. The plans in lines 5–8 sequentially create solve_bt subgoals for each body term ("bt" for short) in the plan body, and these are handled by the plans in lines 11–47. For test goals, belief additions and deletions, and internal and (standard) external actions, lines 11–12 and 47 call these body terms directly to invoke the standard Jason interpreter. Line 13 ensures that the metainterpreter can handle plans containing solve subgoals to explicitly make use of the meta-interpreter's extensions. The remaining plans provide extended BDI semantics, as outlined below.

– As explained in Sect. 5.1, when a landmark in a social practice includes an action associated with the current agent, the plan to activate a landmark attempts to find an existing set of plans that can achieve the landmark's purpose while also including the specified action. This is a recursive search through plans and their subgoals, and it results in a pre-selected path through the goal-plan tree [11] representing the search space for satisfying the landmark's purpose. This differs from the standard Jason goal execution mechanism, in which a set of *relevant* plans (those triggered by a goal matching the current one) is determined, these are filtered by evaluating the plans' context conditions to produce the *applicable* plans, and one is selected to be executed (the first-listed one, by default). This process is then repeated for each subgoal appearing in the body of a plan being executed. This standard process will not guarantee that the landmark's associated action will be performed. Thus, the metainterpreter allows a predetermined goal-plan tree path to be passed as an optional argument to a solve goal (see line 55 in Listing 2), to guide it directly to the pre-chosen subplans, and eventually the desired action. This feature is useful for plan pre-selection in other meta-reasoning contexts as well, e.g. choosing plans based on their effect on the values of a human user [4]. If no path is provided as

---

[9] The metainterpreter requires version 2.4 of Jason.

an argument to `solve`, a default value of `no_path` is used (line 3 of Listing 3). When a path is provided, lines 16 to 19 select the requested plan for the current goal, if its context condition holds, and call its body via `solve`. Otherwise, the list of applicable plans (those whose context conditions are true) are computed (lines 21 and 59–64[10]), the first (in order of appearance in the agent's code) is chosen (second argument in line 21), and its plan body is called via `solve` (line 22). If there are no applicable plans, this plan fails, as does the original `solve` goal.

- Durative actions, as required by our scenario, are supported (lines 25–45 and 49–57)[11]. A continuation predicate, and optionally a clean-up goal, for the action are looked up (lines 27–32), the time the action was started is recorded as a belief (lines 43–44), and a `solve_durative` goal is created (line 45) to trigger the performance of the action. The plan for this goal (lines 49–56) checks the continuation condition (passed as variable `Query`). It is intended that the query is a 0-arity predicate defined by a rule in the agent's program. If the query succeeds, the action is executed with a "durative" annotation (which the environment should check for), and possibly an annotation listing the action participants if it is a joint action (see below). The goal is then called recursively. If the query fails, `stop(Act)` is executed (again, with the appropriate annotations). Thus, durative actions are implemented by repeated execution of an action until the corresponding stop action is called.

- Joint actions are also supported. These are durative actions with an annotation listing the intended action participants. The environment should notify all intended participants (via a percept) when a durative action is called for the first time or is stopped, thus enabling the participants to coordinate their actions. It should also keep a history of the time intervals over which the participants perform the action, as its outcome will depend on the existence and length of a period of overlap. Lines 33–34 and 38–42[12] ensure that an action term annotation recording the participants is passed on when starting the action, and line 54 passes the annotation on when performing the stop action.

6   Evaluation

We ran our Jason care robot program, with and without the social practice beliefs and meta-deliberation plan, using a Jason agent to simulate the patient (as outlined at the end of Sect. 3). With the social practice support for the care robot agent, the robot and patient agent could more successfully coordinate their actions across the landmarks of the social practice, ensuring that the patient remains in a good mood, and engages in the newspaper reading for longer (compared to the outcome outlined in the last paragraph

---

[10] Lines 59–64 would be better implemented as Jason rules (Horn clauses), but passing plan bodies to Jason rules via test goals currently causes the goals to fail, even when the rules succeed.

[11] The second context condition in line 26 binds `NoAnnotsA` to the action term `A` with annotations removed.

[12] Lines 39 to 41 are a workaround for a current limitation of Jason: annotations cannot be added to an existing plan body term.

of Sect. 3). Of course, the scenario was designed to produce better outcomes when the social practice is followed, but demonstrating this in practice validates our metadeliberation plan and metainterpreter.

In this paper, we aim to show the promise of using social practices as part of a meta-deliberation cycle for BDI agents in order to cope with real time environments. The main characteristic of using this approach is that we can separate different concerns. One is to deal with a context of an interaction and its consequences for the plans and actions of the agent; the other is to deal with plans within a certain context. It follows from the above that we do not really extend the language or intrinsic capabilities of the agent (as we have shown, the meta-deliberation cycle can indeed be written using Jason rules and plans). Rather we claim that using this separation of concerns will make it more scalable and robust. These are hard properties to prove or evaluate directly.

What would be needed for an evaluation are complex and dynamic scenarios where the agent is interacting with several people and other agents in different roles, and where events in the environment can also influence the interaction. We can then show that in these complex scenarios the agents based on social practices are still programmed in a modular way, with limited complexity, and behaving robustly. Ideally one would show how Jason BDI agents would have to be programmed without the social practices in the meta-deliberation and compare that with a Jason agent including the social practice in the meta-deliberation. That would give some indication of the utility of our architecture. However, one could still object that the specific agent programs should be programmed by people with the same background, using the same information and measuring the time to develop the agents, etc., in order to make a fair comparison.

As first steps in this evaluation process we will develop more complex scenarios for social robots that will act in a physical context in order to evaluate the robustness and efficiency of our approach.

7   Conclusions

We have argued that for interactive settings, as sketched in our scenario, the use of social practices is a good compromise between using a fixed interaction protocol and deliberation and planning from scratch at each point during the interaction. We proposed a mechanism for a BDI agent to maintain awareness about and contribute towards the completion of social practices, and presented this as a meta-deliberation plan for Jason agents. We also presented a Jason metainterpreter to support this plan and our care robot scenario. These contributions provide a specification of potential extensions to the BDI reasoning cycle, but also allow the approach to be directly applied within Jason agents.

Our approach allows BDI agents to use their existing plans to achieve social practice landmarks that do not detail all actions required to achieve the landmark. In future work we intend to investigate more complex interactions between social practices and agent's local plans. We also intend to develop elaborate scenarios that use all aspects of a social practice, and compare these with agent implementations where no social practice is used, both in terms of the outcomes of the agent and the ease of design of the agents.

Acknowledgement. We thank Jomi Hübner for making extensions to Jason in support of the Jason metainterpreter presented in Listing 3.

References

1. Augello, A., Gentile, M., Dignum, F.: Social practices for social driven conversations in serious games. In: de De Gloria, A., Veltkamp, R. (eds.) GALA 2015. LNCS, vol. 9599, pp. 100–110. Springer, Cham (2016). https://doi.org/10.1007/978-3-319-40216-1_11
2. Bordini, R.H., Hübner, J.F., Wooldridge, M.: Programming Multi-Agent Systems in AgentSpeak Using Jason. Wiley, Chichester (2007)
3. Bourdieu (trans. R. Nice), P.: Outline of a Theory of Practice. Cambridge University Press, Cambridge (1972)
4. Cranefield, S., Winikoff, M., Dignum, V., Dignum, F.: No pizza for you: value-based plan selection in BDI agents. In: Proceedings of the Twenty-Sixth International Joint Conference on Artificial Intelligence, pp. 178–184. ijcai.org (2017)
5. Dignum, F.: Interactions as social practices: towards a formalization. arXiv (2018). https://arxiv.org/abs/1809.08751
6. Dignum, V., Dignum, F.: Contextualized planning using social practices. In: Ghose, A., Oren, N., Telang, P., Thangarajah, J. (eds.) COIN 2014. LNCS (LNAI), vol. 9372, pp. 36–52. Springer, Cham (2015). https://doi.org/10.1007/978-3-319-25420-3_3
7. Folsom-Kovarik, J., Schatz, S., Jones, R.M., Bartlett, K., Wray, R.E.: AI challenge problem: scalable models for patterns of life. AI Mag. **35**(1), 10–14 (2014)
8. Giddens, A.: Central Problems in Social Theory: Action, Structure and Contradiction in Social Analysis. University of California Press, Berkeley (1979)
9. Harel, R., Yumak, Z., Dignum, F.: Towards a generic framework for multi-party dialogue with virtual humans. In: Proceedings of the 31st International Conference on Computer Animation and Social Agents, CASA 2018, pp. 1–6. ACM, New York (2018)
10. Logan, B.: An agent programming manifesto. Int. J. Agent-Oriented Softw. Eng. **6**(2), 187–210 (2018)
11. Logan, B., Thangarajah, J., Yorke-Smith, N.: Progressing intention progression: a call for a goal-plan tree contest. In: Proceedings of the 16th Conference on Autonomous Agents and Multiagent Systems, pp. 768–772. IFAAMAS (2017)
12. Mercuur, R., Dignum, F., Kashima, Y.: Changing habits using contextualized decision making. In: Jager, W., Verbrugge, R., Flache, A., de Roo, G., Hoogduin, L., Hemelrijk, C. (eds.) Advances in Social Simulation 2015. AISC, vol. 528, pp. 267–272. Springer, Cham (2017). https://doi.org/10.1007/978-3-319-47253-9_23
13. Miller, T., Dignum, V., Dignum, F.: Planning for human-agent collaboration using social practices. In: First International Workshop on Socio-cognitive Systems at IJCAI 2018 (2018)
14. Minsky, M.: A framework for representing knowledge. In: Smith, A., Collins, E. (eds.) Readings in Cognitive Science, pp. 156–189. Morgan Kaufmann (1988)
15. Narasimhan, K., Roberts, T., Xenitidou, M., Gilbert, N.: Using ABM to clarify and refine social practice theory. In: Jager, W., Verbrugge, R., Flache, A., de Roo, G., Hoogduin, L., Hemelrijk, C. (eds.) Advances in Social Simulation 2015. AISC, vol. 528, pp. 307–319. Springer, Cham (2017). https://doi.org/10.1007/978-3-319-47253-9_27
16. Reckwitz, A.: Toward a theory of social practices. Eur. J. Soc. Theory **5**(2), 243–263 (2002)
17. Schatzki, T.R.: A primer on practices. In: Practice-Based Education, Practice, Education, Work and Society, vol. 6, pp. 13–26. SensePublishers, Rotterdam (2012)
18. Shove, E., Pantzar, M., Watson, M.: The Dynamics of Social Practice. Sage, Thousand Oaks (2012)
19. Winikoff, M.: An AgentSpeak meta-interpreter and its applications. In: Bordini, R.H., Dastani, M.M., Dix, J., El Fallah Seghrouchni, A. (eds.) ProMAS 2005. LNCS (LNAI), vol. 3862, pp. 123–138. Springer, Heidelberg (2006). https://doi.org/10.1007/11678823_8

Who's That? - Social Situation Awareness for Behaviour Support Agents
A Feasibility Study

Ilir Kola[1]([✉])(iD), Catholijn M. Jonker[1,2](iD), and M. Birna van Riemsdijk[3](iD)

[1] Interactive Intelligence Group, Delft University of Technology,
Delft, The Netherlands
{i.kola,c.m.jonker}@tudelft.nl
[2] Leiden Institute of Advanced Computer Science, Leiden, The Netherlands
[3] Human Media Interaction Lab, University of Twente, Enschede, The Netherlands
m.b.vanriemsdijk@utwente.nl

Abstract. Behaviour support agents need to be aware of the social environment of the user in order to be able to provide comprehensive support. However, this is a feature that is currently lacking in existing systems. To tackle it, first of all we explore literature from social sciences in order to find which elements of the social environment need to be represented. We structure this knowledge as a two-level ontology that models social situations. We formalize the elements that are needed to model social situations, which consist of different types of meetings between two people. We conduct an experiment to evaluate the lower level of the ontology using feedback from the subjects, and to test whether we can use the data to reason about the priority of different situations. Subjects found our proposed features of social relationships to be understandable and representative. Furthermore, we show these features can be combined in a decision tree to predict the priority of social situations.

Keywords: Socially aware agents · Social situation modelling · Knowledge representation

1 Introduction

Artificial agents that support people in their daily lives, for example to live healthier lifestyles or help them in the execution of daily tasks, are becoming a reality (e.g. [32,43]). Such behaviour support agents need to be aware of a user's *social context* to function effectively [46]: a user's social network may need to play a role in providing support, and a user's activities may involve other people which affects the type of support that is needed [41]. For instance, an app that helps its user be more punctual might send reminders at different intervals when it sees that a meeting is approaching. However, not all meetings have the same

This work is part of the research programme *CoreSAEP* (project no. 639.022.416), supported by the Netherlands Organisation for Scientific Research (NWO).

L. A. Dennis et al. (Eds.): EMAS 2019, LNAI 12058, pp. 127–151, 2020.
https://doi.org/10.1007/978-3-030-51417-4_7

128   I. Kola et al.

priority: for most people, being on time for a job interview is more important than being on time for an informal dinner with friends. Effective support may require taking this into account in the frequency or type of reminders that are generated.

Existing behaviour support agents however mostly focus on modelling internal aspects of the users (e.g. their goals, values, abilities, etc.) [36,44], while paying less attention to users' social context. In this paper we take first steps towards developing a *generic framework* that enables behaviour support agents to take into account the user's social environment in order to provide personalized and socially-aware behaviour support [46].

The main idea underlying our approach is to take research on situation awareness, which offers ways to model and reason about the physical environment, and adapt it for realizing *social situation awareness*. Specifically, we take the well-known situation awareness model by Endsley [17] as a starting point. Endsley's model distinguishes three levels of situation awareness: 1) *perception* of relevant elements in the environment, 2) *comprehension* to understand their significance, and 3) *projection* towards future states of the environment. Inspired by these levels, we put forward the idea that a behaviour support agent should similarly be able to represent relevant aspects of social situations, be able to reason about their meaning, and lastly project how these situations will affect the behaviour of the user. These three levels are in line with the classic sense-reason-act cycle in multi-agent systems.

While there are many socially relevant dimensions to behaviour support, in this paper we focus on handling *social settings* such as meetings or social gatherings. Moreover, we focus on behaviour relevant for arranging these social settings, rather than how to behave whilst participating in one. One may think of a personal assistant agent that can schedule social events for its user [41], or an agent to support people with cognitive impairments in arranging their social life. Furthermore, we need to determine which dimensions of a social situation may be used to interpret their meaning, i.e., what is the "output" of the comprehension process. In this case we focus on *priority* of social situations. We expect that priority, among other things, may be used for dealing with conflicts in a user's schedule. Putting this together, in this paper we address the following research questions and hypothesis, corresponding with the three levels of situation awareness:

- **RQ1: Perception** - Which features can be used to describe a social situation from the perspective of a user for the purpose of behaviour support?
- **RQ2: Comprehension** - How can features of a social situation be used to assess its priority?
- **H3: Projection** - Priority of social situations can be used for resolving conflicts between two social settings if they cannot both be attended.

While these research questions and hypothesis guide the work presented in this paper, we do not aim to provide definitive answers here. Rather, as this is a novel research direction, our aim is to assess the feasibility of the approach as a basis for future work that considers other dimensions besides priority, as well as a more extensive investigation into their translation to support actions by the agent.

Addressing these questions involves creating knowledge structures and reasoning techniques for representation and interpretation of social situations, as well as evaluation with users. We further detail this approach and the envisaged software architecture for our support agent in Sect. 2. We present a knowledge structure for describing features of social situations in Sect. 3. We present our user study to evaluate this knowledge structure and gather data for addressing RQ2 and H3 in Sect. 4. Our reasoning model for addressing RQ2 is presented in Sect. 5. We conclude the paper and discuss our findings in Sect. 6.

2   Research Approach and Agent Architecture

The overall objective of this work is to assess the feasibility of realizing social situation awareness for behaviour support agents based on the three levels of situation awareness of Endsley [17]. For this reason, we touch on each of these three levels in this work (albeit less comprehensively for the higher levels), i.e., we take a "breadth-first" approach, rather than first going into depth on the first level. In this way we get a sense of how the different levels of the framework could work together to achieve social situation awareness early on in the research, and it allows us to identify aspects that require a more in-depth study in follow-up research. Specifically, we address the research questions and hypothesis in the following way:

- RQ1: Which features can be used to describe a social situation from the perspective of a user for the purpose of behaviour support?
  - Model building: based on research in social sciences, we propose an ontology for modelling the high-level structure of social situations, as well as a set of low level features that can be used to describe daily life social situations (Sect. 3).
  - Evaluation: Assessing whether the social features identified in the modelling step are suitable, consists of two parts: i) assessing the understandability and expressivity of these features for users; this is important, since we envisage that we will (partly) elicit these features from users through interaction with the support agent, and explaining the support agent's actions to the user requires that these features are meaningful to users (Sect. 4); ii) assessing the usefulness of these features for situation comprehension; this is assessed via RQ2 (Sect. 5).
- RQ2: How can features of a social situation be used to assess its priority?
  - Model building: One may envisage different ways of building a model that can take features of a social situation and derive a corresponding priority, for example by pre-specified rules, through machine learning, or a combination. Since an important requirement for this model is its explainability for users, in this paper we choose a learning method that

yields an interpretable model: decision trees. To create this decision tree, we collect data from people via a user study (Sect. 4), and then use the data to learn a decision tree that predicts priority of social situations (Sect. 5).

- Evaluation: We evaluate the predictive capacity of the decision tree by taking a test data set from the data collected for building the model, and evaluating its capacity in predicting the right priority for a specific event based on information about social features of the situation.

- H3: Priority of social situations can be used for resolving conflicts between two social settings if they cannot both be attended.
  - Data collection: First, we ask subjects about their relationship with people in their social circle. Then, we present them with social situations involving these people, and ask them what priority they would assign to these situations. Lastly, we show them pairs of these situations and ask them which one they would attend if the meeting times would overlap and they had to choose only one (Sect. 4).
  - Hypothesis testing: To test this hypothesis, we check whether the proportion of meetings with higher priority that was chosen when breaking the ties is higher than chance.

Figure 1[1] depicts a high level architecture of how our proposed behaviour support agent can be used in practice. The first part of the work consists in learning a model which given data from different social situations (in our case, the experiment data), it learns priority rules based on the answers of the participants. When the user is faced with a future social situation, it gives the behaviour support agent a description of the situation (*situation cues*) and relationship with the other person (*social background features*). The agent uses this information, as well as the learned priority rules, to reason about the priority of this situation. In future work, the priority level will be fed to a support reasoner, which will then output a support action to be of assistance to the user. In this work, we hypothesize that priority can be used to break ties when different meetings overlap. In that case, the support reasoner can compare the priority of the different meetings, and suggest to the user which one to attend.

3   Modelling Social Situations

In this section we outline which features can be used to describe a social situation from the perspective of a user of the behaviour support agent. We distinguish between a description of the main components, i.e., the overall structure of a social situation (Sect. 3.1) which we refer to as the upper ontology following [24], while the concrete features of the social situation that are the result of the perception process are described in a lower ontology (Sect. 3.2).

---

[1] Icons used in the architecture were made by Freepik and retrieved from www.flaticon. com.

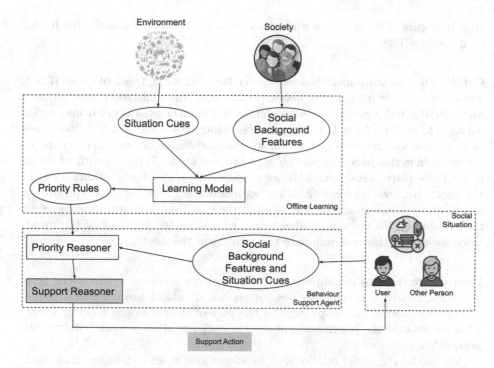

Fig. 1. High level architecture of the proposed approach. Boxes marked in blue are parts which we do not explicitly tackle in this paper. (Color figure online)

3.1 Structure of Social Situations: Upper Ontology

Research in social psychology by Rauthmann and colleagues [37] proposes that features of situations can be discussed on three different levels: *cues*, which are physical and objective elements (who is present, what activity is taking place, etc.), *psychological characteristics*, which are dimensions that can be used to describe situations (such as duty, intellect, etc.), as well as *classes*, which are abstract types of situations (such as social situations, work situations, etc.). For the scope of this work, we will focus on situation cues and classes, since these are concrete concepts that can be elicited from the user, i.e., that are the result of the perception process. Psychological characteristics, and how to automatically infer them, will be explored in future work.

Cues in turn can be divided into three categories according to [37]: persons, events/activities, and locations. Saucier et al. [39] identify similar categories in an experiment in which students describe their daily situations, namely locations, associations (i.e. people/interactions), as well as actions and positions. Thus we can see that in the literature information about people in the situation is considered to be a specific kind of situation cue. Since in this paper we focus on modelling *social* situations, meaning that the relation to the people in the situation is of specific interest, we decide to model people separately from other situation cues. This is in line with other work in the field of socially intelligent technologies [1,2].

Cues. The literature identifies essentially two remaining types of cues [37,39], when we separate information about people from other situation cues: *location* and *activity*. In this paper we also model the situation class as a type of cue, which we refer to as the *setting*. Furthermore, we introduce a number of additional cues that we consider specifically relevant for comprehension of organized events, as we focus on in this paper. In particular, we represent the *frequency* with which an event takes place. This variable is not explicitly mentioned as a situation cue in the literature, however some situation taxonomies, e.g., [33], suggest typicality as one of the psychological characteristics of the situation. Moreover, we represent the *time* at which the event takes place, as well as the *initiator* of the event, since we expect this may influence the priority of the meeting.

People. For reasons of simplicity, in this work we focus on dyadic social relationships, i.e., we concern ourselves with social situations involving two people. In our case, one of the people will be the user of the behaviour support agent. This means that the information about the social relation is modelled *from the perspective of the user*.

We model the social relationship by identifying a set of features that characterize this relationship. We distinguish between *social background features* and *situation-specific social features*. The former concern features that describe aspects of the relationship in general, while the latter describe aspects that are specific to the situation at hand. We distinguish two kinds of social background features, namely *structural features* and *personal features*. The former concern what may be referred to as "objective" characteristics such as the user's role in relation to the other person, while the latter concern "subjective" relationship characteristics from the perspective of the user, such as the quality of the relationship. This distinction is in line with research in social science on relationships in organizations [30] and social support [25], which considers the difference between relationship characteristics that are derived from formal requirements of a role, and interpersonal characteristics. These features are further detailed in Sect. 3.2.

Putting this all together, Fig. 2 offers a schematic representation of the upper ontology.

Related Work. Context and situations are well studied concepts in computer science. Kokar and colleagues [27] present an ontology for formalization of situations based on the situation theory developed by Barwise [5] and extended by Devlin [10]. This formalization is compatible with the interpretation of situation awareness provided by Endsley [18], which also forms the basis of our work. Yau and Liu [48] offer another ontological approach that models situations for pervasive computing applications. They differentiate between situations, defined as

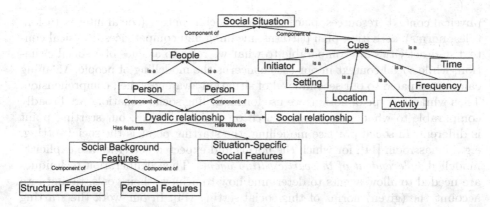

Fig. 2. Schematic representation of an upper ontology of dyadic social situations.

"a set of contexts in the application over a period of time that affects future system behavior" and contexts, defined as "any instantaneous, detectable, and relevant property of the environment, system, or users". Their ontology is based on this division, and they specify a context layer, which models context definition and contextual data, and a situation layer which is built on top of the context layer and aggregates context into situations. This forms the core of their upper ontology, whereas the elements of the lower ontology can be specified depending on the domain. Their definition of context can be compared to our notion of situation cues. However, these approaches are very abstract in the concepts used in the ontology since they focus on modelling a generic type of situations. Building the lower level ontologies, specifically concerning the modelling of social situations as we focus on in this paper, is not a trivial task.

Zavala and colleagues [50] offer a framework which can be used to build *place-aware mobile applications*. To do so, they build a place ontology which models the concept of place not only as a geographical location, but also in terms of activities that occur there. For instance, someone can have an office in two different cities, but both of them would count as a *workplace* since similar activities occur there. This is comparable to the cues "location" and "setting" in our ontology. In Murukannaiah et al. [31] this approach is extended and social circles are learned based on the places in which people are meeting: following the previous example, people meeting in workplaces would be classified as colleagues. This can be viewed as a kind of structural relationship feature, as we refer to it in our ontology. Similar to our work, their approach goes beyond modelling very abstract concepts for representing generic situations. However, the concept of places and associated types of relationship is just one aspect relevant to comprehending social situations. Our approach aims at providing a more comprehensive knowledge structure for modelling social situations, as well as development of methods for interpreting these.

Another related line of research is work on modelling and reasoning about *social practices* [11,14]. In [14], social practices are represented by distinguishing physical context (resources, places, actors), social context (social interpretation, roles, norms), activities, plan patterns, meaning and competences. Physical context and activities are comparable to what we refer to as cues of a social situation, while social context in our case concerns the modelling of people. Meaning can be compared to our second level of situation awareness, i.e., comprehension. Thus while the type of notions we use for modelling social situations are broadly comparable to what is used in research on social practices, our starting point is different. In social practice modelling, the starting point is the social setting, e.g., a classroom [11], for which the norms and expected activities are explicitly modelled *independent of the participating agents*. Then deliberation techniques are needed to allow agents to determine how to achieve their goals, taking into account the (given) norms of this social setting [14]. In our work the starting point is the social relation between the (human) *agents*. For this reason we go in detail regarding the modelling of social background features (Sect. 3.2) that characterize from the (subjective) user's point of view their relation with the other person in the social situation. Based on these features, we then interpret in a bottom-up way the social situation in terms of more abstract general characteristics, in this case priority of a social event. From that we then determine appropriate support actions for the user. Moreover, since our aim is to create behaviour support agents for *people*, we develop our models taking into account results from user studies.

In our previous work [28] we provide an extension of the ontology of [27] with relations that support modelling social relationships, and explore how these can be used for decision making in social situations. However, in that paper we model social relations based on only four abstract relationship types from [19] that can be used to model social decision making: communal sharing, authority ranking, equality matching, and market pricing. These can be viewed as a type of structural relationship feature. However, these do not capture personal features that describe more subjective aspects of interpersonal relationships. Moreover, in that paper we do not investigate comprehension of a social situation based on these features, but rather model decision making directly using pre-specified rules.

3.2   Features of Social Situations: Lower Ontology

In this section we go more in detail regarding the modelling of situation cues, and we introduce features of dyadic social relationships that a behaviour support agent can use to model daily life social situations of a user. The list of features presented in this section is not exhaustive, and depending on the type of behaviour support different features may be relevant. However it highlights the type of features that may be considered, and serves as an example of the concrete features that can be used. Moreover, we use these features to model the scenarios in our experiment.

We represent features of social situations by means of relations over situation instances ($\mathcal{SI}$) and dyadic social relationships ($\mathcal{A} \times \mathcal{A}$ where $\mathcal{A}$ is the set of people) for cues and social features respectively, and a domain ($\mathcal{D}$) that specifies the value-ranges the feature can take. This is in line with situation theory ontology [27] in which the modelling of perceived aspects of a situation is done by means of so-called *infons* which describe the relations between objects in a situation. The appropriateness of the chosen value-ranges is also subject to evaluation, and may be changed depending on the domain.

Cues. For simplicity in this paper we focus on three out of six cues that have been introduced in Sect. 3.1: the initiator of an event, the setting of a social situation, and frequency of the event. A good starting point for modelling locations and activities can be the work of Zavala et al. [50].

The initiator is a person from the set $\mathcal{A}$, or **none** if no initiator is identified. For the selection of types of setting of a situation we choose common situation classes that users may face in their daily life. In this paper, we base the types of settings on Pervin [35], who identifies work situations, family situations, friends/recreation situations, and private recreation situations. We omit the latter since we are concerned with social situations, and add sports activity as a specific type of setting. The situation classes proposed in Rauthmann et al. [37] can also be clustered into these settings. We distinguish two frequencies, **regular** and **occasional**. While more fine-grained distinctions can be made, we expect that this broad categorization suffices in many cases. We list the corresponding relations in Table 1 below.

Table 1. Relations to model cues of social situations. For a relation $\langle name \rangle$, set of situation instances $\mathcal{SI}$ and domain $\mathcal{D}$, the relation is defined as $\langle name \rangle : \mathcal{SI} \times \mathcal{D}_{\langle name \rangle}$.

Relation name	Domain ($\mathcal{D}$)
event_initiator	$\mathcal{A} \cup \{\text{none}\}$
setting	$\{\text{work\_related, casual\_meeting, sports\_activity, family\_related}\}$
event_frequency	$\{\text{regular, occasional}\}$

Social Background Features. While there is a lot work in the social sciences on understanding social relationships, in this paper we mainly use the following two lines of work as the basis for selecting structural and personal social features for our model. First, Kahn and Antonucci [3,4,25] explore the role of social relations as a form of social support for (elderly) people. Enabling social support is an important purpose of the behaviour support agents we aim to create [46]. We select our structural features mainly from this line of work. Second, social relations are also considered from the organizational point of view. Specifically, we use the work of Mainela [30] which gives an overview of types and functions of social relationships that can be relevant in the organization of a joint venture. Organizational relationships are an important type of relation that our behaviour support agent may take into consideration. We select our personal features mainly from this work.

Structural Features. Kahn and Antonucci conceptualize support systems as a so-called Convoy model - three concentric circles representing three levels of closeness between the supported person and their "convoy" of supporters. Different aspects of the relationship are considered in order to establish someone's position within the convoy model. The Convoy model [4] distinguishes between structural (age, sex, years known, proximity, contact frequency, relationship (role)) and functional characteristics (types of support received and provided) of social support networks.

For this paper we use *role*, *contact frequency*, and *default geographical distance* (proximity) as structural features. The feature *role* refers to the role of the other person towards the user in dyadic relations. Knowing this is important since it can help inferring the expectations that come with the role. The range of roles we use is taken from the general social survey [8]. The geographical distance refers to the physical proximity of the two actors in terms of their default home location. Proximity can influence the relationship of two people since it affects how often they can see each other. For the range we opted to measure distance in terms of time that it usually takes to get to that person.

Besides the above three structural features, we introduce a fourth one, namely *hierarchy*, to express the type of relation between the user and the other person. Hierarchy affects the power dynamics between the first and second actor. Higher (respectively same and lower) means that the other person is higher up (resp. at the same level, and lower) in the hierarchy than the user. In case there is no hierarchy amongst the actors, this is indicated by "n.a.". We expect this feature to be relevant when assessing the priority of meetings, especially for users who are in working relations, or actors that come from a culture with some sort of caste system. More information on the concept of hierarchical ranking can be found in, e.g., [19,47].

Personal Features. The first of our personal features is also taken from the Convoy model [3]. In addition to structural and functional aspects of relationships, this paper emphasizes the importance of *relationship quality* in characterizing social relations. The remaining three personal features we consider in this paper are taken from Mainela [30]. The paper gives an overview of how types of social relationships in business dyads have been characterized in the literature. For example, Granovetter [22,23] talks about strong ties and weak ties in work relationships. The strength of a tie in a network depends on aspects such as the amount of time spent on it, the emotional intensity, the intimacy, and the reciprocity. Furthermore, the author argues that ties are stronger when the level of acquaintance is deeper.

From the list of features for characterizing social relations identified through the literature study of Mainela, we select three, namely *acquaintance depth* [22] of the user towards the other person, *level of formality* of the relationship [38], and *trust* [45] of the user towards the other person as personal features. These features can inform the expectations of the relationship between user and the other person, and consequently are relevant for comprehending social situations.

Other features mentioned by Mainela can be used to distinguish different types of social relationships in a business context, but seem too specific for social situation awareness of our envisaged behaviour support agent, e.g., legal questions, attendant consequences, activation of a relation, outcome expectations, and scope of economic issues. The features continuity of interaction and amount of time spent are closely related to event frequency, contact frequency and acquaintance depth. Features like personal nature, intimacy and emotional intensity seem closely related to level of formality and acquaintance depth. Finally, reciprocity may also be relevant for our purposes, however refers more to functional aspects of the relationship and may be difficult to characterize directly in these terms by users. Therefore we leave it out in this paper.

We summarize these social background features in Table 2 below. The range of some features is Likert_5, which denotes a 5-point Likert-type scale, where 1 is the lowest/most negative value and 5 the highest/most positive value.

Table 2. Relations to model social background features of social situations. The upper part concerns structural features, the bottom part personal features. For a relation $\langle name \rangle$, and domain $\mathcal{D}$, the relation is defined as $\langle name \rangle : \mathcal{A} \times \mathcal{A} \times \mathcal{D}_{\langle name \rangle}$ where $\mathcal{A}$ denotes the set of persons.

Relation name	Domain ($\mathcal{D}$)
role	{partner, parent, sibling, child, extended_family, coworker, neighbor, friend, supervisor, group_member, other}
contact_frequency	Likert_5
def_geo_distance	{0-1 h, 1-2 h, 2-4 h, flight needed}
hierarchy	{higher, same, lower, n.a.}
rel_quality	Likert_5
acq_depth	Likert_5
rel_formality	Likert_5
trust	Likert_5

Situation-Specific Social Features. Several of the social background features may have a situation-specific variant, for example if you go to a basketball game with your boss, in that situation you are both team-mates, and if you are the captain you are the one holding a higher hierarchy level in that situation. However for reasons of simplicity we do not further elaborate on these in this paper.

We do introduce another situation-specific social feature, which we call the *help dynamic*. It refers to whether in the specific event the user is giving to or receiving help from the other person. The fact that they have to give or receive help can influence how obligated the actors feel to attend a certain event. It is defined as a relation $help\_dynam : SI \times A \times A \times D_{help\_dynam}$, where $D_{help\_dynam} = \{\texttt{giving, receiving, neither}\}$.

Related Work. Different aspects of modelling social relationships have been studied in sub-fields of multi-agent systems. In particular, when talking about organizations of agents, "role" is one of the central concepts. In the OperA model [13], agents form societies with different organizational structures, and they take up roles in these societies. These roles, in combination with social contracts, define what an agent should and should not do. Singh [40] follows a similar approach, and proposes that "Org(anization)s are finely structured through the notion of a role, which codifies a set of related interactions that a member of an Org may enact". D'Inverno and colleagues [16], in their quest to weave a fabric for socially aware agents, also introduce the concept of roles in order to represent agents in the context of a social setting. Roles in these works are used to describe, design and understand interactions in an abstract and re-usable sense, independent from the agents that will eventually play the roles. In our case we combine abstract information about roles with information about the concrete relation between the user and the other person, i.e., between the specific (human) agents in the interaction, in order to assess how best to support the user this social situation.

The notion of hierarchy is used in [13] to describe a type of relation between roles in an organization. Although not the same thing, hierarchy can be connected to the notion of power. Pereira and colleagues [34] argue for the importance of modelling social power into the decision making of cognitive agents. The importance of modelling social power is also proposed in [12].

Another well studied concept within the multi-agent systems field is trust. Mostly, it is considered from the point of view of software agents trusting each other. The focus is on determining the level of trust in another agent by taking into consideration the agent's previous interactions with another agent, or by relying on other agents' opinions about that agent [20,49]. In our case, once we have information about the trust the user has towards the other person, we use it for interpreting the social situation and allowing our support agent to determine the appropriate support actions in this situation.

The virtual agents research area has also studied modelling and use of various features that describe social relationships. Zhao and colleagues [51] argue for the importance of representing rapport in a virtual agent that interacts with a human. Rapport is a feeling of connection and closeness to another person, which can be compared with depth of acquaintance. Dudzik and colleagues [15] provide a review of literature that deals with contextual features of human emotion perception for automatic affect recognition. As contextual factors they identify characteristics of the sender or receiver of the emotion, such as age, gender and occupation, as well as situation features such as cause of the emotion, conversation content and language, information about the conversation partner in the social interaction, location, and lighting conditions during the interaction. Our work is complementary in that it focuses on characterizing the social relationship itself between people in the social situation, and from that derive higher-level understanding of the social situation, in this case in terms of its priority.

Thus our framework for modelling social situations includes a number of features that have been studied in various parts of the agent systems literature. Based on social science literature we add several features that are specifically relevant for characterizing human social relations, such as contact frequency, geographical distance, and relationship formality. Moreover, our work differs from existing work in multi-agent systems in that we investigate how we can *combine* features of social situations for the purpose of comprehension in order to allow an agent to provide appropriate socially-aware support.

4   User Study

In order to evaluate how well we can use our proposed low level features to model and interpret daily social situations, we conducted a pilot experiment in which subjects had to answer a survey about the social relations in their life [29]. The survey consisted of three parts, through which we explore RQ1 and evaluate H3. Furthermore, we use the data from survey to create and evaluate a model that addresses RQ2. We present our experimental setting in Sect. 4.1 and our results in Sect. 4.2.

4.1   Experimental Setting

Pilot Subjects. We tested 20 subjects (15 male, 5 female) who answered to all three parts of the experiment. Subjects were university employees (mostly PhD candidates). The average age was 31.1 years old (SD = 7.6yo).

Design and Procedure.[2] The experiment was implemented as an online survey, and consisted of three parts. In *Part I – Perception*, subjects were asked to think about six people from their social circle. For the purpose of the study, they were instructed to select at least one family member, one friend, and one person who had a higher hierarchy level than them. In follow-up research, we will also ask for information on relationships with people lower in the hierarchy. For each of these people, subjects were asked to provide all social background features (Sect. 3.2). The first part was concluded with an evaluation section in which the subjects were asked whether the questions were understandable, whether the amount of questions was appropriate, and how well they thought the questions represent their social relationship with someone. Through these questions, we test how understandable and expressive our proposed features are (RQ1). Furthermore, they had the option to propose more aspects of social relationships which they thought are relevant.

---

[2] The questions for each part of the experiment can be found in the Appendix.

In *Part II – Comprehension*, subjects were shown 20 scenarios of daily life social situations. Each scenario involved one of the six people that subjects had mentioned in Part I, selected randomly[3]. We made the study subject-specific to enable them to reflect on their own relationships, instead of presenting them with hypothetical relationships. Scenarios consisted of different parameters of the situation cues and situation specific features of social relationships. A scenario could represent a social situation such as:

"You have invited *Person X* for a work meeting on Tuesday morning because you need some feedback on your recent project".

In this case it is a work setting, the event is occasional, the subject is the initiator and he/she is expected to receive help. For each scenario, subjects were asked about the priority of the meeting, how obligated they would feel to attend the meeting and how much they would enjoy it. We need the information on priority to answer RQ2. Obligation and enjoyment were asked for exploratory purposes to inform future research. Furthermore, subjects were asked how they think the other person would answer these questions. This was done because in future work, we want to explore the reciprocity of these decisions. Lastly, they were asked about the likelihood of that scenario happening in their daily life in order to assess the appropriateness of the scenarios we have chosen. Subjects had to answer on a 5-point Likert scale. In order to assess priority, they were instructed to take into account how difficult it would be for them to cancel the meeting, how important they think it is to be punctual, and any other thing they would consider relevant.

In *Part III – Projection*, scenarios were paired randomly and subjects were asked which of the two meetings would they choose to attend in case of a conflict between the two scenarios meaning that they could not attend both meetings. We will use this information to evaluate H3. Furthermore, they were asked what reason would they give to the person whose meeting they were canceling: the real reason, some other reason, or no reason. This was asked in order to have some more insight in case our hypothesis is not corroborated from the data. Each subject was presented with six pairs of scenarios.

4.2   Results

In this subsection, we will present and discuss the results of each part of the experiment separately.

Part I – Perception. The selected people from the subjects' social circle had an average age of 37.6 years old (SD = 13.55 yo). They were mostly friends (29%), followed by people from work (18% supervisors and 10% coworkers) and family

---

[3] Apart from the scenarios in which a family setting or a higher hierarchy work setting were being tested, which were restricted to family members and people with higher hierarchy, respectively.

members (11% parents, 8% siblings and 7% members of the extended family). Partners consisted of 10% of the selected people. Overall 74% of the people were not in a hierarchical relation with the subjects, 22% were on a higher level and 4% on a lower level. 36% lived within an hour of distance from the subjects, 18% between 1–2 h, 4% between 2–4 h, and for the remaining 32%, the subjects would need to take a flight in order to meet them. The subjects' answers for social background features that have a Likert-scale as the domain are shown in Table 3 below.

Table 3. Percentage of subjects that gave each specific answer for different social background features. The answer options were Likert-type scale values ranging from 1 to 5. For relationship quality 1 = very negative and 5 = very positive. For the rest, 1 = very low and 5 = very high.

Feature\Answer	1	2	3	4	5
Contact frequency	0	23.82	25.59	25.59	25
Relationship quality	2.06	5	10.88	49.41	32.65
Acquaintance depth	0	15.59	34.12	25.59	24.71
Relationship formality	46.76	16.18	26.18	7.06	3.82
Trust	1.76	1.47	25	37.25	34.41

As seen in Table 3, subjects mostly choose people with whom they have strongly positive relationships. Furthermore, they chose people whom they trust, and the relationships have a low level of formality. In future work, in order to have more representative data from a larger variety of relationships, we will control some features when asking the subjects to think of people from their social circle. For instance, we will ask some subjects to think about a coworker with whom they do not have a positive relationship.

The evaluation questions (all posed with a 5-point Likert scale in possible answers) showed that the subjects found the questionnaire understandable, with an average of 4.59 (SD = 0.51). The number of asked questions was appropriate (the average answer was 3, SD = 0.61, on a 5-point scale where 3 = `appropriate`). When asked how much this information represents their relationship with someone (Likert range from 1 = `very little` to 5 = `very much`), the average answer was 3 (SD = 0.79), confirming that social relationships have subtle aspects not captured in our questionnaire. Whether we need to add more features, depends on the strength of the correlations between the current features and the choices the subjects make in Part II of the questionnaire. The subjects (mostly being PhD students), seemed to understand this point, as some subjects indicated that the answer to this question depends on the purpose of the study. This is something that we will take into account in future experiments.

When asked whether they could think of additional aspects of social relationships which should be present in the survey, 35% of subjects answered with

"Yes". Some of the suggestions included: dependability, understanding, fun, respect, how important is the other person, common interests, etc. However, none of the suggestions appeared consistently.

Part II – Comprehension. In this section subjects were asked to evaluate different scenarios with respect to their priority (and additionally obligation and enjoyment). Subjects mostly give a high priority to the meetings, with 37% of scenarios being assigned a 5, 41% a 4 and 16% a 3, with only 6% having a 1 or a 2. This was expected given that scenarios included people with whom the subjects have a close and positive relationship. This is also reflected in how much they enjoy these meetings (65% of scenarios being assigned a 4 or a 5). For obligation, the results were more balanced, with 14% of scenarios being assigned a 2, 21% a 3, 37% a 4 and 25% a 5. The average likelihood of the scenarios was 3.14 (SD = 1.42), which means the scenarios were relatively likely despite being chosen randomly in terms of the combination of person with whom the subject relates, and scenario. We notice a high standard deviation, caused by the fact that some of the scenarios had a low likelihood, possibly because of the random person-meeting combination.

Part III – Projection. In this part, subjects were given pairs of scenarios (from Part II), and they had to select which one they would attend if they could attend only one. We notice that in 69% of the cases, subjects would select the meeting to which they had assigned a higher priority in Part II. This suggests that priority is a good indicator of how people break ties. However, it is not the only thing. We noticed that in most of the cases in which subjects select meetings to which they had assigned a lower priority, those meetings have also a low likelihood. This suggests that when breaking ties between different meetings, subjects also take into account how difficult it would be to reschedule each of the meetings. Also, in this section we see differences between individuals, since there were subjects who consistently chose a certain type of meetings. This can link to the subjects' *personal values* (see also [26,44]). For instance, some subjects consistently picked work meetings or family meetings, which indicates a tie to their value system. This will be explored in future work.

Subjects were also asked about the justification that they would give to the person whose meeting they would cancel. In 89% of the cases, subjects reported that they would give the real reason. Most of the cases in which the subjects would give no reason or a different reason (and not the real one) took place when they chose to attend meetings with a lower priority. Furthermore, many cases involve either not reporting to someone with a higher rank, or not giving details about their meetings with family members.

5 Predicting Priority of Social Situations

In order to address RQ2, we will investigate how to use data from Part II of the user study in order to predict the priority level of social situations based on information about social features. First we will discuss possible options on how to achieve this (Sect. 5.1), and then we will introduce and evaluate our proposed approach (Sect. 5.2).

5.1   Reasoning About Situations

Different strategies can be used to reason about the priority of an event. The most straightforward approach would be to combine the situation cues in an Expected Priority (EP) function, such as:

$$EP = \sum_{f \in \mathcal{F}} w_f v_f$$

where $\mathcal{F}$ is the set of all features considered, and where for all $f \in \mathcal{F}$, v_f refers to the feature value and w_f to the relative weight of feature f in this computation. However, there are two main issues with this approach. First of all, most of the features that we are dealing with have nominal values, so quantifying them is difficult. Furthermore, based on the literature on preference profiles, see e.g., [6], in many decision situations, we hypothesize the weights to be dependent on the individual, making the correct initialization of the weights a challenge.

Another option is to learn a model from our data, and use it to classify new instances. Our proposed approach to do this is to use decision trees [7], because literature suggests that the structure of decision trees is appropriate for reasoning about social relations. First of all, cognitive psychology proposes that social intelligence can have a modular nature [21]. This means different "scripts" are activated in different settings. People recognize these settings from environmental cues, and in turn decide to behave in a certain way. This is similar to the concept of decision trees, in which different combinations of features lead to different decisions. Endsley also suggests that people use different "schemata" to organize and combine knowledge and perceptions in order to comprehend the situation [17]. Moreover, the decision process of decision trees is predictable and transparent. This would allow the agent to *explain* to the user why a certain priority level is assigned to a specific event, which is important since we focus on behaviour support.

Decision trees are graphical representations of a set of rules which can be used to make classifications. Each node of the tree represents a question regarding certain features of the object that is being classified, in this case a social situation, and each branch represents a different answer to that question, in this case the priority level. Nodes below a given node either contain another question, or are given a *label* which assigns a class to the object. The latter are called *leaf-nodes*. Given an object with a set of features and a decision tree, in order to classify the object we traverse the tree until we reach a leaf.

5.2   Model

So far, we have represented the features of the social situations. However, this raw information is not sufficient to draw conclusions about how people evaluate situations. As explained in Sect. 1, in situation awareness literature, this process is called *comprehension* [18]. In this work we explore one general and abstract characteristic of a given situation, namely its *priority*.

As mentioned in the previous section, we will use decision trees to predict priority of social situations. One of the most used methods because of its high accuracy is the Classification and Regression Trees algorithm (*CART*) [7]. CART models are binary trees, which means for every parent node there are two child nodes. Learning a CART model involves selecting features and split points on those features until a suitable tree is constructed. This selection is performed by using a greedy algorithm which minimizes a cost function. We build the model using the R package `rpart` [42]. We use 70% of the data as a training set from which the tree structure was learned, and then test it on the remaining 30%. As a pruning mechanism we limit the maximal depth of the tree to 4.[4]

The learned model is shown in Fig. 3. We remark that, to us, many of the tree splits are intuitive. For instance, the first information that is checked is the setting of the meeting, with casual and sport events on one hand (the left branch) and family and work events on the other (the right branch). This split was to be expected since subjects assigned higher priorities to family and work events.

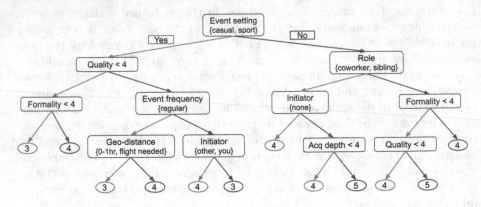

Fig. 3. Decision tree built based on the data. Nodes with categorical features, such as event setting, should be interpreted as "is *event_setting*=`casual` OR `sport`?"

Since we lack a benchmark in this domain in order to evaluate our model, we compare our result with an algorithm which would predict a random priority (as we offered 5-point scale, chance corresponds to 20%) and with an algorithm which always picks the most selected class, i.e., priority 4, which was selected in 41% of cases. To determine the accuracy of the models, we use the following definition:

---

[4] The code can be found in: https://github.com/ilir-kola/decisiontree-socialsit.git.

$$accuracy = \frac{Number\_correct\_predictions}{Number\_overall\_predictions}$$

The accuracy of our model on the test set is 47%, thus performing better than the other two algorithms that we used as a benchmark. This means that information about social features can be used to predict priority of a social situation.

6   Discussion and Conclusions

6.1   Research Questions and Hypothesis

Regarding RQ1, in Sect. 4.2 we notice that subjects find our proposed set of features understandable and their quantity appropriate. Furthermore, they find the features relatively expressive. In Sect. 5, we tackle RQ2 by proposing a model which learns a decision tree to predict priority of meetings. We observe that the model performs better than chance, which shows that while this can be a way to predict priority of social situations, more works needs to be done in order to achieve a higher accuracy. This may involve introduction of additional features. The result also contributes in the answer of RQ1, since it suggests that the features allow us to represent social situations in order to learn information about them. Regarding H3, in Sect. 4.2 we see that in 69% of the cases, priority is a good predictor for choosing between overlapping meetings. However, it also shows that it is not the only element, and more dimensions of situations need to be assessed to identify where this difference comes from.

6.2   Contributions

For the benefit of the development of behaviour support·agents with social situation awareness, this paper provides the following contributions:

- an upper ontology for representing the salient situation cues and types of features for characterizing dyadic social relationships.
- a set of lower level features which can be used to represent daily life social situations.
- an evaluation of social features via a user study, showing that subjects find the concepts understandable and expressive.
- an evaluation whether decision trees can be used to predict the priority of social situations based on features of social situations, which proved to be the case.

Results presented in this work tend to support the feasibility of our overall approach, but in parallel they open the way for different research questions which need to be explored in more depth in future work.

6.3 Limitations

First of all, the number of people in our user study via which we evaluate our proposed features is relatively small, and the subjects are mostly PhD candidates. This does not allow for a conclusive answer when it comes to understandability and expressiveness among other types of people with, for example, other levels of education. In turn, this also creates limitations when tackling RQ2. First of all, we built the model using a small data set, and learning algorithms need more data in order to generalize better. This is also shown by the high level of overfitting which takes place, as noticed by the fact that the accuracy on the training set is 65%. Moreover, the data is unbalanced, since people mostly give a priority of 4 or 5 to events. The presence of lower priorities would make the evaluation of the algorithm more realistic since we would be able to measure not only the number of correct predictions, but also how far off the incorrect predictions are. The low variance in the data can be explained by the fact that subjects chose people who are very close to them, thus they would prioritize those events.

6.4 Proposed Future Work

Based on the findings reported in this paper, a more extensive experiment can be confidently carried out to obtain a detailed social model that can serve as a background model for behaviour support agents to advise on how to choose between social situations. More data can help not only in building a more accurate model, but also to try out more techniques. Furthermore, that data can also be used to study the correlations between the different features, in order to select a minimal set of features for which to ask the users.

Another interesting approach is to analyze how *personal values* [26,44] affect the way in which subjects think about social situations. Part III of our experiment suggested the existence of individual differences in how people decide which meetings to attend. We will explore whether people with shared personal values make similar choices.

The current model relies fully on information that is acquired directly from the users. In future work, we would like to add sensory data to inform our model. Literature shows that sensory data can be used to perceive social information (e.g., [9]). This line of research would provide useful ways to acquire information without interrupting the user.

Finally, in this work we mostly focus on the modelling of social situations. The next step is to dive deeper into situation comprehension, and reason about different dimensions of social situations (other than priority). Data from the user study suggests that both enjoyment and obligation correlate well with priority, and this correlation is stronger when considering situations in specific settings (enjoyment for casual situations and obligation for work situations). Representing more dimensions of social situations would lead to having a more complete profile of the situation, which in turn enables behaviour support agents to provide more comprehensive help.

Appendix

Part 1
For each person, the following questions were asked:

- What's the name of this person? (e.g. Alice)
- What is the role of Alice towards you? options: {partner, parent, sibling, child, friend, extended family member, neighbor, coworker, supervisor, member of the same group (e.g., sports team), other}
- What's the hierarchy rank (from a formal point of view) of Alice towards you? options: {higher, lower, same, n.a.}
- How would you consider the quality of your relationship with Alice? options: Likert$_5$
- What's the geographical distance between you and Alice? options: {0-1 h, 1-2 h, 2-4 h, I would need to take a flight}
- How well do you know Alice? options: Likert$_5$
- How often are you in touch with Alice? options: Likert$_5$
- How much do you trust Alice? options: Likert$_5$
- How formal is your relationship with Alice? options: Likert$_5$

Part 2
For each scenario, the following questions were asked. For all, the answer option was a 5-point Likert scale:

- What priority would you assign to this meeting?
- What priority do you think the other person would assign to this meeting?
- To what extent would you feel obligated to attend this meeting?
- To what extent do you think the other person would feel obligated to attend this meeting?
- To what extent would you enjoy attending this meeting?
- To what extent do you think the other person would enjoy attending this meeting?
- How likely are you to encounter this scenario in your life?

Part 3
Two scenarios were chosen randomly and shown to the subject, and the following questions were asked:

- If they were planned to happen at the same time, which of the two scenarios would you attend? options: {Scenario 1, Scenario 2}
- What explanation would you give to the person whose meeting you would have to cancel? options: {no explanation, the real reason, some other reason}.

References

1. Ajmeri, N., Guo, H., Murukannaiah, P.K., Singh, M.P.: Designing ethical personal agents. IEEE Internet Comput. **22**(2), 16–22 (2018)
2. Ajmeri, N., Murukannaiah, P.K., Guo, H., Singh, M.P.: Arnor: modeling social intelligence via norms to engineer privacy-aware personal agents. In: Proceedings of the 16th Conference on Autonomous Agents and MultiAgent Systems, pp. 230–238. International Foundation for Autonomous Agents and Multiagent Systems (2017)
3. Antonucci, T.C., Ajrouch, K.J., Birditt, K.S.: The convoy model: explaining social relations from a multidisciplinary perspective. Gerontologist **54**(1), 82–92 (2013)
4. Antonucci, T.C., Akiyama, H.: Social networks in adult life and a preliminary examination of the convoy model. J. Gerontol. **42**(5), 519–527 (1987)
5. Barwise, J., Perry, J.: Situations and attitudes. J. Philos. **78**(11), 668–691 (1981)
6. Boutilier, C.: A POMDP formulation of preference elicitation problems. In: Eighteenth National Conference on Artificial Intelligence, pp. 239–246. American Association for Artificial Intelligence, Menlo Park (2002). http://dl.acm.org/citation.cfm?id=777092.777132
7. Breiman, L., Friedman, J., Olshen, R., Stone, C.: Classification and Regression Trees. Routledge, Abingdon (1994)
8. Burt, R.S.: Network items and the general social survey. Soc. Netw. **6**(4), 293–339 (1984)
9. Cabrera-Quiros, L., Demetriou, A., Gedik, E., van der Meij, L., Hung, H.: The MatchNMingle dataset: a novel multi-sensor resource for the analysis of social interactions and group dynamics in-the-wild during free-standing conversations and speed dates. IEEE Trans. Affect. Comput. (2018). https://doi.org/10.1109/TAFFC.2018.2848914
10. Devlin, K.: Logic and Information. Cambridge University Press, Cambridge (1995)
11. Dignum, F.: Interactions as social practices: towards a formalization. arXiv preprint arXiv:1809.08751 (2018)
12. Dignum, F., Prada, R., Hofstede, G.J.: From autistic to social agents. In: Proceedings of the 2014 International Conference on Autonomous Agents and Multi-Agent Systems, pp. 1161–1164. International Foundation for Autonomous Agents and Multiagent Systems (2014)
13. Dignum, V.: A Model for Organizational Interaction: Based on Agents, Founded in Logic. SIKS (2004)
14. Dignum, V., Dignum, F.: Contextualized planning using social practices. In: Ghose, A., Oren, N., Telang, P., Thangarajah, J. (eds.) COIN 2014. LNCS (LNAI), vol. 9372, pp. 36–52. Springer, Cham (2015). https://doi.org/10.1007/978-3-319-25420-3_3
15. Dudzik, B., et al.: Context in human emotion perception for automatic affect detection: a survey of audiovisual databases. In: Proceedings of the 8th International Conference on Affective Computing & Intelligent Interaction. Association for the Advancement of Affective Computing (2019)
16. d'Inverno, M., Luck, M., Noriega, P., Rodriguez-Aguilar, J.A., Sierra, C.: Weaving a fabric of socially aware agents. In: Kinny, D., Hsu, J.Y., Governatori, G., Ghose, A.K. (eds.) PRIMA 2011. LNCS (LNAI), vol. 7047, pp. 263–274. Springer, Heidelberg (2011). https://doi.org/10.1007/978-3-642-25044-6_21
17. Endsley, M.R.: Toward a theory of situation awareness in dynamic systems. Hum. Factors **37**(1), 32–64 (1995)

18. Endsley, M.R.: Theoretical underpinnings of situation awareness: a critical review. Situat. Aware. Anal. Meas. **1**, 24 (2000)
19. Fiske, A.P.: The four elementary forms of sociality: framework for a unified theory of social relations. Psychol. Rev. **99**(4), 689 (1992)
20. Fullam, K.K., Klos, T., Muller, G., Sabater-Mir, J., Barber, K.S., Vercouter, L.: The agent reputation and trust (ART) testbed. In: Stølen, K., Winsborough, W.H., Martinelli, F., Massacci, F. (eds.) iTrust 2006. LNCS, vol. 3986, pp. 439–442. Springer, Heidelberg (2006). https://doi.org/10.1007/11755593_32
21. Gigerenzer, G.: The modularity of social intelligence. In: Machiavellian Intelligence II: Extensions and Evaluations, vol. 2, no. 264, pp. 264–288 (1997)
22. Granovetter, M.: The strength of weak ties: a network theory revisited. In: Sociological Theory pp. 201–233 (1983)
23. Granovetter, M.: Weak ties and strong ties. Am. J. Sociol. **78**, 1360–1380 (1973)
24. Hoekstra, R.: Ontology representation design patterns and ontologies that make sense. In: Proceedings of the 2009 Conference on Ontology Representation: Design Patterns and Ontologies that Make Sense, pp. 1–236. IOS Press (2009)
25. Kahn, R., Antonucci, T.: Convoys over the life course: attachment, roles, and social support. In: Life-Span Development and Behavior (1980)
26. Kayal, A., Brinkman, W.P., Neerincx, M.A., Riemsdijk, M.B.V.: Automatic resolution of normative conflicts in supportive technology based on user values. ACM Trans. Internet Technol. **18**(4), 41:1–41:21 (2018)
27. Kokar, M.M., Matheus, C.J., Baclawski, K.: Ontology-based situation awareness. Inf. Fusion **10**(1), 83–98 (2009)
28. Kola, I., Jonker, C.M., van Riemsdijk, M.B.: Modelling the social environment: towards socially adaptive electronic partners. In: 10th International Workshop on Modelling and Reasoning in Context (2018)
29. Kola, I., Jonker, C.M., van Riemsdijk, M.B.: Pilot experiment exploring the priority of social situations (2019). https://doi.org/10.4121/uuid:e18fb318-c1d4-4ccc-9b4f-be48e1ee49e2
30. Mainela, T.: Types and functions of social relationships in the organizing of an international joint venture. Ind. Mark. Manag. **36**(1), 87–98 (2007)
31. Murukannaiah, P.K., Singh, M.P.: Platys social: relating shared places and private social circles. IEEE Internet Comput. **16**(3), 53–59 (2012)
32. Myers, K.L., Yorke-Smith, N.: Proactivity in an intentionally helpful personal assistive agent. In: AAAI Spring Symposium: Intentions in Intelligent Systems, pp. 34–37 (2007)
33. Parrigon, S., Woo, S.E., Tay, L., Wang, T.: Caption-ing the situation: a lexically-derived taxonomy of psychological situation characteristics. J. Pers. Soc. Psychol. **112**(4), 642 (2017)
34. Pereira, G., Prada, R., Santos, P.A.: Integrating social power into the decision-making of cognitive agents. Artif. Intell. **241**, 1–44 (2016)
35. Pervin, L.A.: A free-response description approach to the analysis of person-situation interaction. ETS Res. Bull. Ser. **1975**(2), i-26 (1975)
36. Pinder, C., Vermeulen, J., Cowan, B.R., Beale, R.: Digital behaviour change interventions to break and form habits. ACM Trans. Comput.-Hum. Interact. (TOCHI) **25**(3), 15 (2018)
37. Rauthmann, J.F., et al.: The situational eight diamonds: a taxonomy of major dimensions of situation characteristics. J. Pers. Soc. Psychol. **107**(4), 677 (2014)
38. Ring, P.S., Van de Ven, A.H.: Developmental processes of cooperative interorganizational relationships. Acad. Manag. Rev. **19**(1), 90–118 (1994)

39. Saucier, G., Bel-Bahar, T., Fernandez, C.: What modifies the expression of personality tendencies? Defining basic domains of situation variables. J. Pers. **75**(3), 479–504 (2007)
40. Singh, M.P.: Norms as a basis for governing sociotechnical systems. ACM Trans. Intell. Syst. Technol. (TIST) **5**(1), 21 (2013)
41. Tambe, M., Bowring, E., Pearce, J.P., Varakantham, P., Scerri, P., Pynadeth, D.V.: Electric elves: what went wrong and why. AI Mag. **29**, 23 (2008)
42. Therneau, T., Atkinson, B.: rpart: Recursive Partitioning and Regression Trees (2018). https://CRAN.R-project.org/package=rpart. R Package Version 4.1-13
43. Tielman, M., Brinkman, W.-P., Neerincx, M.A.: Design guidelines for a virtual coach for post-traumatic stress disorder patients. In: Bickmore, T., Marsella, S., Sidner, C. (eds.) IVA 2014. LNCS (LNAI), vol. 8637, pp. 434–437. Springer, Cham (2014). https://doi.org/10.1007/978-3-319-09767-1_54
44. Tielman, M.L., Jonker, C.M., van Riemsdijk, M.B.: What should i do? Deriving norms from actions, values and context. In: Proceedings of the 10th International Workshop on Modelling and Reasoning in Context, MRC 2018, pp. 35–40. CEUR Workshop Proceedings (2018)
45. Uzzi, B.: Social structure and competition in interfirm networks: the paradox of embeddedness. Adm. Sci. Q. **42**, 35–67 (1997)
46. Van Riemsdijk, M.B., Jonker, C.M., Lesser, V.: Creating socially adaptive electronic partners: interaction, reasoning and ethical challenges. In: Proceedings of the 2015 International Conference on Autonomous Agents and Multiagent Systems, pp. 1201–1206. International Foundation for Autonomous Agents and Multiagent Systems (2015)
47. Williamson, O.E.: Markets and Hierarchies: Analysis and Antitrust Implications. Free Press, New York (1975)
48. Yau, S.S., Liu, J.: Hierarchical situation modeling and reasoning for pervasive computing. In: The Fourth IEEE Workshop on Software Technologies for Future Embedded and Ubiquitous Systems, p. 6. IEEE (2006)
49. Yolum, P., Singh, M.P.: Service graphs for building trust. In: Meersman, R., Tari, Z. (eds.) OTM 2004. LNCS, vol. 3290, pp. 509–525. Springer, Heidelberg (2004). https://doi.org/10.1007/978-3-540-30468-5_32
50. Zavala, L., et al.: Platys: from position to place-oriented mobile computing. AI Mag. **36**(2), 50–62 (2015)
51. Zhao, R., Papangelis, A., Cassell, J.: Towards a dyadic computational model of rapport management for human-virtual agent interaction. In: Bickmore, T., Marsella, S., Sidner, C. (eds.) IVA 2014. LNCS (LNAI), vol. 8637, pp. 514–527. Springer, Cham (2014). https://doi.org/10.1007/978-3-319-09767-1_62

The "Why Did You Do That?" Button: Answering Why-Questions for End Users of Robotic Systems

Vincent J. Koeman[1], Louise A. Dennis[2]([⊠]), Matt Webster[2],
Michael Fisher[2], and Koen Hindriks[3]

[1] Delft University of Technology, Delft, The Netherlands
v.j.koeman@tudelft.nl
[2] University of Liverpool, Liverpool, UK
{L.A.Dennis,M.Webster,MFisher}@liverpool.ac.uk
[3] Vrije Universiteit Amsterdam, Amsterdam, The Netherlands
k.v.hindriks@vu.nl

Abstract. The issue of explainability for autonomous systems is becoming increasingly prominent. Several researchers and organisations have advocated the provision of a "Why did you do that?" button which allows a user to interrogate a robot about its choices and actions. We take previous work on debugging cognitive agent programs and apply it to the question of supplying explanations to end users in the form of answers to *why-questions*. These previous approaches are based on the generation of a trace of events in the execution of the program and then answering why-questions using the trace. We implemented this framework in the *agent infrastructure layer* and, in particular, the GWENDOLEN programming language it supports – extending it in the process to handle the generation of applicable plans and multiple intentions. In order to make the answers to why-questions comprehensible to end users we advocate a two step process in which first a representation of an explanation is created and this is subsequently converted into natural language in a way which abstracts away from some events in the trace and employs application specific *predicate dictionaries* in order to translate the first-order logic presentation of concepts within the cognitive agent program in natural language. A prototype implementation of these ideas is provided.

1 Introduction

As autonomous systems become more prevalent in society, issues related to the ways in which humans interact with such systems become more important. Among these issues is the question of transparency and, in particular, explainability. Wortham and Theodorou [35], and Sheh [24] (among others) have argued that the ability for a robot (and by extension any autonomous system) to provide explanations of its behaviour helps users develop accurate mental models of the robot's reasoning and so interact better with the robot and develop trust. Charisi

© Springer Nature Switzerland AG 2020
L. A. Dennis et al. (Eds.): EMAS 2019, LNAI 12058, pp. 152–172, 2020.
https://doi.org/10.1007/978-3-030-51417-4_8

et al. [5], Turner [26] and The IEEE Global Initiative on Ethics of Autonomous and Intelligent Systems [25] in particular advocate the provision of a "why did you do that?" button to help the user understand a robot's behaviour.

We take as our focus autonomous systems which employ a cognitive agent to make high level decisions such as [27,28,36]. One of the reasons often put forward for the employment of cognitive agents in this role is their in principle ability to explain their decisions to end users. However, in practice, little research has been performed in actually providing such explanations of reasoning.

There are a number of key problems in the provision of explanations. Firstly, they require a backward view of the program execution (in contrast to common debugging practice in which a breakpoint is set and the program is then run forwards from the breakpoint). Secondly, log files, which are the obvious solution to the first problem tend to be verbose and their production can cause significant performance overheads. These problems are exacerbated when all the information needed to understand why something is taking place must be captured.

In this paper we combine work on the debugging of cognitive agent programs in the Beliefs-Desires-Intentions (BDI) paradigm [17] with work on the provision of explanations for programmers in GOAL [15] and AgentSpeak [31]. Koeman et al. [17] generate an omniscient trace of key events that take place during program execution in a manner which limits the overhead cost of producing the trace. Each event stores enough information about the agent's mental state to reconstruct the state of the program execution at that point. This trace is supported by tools allowing it to be viewed at a high-level of abstraction hiding extraneous information unless a user wants to see it.

We have implemented omniscient tracing in the *Agent Infrastructure Layer* (AIL) [7,9], a prototyping tool for verifiable interpreters for cognitive agent programming languages, with particular attention to the GWENDOLEN programming language [8] but with attention paid to keeping the framework generic where possible. In applying this framework to the AIL we extended the key events considered beyond changes to the agent's mental state to include a number of events involved in the generation of plans and the handling of intentions.

The development of omniscient debugging was driven, in part, by a desire to support programmers in answering why-questions. Programmers can interrogate the high level trace at specific points in the program execution and ask "why did you do that" (as outlined in [15]). Winikoff [31] reports on a similar system constructing why and why-not explanations over traces for AgentSpeak.

We implemented this idea in our AIL-based omniscient debugging framework. We developed an explanation generation framework for end users that is specific to GWENDOLEN, providing explanations at a higher level of abstraction than previously considered, and using *predicate dictionaries* to provide natural language substitutes for application specific logical predicates. This implementation generates explanations when multiple intentions are being executed in an interleaved fashion (something omitted from [31]).

2   Background and Related Work

2.1   Cognitive Agent Programming

At its most general, an *agent* is an abstract concept that represents an *autonomous* computational entity that makes its own decisions [33]. A general agent is simply the encapsulation of some distributed computational component within a larger system. However, in many settings, something more is needed. Rather than just having a system which makes its own decisions in an opaque way, it is increasingly important for the agent to have explicit *reasons* (that it could explain, if necessary) for making one choice over another.

Cognitive agents [3,21,34] enable the representation of this kind of reasoning. Such an agent has explicit reasons for making the choices it does. We often describe a cognitive agent's *beliefs* and *goals*, which in turn determine the agent's *intentions*. Such agents make decisions about what action to perform, given their current beliefs, goals and intentions. This view of cognitive agents is encapsulated within the Beliefs-Desires-Intentions (BDI) model [20–22]. Beliefs represent the agent's (possibly incomplete, possibly incorrect) information about itself, other agents, and its environment, desires represent the agent's long-term goals while intentions represent the goals that the agent is actively pursuing (the representation of intentions often includes partially instantiated and/or executed plans and so combines the goal with its intended means).

There are *many* different agent programming languages and agent platforms based, at least in part, on the BDI approach [1,6,14,19,23]. Agents programmed in these languages commonly contain a set of *beliefs*, a set of *goals*, and a set of *plans*. Plans determine how an agent acts based on its beliefs and goals and form the basis for *practical reasoning* (i.e., reasoning about actions) in such agents. As a result of executing a plan, the beliefs and goals of an agent may change and actions may be executed.

It is generally recognised that debugging BDI agent programs is hard [29,30] (and by extension that agent behaviour can be difficult to understand even when performing as desired). In particular agents react to exogenous events in dynamic environments; exogenous events which may combine in unexpected ways and which may be handled by the agent "in parallel" with each other. Furthermore many cognitive agent languages have provision for failure handling which, again, may interact in complex ways with the behaviour of the rest of the program.

2.2   Explanations in Cognitive Agent Systems and "Why" Questions

Ko and Myers [16] created the WHY-LINE tool, which allows developers to pose "why did" or "why didn't" questions about the output of Java programs. A trace is generated in memory through bytecode instrumentation, containing everything necessary for reproducing a specific execution. From this trace, a set of questions and associated answers is generated. The authors note that their approach is not suited for executions that span more than a few minutes or executions that process or produce substantial amounts of data. However, their results do show that the approach enables developers to debug failures substantially faster.

Hindriks [15] and Winikoff [31] both consider a similar model applied to the debugging of cognitive agent programs in GOAL and AgentSpeak respectively. Of these [15] is the earlier and has a more informal treatment than [31] which sought to extend, formalise and implement the proposal. The two approaches are therefore similar in their underlying conception and we use them as the basis for our work. The key idea is that a trace of events is stored as a log. Each event in the trace can be interrogated and an explanation constructed in a systematic way using information either stored in that event and/or by referring to a previous event in the log. For instance the explanation for why some action was executed might be that "the action's preconditions held and a plan was previously selected which contained the action". Explanations can then also be given for why the preconditions succeeded and/or why the plan was selected.

Koeman et al. [17] propose a trace based mechanism for debugging cognitive agent programs. Although concerned with many of the same issues as [15] and [31] (and indeed, intended as support for the mechanisms proposed in [15]) the authors focus on more foundational questions of what information needs to be stored in a trace in order to reconstruct the state of an agent at that point, and the performance overhead of storing such traces for a program. They conclude that if a trace stored the key events in agent execution, namely the changes to the agent's mental state, then the program run could be reconstructed without the significant performance impact associated with storing the full state of an agent at each step in execution. They develop a *space-time visualiser* for these traces which allows a programmer to inspect the trace and query the state of the underlying program at any point.

Hindriks [15] and Koeman et al. [17] consider primarily changes to an agent's mental state (i.e., beliefs and goals) in their tracing and debugging frameworks. Winikoff [31] extends this to include traces and explanations for the selection of plans but assumes that the entirety of a plan is executed before anything else happens. The AIL allows interleaved execution of plans by manipulating intentions. In our work therefore, we integrated the approach in [31] with that of [17] and then extended it to the handling of multiple intentions[1].

A few systems have considered the question of providing explanations specifically for end users of cognitive agent systems. In Harbers [13] explanations of agent behaviour are generated based on the beliefs and goals of the agents using a goal hierarchy paired with a behaviour log. Winikoff et al. [32] presents a similar system but adds the concept of preferences (or *valuings*) to the explanations presented to end users. The use of goal heirarchies can be viewed as a more abstract approach than ours which considers the concept of plans and their selection as an important part of explanation generation beyond their use

---

[1] Though it should be noted that the implementation of omniscient debugging in GOAL also handles GOAL's module mechanism (although this is not reported in depth in [17]) which is not entirely dissimilar to the concept of intention in the AIL.

to decompose goals into sub-goals. We hypothesise that many users will find the concept of plan a useful one but have yet to evaluate this hypothesis in any way.

2.3   The Agent Infrastructure Layer and Gwendolen

The Agent Infrastructure Layer (AIL) [7] is a set of Java classes intended to assist in the development of BDI-style programming languages. GWENDOLEN [8] is the most mature language in this framework.

Aside: It is unfortunate that the literature on tracing programs refers to storing key events in a trace, while the BDI literature refers to events that trigger plans (which may be either external or internal to the program). We distinguish between these two uses of the word "event" in what follows by using *trace event* for events stored in traces and *BDI event* for events that may trigger plans during program execution.

The AIL provides default data structures for agents, beliefs, goals, plans and intentions. Individual languages implemented in the AIL define custom reasoning cycles for agent deliberation. However the toolkit has an underlying assumption that such reasoning cycles will typically involve the following steps in some order:

- Perception which creates sets of new beliefs and removes beliefs that no longer hold.
- Posting BDI events (either as new intentions, or added to existing intentions) when beliefs are acquired or removed and goals are acquired or removed.
- Selecting plans to react to BDI events.
- Selecting among intentions which represent partially processed plans or unhandled BDI events.
- Processing one (or more) steps in an intention which include adding and removing beliefs and goals and executing actions.

These default steps therefore form the core events supported by our implementation of omniscient debugging within the AIL.

Gwendolen Operational Semantics. We use GWENDOLEN as our key implementation language. We present here a simplified version of the GWENDOLEN operational semantics which is presented in full in [8]. The semantics presented here assumes all terms are ground (so ignores issues surrounding the handling of unifiers), and ignores a number of language features such as locking and suspending intentions, dropping goals, agent sleeping and waking behaviour, message handling and special cases such as transitions for handling goals that can't be planned. The intention is to present enough information to allow our framework to be understood. This operational semantics is shown in Fig. 1. Following [31] we annotate the transitions (expressions above the arrow) with the trace events that are stored by the omniscient debugger. These are discussed further in Sect. 3.

$$\frac{\mathcal{S}_{\text{int}}(I \cup \{i_k\}) = (i'_{k'}, I')}{\langle i_k, I, B, \emptyset \rangle \xrightarrow{seli(i'_{k'})} \langle i'_{k'}, I', B, \emptyset \rangle} \mathbf{A} \qquad (1)$$

$$\frac{\mathcal{G}(i_k, I, B) = A}{\langle i_k, I, B, \emptyset \rangle \xrightarrow{\Gamma} \langle i_k, I, B, A \rangle} \mathbf{B} \qquad (2)$$

$$\frac{(e, ds) = \mathcal{S}_{\text{plan}}(A)}{\langle i_k, I, B, A \rangle \xrightarrow{selp((e,ds),k)} \langle (e, ds) \, \texttt{@} \, \texttt{tl}_i(i_k), I, B, \emptyset \rangle} \mathbf{C} \qquad (3)$$

$$\frac{B \models g}{\langle (e, +!g);_i i_k, I, B, \emptyset \rangle \to \langle i_k, I, B, \emptyset \rangle} \mathbf{D} \qquad (4)$$

$$\frac{B \not\models g}{\langle (e, +!g);_i i_k, I, B, \emptyset \rangle \xrightarrow{add((e,+!g),k)} \langle (+!g, \epsilon);_i (e, +!g);_i i_k, I, B, \emptyset \rangle} \mathbf{D} \qquad (5)$$

$$\frac{}{\langle (e, +b);_i i_k, I, B, \emptyset \rangle \xrightarrow{addb(+b,k);crei((+b,\epsilon),k')} \langle i_k, I \cup (+b, \epsilon)_{k'}, B \cup \{b\}, \emptyset \rangle} \mathbf{D} \qquad (6)$$

$$\frac{}{\langle (e, -b);_i i_k, I, B, \emptyset \ldots \rangle \xrightarrow{delb(-b,k);crei((-b,\epsilon),k')} \langle i_k, I \cup (-b, \epsilon)_{k'}, B \backslash \{b\}, \emptyset \rangle} \mathbf{D} \qquad (7)$$

$$\frac{\mathbf{do}(a)}{\langle (e, a);_i i_k, I, B, \emptyset \rangle \xrightarrow{act(a,k)} \langle i_k, I, B, \emptyset \rangle} \mathbf{D} \qquad (8)$$

$$\frac{P = \mathbf{Percepts} \quad OP = \{b \mid b \in B \backslash P \land percept(b)\}}{\langle i_k, I, A, B \rangle \xrightarrow{\Pi}} \mathbf{E} \qquad (9)$$
$$\langle i, I \cup \{(\mathbf{percept}, +b)_{k'} \mid b \in P \backslash B \land fresh(k')\} \cup$$
$$\{(\mathbf{percept}, -b)_{k'} \mid b \in OP \land fresh(k')\}, B, A \rangle$$

Fig. 1. Simplified GWENDOLEN Semantics

The GWENDOLEN reasoning cycle shown here has five stages $\mathbf{A}, \mathbf{B}, \mathbf{C}, \mathbf{D}$ and $\mathbf{E}$[2]. One transition in each stage is executed in turn. In the semantics we show the stage that a transition applies to with a letter to the right of the rule. A GWENDOLEN agent starts in stage $\mathbf{A}$ and so (1) is the first rule to apply, followed by (2) and so on. In stage $\mathbf{D}$ whichever rule applies to the top of the current intention is applied and then the reasoning cycle moves on to stage $\mathbf{E}$.

BDI languages use intentions to store the *intended means* for achieving goals – this is generally represented as some form of *deed stack* (deeds include actions, belief updates, and the commitment to goals). In GWENDOLEN, intention structures[3] also maintain information about the BDI event that triggered them (the addition or removal of a belief or the posting of a (sub-)goal). GWENDOLEN aggregates this information: an intention becomes a stack of tuples of an event and a deed. Each tuple associates a particular deed with the BDI event that triggered the plan that placed the deed in the intention. Unplanned BDI events are associated with an empty deed, ϵ, which can be thought of a marker indicating "no plan yet".

---

[2] The implementation of GWENDOLEN contains a sixth stage for message handling.
[3] A refinement of the AIL's intention structure which is more general.

In order to track the evolution of intentions in traces more easily, we extended the AIL implementation of intentions with an ID number, k, and will use the notation i_k to represent that intention, i, has ID number, k. This ID number is frequently stored in trace events (see, for instance, (3) in Fig. 1).

We represent an agent state as a tuple $\langle i, I, B, A \rangle$ where: i is the current intention; I is a queue of intentions $\{i_1, i_2, ..\}$; B is a set of the agent's beliefs; and A is a set of currently applicable plans for the current intention i.

A GWENDOLEN program consists of a set of plans, Δ, of the form, $e : \{g\} \leftarrow ds$ (where ds is a sequence of deeds to be executed if BDI event, e is posted and guard, g, follows from the agent's beliefs and goals), a set of initial beliefs, $\mathcal{B}$, and a set of initial goals, Gs. In an agent's initial state the current intention is *null*, the intention set consists of one intention for each of the initial goals provided by the programmer of the form $(\texttt{start}, +!g)$. The belief base is $\mathcal{B}$ and the applicable plans are empty.

(1) governs the selection of intentions. $\mathcal{S}_{\mathrm{int}}$ is an application specific function that selects one intention out of a set of intentions and returns a tuple of the selected intention and the set without that intention in it. By default $\mathcal{S}_{\mathrm{int}}$ operates on a queue data structure and so in general the current intention is placed at the end of the queue and the intention at the top of the queue is selected. Also by default empty intentions which have been fully executed are removed at this point.

(2) represents the process of inspecting the plan library and finding plans that match the current intention. These are transformed into *applicable plans* and returned by the function $\mathcal{G}$. A plan, $e : \{g\} \leftarrow ds$ matches an intention if e matches the BDI event in the top tuple of the intention, g is a logical consequence of the agent's beliefs and goals (goals are inferred from the BDI events posted in all intentions) and the deed in the top tuple of the intention is ϵ. Applicable plans are an interim data structure that describe how the plan changes the current intention. An applicable plan describes new tuples to be placed on the top of the intention stack (replacing the existing top tuple). A tuple is created for each deed in ds and associated with e[4].

(3) uses the application specific function $\mathcal{S}_{\mathrm{plan}}$ to pick an applicable plan to be applied. By default, this treats the set as a list and picks the first plan based on the order they appear in the GWENDOLEN program. We use the syntax $(e, ds) \mathbin{@} \mathtt{tl}_i(i)$ to represent the replacement of the top tuple in intention, i, by the tuples in the applicable plan, $e : \{g\} \leftarrow ds$.

(4), (5), (6), (7) and (8) process the top deed in the intention handling the instruction to add a goal (depending upon whether the goal is already achieved or not), add a belief, drop a belief and execute an action respectively. $(e, d);_i i$

---

[4] In order to handle situations where the top deed on the intention is not ϵ ("no plan yet") then $\mathcal{G}$ returns the existing top tuple so there is no change to the intention and it continues to be processed as normal. This somewhat baroque mechanism has its roots in GWENDOLEN's origin as an intermediate language into which all BDI languages could be translated [10]. We ignore this type of applicable plan in our explanation mechanism and so do not refer to them further here.

represents the addition of the tuple (e, d) to the top of the intention i. $\mathbf{do}(a)$ represents the execution of an action in some external environment. These rules make a check on the top deed in the intention to see what type it is (e.g., the addition of a belief, the deletion of a goal). We represent these checks implicitly using the notation: a for an action; $+b$ for a belief addition; $-b$ for a belief removal; and $+!g$ for a goal addition. (6) and (7) both add two trace events to the trace representing that both the belief base has been changed and that a new intention has been created. This new intention has a new ID number k'.

(9) handles perception. A set of **Percepts** are gathered from the environment. New percepts are added as intentions to add a belief (each with a new ID number indicated by $fresh(k')$). Out of date percepts (i.e., percepts in the belief base that can no longer be perceived) are handled by creating a new intention to remove them.

3   An AIL-Based Framework for Omniscient Debugging Driven Explanations for Cognitive Agents

As noted above, omniscient debugging was developed with the intention of supporting explanations in the form of answering why- and why-not-questions as outlined in [15] and [31].

Omniscient debugging for GOAL focused on the changes in agent goals and beliefs as the key trace events underpinning a trace. We used the analysis from Sect. 2.3 to extend[5] this to:

1. Creation of intention, i_k: $crei(i, k)$.
2. Selection of intention, i_k: $seli(k)$.
3. Successful evaluation of guard, g for (applicable) plan π, with unifier, θ in intention, i_k: $bel(\pi, g, \theta, k)$.
4. Selection of an applicable plan, (e, ds) in intention, i_k: $selp((e, ds), k)$.
5. Execution of action, a, by intention i_k: $act(a, k)$.
6. Adding or removing goal, g, by intention i_k: $addg(g, k), delg(g, k)$.
7. Adding or removing belief, b by intention i_k: $addb(b, k), delb(b, k)$.
8. Modification of intention, i_k, by adding or removing tuples, ts: $add(ts, k), del(ts, k)$.

We used the work of Koeman et al. [17] for trace construction and visualisation to implement tracing in the AIL. Since both GOAL and the AIL were implemented in Java it was possible to port much of the framework directly.

3.1   Adaptation to GWENDOLEN

Commands to log these trace events were embedded in relevant parts of the AIL toolkit, primarily in classes used to implement transition rules in reasoning

---

[5] Note this is not the complete set of trace events shown in Fig. 1. This is elaborated further in Sect. 3.1.

cycles. This is why in Fig. 1 we were able to annotate the transitions in the
GWENDOLEN semantics with the associated trace events. Given GWENDOLEN
modifies the current intention when a goal is posted instead of maintaining a
goal base we do not use $addg(g, k)$ or $delg(g, k)$.

In Fig. 1 we reference two further constructs, Γ and Π, these represent situations where one transition in the semantics generates several trace events in
the trace. Γ logs each successful guard evaluation for plans in Δ as an event
in the trace and associates them with the relevant applicable plan. Π logs the
creation of the intentions caused by the addition and removal of beliefs following
perception.

3.2 Example

As an example of a simple GWENDOLEN trace we consider the excution of a
GWENDOLEN program that consists of a single plan $+b : \{a\} \leftarrow +d; e$ (if the
BDI event that b is believed is posted and a is already believed then add the
belief d and do e). We will omit the gory details of the GWENDOLEN agent
state, but hope the process of execution is nevertheless comprehensible from the
example trace.

In the trace a number of beliefs are added following perception steps in the
program execution. Some of these beliefs are relevant to the plan execution
and some are not. We have included them to help illustrate the use of multiple
intentions.

Subscripts on trace events indicate the step in the trace.

$$crei((\texttt{percept}, +a), 1)_1$$
$$seli(1)_2$$
$$addb(a, 1)_3$$
$$crei((+a, \epsilon), 2)_4$$
$$crei((\texttt{percept}, +b), 3)_5$$

Steps 1–5 in the trace represent two rounds of the reasoning cycle. a is perceived
in step 1 and creates an intention (intention 1). Intention 1 is selected (step 2).
a is added as a belief and a new intention (intention 2) is created (steps 3 and
4). At the end of the round b is perceived and this creates intention 3 (step 5).

In the next cycle intention 2 is selected. There is no plan for responding to
the belief a and so nothing else happens. We get a single addition to the trace:
$seli(2)_6$ (intention 1 is empty and is removed. This isn't recorded in the trace).

In the fourth cycle the following steps are added to the trace:

$$seli(3)_7$$
$$addb(b, 3)_8$$
$$crei((+b, \epsilon), 4)_9$$
$$crei((\texttt{percept}, +c), 5)_{10}$$

Intention 3 is selected (step 7); b is added to the belief base (step 8); a new
intention is created recording the fact (step 9) and; finally, c is perceived (step
10).

In the fifth cycle the following steps are added to the trace:

$$seli(4)_{11}$$
$$bel((+b, +d; do(e)), a, \emptyset, 4)_{12}$$
$$selp((+b, +d; do(e)), 4)_{13}$$
$$addb(d, 4)_{14}$$
$$crei((+d, \epsilon), 6)_{15}$$

Intention 4 is selected (step 11). This triggers the plan and the trace records that the plan's guard, a, holds (step 12) and that the plan has been selected (step 13). The first deed in the plan is executed (d is added to the belief base) (step 14) and this creates intention 6 (step 15).

$$seli(5)_{16}$$
$$addb(c, 5)_{17} \qquad (10)$$
$$crei((+c, \epsilon), 7)_{18}$$

The sixth cycle processes the perception, c.

$$seli(4)_{19}$$
$$act(e, 4)_{20} \qquad (11)$$

The seventh cycle selects intention 4 again and this time executes e.

$$seli(6)_{21}$$
$$seli(7)_{22} \qquad (12)$$

Finally intentions 6 and 7 are selected in turn. There is no processing to do in relation to them and they are removed.

The agent now has no intentions and execution stops until something new is perceived.

3.3 From Traces to Explanations: Why-Questions in GWENDOLEN

For answering a why-question, a trace is mapped to a chain of reasons (i.e., an explanation). Reasons thus represent a selection of directly connected trace events that might span over large parts of the trace. For example, the trace event of adopting a goal can be directly connected to the event of evaluating the guard of the plan whose body contained that goal, in between evaluating the guard and actually adopting the goal many other trace events could occur (e.g., the evaluations of guards for other plans).

In order to generate explanations we need to link each of the traced events to a local explanation as outlined particularly in [31] but also implied in [15]. To do this the explanation had to be grounded in the specific language, GWENDOLEN, under consideration but nevertheless could be fitted into a general framework.

We consider some event e occurring at step, N, in a trace t and assume, following [31], the existence of a language specific function why such that $why(e_N, t)$

returns some representation of an explanation. In our case we represent an explanation as a tree where each node represents a trace event and its children represent previous trace events that explain this one. This tree structures a subset of the trace events that appear in the trace.

Our focus on end users, however, means that explanations should have a default cut-off point and are not unwrapped further unless requested by the user. So we perform further processing on the tree in order to generate our explanations.

Figure 2 shows the algorithm for constructing an explanation tree for GWEN-DOLEN and Fig. 3 shows the algorithm for converting the tree into a text based explanation.

$why(e_N, \tau)$ can be read as "why did e occur at step N in trace τ" where e is one of our traced events. We can also ask why some formula is believed at step N, $why(b_N, \tau)$, and why some formula is a goal at step N, $why(!g_N, \tau)$.

Definition 1. *An explanation tree is a tree structure*

$$t ::= \mathbf{n_e}(e_N, [t, \ldots, t]) \mid \mathbf{n_e}(b_N, [t, \ldots, t]) \mid \mathbf{n_e}(!g_N, [t, \ldots, t]) \mid \mathbf{l_e}(e_N)$$

where e is a trace event, b is a belief formula, g is a goal formula and N is a step in a trace.

Leaves, $\mathbf{l_e}(e_N)$, can be considered as events that require no explanation (such as perceptions) or are to be expanded by a further "top level" question (e.g., "why did you believe that") and nodes, $\mathbf{n_e}(e_n, l)$ are an explanation for trace event e. In selecting the trace events to form part of the explanation tree we typically move backwards along the trace from N looking for an event of some particular kind. We introduce the notation $\uparrow_{N,\tau} S$ to represent this process where S is a set of event specifications. An event specification is either an event expression (with capital letters used Prolog-style to indicate variables to be instantiated when a matching event is found) or an event with some side condition – e.g., the event specification $selp((E, D), k) \mid e \in D$ matches a select plan event in intention, k, where e appears in the set of deeds, D, of the plan.

In Fig. 2 we see in equation (13) that an action is taken because some plan was selected that included the action in its deeds. An explanation tree node is constructed with one child – an explanation for why that plan was selected. Note that we need the select plan events to have operated on the same intention (and GWENDOLEN's intention selection mechanism means that other intentions may have been manipulated in between selecting a plan and performing the action) so we track the intention ID number, k, to ensure we are considering the events occurring in the correct intention.

(14) and (15) ask why something is believed at step N or is a goal at step N. In the first case the explanation is that a belief was added to the belief base at some previous step and, in the second case, that an achieve goal event was added to the top of some intention.

The reason an applicable plan is selected (16) is because the guard g was believed and *either* the BDI event e appeared when a new intention was created

$$why(act(a,k)_N, \tau) = \mathbf{n_e}(act(a,k)_N,$$
$$[why(\uparrow_{N,\tau}\{selp((E, Ds), k) \text{ s.t. } a \in Ds\}, \tau)]) \tag{13}$$
$$why(b_N, \tau) = \mathbf{n_e}(b_N, [why(\uparrow_{N,\tau}\{addb(+b, K)\}, \tau)]) \tag{14}$$
$$why(!g_N, \tau) = \mathbf{n_e}(!g_N, [why(\uparrow_{N,\tau}\{add((+!g, \epsilon), K)\}, \tau)]) \tag{15}$$

$$why(selp((e, ds), k)_N, \tau) = \mathbf{n_e}(selp((e, ds), k)_N,$$
$$[\mathbf{l_e}(\uparrow_{N,\tau}\{bel((e, ds), g, \theta, k)\}), why(e_\tau, \tau)])$$
$$\text{where} \quad e_\tau = \uparrow_{N,\tau}\{crei((E, \epsilon), k), add((E, \epsilon), k), addb(B, k)\} \tag{16}$$

$$why(addb(+b, k)_N, \tau) = \mathbf{n_e}(addb(+b, k)_N, [why(e_\tau, \tau)])$$
$$\text{where} \quad e_\tau = \uparrow_{N,\tau}\{crei((E, +b), k), selp((E, D), k) \mid +b \in D\} \tag{17}$$

$$why(add((+!g, \epsilon), k)_N, \tau) = \mathbf{n_e}(add((+!g, \epsilon), k)_N, [why(e_\tau, \tau)])$$
$$\text{where} \quad e_\tau = \uparrow_{N,\tau}\{crei((E, +!g), k), selp((E, D), k) \mid +!g \in D\} \tag{18}$$

$$why(crei((a, b), k)_N, \tau) = \begin{cases} \mathbf{l_e}(crei((a, b), k)_N) & a = \mathbf{start} \lor \\ & a = \mathbf{percept} \\ \mathbf{n_e}(crei((a, b), k)_N, [why(e_\tau, \tau)]) & b = \epsilon \end{cases}$$
$$\text{where} \quad e_\tau = \uparrow_{N,\tau}\{selp((E, D), K) \mid e \in D, crei((E, e), K)\} \tag{19}$$

Fig. 2. Generating explanation trees

(as happens when beliefs are posted in GWENDOLEN) *or e* was posted to the top of an intention (as happens when goals are posted in GWENDOLEN). We construct a node for the select plan event with two children, the guard event created when the plan's guard was evaluated (for which we do not generate an explanation, though one can be produced if the user wishes) and an explanation for the created intention or posted goal.

(17) and (18) ask why either a belief was added to the belief base or a goal was posted to the top of an intention, this is either because an intention was created to perform that deed (for instance in the case of an initial goal) or a plan was selected previously in the intention which included the posting of the belief or goal as a deed.

There are four reasons why an intention (a, b) may have been created (19): if a is **start** then b was an initial belief or goal, if a is **percept** then b is something perceived. In all other cases $b = \epsilon$ and a is the addition of a belief, and the intention was created either as part of processing an initial belief or percept (i.e., another create-intention event though this time with a on the left hand side) or because a plan was selected which included posting a new belief in its deed stack.

If we look at our running example then if we ask for an explanation for why e was performed in state 20. We get the following explanation tree:

$$\mathbf{n_e}(act(e,4)_{20}, [\mathbf{n_e}(selp((+b,+d;e),4)_{13},$$
$$[\mathbf{l_e}(bel((+b,+d;e),a,\emptyset,4)), \mathbf{n_e}(crei((+b,\epsilon),4)_9,$$
$$[\mathbf{n_e}(addb(b,3)_8, [\mathbf{l_e}(crei((\texttt{percept},+b),3)_5)])])])]) \quad (20)$$

Once we have successfully generated an explanation tree we need to process it into an explanation for presentation to end users. This involves deciding how far down the branches of the tree to progress as part of explanation generation. The algorithm for this is shown in Fig. 3.

In our presentation of explanations we introduce a function $describe(e)$ where e is a trace event, a belief formula or a goal formula. We don't present $describe(e)$ in full here since it may be application specific. In brief however, we first introduce a *predicate dictionary* for each application that provides a mapping of predicates to strings (e.g., 'state(X)' to 'the robot is in state X'). Second, an internal translation of specific programming symbols is used (e.g., '+!' to 'added the goal').

Key features of the explanation algorithm are that where an explanation involves the selection of a plan we do not always explain why the plan was selected, theoretically leaving the user to expand the explanation if they choose[6]. Secondly explanations never refer to manipulation of intentions (we consider these to be low level details of little interest to most users) so where new intentions are created we do not mention the fact just recursing through to the reason the intention was created (generally the perception of a belief of the posting of an initial goal).

Returning to our running example we generate the following explanation from our explanation tree:

e was executed because $+b : \{a\} \leftarrow +d; e$ was selected in state 13 because a was believed and b was added in state 8 because b was perceived in state 5.

Our framework is similar in conception and to that in [31] but our focus on end users has caused us to introduce the two step process of buildling an explanation tree structure and then using the *explain* and *describe* functions to present an explanation. That said the actual trace events identified as important to the explanation are generally in agreement with those identified by Winikoff, given our extension to multiple intentions.

Winikoff [31] also treats a number of other trace events—for instance where some deed is not the first to be executed in the body of a plan, then part of the explanation for its execution includes that the previous deeds were successful. We have taken the view that end users will not generally consider "and the parts

---

[6] It should be noted that our implementation does not yet enable such expansion of explanations.

$$explain(\mathbf{n_e}(act(a,k)_N,[e]) = describe(a) \text{ was executed because } explain(e) \quad (21)$$

$$explain(\mathbf{n_e}(b_N,[e])) =$$
$$describe(b) \text{ was believed in state } N \text{ because } explain(e) \quad (22)$$

$$explain(\mathbf{n_e}(!g_N,[e])) =$$
$$describe(g) \text{ was a goal in state } N \text{ because } explain(e) \quad (23)$$

$$explain(\mathbf{n_e}(selp((e,ds),k)_N,[\mathbf{l_e}(g'_N),e])) =$$
$$describe((e,ds)) \text{ was selected in state } N \text{ because}$$
$$describe(g) \text{ and } explain(e) \quad (24)$$

$$explain(\mathbf{n_e}(add((+b,\epsilon),k)_N,[crei((e,ds),k)_{N'}]) =$$
$$describe(+b) \text{ was added in state } N \text{ because } explain(crei((e,ds),k)_{N'})) \quad (25)$$

$$explain(\mathbf{n_e}(add((+b,\epsilon),k)_N,[selp((e,ds),k)'_N]) =$$
$$describe(+b) \text{ was added in state } N \text{ because}$$
$$describe(selp((e,ds),k)) \text{ was selected in state } N' \quad (26)$$

$$explain(\mathbf{n_e}(addb((+b,\epsilon),k)_N,[]) =$$
$$\text{the belief } describe(b) \text{ was added upon starting the agent} \quad (27)$$

$$explain(\mathbf{n_e}(add((+!g,\epsilon),k)_N,[crei((e,ds),k)_{N'}]) =$$
$$describe(+!g) \text{ was posted in state } N \text{ because } explain(crei((e,ds),k)_{N'})) \quad (28)$$

$$explain(\mathbf{n_e}(add((+!g,\epsilon),k)_N,[selp((e,ds),k)'_N]) =$$
$$describe(+!g) \text{ was posted in state } N \text{ because}$$
$$describe(selp((e,ds),k)) \text{ was selected in state } N' \quad (29)$$

$$explain(\mathbf{l_e}(crei(\mathbf{percept},+b)_N)) = describe(+b) \text{ was perceived in state } N \quad (30)$$

$$explain(\mathbf{l_e}(crei(\mathbf{start},+!g)_N)) = describe(+!g) \text{ was an initial goal} \quad (31)$$

$$explain(\mathbf{n_e}(crei((c,c),k)_N),[e]) = explain(e) \quad (32)$$

Fig. 3. Generating explanations from an explanation tree

of the plan before this succeeded" as part of an explanation, though we may well need to incorporate aspects of this when we look at why-not-questions (i.e., something may not have happened because a previous deed failed). In general, our treatment extends that of Winikoff [31] to multiple intentions but does not yet consider why-not questions.

3.4 Implementation

The AIL is implemented in Java. Therefore we were able to create an abstract class for events and a framework for storing and presenting visualisations based on the work in [17]. We were then able to create specific event types for the events of interest. We extended the visualiser with an interface to allow why-questions to be asked—specifically "why did you perform this action?", "why did you hold this belief?" and "why did you have this goal?".

We then constructed a specific explanation mechanism for the GWENDOLEN language based on the algorithms in Figs. 2 and 3.

We also implemented a pretty printing mechanism which utilised the *describe* mechanism to print out traces for user inspection.

This gave us a flexible and extensible framework for implementing omniscient debugging in order to enable why-questions in AIL languages.

4 Test Examples and Evaluation

Our current implementation is a prototype only so a full evaluation has yet to be undertaken. However, it is possible to present initial results.

4.1 Traces in GWENDOLEN for Tutorial Examples

The AIL comes with an extensive set of examples based on tutorials for the framework, the GWENDOLEN language, and the AJPF model-checker [9]. We used these as an ongoing driver for development of our framework—in particular to help settle on appropriate pretty printing conventions. Figure 4 shows part of a pretty printed version of the event trace for one of these examples as it is constructed[7]. The visualiser for traces is shown in Fig. 5. The trace is read from left to right with specifics of various trace events shown on the left.

Figure 6 shows an example explanation (for why the robot performed the action lift_rubble).

4.2 Potential Use Case: Self-certifying Offshore Assets

In order to validate our intuitions about appropriate explanations for end users we investigated a prototype agent program for surveying offshore assets such as oil rigs and wind farms [11, 12]. This agent guides an unmanned aircraft that must

---

[7] It is generally accepted that end users prefer natural language presentations while developers often prefer something more compact so this log presents the events with end users in mind, though it remains much more verbose than is required for an explanation.

```
selected Intention 1: add the goal achieve "the robot is holding rubble".
confirmed Intention 1: add the goal achieve "the robot is holding rubble"
can still be processed.
generated 1 applicable plan(s): continue processing: add the goal achieve
"the robot is holding rubble" for an event.
selected continue processing: add the goal achieve "the robot is holding rubble".
added achieve "the robot is holding rubble" to the agent's goals.
modified intention by posting an event to become Intention 1: respond to the
event added the goal achieve "the robot is holding rubble" which has no plan
yet THEN add the goal achieve "the robot is holding rubble".
selected Intention 1: respond to the event added the goal achieve "the robot is
holding rubble" which has no plan yet THEN add the goal achieve "the robot is
holding rubble".
```

Fig. 4. A pretty printed event trace for a GWENDOLEN program

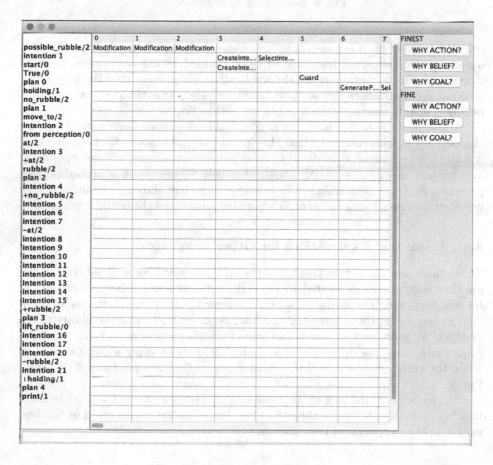

Fig. 5. Trace visualiser

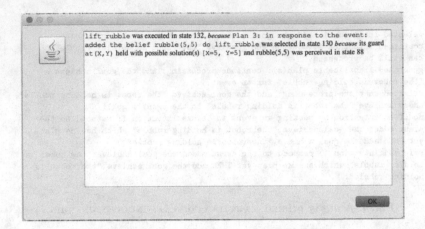

Fig. 6. Generating an explanation

select a suitable path between the legs of an oil rig based on wind speed, wind direction, and perceived tolerance to risks. Guided by the developers, we produced a predicate dictionary for the application which converted the program's internal representation into natural language—e.g., `enactRoute(route2, t2)` becomes `enact route2 with target t2` and so on.

A sample explanation is shown in Fig. 7. These explanations were shown to the developers who confirmed that they provided explanations likely to prove of use to their end users (considered to be experts in unmanned aircraft operation and offshore asset inspection), though obviously further work is needed on the presentation (e.g., performing unifications rather than showing the unifier) and possibly further refining the *explain* algorithm to shorten the initial explanation.

4.3   Traces and Explanations for Other Languages

To evaluate our claim that tracing in the AIL is generic we enabled tracing for another language implemented in the AIL, without any further customisation for the language. The language selected was `pbdi` [4], a reimplementation of a BDI library for Python[8] intended to allow agents written using the library to be verified. We generated an omniscient trace for a simple program in this language (one which stops the operation of a small Pi2Go robot using a command done when the switch on the side of the robot is pressed). A sample trace is shown in Fig. 8.

As can be seen, the lack of language specific pretty printing for plans renders this less readable, but nevertheless a clear trace has been generated of the key events in the execution of the program.

---

[8] https://github.com/VerifiableAutonomy/BDIPython.

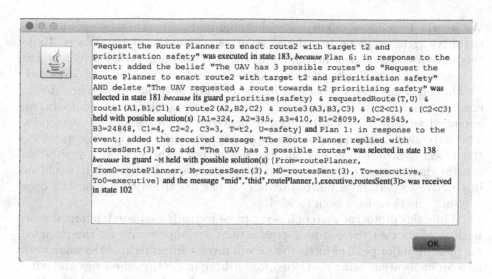

Fig. 7. Explanation of route selection

```
added obstacle_left to the agent's beliefs.
added switch_pressed to the agent's beliefs.
evaluating the guard of 1 :: +!_aAny||True||done||[]
1 :: +!_aAny||switch_pressed||print("Stopping Agent")||[]
 resulted in True.
evaluating the guard of 2 :: +!_aAny||True||print("Obstacle: ",
 agent.sensor_value("obstacle_centre"))||[] resulted in True.
selected 1 :: +!_aAny||True||done||[]
1 :: +!_aAny||switch_pressed||print("Stopping Agent")||[] .
created [empty]::
   * +state||True||print("Stopping Agent")||[]
     +state||True||done||[] .
selected [empty]::
   * +state||True||print("Stopping Agent")||[]
     +state||True||done||[] .
Stopping Agent
performed print("Stopping Agent").
performed done.
removed obstacle_left from the agent's beliefs.
removed switch_pressed from the agent's beliefs.
```

Fig. 8. A sample trace for *BDIPython*

5   Conclusion

We sought to combine omniscient debugging and answering why-questions for cognitive agent programs in order to generate explanations for end users. To do this we ported omniscient debugging to the AIL toolkit and thus demonstrated its general applicability beyond the GOAL language for which it was developed.

On top of the traces generated by the omniscient debugger we were able to construct explanations for programs in the GWENDOLEN language. To do this we extended work by [15] and [31] aimed at answering why-questions for developers. This extension involved adding the capability to handle multiple intentions via the tracking of intention IDs and the use of pretty printing and application specific dictionaries to render explanations into natural language. It would be instructive to perform a full comparison of our algorithm to that in [31] once why-not questions have been tackled.

While this prototype system has yet to be formally evaluated, informal feedback suggests that the end user explanations are appropriate for the intended purpose. A major piece of further work will involve integration of the framework into an application being developed for offshore inspection of oil rigs and wind farms [11,12] and the evaluation of the generated explanations by the application's users. Work is also needed to integrate the answering of why-not-questions into the framework in order to provide *constrastive explanations* as discussed in [18] which argues that why-questions answer counter-factuals.

Work is needed to improve the presentation of traces and explanations and to allow the expansion of explanations if the user wishes to explore further back in a trace. We would also like to investigate the use of tracing/explanation levels analogous to the logging levels used by Java in order to increase the flexibility of the provided explanations allowing users to "drill down" into more detail if the provided explanation does not meet their needs or alternatively to move outward to a presentation similiar to the goal heirarchies used in [13] and [32].

Open Data. The source code for the AIL is available from http://mcapl. sourceforge.net where the work in this paper can be found in the `omniscient` branch of the git repository. The specific examples discussed in the paper can be found in the University of Liverpool Data Catalgue DOI: https://doi.org/10. 17638/datacat.liverpool.ac.uk/751

Acknowledgments. This research was partially funded by EPSRC grants Verifiable Autonomy (EP/LO24845/1) and the Offshore Robotics for Certification of Assets (EP/RO26173) Robotics and Artificial Intelligence Hub.

References

1. Bordini, R.H., Hübner, J.F., Wooldridge, M.: Programming Multi-agent Systems in AgentSpeak Using Jason. Wiley, Hoboken (2007)

2. Bordini, R.H., Dastani, M., Dix, J., El Fallah-Seghrouchni, A. (eds.): Multi-Agent Programming: Languages, Platforms and Applications. Springer, Heidelberg (2005). https://doi.org/10.1007/b137449

3. Bratman, M.E.: Intentions, Plans, and Practical Reason. Harvard University Press, Cambridge (1987)

4. Bremner, P., Dennis, L.A., Fisher, M., Winfiled, A.F.: On proactive, transparent and verifiable ethical reasoning for robots. In: Proceedings of the IEEE special issue on Machine Ethics: The Design and Governance of Ethical AI and Autonomous Systems (2019, to appear)

5. Charisi, V., et al.: Towards moral autonomous systems. CoRR abs/1703.04741 (2017). http://arxiv.org/abs/1703.04741

6. Dastani, M., van Riemsdijk, M.B., Meyer, J.J.C.: Programming multi-agent systems in 3APL. In: [2], chap. 2, pp. 39–67

7. Dennis, L., Fisher, M., Webster, M., Bordini, R.: Model checking agent programming languages. Autom. Softw. Eng. **19**, 1–59 (2011). https://doi.org/10.1007/s10515-011-0088-x

8. Dennis, L.A.: Gwendolen semantics: 2017. Technical report ULCS-17-001, University of Liverpool, Department of Computer Science (2017)

9. Dennis, L.A.: The MCAPL framework including the agent infrastructure layer and agent java pathfinder. J. Open Source Softw. **3**(24), 617 (2018)

10. Dennis, L.A., Farwer, B., Bordini, R.H., Fisher, M., Wooldridge, M.: A common semantic basis for BDI languages. In: Dastani, M., El Fallah Seghrouchni, A., Ricci, A., Winikoff, M. (eds.) ProMAS 2007. LNCS (LNAI), vol. 4908, pp. 124–139. Springer, Heidelberg (2008). https://doi.org/10.1007/978-3-540-79043-3_8

11. Dinmohammadi, F., et al.: Certification of safe and trusted robotic inspection of assets. In: 2018 Prognostics and System Health Management Conference (PHM-Chongqing), pp. 276–284, October 2018

12. Fisher, M., et al.: Verifiable self-certifying autonomous systems. In: 2018 IEEE International Symposium on Software Reliability Engineering Workshops (ISSREW), pp. 341–348, October 2018

13. Harbers, M.: Explaining agent behaviour in virtual training. Ph.D. thesis, SIKS Dissertation Series (2011). no. 2011–35

14. Hindriks, K.V.: Programming rational agents in GOAL. In: El Fallah Seghrouchni, A., Dix, J., Dastani, M., Bordini, R.H. (eds.) Multi-Agent Programming, pp. 119–157. Springer, Boston (2009). https://doi.org/10.1007/978-0-387-89299-3_4

15. Hindriks, K.V.: Debugging is explaining. In: Rahwan, I., Wobcke, W., Sen, S., Sugawara, T. (eds.) PRIMA 2012. LNCS (LNAI), vol. 7455, pp. 31–45. Springer, Heidelberg (2012). https://doi.org/10.1007/978-3-642-32729-2_3

16. Ko, A.J., Myers, B.A.: Extracting and answering why and why not questions about Java program output. ACM Trans. Softw. Eng. Methodol. **20**(2), 4:1–4:36 (2010)

17. Koeman, V.J., Hindriks, K.V., Jonker, C.M.: Omniscient debugging for cognitive agent programs. In: Proceedings of the 26th International Joint Conference on Artificial Intelligence, IJCAI 2017, pp. 265–272. AAAI Press (2017)

18. Miller, T.: Explanation in artificial intelligence: insights from the social sciences. Artif. Intell. **267**, 1–38 (2017)

19. Pokahr, A., Braubach, L., Lamersdorf, W.: Jadex: a BDI reasoning engine. In: [2], pp. 149–174

20. Rao, A.S., Georgeff, M.P.: Modeling agents within a BDI-architecture. In: Proceedings of 2nd International Conference on Principles of Knowledge Representation and Reasoning (KR&R), pp. 473–484. Morgan Kaufmann (1991)

21. Rao, A.S., Georgeff, M.P.: An abstract architecture for rational agents. In: Proceedings of International Conference on Knowledge Representation and Reasoning (KR&R), pp. 439–449. Morgan Kaufmann (1992)

22. Rao, A.S., Georgeff, M.P.: BDI agents: from theory to practice. In: Proceedings of 1st International Conference on Multi-Agent Systems (ICMAS), San Francisco, USA, pp. 312–319 (1995)

23. Rao, A.S.: AgentSpeak(L): BDI agents speak out in a logical computable language. In: Van de Velde, W., Perram, J.W. (eds.) MAAMAW 1996. LNCS, vol. 1038, pp. 42–55. Springer, Heidelberg (1996). https://doi.org/10.1007/BFb0031845

24. Sheh, R.K.: "Why did you do that?" Explainable intelligent robots. In: AAAI-17 Workshop on Human-Aware Artificial Intelligence (2017)

25. The IEEE global initiative on ethics of autonomous and intelligent systems: ethically aligned design: a vision for prioritizing human well-being with autonomous and intelligent systems. version 2. Report. IEEE (2017)

26. Turner, J.: Robot Rules: Regulating Artificial Intelligence. Palgrave Macmillan, London (2019)

27. Webster, M., Fisher, M., Cameron, N., Jump, M.: Formal methods for the certification of autonomous unmanned aircraft systems. In: Flammini, F., Bologna, S., Vittorini, V. (eds.) SAFECOMP 2011. LNCS, vol. 6894, pp. 228–242. Springer, Heidelberg (2011). https://doi.org/10.1007/978-3-642-24270-0_17

28. Wei, C., Hindriks, K.V.: An agent-based cognitive robot architecture. In: Dastani, M., Hübner, J.F., Logan, B. (eds.) ProMAS 2012. LNCS (LNAI), vol. 7837, pp. 54–71. Springer, Heidelberg (2013). https://doi.org/10.1007/978-3-642-38700-5_4

29. Winikoff, M., Cranefield, S.: On the testability of BDI agent systems. J. Artif. Intell. Res. **51**, 71–131 (2015)

30. Winikoff, M.: BDI agent testability revisited. Auton. Agents Multi-agent Syst. **31**(1094), 1094–1132 (2017). https://doi.org/10.1007/s10458-016-9356-2

31. Winikoff, M.: Debugging agent programs with Why? questions. In: Proceedings of the 16th Conference on Autonomous Agents and MultiAgent Systems, AAMAS 2017, pp. 251–259. International Foundation for Autonomous Agents and Multiagent Systems, Richland (2017)

32. Winikoff, M., Dignum, V., Dignum, F.: Why bad coffee? Explaining agent plans with valuings. In: Gallina, B., Skavhaug, A., Schoitsch, E., Bitsch, F. (eds.) SAFECOMP 2018. LNCS, vol. 11094, pp. 521–534. Springer, Cham (2018). https://doi.org/10.1007/978-3-319-99229-7_47

33. Wooldridge, M.: An Introduction to Multiagent Systems. Wiley, Hoboken (2002)

34. Wooldridge, M., Rao, A. (eds.): Foundations of Rational Agency. Applied Logic Series. Kluwer Academic Publishers, Berlin (1999)

35. Wortham, R.H., Theodorou, A.: Robot transparency, trust and utility. Connect. Sci. **29**(3), 24200247 (2017)

36. Ziafati, P., Dastani, M., Meyer, J.-J., van der Torre, L.: Agent programming languages requirements for programming autonomous robots. In: Dastani, M., Hübner, J.F., Logan, B. (eds.) ProMAS 2012. LNCS (LNAI), vol. 7837, pp. 35–53. Springer, Heidelberg (2013). https://doi.org/10.1007/978-3-642-38700-5_3

Learning and Reconfiguration

From Programming Agents to *Educating* Agents – A Jason-Based Framework for Integrating Learning in the Development of Cognitive Agents

Michael Bosello[iD] and Alessandro Ricci[✉][iD]

Department of Computer Science and Engineering,
Alma Mater Studiorum – Università di Bologna, Cesena Campus, Cesena, Italy
michael.bosello@studio.unibo.it, a.ricci@unibo.it

Abstract. Recent advances and successes of machine learning techniques are paving the way to what is referred as *Software 2.0 era* and *cognitive computing*, in which traditional programming and software development is meant to be replaced by such techniques for many applications. If we consider agent-oriented programming, we believe that such developments trigger new interesting scenarios blending cognitive architecture such as the BDI one and techniques like Reinforcement Learning (RL) even more deeply compared to what has been proposed so far in the literature. In that perspective, we aim at exploring the integration of cognitive agent-oriented programming based on BDI with learning techniques so as to systematically exploit them in the agent development stage. The approach should support the design of BDI agents in which some plans can be explicitly programmed and others instead can be learned by the agent during the development/engineering stage. In that view, the development of an agent is metaphorically similar to an *education process*, in which first an agent is created with a set of basic programmed plans and then grow up in order to learn plans to achieve the goals for which the agent is meant to be designed. This paper presents and discusses this medium-term view, introducing a first model for a BDI agent programming framework integrating RL, a first implementation based on Jason programming language/platform and sketching a roadmap for this research line.

1 Introduction

Machine learning and cognitive computing techniques have been getting a momentum in recent years, thanks to several factors, including theoretical developments in contexts such as (deep) neural networks, reinforcement learning, Bayesian networks, the availability of big data and the availability of more and more powerful parallel computing machinery (GPU, cloud) [3, 13, 14, 17]. Their deeper and deeper impact in real-world applications is celebrating a new "AI Spring" era, which is generating a strong debate in the literature as well [22]. Actually, the impact is not only about the kind of applications but also about *how applications are programmed and engineered*. In particular, a vision of *Software 2.0* era is emerging [18], in which traditional programming and software development is meant to be more and more replaced by e.g. machine learning and cognitive computing techniques, towards the "the end of programming" era [17, 32].

ⓒ Springer Nature Switzerland AG 2020
L. A. Dennis et al. (Eds.): EMAS 2019, LNAI 12058, pp. 175–194, 2020.
https://doi.org/10.1007/978-3-030-51417-4_9

Besides the hype and the marketing-oriented claims, if we consider *agent-oriented programming* [27], and – more generally – multi-agent systems (MAS) engineering, we believe that such recent developments would trigger new interesting scenarios blending cognitive architectures such as the BDI one [24] and techniques like Reinforcement Learning (RL) [30] even more deeply than what has been already proposed so far in literature. As far as authors' knowledge, existing research integrating BDI-based agents and MAS with learning techniques mainly focused on improving agent adaptation, exploiting learning to improve e.g. plan or action selection at runtime. As a further approach, our objective is to explore the integration of cognitive agent-oriented programming based on BDI with learning techniques so as to systematically exploit them in the agent development stage. The basic idea is that an agent developer could integrate the explicit programming of plans – when developing a BDI agent – with the possibility that, for some goals, it would be the agent itself to learn the plans to achieve them, by exploiting reinforcement learning based techniques. This is not only for a specific ad hoc problem, but as a general feature of the agent platform.

In that view, the development of an agent is metaphorically similar to an *education process*, in which first an agent is created with a set of basic programmed plans and then *grow up* in order to learn plans to achieve the goals for which the agent is meant to be designed. We believe that this vision would trigger interesting research directions about the evolution of agent-oriented programming in the *software 2.0 era*. In the remainder of the paper, we present and discuss this view, with a first proof-of-concept framework based on the Jason agent platform [7,8].

After giving a background and an account about related works (Sect. 2), we first describe our approach integrating learning in the loop of BDI agent programming, using AgentSpeak(L) [23] as reference model (Sect. 3). Then, we describe an implementation of the framework on top of the Jason agent language/platform (Sect. 4), including some testing using a simple example and a discussion (Sect. 5). We close the paper sketching a roadmap for this research line (Sect. 6).

2   Background and Related Work

In this section, we first provide an overview about basic concepts of Reinforcement Learning (RL) – taking [30] as main reference – and then an account of existing research works in the context of agent-oriented programming – especially focusing on BDI-based model [24] – proposing an integration with RL. It is worth remarking that in this setting we do not intend to consider the latest advances in RL, but just the core foundational layer useful to present and discuss our approach.

2.1   Reinforcement Learning

Reinforcement Learning (RL) is a machine learning method with the key idea that a goal-oriented agent learns how to fulfill a task by interacting with its environment. Any problem of learning *goal-directed* behavior can be reduced to three signals passing back and forth between an agent and its environment: one signal to represent the choices made by the agent (the *actions*), one signal to describe the basis on which the choices are made (the *states*), and one signal to define the agent's goal (the *rewards*). A state is defined as whatever information is available to the agent about its environment, some of what makes up a state could be based on the memory of past perceptions or even be entirely mental or subjective, i.e. the states can be anything we can know that might be useful in the decision process. The agent must decide what action to take as a function of whatever state signal is available. The actions too might be either internal – changing the agent's mental state – or external – affecting the environment. For example, some actions might control what an agent chooses to think about, or where it focuses its attention. The reward is a single real number obtained at each interaction step that the agent seeks to maximise *over time*. The reward signal thus defines what the good and bad events for the agent are, i.e. it is your way of communicating to the agent what it must achieve.

We refer to each successive stages of interaction between the agent and the environment as *time steps*. In the case of a BDI agent, a reasoning cycle can be pretty assumed as a step. In some applications, there is a natural notion of final time step, that is, when the agent-environment interaction breaks naturally into subsequences that are referred as *episodes*. Related to BDI, this is the case of agents pursuing *achievement goals*. In many cases, the agent-environment interaction does not break naturally into identifiable episodes but goes on continually without limit—these are called *continuing tasks*—i.e., *maintenance goals* in the BDI case.

The agent learns a *policy* as a result of the learning process. A policy is a function that maps states to actions. we seek to learn and exploit an optimal policy, but we need to behave non-optimally to explore all the possibilities. A classic method to balance the *exploitation* and *exploration* phases is to use an ε-greedy policy with which the agent behaves greedily but there is a (small) ε probability to select a random action.

In many cases of interest, the agent has only *partial* information about the state of the world, so, the states signal is replaced by an *observations signal* that depend on the environment state but provide only partial information about it. In the BDI case, this is directly modelled by percepts and, therefore, by beliefs about the environment. The fundamental property of a state, known as the Markov property, is that it can be used to predict the future. A stochastic process has the Markov property if the conditional probability distribution of future states depends only upon the current state, not on the sequence of events that preceded it. From the observations, the agent recovers an approximate state i.e., a state that may not be Markov. Actually, we can partially drop the Markov property; however, this implies that long-term prediction performance can degrade dramatically. An approximate state will play the same role in RL algorithms as before, so we simply continue to call it a state.

2.2 Integrating RL into BDI Agents and AOP

Generally speaking, the integration of learning capabilities has been a main research topic in agents and MAS literature since their roots [33]. A first work providing preliminary results about integrating learning in BDI multi-agent systems is [15], proposing an extension of the BDI architecture to endow agents with learning skills, based on induction of logical decision trees. Learning, in that case, is about plan failures, that an agent should reconsider after its experience.

Other works in literature exploits RL to improve plan/action selection capability in BDI agent, making them more adaptive [2,28,29]. In [21] an extension of BDI is proposed so as to get a model of decision making by exploiting the ability to learn to recognise situations and select the appropriate plan based upon this.

In [4,5], Jason is used to realise Temporal Difference (TD) and SARSA, two reinforcement learning methods, in order to face the RL problem with a more appropriate paradigm which has been remarkably effective. [31] proposes a hybrid framework that integrates BDI and TD-FALCON, a neural network based reinforcement learner. BDI-FALCON architecture extends the low-level RL agent with a desire and intention modules. In this way, the agent has explicit goals in the desire module instead of relying on an external signal, enhancing the agent with a higher level of self-awareness. The intention module and its plan library permit to reason about a course of actions instead of individual reactive responses. If there isn't a plan for a situation, the agent performs the steps suggested by the FALCON module and, if the sequence succeeds, a new plan is created with indications about the starting state, the goal state, and the actions sequence. When the agent uses a plan, it updates the confidence of the plan according to the outcome.

Also in [16] a hybrid approach BDI-FALCON is proposed. Here, the focus is on the abstraction level: BDI provides a high-level knowledge representation but lacks learning capabilities, meanwhile low-level RL agents are more adept at learning. The layered proposal wants to retain both advantages. An alternative vision is provided in [12], where a policy is learned and then is used to generate a BDI agent.

Compared to this literature, in this paper we consider the problem of extending BDI agents with RL from a slightly different perspective, more focused on programming and the software 2.0 vision, that is: how learning – reinforcement learning, in this case – could be exploited by a developer in the process of developing an agent, so as to integrate plans explicitly written by the agent programmer with plans designed to be learnt.

3   The Basic Idea

The simple idea of this paper is to extend the BDI agent development process with a learning stage in which we can specify plans in the plan library whose body is not meant to be explicitly programmed but learned, using a learning by experience technique. In so doing, the development of an agent accounts for: (i) explicitly programming plans as in the traditional way—we will refer to them as *hard plans*[1]; and (ii) implicitly defining plans by allowing the agent itself to learn them by experience—referenced as *soft* plans. Soft plans are meant to become part of the plan library like hard plans and can be selected and used at runtime – in terms of instantiated intentions – without any difference (but allowing for *continuous learning*, if wanted). At runtime, soft and hard plans are treated in a uniform way: intentions are created to carry on plan execution, hard plans could trigger the execution of soft plans and vice versa.

With soft plans we obtain a notion of *learning module*, that is, a soft plan is like a module that defines the boundaries of a learned behavior. A learning module can be

---

[1] *hard* in this case stands for *hard-coded*.

replaced without affecting the rest of the agent. It can be *reused* in other agents and for other tasks as happens with standard hard plans. It can be *tested* at the unit level and in a natural way with the support of the BDI abstractions.

To support the learning stage, we would need to run the agent in a proper environment supporting this learning by experience, like the simulated environments typically used in RL scenarios. Besides, before deploying the agent, there could be some *assessment* of the soft plans, eventually using an assessment environment which could be different from the one used for training. The assessment is actually very similar to a traditional validation stage, including tests that consider the soft plans and their integration with hard plans. If the agent overcomes the assessment, it can be deployed—otherwise, the process goes back to the learning stage, possibly changing also plans in the hard part.

Given this general idea, in the remainder of the section we first introduce the model integrating key concepts of RL into a BDI framework, and then we describe an extension of the BDI reasoning cycle supporting the learning process. We will use AgentSpeak(L) [24] and Jason [7] as concrete abstract and practical BDI-based languages—nevertheless, we believe that the core idea is largely independent of the specific BDI agent programming language or framework adopted.

To exemplify the approach, we will use the simple gridworld example (p. 80, [30]), in which an agent is located into a bi-dimensional grid environment, where it has to reach some destination cells without knowing in advance the best path for doing it.

3.1 A First Model

In devising the model, we aim at abstracting from the specific RL algorithm that can be used. To that purpose, we consider key common RL concepts – observations, actions, rewards, episodes – and how they are represented into a BDI setting (see Fig. 1, top). These concepts are used by a component – referred as *RL reasoner* – extending the BDI reasoner (interpreter) (see Fig. 1, bottom). The classic BDI reasoner handles the hard plans – i.e., with a body – and the RL reasoner handles the soft plans—whose behavior is learned.

Observations are modeled as a subset of the agent beliefs that will be used by the particular algorithm to construct the state, including those that are necessary to understand when a goal is achieved. Recall that the observations are a generalization of states and if we want to represent a Markov state we just need to include all its aspects as observations. In the gridworld case, for instance, the agent must reach a specific position moving towards four directions. In this case, the observations include the current position of the agent (pos(X, Y)) and a belief about having reached the target (finish_line)—if this belief is missing, it means that the agent has not achieved the target in the current state.

The *action set* can contain both primitive actions (a BDI agent action) and compound actions (a BDI agent plan) so that representing different levels of planning granularity. To have a common representation for both cases, we represent actions as plans, i.e. the set of actions selectable by the RL reasoner is a subset of the plan library defined by the plans which are relevant for the goal and applicable in the current context. In Fig. 1, these plans are still referred as *Actions* in the plan library, and as *Behavior* (i.e.,

RL	Proposed BDI+ construct	Representation in BDI
Observations	Belief about Learning	Belief subset
Actions	Actions	Relevant Plans
Rewards	Motivational Rule	Belief Rule
Episode	Terminal Rule	Belief Rule
Policy	Learning Module	Plan
Behavior	Behavior	Intention

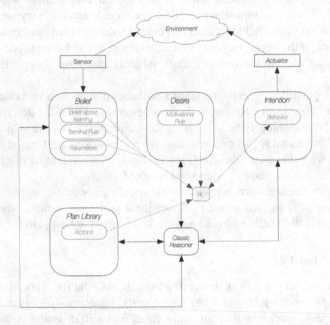

Fig. 1. (Top) The mapping between RL concepts and their counterpart in the BDI model. (Bottom) A graphic representation of the BDI model with the addition of our constructs.

the learned policy) when instantiated at runtime, wrapped into an intention. In the grid-world example, the action set has one parametric plan to move the agent in one direction: !move(D), where D could be up, down, left, right.

Rewards are represented by rules reflecting agent desires—we call them *Motivational Rules*. These rules make it possible to weight the current situation of an agent according to some goal to be achieved. We can see these rules as the generators of internal stimuli in the agent like a reward signal in neuroscience, which is a signal internal to the brain that influences decision making and learning. The signal might be triggered by the external environment, but it can also be triggered by things that do not exist outside the agent and which can be represented as beliefs as well. We move the reward, that in RL comes from the environment, into the agent. This is crucial to separate the agent desires from the environment so as to allow an agent to define its own goals and rewards about them.

In the AgentSpeak(L)/Jason model that will be detailed in next section, we can represent Motivational Rules as Prolog-like rules in the belief base:

```
reward(Goal, Reward) :- < some condition over the belief base >
```

In the gridworld example, the motivational rule will give a positive reward when the finish line is reached (while pursuing a reach_end goal) and a negative reward in other steps.

```
reward(reach_end, 10) :- finish_line.
reward(reach_end, -1) :- not finish_line.
```

It is worth remarking that Motivational Rules are meant to model also the reward signal that comes from the environment, as in the classic view. In this case the reward can be seen more like suggestion coming from a teacher (or a coach) which is assisting the agent during the learning/training process. The teacher conceptually knows both the goal of the agent and the structure of the (task) environment. Since the agent has the objective of learning how to achieve the goal, it is part of its motivation to follow the suggestions given by its teacher/coach.

Finally, we must include a notion of *episode*. An episode is an event or a group of events occurring as part of a sequence. Like in the case of rewards, we can assume that the agent designer may have her vision about how to define episodes, starting from a relevant ensemble of situations. This condition is well established by a rule that asserts in which belief state a coherent group of events ends up in an episode i.e., it defines when the task ends, regardless of whether the agent accomplishes or fails the goal. We refer to this rule as a *Terminal Rule*:

```
episode_end(Goal) :- < some condition over the belief base >
```

In the gridworld example, the episode for achieving a reach_end goal ends when the finish line is reached:

```
episode_end(reach_end) :- finish_line.
```

It is worth noting that this approach could be applied only in the case of achievement goals. In the case of maintenance goals (*continuing tasks* in [30]) we would need to reconsider how an episode is modeled.

3.2 Extending the Reasoning Cycle

In our framework, a BDI agent is then equipped with general-purpose learning capabilities that are triggered as soon as a soft plan must be learned or adapted, for some goal. Figure 1 shows the pseudo-code of a classic BDI agent reasoning cycle (as defined in [8,35]) extended with such learning capabilities. This pseudo-code does not depend on a specific RL algorithm, which is encapsulated inside a separate module – referenced in the following as *learning strategy module* – whose methods are called by the reasoning cycle.

The beginning (lines 1–8) and the end (lines 22–36) of the reasoning cycle have not been modified. We briefly recall those parts, please refer to [8,35] for more details. At the beginning of the reasoning cycle, the agent reviews its beliefs, desires, and intentions according to the new perception from the environment. At the end of the plan cycle, after

Algorithm 1. BDI practical reasoning extended with RL, in pseudo-code.

```
 1: B ← B'                                                    ▷ B' are the initial beliefs
 2: I ← I'                                                    ▷ I' are the initial intentions
 3: loop
 4:     ρ ← GETNEXTPERCEPT
 5:     B ← BRF(B, ρ)                                         ▷ Belief Revision Function
 6:     D ← OPTIONS(B, I)
 7:     I ← FILTER(B, D, I)
 8:     π ← PLAN(B, I, Ac)                               ▷ Ac is the set of available actions
 9:     if SOFTPLAN(π) ∧ LEARNING(π, B) then
10:         A ← INITEPISODE(π, B, I)
11:     end if
              ((SOFTPLAN(π) ∧ LEARNING(π, B) ∧ ¬EPISODEFINISHED(π, B, I))
                ∨ (SOFTPLAN(π) ∧ ¬LEARNING(π, B))
12:     while                                                                              do
                ∨ (¬SOFTPLAN(π) ∧ ¬EMPTY(π)))
              ∧¬((SUCCEEDED(I, B) ∨ IMPOSSIBLE(I, B)))
13:         if ISSOFTPLAN(π) then
14:             if LEARNING(π, B) ∧ ¬EPISODEFINISHED(π, B, I) then
15:                 EXECUTE(A)
16:                 A ← DOLEARNSTEP(π, B, I, A)
17:             else
18:                 A ← CHOOSELEARNTACTION(π, B, I)
19:                 EXECUTE(A)
20:             end if
21:         else
22:             A ← HEAD(π)
23:             EXECUTE(A)
24:             π ← TAIL(π)
25:         end if
26:         ρ ← GETNEXTPERCEPT
27:         B ← BRF(B, ρ)
28:         if RECONSIDER(I, B) then
29:             D ← OPTIONS(B, I)
30:             I ← FILTER(B, D, I)
31:         end if
32:         if ¬SOUND(π, I, B) then
33:             π ← PLAN(B, I, Ac)
34:         end if
35:     end while
36: end loop
```

each action execution, the agent acquires a new percept and uses the new knowledge to reconsider its desires, intentions, and the plan itself.

In the standard cycle, the function *plan* (line 8) generates a plan to achieve the intention I. In our extension, the plan could be either a soft plan or a hard plan. If it is a soft plan and we are in the learning stage, then a new learning episode is initialized (line 10), producing the initial action to be executed. The initialization of the episode depends on the specific learning strategy adopted.

The execution loop condition remains the same for the hard plans (continue until the plan is empty or it succeeds or fails). Instead, a soft plan (in the learning stage) continues until the learning episode finishes – i.e., a terminal state is met. A soft plan in the exploitation stage continues to produce new actions until the intention succeeds or becomes impossible to reach. Inside the loop, in the case of a soft plan in the learning stage, the currently selected action is executed (line 15). and then a learning step is performed (line 16) which also returns the next action to be executed. The learning step depends on the specific learning strategy adopted. If we are not in the learning stage but instead we are in the exploitation stage, the soft plan is used almost like a hard plan: the soft plan is used to decide which action to do (line 18) and the action is executed (line 19). In the case of a hard plan, the action is retrieved from the plan and executed as in the original cycle (lines 22–24).

We must stress that learning and exploitation are two distinct phases at different times. At first, the developer needs to design a teaching stage performed in a simulated environment in which the agent learns how to perform the soft plan. After that, the developer must validate the learning result to ensure it is suitable for the real scenario. From the agent cycle point of view, there is no difference between the two phases: it is the developer's job to assess the agent's capabilities before deploying it. The developer can also freely decide if the agent, after the deployment, will only exploit plans or also adapt to new experiences.

Figure 2 shows the implementation of a learning strategy module based on SARSA [30] as concrete RL algorithm. SARSA is based on an action-value function Q which is built during the learning process. Besides the Q function the module keeps track of the current state, which is built from the observations (line 4 during the initialisation of an episode, line 13 in performing a learning step and line 21 when choosing an action during the exploitation stage). Observations are extracted from the belief base according to the goal to achieve (line 3 and line 12). The reward in a learning step is obtained from the motivational rule that quantifies the fulfilment of the goal in accordance with the current beliefs (line 11). Action selection follows the RL policy and the current value function Q (line 14 and line 22). The core part of the learning step is the value-action function update (line 15).

4   Proof-of-Concept Implementation in Jason

We developed a first proof-of-concept implementation on top of Jason, exploiting its extensibility. Knowledge required by the RL part is uniformly represented by specific beliefs, referred as *beliefs about learning*. The framework abstracts from the specific RL algorithm but, depending on the characteristics of the problem, there will be different constraints on it. Critical factors are the knowledge about the environment and the state/action space dimensionality: if the state/action space dimensionality increases or more environment features are hidden (Markov property), then the constraints on the algorithm will be more stringent. To deal with this problem, we consider the possibility for the programmer to specify some domain knowledge so as to reduce state/action space and thus obtaining a more efficient/effective learning.

Algorithm 2. Learning strategy module based on SARSA

```
1:  Q(S,A), S, α, ε, γ                                    ▷ Module state variables and params

2:  procedure INITEPISODE(π,B,I)                          ▷ To initialise a learning episode
3:      O ← π_obs(B,I)
4:      S ← STATE(O)
5:      return Q_policy(S,ε)          ▷ action chosen using a policy derived from Q (e.g., ε-greedy)
6:  end procedure

7:  function EPISODEFINISHED(π,B,I)                        ▷ To check if an episode is finished
8:      return S = π_term(B,I)
9:  end function

10: procedure DOLEARNSTEP(π,B,I,A)    ▷ To do a learning step of an episode, using SARSA
11:     R ← MR(π,B,I)                       ▷ Getting the reward using the motivational rules
12:     O ← OBS(π,B,I)              ▷ Getting the observations relevant for the learning task
13:     S' ← STATE(O)                       ▷ Reconstruct the state given the observations
14:     A' ← Q_policy(S',ε)               ▷ Choose A' from S' using a policy derived from Q
15:     Q(S,A) ← Q(S,A) + α[R + γQ(S',A') − Q(S,A)]       ▷ Q update, according to SARSA
16:     S ← S'                                      ▷ Updating the new current state S
17:     return A'
18: end procedure

19: function CHOOSELEARNTACTION(π,B,I)
20:     O ← π_obs(B,I)
21:     S ← STATE(O)
22:     return Q_policy(S)          ▷ action chosen from S using Q action-value function
23: end function
```

All the RL items are represented as beliefs, including rules, and plans. In this way, the agent can control everything related to the reinforcement learning process. For the BDI agent, RL is a black box and vice versa. We can see the black box as a block that we can change without affecting the agent and that can implement any RL algorithm.

4.1 RL Concepts Representation in Jason

All beliefs about learning include as the first parameter a ground term representing the goal for which we want a soft plan, i.e. whose plan is learned. This is useful to support multiple goals with soft plans at the same time. In the gridworld, for instance, we identify the goal with reach_end.

In order to reduce the state space, we need to declare which beliefs shall be considered relevant for a goal, so that they will be used as observations. We do this with the beliefs rl_observe(G, O), where G is a ground term that refers to the goal and O is the list of the beliefs that will be considered for the goal. In gridworld example:

```
rl_observe(reach_end, [ pos(_,_) ]).
```

As introduced in the previous section, Motivational Rules define the rewards for some goal given the current context:

```
rl_reward(G, R) :- ...
```

where *G* is the goal and R is a real number. The body of the rule represents the state for which this reward must be generated. In the gridworld example:

```
rl_reward(reach_end, 10) :- finish_line.
rl_reward(reach_end, -1) :- not finish_line.
```

At each execution, the RL reasoner gets the sum of all the rewards of the Motivational Rules for which the body is true on the basis of the agent beliefs.

Similarly, Terminal Rules are in the form of rl_terminal(G) :- ..., asserting when the end of an episode is reached. In the gridworld example:

```
rl_terminal(reach_end) :- finish_line.
```

The action set is represented as a set of (hard) plans, identified by an @action annotation: @action[rl_goal(g_1, ..., g_n)] where g_1, ..., g_n is the list of goals for which the plan/action can be used. In the gridworld example:

```
@action[rl_goal(reach_end),
    rl_param(direction(set(right, left, up, down)))]
+!move(Direction) <- move(Direction).
```

This is used to inform the RL reasoner that the move action, wrapped into the corresponding plan, is relevant for learning how to achieve the reach_end goal. The annotation allows for specifying also parameters that are used in the action/plan, specifying the range of the values: @action[rl_goal(g_1, ..., g_n), rl_param(p_1, ..., p_m)] where p_1, ..., p_m is the list of literals whose names match the names of the variables—these literals must contain a predicate that defines the type of the parameter and its range. To define an action space in which the action set is not the same in all states we can use the context of the plan—if the context is not satisfied for the current state, the plan will not be considered by the RL algorithm.

RL algorithm parameters can be specified as beliefs, enabling the complete control of the learning process by the programmer and the agent. In the gridworld example, some parameters are:

```
rl_parameter(alpha, 0.26).
rl_parameter(gamma, 0.9).
rl_parameter(policy, egreedy).
```

Finally, a couple of internal actions are provided to drive and inspect the learning process: rl.execute(G) and rl.expected_return(G,R).

The internal action rl.execute(G) makes it possible to perform one run (episode) of the learning process – if we are in the learning stage – or execute the soft plan – in the exploitation stage. The belief about policy parameter rl_parameter(policy,P) can be used to specify if the agent is in learning stage or exploitation stage. Exploitation occurs when the policy P is set to exploit. When rl.execute(G) is executed, if the policy is set to exploit, then the soft plan is executed without learning.

The action `rl.execute(G)`, implemented in Java, wraps the core part of the RL algorithm. To that purpose, the Java bridge makes it possible to reuse existing RL libraries, when useful, including libraries written in other languages such as Python ones. The action carries on and improves the soft plan under learning and its execution completes when the episode is completed (or until an action failure). The soft plan intention is carried out like any other intention—so the RL execution competes with the other intentions for the agent attention and further execution. Typically, a full learning process involves the repeated execution of learning episodes, in this case by executing multiple times the `rl.execute` action.

The internal action `rl.expected_return(G, R)` gets the estimate of future rewards R for the goal G on the basis of the current state and learned policy, i.e. the *expected return*. This could be used to understand the performance of the learnt soft plan for some goal, given the current situation of the agent. For instance, if the expectation of the learnt behaviour in the current state is poor, we can fall back on another plan. As a result, we obtain a notion of *context* for soft plans.

A simple example of learning process, related to the gridworld example, using `rl.execute(G)` and `rl.expected_return(G, R)` follows:

```
+!reach_end: rl.expected_return(reach_end, R) & R >= 10
  <- rl.execute(reach_end).

+!reach_end: rl.expected_return(reach_end, R) & R < 10
  <- -+rl_parameter(policy, egreedy);
     !do_learning(reach_end,10).

+!do_learning(G,TargetRew) :
     rl.expected_return(reach_end, R) & R < TargetRew
  <- rl.execute(reach_end);
     !do_learning(G,TargetRew).

+!do_learning(G,TargetRew) :
     rl.expected_return(reach_end, R) & R >= TargetRew
  <- -+rl_parameter(policy, exploit).
```

In this case, if a new `reach_end` goal is requested and we have a good expected return, then we execute the soft plan (which is supposed to be in exploitation mode). Otherwise, we start a learning process, until the target reward is achieved.

4.2 Jason-RL Reasoning Cycle

The Jason reasoning cycle defines how the Jason interpreter runs an agent program, it can be seen as a refinement of the BDI decision loop [8]. There are ten main steps: in our framework, some of these steps are extended to include learning aspects. Figure 2 shows our extended architecture based on the original one; the red components are the extensions. The detailed description of the original cycle can be found in [8]. In the following we focus on our extensions.

In a learning agent, after the update of the belief base (2a), the maps that track the *Belief about Learning* are updated to reflect the new belief; we call this process *Observation Update Function* OUF (2b). In this way, when the observations are required, the agent doesn't need to iterate multiple times over the belief base. In step (7a), when the plan's context is bound to the expected reward, the value is asked to the RL black box and then verified against the threshold (7b). Finally, a new step (11) shall be added to the sequence when the next action of the intention selected in (9) is the RL execution. At this stage, the information that the RL process needs in order to continue shall be provided to it. The observations and the parameters are taken from the belief base, plus, the Motivational Rules and the Terminal Rules are checked against the belief base to retrieve the reward and the terminal status.

The RL reasoner needs also the set of relevant actions; this is formed by the action set defined in the plan library after the non-applicable actions are eliminated through the same check context function of (7). So, the agent provides these data to the RL black box and then obtain the next suggested action (12). This action is pushed on top of the intention queue and, if the state is not terminal, under this action is put a new call to the RL execution action (13). The next time this intention is further executed, the selected action will be performed, at the subsequent intention execution, another action will be requested and so on.

The full implementation of the framework, along with some documentation, is available as open-source project[2].

5   First Evaluation and Discussion

Agentspeak has both a declarative nature (the reasoning) and an imperative one (plans, i.e sequences of actions). We worked towards automating the development of the imperative side while maintaining the declarative one. In the developed framework, the concept of soft plan allows the agent to learn plans while preserving the reasoning capabilities of a BDI agent: the framework act on the body of the plan, retaining the declarative attitude derived from event triggering and plans' context, as with traditional plans. As a result, it is not just about calling a policy learned through RL, but it concerns the inclusion of that kind of plan in the reasoning flow of the agent.

The framework aims at modeling the three fundamental RL signals without any assumption on the RL algorithm behind them. Nevertheless, depending on the RL algorithm, different kinds of environments may be considered, with a different impact on the performances. In literature, three main characteristics of the environments are typically considered to properly select the RL algorithms: the Markov property, the type of task (episodic or continuing), and the state and action spaces dimension. A detailed discussion of this aspect is out of the scope of this paper.

Here we found it interesting to consider if and how our model/framework would be expressive and flexible enough to include more advanced RL approaches used to tackle complex environments. For instance, in literature function approximation is exploited to tackle partial observability, possibly using nonlinear methods such as neural networks,

---

[2] https://github.com/MichaelBosello/jacamo-rl.

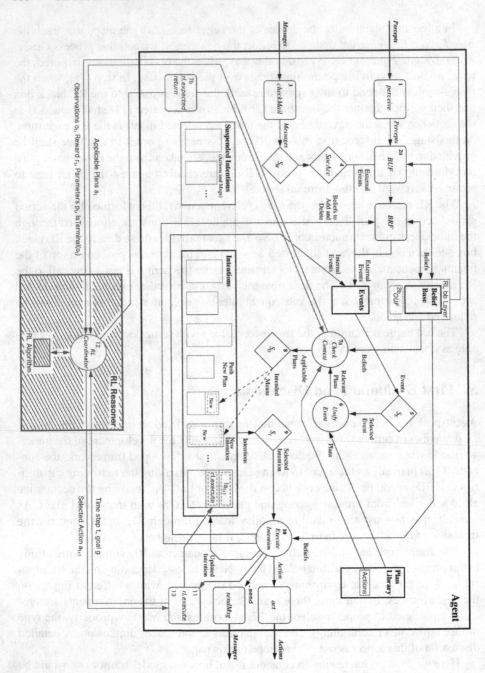

Fig. 2. The Jason Reasoning Cycle extended with learning aspects.

in particular *deep* networks—such as in *deep* reinforcement learning. In our framework, this accounts for changing/plugging a proper RL reasoner component, without changing the whole interpreter architecture.

RL algorithms may have different characteristics and features. It is an action-value method if it selects the actions based on their estimated action values. It is a policy gradient method if it learns a parameterized policy that can select actions without consulting a value function. It is on-policy if it learns the behavior policy i.e., the (near-optimal) policy used to generate behavior. It is off-policy if it learns the target policy i.e., the optimal policy. It is tabular if the value-function is represented with a table. It is approximated if it uses some kind of function approximation. Given such a spectrum of characteristics, to provide a first evaluation of our approach we implemented three RL algorithms which represent three families of RL approaches: (i) SARSA, an on-policy action-value method; (ii) DQN, an off-policy action-value method with approximation i.e. the neural network; (iii) REINFORCE, a policy gradient method.

As we can see, our approach generalizes quite well with respect to the various RL algorithms. The developer needs only to change a belief to change the algorithm used by the agent. In the remainder of the section, we first provide some implementation details about the algorithms used and then we describe the set of tests that we performed, based on simple well-known problems, along with the obtained results. The full source code of the examples is available within the distribution of the framework.

5.1 Details About the Algorithms Used

As a first extension of the framework, we implemented a RESTful service in Python that provides the capability of TF-Agents [26] to our framework. TF-Agents is a library that offers the core elements of RL and several RL algorithms, which is built on top of TensorFlow [1], the popular machine learning open source platform. A Java class that implements the interface requested by our framework consumes the above-mentioned service, completing the bridge between our framework and TF-Agents. We tested two algorithms offered by the library: DQN [19] and REINFORCE [34]. SARSA instead has been implemented directly in Java.

5.2 Tests Performed and Results

In order to test our proof-of-concept implementation, we used the gridworld problem introduced in Sect. 3, performing first simple tests over small (5×5) grids. This problem has been used essentially for testing the framework in its early stages. At every episode, the agent appears in a random place and seek to reach a fixed target position. SARSA algorithm performs properly in this task with a ε-greedy policy with epsilon decay (i.e., the exploration probability decreases with increasing steps). Parameters used: alpha = 0.26, gamma = 0.9, epsilon = 0.22, epsilon decay = 0.99992. The agent learns the policy in about 1000 episodes, and when epsilon decreases under 0.05 (with this decay, approximately after 5000 episodes), the behaviour becomes near optimal. The chart in Fig. 3 shows the average error (how many extra steps were made compared to the minimum path) on five trials with 6000 episodes.

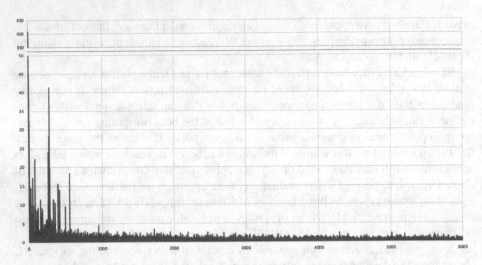

Fig. 3. Chart of simulation results: x is the episode number and y is the average error.

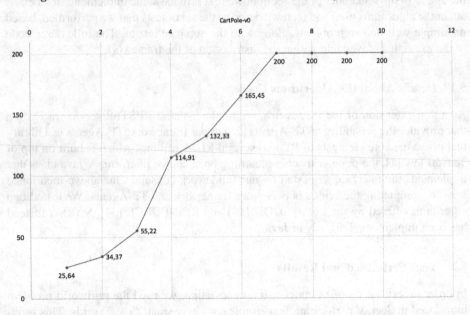

Fig. 4. Chart of CartPole results: x is the validation phase and y is the average reward on 100 episodes.

We tested the other algorithms in two classic control environments, namely Cart-Pole [6] and MountainCar [20]. To obtain an ensemble of test tasks, we implemented a bridge – with a REST service, in the same way as for the algorithms – between the Jason environment and Gym [10], a suite of RL tasks.

In the CartPole quest, a movable pole is attached to a cart. The BDI agent gets four observations from the environment: the cart's position and velocity as well as the

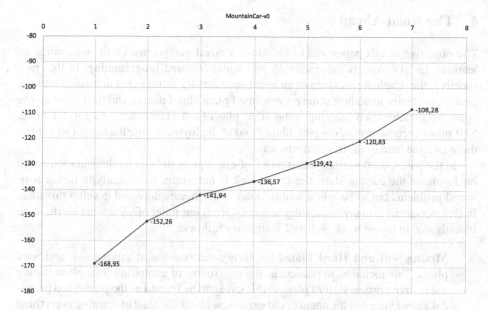

Fig. 5. Chart of MountainCar results: x is the validation phase and y is the average reward on 100 episodes.

position and velocity of the pole. It desires to keep the pole upright and prevent it from falling over by moving the cart. The plan move takes the direction, right or left, as a parameter. At every time-step, the agent receives a positive reward with a cumulative maximum of 200 per episode. The episode ends when the pole is more than 15 degrees from vertical, the cart moves more than 2.4 units from the center, or more than 200 time-steps have passed. CartPole defines "solving" as getting an average reward of 195.0 over 100 consecutive trials. We solved the CartPole problem with the REINFORCE algorithm and the following parameters: learning rate = 0.001, gamma = 1, epsilon = 0.1, one hidden layer with 100 neurons.

In the MountainCar problem, a car is between two mountains in a one-dimensional track. The agent seeks to reach the top of the right one. The car's engine is not strong enough to scale the mountain, so, the agent must build up momentum going back and forth to reach the top. The agent gets as beliefs the position and speed of the car. Its desire is reach_top. It uses the plan move by selecting one of the three directions: back, none, and forth. At every time-step, the agent receives a negative reward. MountainCar-v0 is solved with an average reward of −110.0 over 100 consecutive trials. We used DQN to solve MountainCar. Parameters have been: learning rate = 0.0008, gamma = 0.99, epsilon = 0.1, two hidden layers with 256 neurons each, batch size = 64. The charts in Figs. 4 and 5 display the trend of the average cumulative return. The agent alternate a phase of training and a phase of evaluation. Every column of the charts shows the value of the average reward on 100 episodes of evaluation. Between every evaluation phase, the agent performs 100 episodes of training for the CartPole case and 50 episodes for the MountainCar one.

6   The Road Ahead

The objective of this paper was to introduce a novel perspective on the integration of learning in BDI Agents programming and agent-oriented programming. In that perspective, the development stage of an agent accounts for setting up a first version of the agent, eventually including some programmed plans (hard plans), and then *grow up* the agent by making itself learning some other plans (soft plans), according to the need. Soft plans become part of the plan library and at deployment time the agent can exploit them like the hard ones, in a uniform way.

In the paper, we described a first proof-of-concept model and implementation based on Jason. In the current state, the framework is not meant to be ready to tackle real-world problems but to be a first tool in order to further explore and develop this idea. In that perspective, many interesting aspects – from our point of view – are worth to be investigated in future work. A list of main ones follows:

Mixing Soft and Hard Plans. Exploring the benefits of mixing soft and hard plans. This includes, in particular, the possibility of exploiting hard plans during the learning process. Hard plans in this case can be framed as the predefined practical knowledge that the agent could exploit, without the need of learning everything necessarily from scratch. We believe that this may have a positive impact on both the time required to learn and of the quality of the learnt plans itself. To effectively explore this point, we need both to further extend the basic framework and to identify a proper set of problems of incremental complexity.

Hierarchical RL and Reward Shaping. Further extending the set of RL algorithms used and examples/problems as well, eventually doing a rigorous analysis of the computational complexity and properties of the computations performed by the extended reasoning cycle. Among the large spectrum of RL-based approaches, two are particularly interesting with respect to the objective of our research line. The first is about Hierarchical Reinforcement Learning, extending the reinforcement learning paradigm by allowing the learning agent to aggregate actions into reusable subroutines or skills [9]. In BDI case, reusable subroutines or skills are modelled as plans triggered by subgoals. The second one is about reward shaping in reinforcement learning[3] [11]. There, "education" is realised through the creation of a proper learning environment and, in particular, through demonstration.

Education Process. Exploring further the *development/education process lifecycle*, analysing how the different stages – development/training, validation/assessment, deployment/monitoring – are related.

New Generation of Tools and IDE. Designing and developing proper tools to be embedded in existing IDEs – or extending them – to support this process. Including simulators, which become an essential part of the picture.

Software Engineering. Exploring how software engineering aspects such as modularity, extensibility, reusability, composability can be framed when dealing with soft plans, aside to hard plans. Can we introduce kind of *incremental* learning to extend existing soft plans?

---

[3] We thank the reviewers for this suggestion.

Artifact-Based Environments. Exploring how environment first-class abstractions such as artifacts [25] could be useful to better structure, modularise and make the way in which actions – and observations as well – are currently considered more dynamic.

Beyond the Single Agent Perspective. What does it mean an education process for a multi-agent system? what does it mean an education process for an agent *organisation*?

Methodologies. What's the impact on AOSE methodology. Or, can we exploit existing AOSE methodology to effectively support this process or do we need to extend them?

Planning. In the paper we did not consider at all planning, being our framework focused on learning. Nevertheless, it would be interesting and important to extend the conceptual framework to consider also the role that planning can do in such agent education process.

References

1. Abadi, M., et al.: TensorFlow: Large-scale machine learning on heterogeneous systems (2015). http://tensorflow.org/. Software available from tensorflow.org
2. Airiau, S., Padgham, L., Sardina, S., Sen, S.: Enhancing the adaptation of BDI agents using learning techniques. Int. J. Agent Technol. Syst. 1(2), 1–18 (2009)
3. Andrew McAfee, E.B.: The Second Machine Age: Work, Progress, and Prosperity in a Time of Brilliant Technologies. W. W. Norton & Company, New York (2014)
4. Badica, A., Badica, C., Ivanovic, M., Mitrovic, D.: An approach of temporal difference learning using agent-oriented programming. In: 20th International Conference on Control Systems and Computer Science, pp. 735–742, May 2015
5. Badica, C., Becheru, A., Felton, S.: Integration of jason reinforcement learning agents into an interactive application. In: 19th International Symposium on Symbolic and Numeric Algorithms for Scientific Computing (SYNASC), pp. 361–368, September 2017
6. Barto, A.G., Sutton, R.S., Anderson, C.W.: Neuronlike adaptive elements that can solve difficult learning control problems. IEEE Trans. Syst. Man Cybern. **SMC-13**(5), 834–846 (1983)
7. Bordini, R.H., Hübner, J.F., Vieira, R.: Jason and the golden fleece of agent-oriented programming. In: Bordini, R.H., et al. (eds.) Multi-Agent Programming: Languages, Platforms and Applications, pp. 3–37. Springer, Boston (2005). https://doi.org/10.1007/0-387-26350-0_1
8. Bordini, R.H., Hübner, J.F., Wooldridge, M.: Programming Multi-Agent Systems in AgentSpeak Using Jason (Wiley Series in Agent Technology). Wiley, Hoboken (2007)
9. Botvinick, M., Niv, Y., C Barto, A.: Hierarchically organized behavior and its neural foundations: a reinforcement learning perspective. Cognition **113**, 262–280 (2008)
10. Brockman, G., et al.: OpenAI Gym (2016)
11. Brys, T., Harutyunyan, A., Suay, H.B., Chernova, S., Taylor, M.E., Nowé, A.: Reinforcement learning from demonstration through shaping. In: Proceedings of the 24th International Conference on Artificial Intelligence (IJCAI 2015), pp. 3352–3358. AAAI Press (2015)
12. Feliú, J.L.S.: Use of Reinforcement Learning (RL) for plan generation in Belief-Desire-Intention (BDI) agent systems. University of Rhode Island (2013)
13. Ford, M.: Architects of Intelligence: The Truth About AI from the People Building It. Packt Publishing, Birmingham (2018)
14. Gerrish, S.: How Smart Machines Think. MIT Press, Cambridge (2018)

15. Guerra-Hernández, A., El Fallah-Seghrouchni, A., Soldano, H.: Learning in BDI multi-agent systems. In: Dix, J., Leite, J. (eds.) CLIMA 2004. LNCS (LNAI), vol. 3259, pp. 218–233. Springer, Heidelberg (2004). https://doi.org/10.1007/978-3-540-30200-1_12

16. Karim, S., Sonenberg, L., Tan, A.-H.: A hybrid architecture combining reactive plan execution and reactive learning. In: Yang, Q., Webb, G. (eds.) PRICAI 2006. LNCS (LNAI), vol. 4099, pp. 200–211. Springer, Heidelberg (2006). https://doi.org/10.1007/978-3-540-36668-3_23

17. Kelly, J.E.: Computing, cognition and the future of knowing (2015). IBM Research and Solutions, white paper

18. Meijer, E.: Behind every great deep learning framework is an even greater programming languages concept (2018). Invited Talk at the 26th ACM Joint European Software Engineering Conference and Symposium on the Foundations of Software Engineering (ESEC/FSE)

19. Mnih, V., et al.: Human-level control through deep reinforcement learning. Nature **518** (2015)

20. Moore, A.: Efficient memory-based learning for robot control. Ph.D. thesis, Carnegie Mellon University, Pittsburgh, PA, March 1991

21. Norling, E.: Folk psychology for human modelling: extending the BDI paradigm. In: Proceedings of the Third International Joint Conference on Autonomous Agents and Multiagent Systems (AAMAS 2004), pp. 202–209. IEEE Computer Society, Washington, DC (2004)

22. Parnas, D.L.: The real risks of artificial intelligence. Commun. ACM **60**(10), 27–31 (2017)

23. Rao, A.S.: AgentSpeak(L): BDI agents speak out in a logical computable language. In: Van de Velde, W., Perram, J.W. (eds.) MAAMAW 1996. LNCS, vol. 1038, pp. 42–55. Springer, Heidelberg (1996). https://doi.org/10.1007/BFb0031845

24. Rao, A.S., Georgeff, M.P.: BDI agents: from theory to practice. In: Proceedings of the First International Conference on Multi-Agent Systems (ICMAS 1995), pp. 312–319 (1995)

25. Ricci, A., Piunti, M., Viroli, M.: Environment programming in multi-agent systems: an artifact-based perspective. Auton. Agents Multi-Agent Syst. **23**(2), 158–192 (2011)

26. Guadarrama, S., et al.: TF-Agents: A library for reinforcement learning in tensorflow (2018). https://github.com/tensorflow/agents

27. Shoham, Y.: Agent-oriented programming. Artif. Intell. **60**(1), 51–92 (1993)

28. Singh, D., Hindriks, K.V.: Learning to improve agent behaviours in goal. In: Dastani, M., Hübner, J.F., Logan, B. (eds.) Programming Multi-Agent Systems, pp. 158–173. Springer, Heidelberg (2013)

29. Singh, D., Sardina, S., Padgham, L., James, G.: Integrating learning into a BDI agent for environments with changing dynamics. In: Proceedings of the Twenty-Second International Joint Conference on Artificial Intelligence (IJCAI 2011), pp. 2525–2530. AAAI Press (2011)

30. Sutton, R.S., Barto, A.G.: Reinforcement Learning : An Introduction. The MIT Press, Cambridge (2018)

31. Tan, A.H., Ong, Y.S., Tapanuj, A.: A hybrid agent architecture integrating desire, intention and reinforcement learning. Expert Syst. Appl. **38**(7), 8477–8487 (2011)

32. Tanz, J.: The end of code. Wired (2016)

33. Weiß, G.: Adaptation and learning in multi-agent systems: some remarks and a bibliography. In: Weiß, G., Sen, S. (eds.) IJCAI 1995. LNCS, vol. 1042, pp. 1–21. Springer, Heidelberg (1996). https://doi.org/10.1007/3-540-60923-7_16

34. Williams, R.J.: Simple statistical gradient-following algorithms for connectionist reinforcement learning. Mach. Learn. **8**(3), 229–256 (1992)

35. Wooldridge, M.: Introduction to Multi-Agent Systems. Wiley, Hoboken (2009)

Plan Library Reconfigurability
in BDI Agents

Rafael C. Cardoso(✉) ⓘ, Louise A. Dennis ⓘ, and Michael Fisher ⓘ

University of Liverpool, Liverpool L69 3BX, UK
{rafael.cardoso,L.A.Dennis,mfisher}@liverpool.ac.uk

Abstract. One of the major advantages of modular architectures in robotic systems is the ability to add or replace nodes, without needing to rearrange the whole system. In this type of system, autonomous agents can aid in the decision making and high-level control of the robot. For example, a robot may have a module for each of the effectors and sensors that it has and an agent with a plan library containing high-level plans to aid in the decision making within these modules. However, when autonomously replacing a node it can be difficult to reconfigure plans in the agent's plan library while retaining correctness. In this paper, we exploit the formal concept of capabilities in Belief-Desire-Intention agents and describe how agents can reason about these capabilities in order to reconfigure their plan library while retaining overall correctness constraints. To validate our approach, we show the implementation of our framework and an experiment using a practical example in the Mars rover scenario.

Keywords: Belief-Desire-Intention · Modular architectures · Autonomous agents · Reconfigurability

1 Introduction

Robots have been frequently used in real world applications over the years, from industrial robotics [34] to teleoperated robots in search and rescue [27]. However, there are still many open challenges such as: the German strategic initiative Industrie 4.0 that encourages research in the intelligent networking of machines; and robot assisted disaster response in the TRADR project [21]. The reconfigurability problem originally stemmed from manufacturing systems [20], but has since been expanded to self-reconfigurable robots [6,35] that can adapt to different situations via proper selection and reconfiguration of the functional components and the software that are available.

Due to the complexity present in these challenges modular architectures are typically employed to speed up and make the development of robotic systems

Work supported by UK Research and Innovation, and EPSRC Hubs for "Robotics and AI in Hazardous Environments": EP/R026092 (FAIR-SPACE), and EP/R026084 (RAIN).

L. A. Dennis et al. (Eds.): EMAS 2019, LNAI 12058, pp. 195–212, 2020.
https://doi.org/10.1007/978-3-030-51417-4_10

easier. The Robot Operating System (ROS) [29] is an example of a popular middleware that can be used to develop a modular robotic system. In ROS, nodes are used to effectively capture robotic software in terms of a graph that describes the communication between distinct nodes. Some of the advantages of decoupling the system in this way include: more precise failure handling and recovery mechanisms, since failures can be traced to individual nodes; and the complexity of the code is reduced when compared to monolithic systems, making it easier to add, replace, or remove functionality (i.e., nodes).

Agent-based control allows a system to dynamically adapt to changes in the environment through the use of modularity, decentralisation, autonomy, scalability, and reusability [22]. Many of these systems use cognitive agents, particularly those in the Belief-Desire-Intention (BDI) paradigm [30]. Kohn and Nerode's MAHCA system [19] uses multiple knowledge-based agents as planners which generate the actions performed by the underlying control system. While these agents are not based on the BDI paradigm, which was only in its infancy when MAHCA was originally developed, the approach was designed to represent logical decision-making in a high-level declarative fashion. Recent agent-based approaches have been used in networks of autonomous agents interacting to solve complex and dynamic problems in manufacturing and supply chain decision making [24], and explored in the control of spacecraft [28], Unmanned Aircraft [37], and robotics [38]. Many of these approaches are explicitly BDI-based that aim to model the mission designer's *intent* and to separate the symbolic and non-symbolic reasoning.

Modular architectures for robotic systems often benefit from having a framework for reconfigurability, allowing modules to be added and replaced should the need arise. For example, a node can be replaced if it is under-performing according to a specific measure (e.g., the path planner is wasting too much battery), or due to a failure the node is no longer operational; a new node can be added to deal with some problem that was detected post-deployment, or to improve the functionality of other nodes. Several types of reconfigurability can be identified in these systems [9]: (i) reconfiguration at the hardware level, for instance the dynamic reconfiguration of effectors and sensors to cope with a hardware change; (ii) reconfiguration due to low-level control, such as ROS node reconfiguration and being able to replace nodes while still maintaining a working graph; (iii) reconfiguration due to high-level control, for example reconfiguring an agent's goals, plans, and knowledge.

In this paper, we introduce the reconfigurability of plan libraries in BDI agents. Specifically, our approach is aimed towards modular architectures and applications that detect anomalies or malfunctions in a capability (an extended action specification) and can then reason about replacing it with alternative capabilities that are able to achieve the desired outcome. Our reconfigurability framework consists of formal descriptions of capabilities, plans, and how to perform plan replacement.

We use the BDI-based agent-oriented programming language GWEN-DOLEN [7] to implement our framework. By using this language, we can formally verify our new plan library using a program model checker. This is an important, and necessary [11], step towards the validation and reliability of the framework and its applications. To evaluate the implementation of our framework, we used it to reconfigure plans of a BDI agent controlling a Mars rover.

In the next section we provide a background on BDI agents and clarify the distinction between actions and capabilities in BDI agent programming languages. Section 3 introduces our reconfigurability framework, with an overview of the overall system architecture that it can be applied to and a running example. Then, we provide a formal description of capabilities, plans, and plan replacement in propositional logic. In Sect. 4 we describe our implementation of reconfigurability in the GWENDOLEN language, and then demonstrate its use in a practical experiment in the Mars rover scenario. Section 5 covers the related work, from purely theoretical approaches to application-based solutions. We end the paper in Sect. 6 with our conclusions and future work.

2 BDI Agent Programming Languages and Capabilities

Agents programmed using BDI languages commonly contain a set of *beliefs*, representing the agent's current state and knowledge about the environment in which it is situated; a set of *goals*, tasks that the agent aims to achieve; a set of *intentions*, tasks that the agent is committed to achieve; and a set of *plans*, courses of actions that are triggered by events. *Events* can be related to changes in the agent's belief base or to the addition or removal of goals. The agent reacts to these events by creating new intentions which are generated from the set of applicable plans related to that event.

The body of a plan often contains a set of *actions* that can cause changes in the environment. Languages such as *Jason*, GWENDOLEN, and 2APL delegate these actions' specifications to the environment. Any preconditions or postconditions (i.e., effects) that such actions may have are invisible to the agent and are dealt with at the environment level. The environment may return some value to be unified with an open variable or, for example, in *Jason* it may also return a failure condition which will trigger the removal of the event that started the plan, allowing the user to set plans to handle these failures.

It is possible to specify an action's pre and postconditions at the agent level using these languages, for example by creating a dummy plan with only one action, and writing the preconditions of the actions as the preconditions of the plan. The postconditions, if any, could then be written as belief operations (add or remove) to be executed after the action finishes. However, this is not how BDI agents are traditionally programmed in those languages and it can be difficult to reason about an action's pre and postconditions programmed this way.

In general, to be able to successfully search for replacement actions it is necessary to know the preconditions and postconditions of all available actions. Thus, during reconfiguration it is crucial to be able to access information about the execution of an action. We refer to actions with explicit specifications of *pre* and *post*conditions as *capabilities*. It is important to note that agent languages usually do not use this term and when it is used its meaning can vary depending on the language.

A capability can only be executed when its preconditions are true, and any postconditions that it has are added as beliefs when the capability ends with success. This kind of action theory is more prominent in automated planning, known as actions in classical planning [13] or primitive tasks (also operators) in Hierarchical Task Network (HTN) planning [36]. However, there are some BDI languages that implement this concept of capability, such as GOAL, 3APL, and 2APL (only for belief update actions).

The problem that we are interested in solving is improving the system's ability to adapt its behaviour in the event of a (software) failure or damage to some of its (physical) sub-systems in such a way that it can continue to achieve some, or all, of its goals. In these systems, a BDI-agent is involved at the highest decision-making level, and as such, the agent can *recognise* that a component is no longer behaving as expected, then *invoke* diagnosis subsystems to identify the actions related to the failure, and lastly *reconfigure* its plan library to cope with the failure. We note that failure detection and diagnosis in agents is touched on, for example, with semantics for adding duration and failure information in actions for the life-cycle of goals in [8], and through the use of trace expressions to specify protocols on top of sets of events (such as messages, beliefs, and actions) to be checked at runtime through the use of automatically generated monitors [12]. Such mechanisms are assumed to be in place and are not a part of the framework that we describe in this paper; we focus on the reconfigurability problem.

3   Reconfigurability Framework

Our framework is aimed towards systems that have a similar architecture to the one represented in Fig. 1. The system goes through phases of potentially time critical operations followed by an offline phase in which it can reason about failure, perform reconfiguration, and if necessary reverify any relevant system properties. When such a system is deployed, the execution of its capabilities is monitored (e.g., with runtime monitors [12]). If a capability is detected as faulty, then the reconfiguration process tries to replace calls to the faulty capability with viable alternatives, which may include one or multiple capabilities.

We are particularly interested in applications where a high degree of assurance (ideally formal verification) is required. We assume that the system has an offline period, which is very common in robotic systems with long-term autonomy (see [17] for example). During this period the robot can recharge and perform cleanup operations, among other things. But, more importantly from our point of view, it can also reconfigure itself if any faults were detected and verify any plans that were replaced using, for example, a program model checker for agent programming languages. In this paper, we focus on the formal definition and implementation of the reconfigurability of plan libraries in BDI agent(s) that perform high-level reasoning within the system.

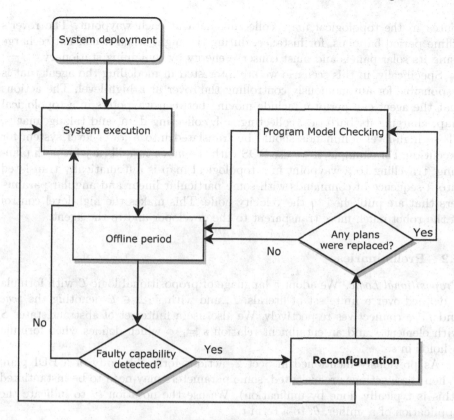

Fig. 1. Overview of the system.

3.1 Running Example

Robots are increasingly deployed to explore hazardous environments that are dangerous for human exploration and often safety-critical, such as areas with extreme temperatures (monitoring of offshore structures [33]), lack of oxygen (both orbital [14] and planetary [39] space exploration), or high radiation (nuclear inspection and decommissioning [3]). Autonomous robots are especially important in scenarios with communication bottlenecks, for example, in planetary space exploration it can take a very long time for human operators to send commands from Earth to the robots. One such example is the Mars rovers used by NASA[1] in several missions. In this scenario an autonomous rover vehicle traverses the surface of Mars collecting image, soil, and rock data. For our example we assume that the rover has access to a topological map, which indicates areas of interest (denoted by waypoints) where the rover can collect data.

The Mars rover scenario can easily be seen as a system that matches the overview depicted in Fig. 1. While in execution mode, the rover traverses through

---

[1] https://mars.nasa.gov/.

routes in the topological map, collecting data at each waypoint. The rover's offline period happens, for instance, during the night when it can not recharge using its solar panels and must conserve energy by remaining stationary.

Specifically, in this scenario we are interested in modelling the agent that is responsible for autonomously controlling the rover at a high-level. The actions that the agent can perform include moving between waypoints in a topological map, charging its batteries, collecting soil, collecting data, and taking images. These high-level commands should be translated into a lower-level system for execution. For example, if we use ROS with the *move base* library for path planning, travelling to a waypoint in a topological map is automatically translated into a sequence of commands with some particular linear and angular parameters that are published to the velocity node. This makes the high-level control of the robot much more transparent to the developer and to the agent.

3.2   Preliminaries

Propositional Logic. We adopt a language of propositional logic $\mathcal{L}$ with formula ϕ defined over a finite set of literals, L, and with $\top, \bot \in \mathcal{L}$ denoting the *true* and *false* connectives respectively. We also use a finite set of abstract states S with element s and an entailment relation $s \models_{\mathcal{L}} \phi$ which defines when formula ϕ holds in s.

As previously mentioned in Sect. 2, actions form the body of a BDI plan. When these actions are executed, some parameters may need to be instantiated (this is typically done by unification). We use the notation $t\theta$ to indicate the application of a unifier, θ, to a term t.

3.3   Capabilities

Our formal representation of capabilities is based on the action theory found in classical automated planning, such as STRIPS reasoning [13], situation calculus [31], and the Planning Domain Definition Language (PDDL) [25]. As such, our formalism is deliberately close to those, but a key difference is that we do not plan from scratch. We discuss the relationship between our work and planning systems in related work (Sect. 5).

A capability specification describes an action that an agent can take and any relation it has to the internal (self) and external (environment) facts of the agent. The specification is in the form of a set of preconditions and postconditions for the action. If the preconditions hold before the action is performed then the action specification states that eventually, if the action terminates with success, the postconditions will hold.

Capability Specification. We use the notation $\{C_{pre}\}\, C\, \{C_{post}\}$ where C is the capability, C_{pre} are the preconditions and C_{post} are the postconditions. C, C_{pre}, and C_{post} are all formulas $\phi \in \mathcal{L}$.

Capability Example. The *move* action of a rover can be represented as:

$$C = \{at(W_1),\, not\, W_1 = W_2\}\, move(W_1, W_2)\, \{not\, at(W_1),\, at(W_2)\}$$

such that W_1 is the current position of the rover, and W_2 is the desired destination. Following the capability specification, we know that the rover must be
$at(W_1)$ (precondition), and after the end of the execution it must be $at(W_2)$
(postcondition). Note that we consider postconditions as belief updates. That
is, $not\, at(W_1)$ in the postcondition is a belief removal of $at(W_1)$. This is needed
to maintain consistency during the search for plan replacements. Consistency
here indicates that the preconditions do not contradict the postconditions.

Reasoning About the Execution of a Capability. The notation $\mathbf{do}(C\theta)$ indicates
the execution of a capability, with its parameters instantiated by the θ unifier.
The execution defines a transition on states in S that is completely specified by
the specification of C. That is, if $s \in S$ and $s \models_{\mathcal{L}} C_{pre}\theta$ there is some unique
state $s' \in S$ such that:

$$s \xrightarrow{\mathbf{do}(C\theta)} s' \text{ and } s' \models_{\mathcal{L}} C_{post}\theta$$

In order to avoid the frame problem, we make the simplifying assumption
that for any $\phi \in \mathcal{L}$, if $s \models_{\mathcal{L}} \phi$ and $\phi \wedge C_{post}\theta$ is consistent then $s' \models_{\mathcal{L}} \phi$. That is,
any formula that is true in state s and is not explicitly effected by the execution
of the capability will still be true in state s'. Thus, if the preconditions hold then
the postconditions will also hold.

As discussed in Sect. 2, many BDI systems employ a simplistic action theory
where the pre and postconditions of actions are not represented at the execution
level of the agent. Thus, it is always possible to execute actions in those systems
as long as the preconditions of the plan hold when the plan was selected. Our
theory of plan validity assumes that capability specifications are complete and
correct and that the preconditions of a capability always hold when the system
attempts to execute the associated action.

Execution Example. Suppose that in state s the proposition $empty(true)$ holds
and the next action in the plan to be executed is the capability *collect_sample*
with postcondition $empty(false)$:

$$s \xrightarrow{\mathbf{do}(collect\_sample)} s'$$

results in a state where $empty(false)$ holds.

3.4 Plans

A BDI plan is a structure which contains a sequence of capabilities as its body,
but may also contain additional elements such as trigger events or guards. For
simplicity, we ignore these additional elements in a plan body when reasoning
about plan replacements, but we point out that most of these elements could be
represented as capabilities.

Plan Specification. Given a plan, P, we write its preconditions as P_{pre} and its postconditions as P_{post}. We use the notation $\overline{C} = [C^1; C^2; \ldots; C^n]$ to indicate a sequence of capabilities that are to be executed as part of the body, $\overline{C}$, of a BDI plan. Our theory assumes that capabilities are guaranteed to execute sequentially, i.e., C^{i+1} is not executed until C^i_{post} holds.

Plan Body Example. We have a plan, P^1 to collect a rock sample at a particular position and then transmit the data. The body of this plan, $\overline{C^1}$, consists of a sequence of four capabilities:

$$\overline{C^1} = [move(W_1, W_2); collect\_sample(S); move(W_2, W_3); transmit\_data(S)]$$

The first moves the rover to a position where it is capable of collecting a rock sample, performs the collection, then moves to a position where it can transmit the data, and finally performs the transmission.

Many BDI-based languages already allow the specification of preconditions in plans (e.g., plan context in Jason, or plan guards in GWENDOLEN), but it is unusual for a BDI plan to have explicit postconditions. However, we believe these can often be understood implicitly from the postconditions of the capabilities in a plan's body.

Pre and Postcondition Example. Using the plan from the previous example, P^1, we can complete the plan specification by adding $P^1_{pre} = [at(W_1), empty(true)]$ and $P^1_{post} = [data\_transmitted(S)]$ as such:

$$P^1 = \{at(W_1), empty(true)\} \, \overline{C^1} \, \{data\_transmitted(S)\}$$

meaning that for the plan to be applicable the rover must be at waypoint W_1 and it must not be carrying any sample, and after the plan's conclusion the data of S will have been transmitted.

We represent pre and postconditions for plans explicitly because even though two capabilities may have different postconditions it may be the case that one can be replaced by another in a plan, without changing what the plan is intended to achieve. In other words, by having the plan's postconditions explicitly specified we can check that they still hold even after replacing a capability for another one with different postconditions. Although it would be possible to enforce capabilities in the body of a plan to be minimal, we prefer to not impose that restriction, since BDI plans are generally constructed by humans rather than automated planning systems.

It may occur that the postcondition of a plan does not include all of the effects from the execution of the capabilities in the plan body (i.e., $P_{post} \neq C^1_{post} \cup \ldots \cup C^n_{post}$). For example, the proposition $at(W_2)$ is not a postcondition of P^1 since in this case we do not care if the final position of the rover is W_2, only that it has successfully transmitted the data. This may be achievable from other waypoints, allowing the plan to be modified in a fashion that would have the rover transmitting data from a different waypoint.

Simple Plan Trace. A simple plan trace is one in which only the capabilities in the plan body cause state transitions in S. That is, the environment does not change apart from the execution of those capabilities and the plan's execution has not been interleaved with the execution of any other plan. Formally, let $[C^1; \ldots; C^n]$ form the body of some plan, P. Then a sequence of states $s_1; \ldots; s_{n+1}$ together with a unifier, θ, forms a simple plan trace for P if for all s_i, $s_i \xrightarrow{\textbf{do}(C^i\theta)} s_{i+1}$.

3.5 Plan Replacement

When reasoning about plan replacement we assume an idealised execution environment for the plan represented by a simple plan trace. We ignore any impact that the environment (or another external factor) might have in the outcome of a capability, as these would be impossible to predict. The end system may still have them and they may make a plan that was replaced fail, but we do not address this issue in this paper, since this is not directly related to the reconfigurability problem.

Definition 1 (Valid Plan). *We say a plan P with a body consisting of the sequence of capabilities $[C^1; \ldots; C^n]$ is valid with regards to the specifications of the capabilities, if for all simple plan traces, $\langle s_1; \ldots; s_{n+1}, \theta \rangle$ where θ instantiates all the parameters of all the specifications for capabilities in the body of P, $s_i \models_{\mathcal{L}} C^i_{pre}\theta$ for all C^i. That is, the precondition in the specification for the next capability in the plan holds when some capability is executed.*

Note that plans in an actual BDI program may not be valid w.r.t. to the actions' specifications since they have been supplied by a programmer, i.e., not constructed from the specifications. In this case, these plans would need to be fixed, either by an automatic algorithm or by hand, to be considered as valid plans and able to be replaced.

Definition 2 (Valid Plan Specification). *We say that a plan specification $P = \{P_{pre}\}\overline{C}\{P_{post}\}$ for a plan with body $[C^1; \ldots; C^n]$ is valid if*
[1.]
1. *P is valid;*
2. *$P_{pre} \rightarrow C^1_{pre}$; and*
3. *for all simple plan traces, $\langle s_1; \ldots; s_{n+1}, \theta \rangle$ where θ instantiates all the parameters in the specifications of capabilities appearing in the body of P and all free variables in P_{pre} and P_{post}, if $s_1 \models_{\mathcal{L}} P_{pre}\theta$ then $s_{n+1} \models_{\mathcal{L}} P_{post}\theta$.*

The first point is covered in Definition 1. The second point states that if the preconditions of the plan holds *before* its execution, then the preconditions of the first capability in that plan's body also hold. The third point declares that a plan specification is valid if it can establish its postconditions on simple plan traces. That is, if the precondition of a plan hold before execution of the plan, then the plan's postconditions hold *after* its execution.

Once again, we assume a static environment where all capabilities behave according to their specification. Note that this does *not* guarantee that the plan always works, only that it has been specified appropriately and sensibly programmed to work in most situations where it is invoked.

Definition 3 (Preservation of Plan Spec. Validity). *Consider a plan specification* $P = \{P_{pre}\}\overline{C}\{P_{post}\}$. *Let* P' *be a plan that has identical pre and post-conditions to* P *except that* P' *has body* $\overline{C'}$. *We say that* P' *preserves the validity of* P *if* $P' = \{P_{pre}\}\overline{C'}\{P_{post}\}$ *is valid.*

We argue that the preservation of plan specification validity is a minimal requirement when replacing plans. It states that if there is a static environment and no interleaved execution of plans, then the new plan will achieve the replaced plan's postconditions.

Definition 4 (Rational Plan Body Replacement). *We say the replacement of plan body* $\overline{C}$ *for* $\overline{C'}$ *in a plan* P *so it becomes a plan* P' *is* rational *if* P' *preserves the validity of* P.

Therefore we seek to implement mechanisms for plan body replacement that are rational.

Plan Body Replacement Example. If we detect a capability in the previous plan P^1 to be faulty, for example, the rover can no longer move from the place it collected the rock sample to a place to transmit the data due to an unavoidable obstacle. Then, the capability $move(W_2, W_3)$ can be exchanged in the plan body replacement:

$$\overline{C^{1'}} = \begin{bmatrix} move(W_1, W_2);\ collect\_sample(S);\ move(W_2, W_4); \\ move(W_4, W_3);\ transmit\_data(S) \end{bmatrix}$$

with W_4 representing an intermediate waypoint between W_2 and the goal position W_3 and that this route is obstacle-free. This is a rational plan body replacement: the new plan $P^{1'} = \{at(W_1),\ empty(true)\}\ \overline{C^{1'}}\ \{data\_transmitted(S)\}$ is a valid plan which achieves P^1 postconditions whenever P^1 preconditions are true, assuming that the environment is static and plan execution is not interleaved.

4   Implementation

We have implemented our theory as an extension of the GWENDOLEN programming language [7], chosen for its association with the Agent Java Pathfinder (AJPF) model-checker [10]. This provides a potential route for verification of a reconfigured plan library. To simplify implementation, we only use grounded capabilities in our practical experiment.

Algorithm 1 shows a high-level abstraction of our implementation for reconfigurability of plan libraries in BDI agents. Due to the availability and accessibility of implementations of fast classical planners, we opted to translate the search for the replacement of plan bodies into a limited planning problem. Limited here

---

Algorithm 1: Implementation of plan library reconfigurability.

```
1  Function replace (capability)
2  │   Capabilities ← get_capabilities;
3  │   Capabilities ← Capabilities \ {capability};
4  │   if Capabilities = ∅ then
5  │   │   return false;
6  │   domain ← create_domain (Capabilities);
7  │   PlanLibrary ← get_plan_library;
8  │   Plans ← get_plans (capability);
9  │   while there exists {plan} ∈ Plans do
10 │   │   InitState ← propagate (plan, capability);
11 │   │   Goals ← get_post_cond (plan);
12 │   │   problem ← create_problem (InitState, Goals);
13 │   │   replacement ← STRIPS_planner (domain, problem);
14 │   │   if replacement = ∅ then
15 │   │   │   return false;
16 │   │   newplan ← replace_cap (plan, replacement);
17 │   │   PlanLibrary ← PlanLibrary \ {plan} ∪ {newplan};
18 │   │   Plans ← Plans \ {plan};
19 │   update_plan_library (PlanLibrary);
20 │   return true;
```

---

refers to the use of a very small subset of information, instead of planning from scratch.

We start the reconfiguration of the plan library when a capability is detected to be faulty and in need of a replacement. First, we retrieve all capabilities that the agent has, except for the one that it wants to replace (lines 2–3). If we are left with an empty set of capabilities, then that capability cannot be replaced. Otherwise, the domain is created, translating all capabilities into STRIPS operators. Next, we fetch all plans from the agent's plan library that have the faulty capability in a plan's body (line 8).

In lines 9–18 we cycle through each of the plans that include the capability to be replaced. We construct the initial state from the propagation of the literals from the preconditions and postconditions starting at the first capability and going up to the last capability before the faulty one in the plan. This propagation is also known as progression in search algorithms. Our *Goals* set contains the postconditions of the plan to be replaced. We create the problem specification and then call a STRIPS planner to find the replacements by providing the domain and problem specifications that were translated from the GWENDOLEN syntax. Although any STRIPS planner would suffice, we chose the SIW+−then-BFSf planner [23], one of the top performing planners from the agile track in the International Planning Competition.

If no replacement is found by the planner, then the faulty capability cannot be replaced in that plan. Otherwise, we swap it with the replacement that was found (which can contain one or more alternative capabilities), remove the old plan from the temporary plan library, and add in the new plan. After we cycled all plans and replaced the faulty capability within them, the plan library is updated with the new modifications.

4.1   Practical Experiment

We use a simple problem in our running example of the Mars rover scenario as a practical experiment. The problem is to replace a faulty movement capability, $moveW1W2$ that represents the route between the topological nodes $W1$ and $W2$. For this experiment we focus only on movement capabilities. Although other actions such as collecting rock data are also represented as capabilities, we omit them since they are not relevant to this experiment.

The capabilities in Fig. 2 represent the topological map that the agent has access to. A precondition list precedes the capability, which is followed by a postcondition list. The topological map consists of the following navigation routes between each waypoint: $W1 \Leftrightarrow W2$, $W1 \Leftrightarrow W3$, $W3 \Leftrightarrow W2$, $W1 \Leftrightarrow W4$, $W2 \Leftrightarrow W5$, and $W5 \Leftrightarrow W4$.

```
 1  :Capabilities:
 2  {  at(waypoint1)  }  moveW1W2  {  −at(waypoint1),  +at(waypoint2)  }
 3  {  at(waypoint2)  }  moveW2W1  {  −at(waypoint2),  +at(waypoint1)  }
 4  {  at(waypoint1)  }  moveW1W3  {  −at(waypoint1),  +at(waypoint3)  }
 5  {  at(waypoint3)  }  moveW3W1  {  −at(waypoint3),  +at(waypoint1)  }
 6  {  at(waypoint3)  }  moveW3W2  {  −at(waypoint3),  +at(waypoint2)  }
 7  {  at(waypoint2)  }  moveW2W3  {  −at(waypoint2),  +at(waypoint3)  }
 8  {  at(waypoint1)  }  moveW1W4  {  −at(waypoint1),  +at(waypoint4)  }
 9  {  at(waypoint4)  }  moveW4W1  {  −at(waypoint4),  +at(waypoint1)  }
10  {  at(waypoint2)  }  moveW2W5  {  −at(waypoint2),  +at(waypoint5)  }
11  {  at(waypoint5)  }  moveW5W2  {  −at(waypoint5),  +at(waypoint2)  }
12  {  at(waypoint5)  }  moveW5W4  {  −at(waypoint5),  +at(waypoint4)  }
13  {  at(waypoint4)  }  moveW4W5  {  −at(waypoint4),  +at(waypoint5)  }
```

Fig. 2. Capabilities of the rover agent in Gwendolen.

The plans for the rover agent are listed in Fig. 3. A plan in Gwendolen is started by an *event*, for example, a plan for completing a mission *mission1* is activated when the goal (!) *mission1* is added (+); this is known as a goal addition event. The plan will be selected and added to the agent's intention base if the formulae present in the *guard* (i.e., the context or precondition of the plan, goes after a colon and between curly brackets) are true. After a plan is selected, a sequence of actions in the plan body (denoted by ←) is executed.

There are plans for three different missions, each applicable when the agent is at a different location. For example, the guard of *mission1* (line 3) states that the agent must have the belief $at(waypoint1)$ expressing that the rover must be currently located in waypoint1. The body of *mission*1 (lines 4–8) contains the capabilities that must be executed in sequential order to successfully achieve the mission's goal.

```
1  :Plans:
2  +!mission1 [perform]  :
3       { B at (waypoint1) }
4  ←
5       moveW1W2,
6       collect_soil,
7       moveW2W5,
8       collect_rock;
9  +!mission2 [perform]  :
10      { B at (waypoint4) }
11 ←
12      moveW4W1,
13      collect_rock,
14      moveW1W2,
15      take_image;
16 +!mission3 [perform]  :
17      { B at (waypoint3) }
18 ←
19      moveW3W1,
20      moveW1W2,
21      collect_rock,
22      moveW2W5,
23      take_image;
```

Fig. 3. Plan library of the rover agent in GWENDOLEN.

Figure 4 shows a simple example in the Mars rover scenario using a representation of all the capabilities described in Fig. 2. A lander spacecraft stays in its original position and acts as a charging station for the rover, which starts next to the lander at waypoint 1 ($W1$). At some point during the system's deployment, either while in execution or in the offline period, the capability *moveW*1*W*2 is detected to be faulty. This could have been caused because, for example, the route between waypoint 1 and waypoint 2 is no longer valid (e.g., there is an unavoidable obstacle), or the route is consuming too much battery (e.g., the terrain became difficult to traverse).

The solution found by the planner was to replace the faulty capability *moveW*1*W*2 for *moveW*1*W*3 and *moveW*3*W*2. Then, we replace all occurrences of that capability in all plans, effectively removing the route between waypoint 1 and waypoint 2, and replacing it with the route from waypoint 1 to waypoint 3, and then from waypoint 3 to waypoint 2. Although this solves the problem caused by the faulty capability in all three mission plans, it also introduces some backtracking in the plan for *mission*3. This would be necessary if the agent was

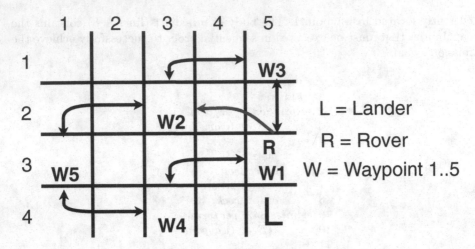

Fig. 4. Mars rover practical example.

executing that plan and had to stop to reconfigure itself, and then resume from that moment onward. However, in most other cases it would result in unnecessary backtracking. This illustrates the trade-off between speed and optimality.

Because we are using an agile planner the solution is not always guaranteed to be optimal. However, as we previously mentioned, the translation from GWENDOLEN can be used in any STRIPS classical planner, including optimal planners. Another, more advanced, option would be to add reasoning plans to be able to choose between different planners depending on the situation that the rover is currently in. A simple example of such feature would be to use an agile planner for generating replacements if the system is running, and an optimal planner if the system is in offline period.

5   Related Work

In [18], an extension of a temporal epistemic logic is used to generalise model checking as a solution to reconfiguring reactive multi-agent systems. In this case the problem was to determine whether a set of reactive robots can combine into a robot that satisfies the functionality of the system. Two scenarios are given, one is a monolithic system and the other is an individual module that is part of a bigger system. Similar to our work, they have also defined a new logic-based language to represent multi-agent systems and reason about reconfigurability at an abstract level, however, our approach is intended as a generic extension applicable to a range of BDI-based agent-oriented programming languages and which, as we have shown, can result directly in an implemented system.

An agent-based framework is proposed for resource reconfiguration in production lines of industrial assembly applications considering product specification and capabilities of production resources [2]. The reconfiguration is goal-based and done through task reallocation. The authors claim that the framework is implemented and runs on a real-world assembly system, however, there is no formal description of the framework or any of its features. Although the concept of reconfigurability and capability is similar to ours, the main difference is that their concepts are intrinsically tied to industrial assembly applications, whilst our framework is domain independent.

An architecture for planning in reconfigurable manufacturing systems is presented in [4]. Reconfiguration in these systems are described to occur in three different scenarios: a production change, physical malfunctions, or a change in production goals. The control system implements a sense-plan-act cycle using ontology-based knowledge to regenerate the planning domain specification when necessary. Similar to the previous approach, this architecture is application specific, and thus, it does not address generic reconfigurability problems.

A reconfigurable agent-based architecture for use in autonomous nuclear waste management is reported in [1]. In this system a BDI-agent controls a ROS-based system for sorting and segregating different types of low radiation level nuclear waste. Reconfiguration is handled by pre-existing plans in the BDI agent rather than by the agent reconfiguring its existing plans. This necessarily limited the extent to which the system could adapt to hardware degradation and changes in its environment.

As previously mentioned, our approach assumes the integration of a planning system with a BDI programming language for implementation purposes. We use the planner strictly to find replacement plans in a limited planning problem. There are many approaches that try to fully incorporate planning in agents, such as in [26]. By extending an AgentSpeak(L) interpreter, agents are able to call a classical planner to create new plans at runtime to respond to unforeseen circumstances at design time. Another example is the work done in [5], that allows agents in a multi-agent system to perform decentralised HTN planning. These approaches do not consider reconfigurability, however it should be possible to use them to implement our reconfigurability framework as long as the agent languages used have (or are extended to have) the same concept of capabilities as in our framework.

The reconfigurability scenarios that we described could be represented as replanning problems or plan[2] repair problems [15]. In plan repair, there are several bodies of work such as: in [16] a plan adaptation approach is used to first analyse the actions, identify inconsistencies, and then repair the plan; and in [32] the authors use a CSP-solver (Constraint Satisfaction Problem) to perform the reconfigurability of a plan. However, formal verification of planning is still an area in its infancy while the verification of BDI agents is well studied in BDI programming languages—hence we have developed a framework in which planning is only part of our approach, namely in the search of capability replacements. If we tried to solve reconfigurability by only using planning, then the complete state

---

[2] The areas of automated planning and BDI agent programming both use the word "plan" but with slightly different meanings.

of the world would have to be passed to a planner. By using our reconfigurability framework this can be avoided, potentially saving computation time.

6   Conclusions

There are different ways that the reconfigurability problem can be solved, such as: preemptively adding plans that cover plan failure; or replanning from scratch. However, the former is prone to human error, and the latter can take substantially longer in complex problems.

In this paper, we have described a formal framework for plan library reconfigurability in BDI agents. We presented a theory based on capabilities and plans, and introduced several definitions concerning how to reason about valid plan replacement. Further to this, we implemented our framework into the GWENDOLEN BDI language and used an agile planner to find capability replacements that are then merged into a plan replacement. As a demonstration of the implementation of our framework we performed a practical experiment on reconfigurability in the Mars rover scenario.

The performance of the implementation of our reconfigurability framework is intrinsically tied to the performance of the planner's implementation that we used to find the proper replacements for a faulty capability. Therefore, future experiments to measure the scalability of our framework should include different planners to better evaluate how well our approach scales by isolating the performance of the planning component. Future work also include considering plan regression to rationally discard redundant capabilities that came before the faulty capability to remove any unnecessary backtracking.

References

1. Aitken, J.M., et al.: Autonomous nuclear waste management. IEEE Intell. Syst. **33**(6), 47–55 (2018)
2. Antzoulatos, N., Castro, E., de Silva, L., Rocha, A.D., Ratchev, S., Barata, J.: A multi-agent framework for capability-based reconfiguration of industrial assembly systems. Int. J. Prod. Res. **55**(10), 2950–2960 (2017)
3. Bogue, R.: Robots in the nuclear industry: a review of technologies and applications. Ind. Robot: Int. J. **38**(2), 113–118 (2011)
4. Borgo, S., Cesta, A., Orlandini, A., Umbrico, A.: A planning-based architecture for a reconfigurable manufacturing system. In: Proceedings of the Twenty-Sixth International Conference on International Conference on Automated Planning and Scheduling, ICAPS 2016, pp. 358–366, AAAI Press, London (2016)
5. Cardoso, R.C., Bordini, R.H.: Decentralised planning for multi-agent programming platforms. In: Proceedings of the 18th International Conference on Autonomous Agents and MultiAgent Systems, AAMAS 2019, International Foundation for Autonomous Agents and Multiagent Systems, pp. 799–818, Richland (2019)
6. Chen, I.M., Yang, G., Yeo, S.H.: Automatic modeling for modular reconfigurable robotic systems: theory and practice. In: Cubero, S. (ed.) Industrial Robotics, chap. 2. IntechOpen, Rijeka (2006)

7. Dennis, L.A., Farwer, B.: Gwendolen: a BDI language for verifiable agents. In: Logic and the Simulation of Interaction and Reasoning, AISB, Aberdeen (2008)
8. Dennis, L.A., Fisher, M.: Actions with durations and failures in BDI languages. In: 21st European Conference on Artificial Intelligence, vol. 263, pp. 995–996. IOS Press (2014)
9. Dennis, L.A., et al.: Reconfigurable autonomy. KI - Künstliche Intelligenz 28(3), 199–207 (2014)
10. Dennis, L.A., Fisher, M., Webster, M.P., Bordini, R.H.: Model checking agent programming languages. Autom. Softw. Eng. 19(1), 5–63 (2012)
11. Farrell, M., Luckcuck, M., Fisher, M.: Robotics and integrated formal methods: necessity meets opportunity. In: Furia, C.A., Winter, K. (eds.) IFM 2018. LNCS, vol. 11023, pp. 161–171. Springer, Cham (2018). https://doi.org/10.1007/978-3-319-98938-9_10
12. Ferrando, A., Dennis, L.A., Ancona, D., Fisher, M., Mascardi, V.: Verifying and validating autonomous systems: towards an integrated approach. In: Colombo, C., Leucker, M. (eds.) RV 2018. LNCS, vol. 11237, pp. 263–281. Springer, Cham (2018). https://doi.org/10.1007/978-3-030-03769-7_15
13. Fikes, R.E., Nilsson, N.J.: STRIPS: a new approach to the application of theorem proving to problem solving. Artif. Intell. 2(3), 189–208 (1971)
14. Flores-Abad, A., Ma, O., Pham, K., Ulrich, S.: A review of space robotics technologies for on-orbit servicing. Prog. Aerosp. Sci. 68, 1–26 (2014)
15. Fox, M., Gerevini, A., Long, D., Serina, I.: Plan stability: replanning versus plan repair. In: Proceedings of the 16th International Conference on Automated Planning and Scheduling, pp. 212–221. AAAI Press, Cumbria (2006)
16. Gerevini, A.E., Serina, I.: Efficient plan adaptation through replanning windows and heuristic goals. Fundam. Inf. 102(3–4), 287–323 (2010)
17. Hawes, N., et al.: The STRANDS project: long-term autonomy in everyday environments. Robot. Autom. Mag. 24(3), 146–156 (2017)
18. Huang, X., Chen, Q., Meng, J., Su, K.: Reconfigurability in reactive multiagent systems. In: Proceedings of the 25th International Joint Conference on Artificial Intelligence, pp. 315–321. AAAI Press, New York (2016)
19. Kohn, W., Nerode, A.: Multiple agent autonomous hybrid control systems. In: Proceedings of the 31st Conference Decision and Control (CDC), pp. 2956–2964. Tucson (1992)
20. Koren, Y., et al.: Reconfigurable manufacturing systems. CIRP Ann. 48(2), 527–540 (1999)
21. Kruijff-Korbayová, I., et al.: TRADR project: long-term human-robot teaming for robot assisted disaster response. KI - Künstliche Intelligenz 29(2), 193–201 (2015)
22. Leitão, P.: Agent-based distributed manufacturing control: a state-of-the-art survey. Eng. Appl. Artif. Intell. 22(7), 979–991 (2009)
23. Lipovetzky, N., Ramirez, M., Muise, C., Geffner, H.: Width and inference based planners: SIW, BFS (f), and PROBE. In: Proceedings of the 8th International Planning Competition (2014)
24. Marik, V., McFarlane, D.: Industrial adoption of agent-based technologies. IEEE Intell. Syst. 20(1), 27–35 (2005)
25. Mcdermott, D., et al.: PDDL - the planning domain definition language. Technical report, TR-98-003, Yale Center for Computational Vision and Control (1998)
26. Meneguzzi, F., Luck, M.: Declarative planning in procedural agent architectures. Expert Syst. Appl. 40(16), 6508–6520 (2013)
27. Murphy, R.R.: Trial by fire [rescue robots]. IEEE Robot. Autom. Mag. 11(3), 50–61 (2004)

28. Muscettola, N., Nayak, P.P., Pell, B., Williams, B.: Remote agent: to boldly go where no AI system has gone before. Artif. Intell. **103**(1–2), 5–48 (1998)
29. Quigley, M., et al.: ROS: an open-source robot operating system. In: Workshop on Open Source Software at the International Conference on Robotics and Automation. IEEE, Japan (2009)
30. Rao, A.S., Georgeff, M.P.: BDI agents: from theory to practice. In: Proceedings of the first International Conference on Multi-Agent Systems, pp. 312–319 (1995)
31. Reiter, R.: The frame problem in situation the calculus: a simple solution (sometimes) and a completeness result for goal regression. In: Lifschitz, V. (ed.) Artificial Intelligence and Mathematical Theory of Computation, pp. 359–380. Academic Press Professional Inc., San Diego (1991)
32. Scala, E., Micalizio, R., Torasso, P.: Robust plan execution via reconfiguration and replanning. AI Commun. **28**(3), 479–509 (2015)
33. Shukla, A., Karki, H.: Application of robotics in offshore oil and gas industry - a review part II. Robot. Auton. Syst. **75**, 508–524 (2016)
34. Singh, B., Sellappan, N.P.K.: Evolution of industrial robots and their applications. Int. J. Emerg. Technol. Adv. Eng. **3**(5), 763–768 (2013)
35. Støy, K., Brandt, D., Christensen, D.J.: Self-Reconfigurable Robots. MIT Press, Cambridge (2010)
36. Tate, A.: Generating project networks. In: Proceedings of the 5th International Joint Conference on Artificial Intelligence, IJCAI 1977, vol. 2, pp. 888–893. Morgan Kaufmann Publishers Inc., San Francisco (1977)
37. Webster, M., Fisher, M., Cameron, N., Jump, M.: Formal methods for the certification of autonomous unmanned aircraft systems. In: Flammini, F., Bologna, S., Vittorini, V. (eds.) SAFECOMP 2011. LNCS, vol. 6894, pp. 228–242. Springer, Heidelberg (2011). https://doi.org/10.1007/978-3-642-24270-0_17
38. Wei, C., Hindriks, K.V.: An agent-based cognitive robot architecture. In: Dastani, M., Hübner, J.F., Logan, B. (eds.) ProMAS 2012. LNCS (LNAI), vol. 7837, pp. 54–71. Springer, Heidelberg (2013). https://doi.org/10.1007/978-3-642-38700-5_4
39. Wilcox, B.H.: Robotic vehicles for planetary exploration. Appl. Intell. **2**(2), 181–193 (1992)

Implementation Techniques and Tools

JS-son - A Lean, Extensible JavaScript Agent Programming Library

Timotheus Kampik(✉) and Juan Carlos Nieves

Umeå University, 901 87 Umeå, Sweden
{tkampik,jcnieves}@cs.umu.se

Abstract. A multitude of agent-oriented software engineering frameworks exist, most of which are developed by the academic multi-agent systems community. However, these frameworks often impose programming paradigms on their users that are challenging to learn for engineers who are used to modern high-level programming languages such as JavaScript and Python. To show how the adoption of agent-oriented programming by the software engineering mainstream can be facilitated, we provide a lean JavaScript library prototype for implementing reasoning-loop agents. The library focuses on core agent programming concepts and refrains from imposing further restrictions on the programming approach. To illustrate its usefulness, we show how the library can be applied to multi-agent systems simulations on the web, deployed to cloud-hosted function-as-a-service environments, and embedded in Python-based data science tools.

Keywords: Reasoning-loop agents · Agent programming · Multi-agent systems

1 Introduction

Many multi-agent system (MAS) platforms have been developed by the scientific community [11]. However, these platforms are rarely applied outside of academia, likely because they require the adoption of design paradigms that are fundamentally different from industry practices and do not integrate well with modern software engineering tool chains. A recent expert report on the status quo and future of *engineering multi-agent systems*[1] concludes that "many frameworks that are frequently used by the MAS community–for example Jason and JaCaMo–have not widely been adopted in practice and are dependent on technologies that are losing traction in the industry" [13]. Another comprehensive assessment of the current state of agent-oriented software engineering and its implications on future research directions is provided in Logan's *Agent Programming Manifesto* [12]. Both the *Manifesto* and the EMAS report recommend developing agent programming languages that are easier to use (as one of several ways to facilitate the impact of multi-agent systems research). The EMAS report highlights, *in particular*, the following issues:

---

[1] The report was assembled as a result of the EMAS 2018 workshop.

L. A. Dennis et al. (Eds.): EMAS 2019, LNAI 12058, pp. 215–234, 2020.
https://doi.org/10.1007/978-3-030-51417-4_11

1. The tooling of academic agent programming lacks maturity for industry adoption. In particular, Logan states that "there is little incentive for developers to switch to current agent programming languages, as the behaviours that can be easily programmed are sufficiently simple to be implementable in mainstream languages with only a small overhead in coding time" [12].
2. Recent trends towards higher-level programming languages have found little consideration by the multi-agent systems community. In contrast, the machine learning community has embraced these programming languages, for example by providing frameworks like Tensorflow.js for JavaScript [16] and Keras for Python [6].
3. Consequently, agent programming lacks strong industry success stories.

Based on these challenges, the following research directions can be derived:

1. Provide agent programming tools that offer useful abstractions in the context of modern technology ecosystems/software stacks, without imposing unnecessarily complex design abstractions or niche languages onto developers.
2. Embrace emerging technology ecosystems that are increasingly adopted by the industry, like Python for data science/machine learning and JavaScript for the web.
3. Evaluate agent programming tools in the context of industry software engineering.

While this work cannot immediately provide practical agent programming success stories, it attempts to provide a contribution to the development of tools and frameworks that are conceptually pragmatic in that they limit the design concepts and technological peculiarities they impose on their users and allow for a better integration into modern software engineering ecosystems. We follow a pragmatic and lean approach: instead of creating a comprehensive multi-agent systems framework, we create *JS-son*, a light-weight library that can be applied in the context of existing industry technology stacks and tool chains and requires little additional, MAS-specific knowledge.

The rest of this chapter is organized as follows. The design approach for JS-son is described in Sect. 2. The architecture of JS-son, as well as the supported reasoning loops, are explained in Sect. 3. Subsequently, Sect. 4 explains how to program JS-son agents using a small, step-by-step example. Section 5 elaborates on scenarios, in which using JS-son can be potentially beneficial; for some of the use case types, simple proof-of-concept examples are presented in Sect. 6. Then, JS-son is put into the context of related work on agent programming libraries and frameworks in high-level programming languages in Sect. 7. Finally, Sect. 8 concludes the chapter by discussing limitations and future work.

2   Design Approach

Programming languages like Lisp and Haskell are rarely used in practice but have influenced the adoption of (functional) features in mainstream languages like JavaScript and C#. It is not uncommon that an intermediate adoption step is enabled by external libraries. For example, before JavaScript's `array.prototype.includes` function was adopted as part of the ECMA Script standard[2], a similar function (`contains` and its aliases `include/includes`) could already be imported with the external library `underscore`[3]. Analogously, JS-son takes the belief-desire-intention (BDI) [15] architecture as popularized in the MAS community by frameworks like Jason [3] (as the name *JS-son* reflects) and provides an abstraction of the BDI architecture (as well as support for other reasoning loops) as a *plug and play* dependency for a widely adopted programming language. Table 1 provides a side-by-side overview of the influence of the functional programming paradigm via Lisp's `MEMBER` function on JavaScript's `includes` function as an analogy to the influence of Jason's (`event, context, body`)-plans on JS-son's (`intention-condition, body`)-plans. To further guide the design and develop-

Table 1. Evolution of a Functional Feature from Lisp to JavaScript and Development of an Agent-oriented Feature from Jason to JS-son.

	Functional programming	Agent-oriented programming
Source technology	Lisp	Jason
Source feature,	`MEMBER` function (list)	(`event, context, body`) plans
Target technology	JavaScript	
Target feature	`includes` functor (array)	(`intention-condition, body`) plans
Library/extension	Lodash (_)	JS-son
Standard feature	`includes` (ES2016)	none

ment of JS-son, we introduce three design principles that are–in their structure, as well as in their intend to avoid unnecessary overhead on the software (agent) engineering process–influenced by the *Agile Manifesto*[4].

Usability over intellectual elegance. JS-son provides a core framework for defining agents and their reasoning loops and environments, while allowing users to stick to pure JavaScript syntax and to apply their preferred libraries and design patterns to implement agent-agnostic functionality.

Flexibility over rigor. Instead of proposing a *one-size-fit-all* reasoning loop, JS-son offers flexibility in that it supports different approaches and is intended to remain open to evolve its reasoning loop as it matures.

Extensibility over out-of-the-box power. To maintain JS-son as a concise library that can be adapted to a large variety of use cases while requiring little additional learning effort, we keep the JS-son core small and abstain from adding complex, special-purpose features, in particular if doing so imposed additional learning effort for JS-son users or required the use of third-party dependencies; *i.e.*, we maintain a lean JS-son core module that is written in

---

[2] https://www.ecma-international.org/ecma-262/7.0/#sec-array.prototype.includes.
[3] https://underscorejs.org/#contains.
[4] http://agilemanifesto.org/.

vanilla JavaScript (does not require dependencies). Additional functionality can be provided as modules that extend the core and are managed as separate packages.

3   Architecture and Reasoning Loops

The library provides object types for creating agent and environment objects, as well as functions for generating agent beliefs, desires, intentions, and plans[5]. The **agent** implements the BDI concepts as follows:

Beliefs: A belief can be any JavaScript Object Notation (JSON[6]) object or JSON data type (string, number, array, boolean, or *null*).

Desires: Desires are generated dynamically by agent-specific desire functions that have a desire identifier assigned to them and determine the value of the desire based on the agent's current beliefs.

Intentions: A `preference` function filters desires and returns *intentions* - an array of JSON objects.

Plans: A plan's *head* specifies which intention needs to be active for the plan to be pursued. The plan body specifies how the plan should update the agent's beliefs and determines the actions the agent should issue to the environment.

Each agent has a `next()` function to run the following process:

1. It applies the belief update as provided by the environment (see below).
2. It applies the agent's preference function that dynamically updates the intentions based on the new beliefs; *i.e.*, the agent is *open-minded* (see Rao and Georgeff [15]).
3. It runs the plans that are active according to the updated intentions, while also updating the agent beliefs (if specified in the plans).
4. It issues action requests that result from the plans to the environment.

It is also possible to implement simpler belief-plan agents; *i.e.*, as a plan's head, one can define a function that determines–based on the agent's current beliefs–if a plan should be executed. Alternatively, belief-desire-plan/belief-intention-plan reasoning loops are supported; these approaches bear similarity to the belief-goal-plan approach of the *GOAL* language [8]. Figure 1a depicts the reasoning loops that are supported by standard JS-son agents.

The **environment** contains the agents, as well as a definition of its own state. It executes the following instructions in a loop:

1. It runs each agent's `next()` function.
2. Once the agent's action request has been received, the environment processes the request. To determine which update requests should, in fact, be applied to the environment state, the environment runs the request through a filter function.

---

[5] The library–including detailed documentation, examples, and tests–is available at https://github.com/TimKam/JS-son.

[6] http://www.ecma-international.org/publications/files/ECMA-ST/ECMA-404.pdf.

3. When an agent's actions are processed, the environment updates its own state and the beliefs of all agents accordingly. Another filter function determines how a specific agent should "perceive" the environment's state.

Figure 1b depicts the environment's agent and state management process[7].

4   Implementing JS-son Agents

This section explains how to implement JS-son agents, by first giving a detailed explanation of the most important parts of the JS-son core API and then providing a programming tutorial.

4.1   JS-son Core API

The JS-son core API provides two major abstractions: one for agents and one for environments[8]. In addition, the agent requires the instantiation of beliefs, desires, and plans. Note that intentions are generated dynamically, as is explained below.

Agents. An agent is instantiated by calling the *Agent* function with parameters that specify the agent's identifier (a text string), as well as its initial beliefs, desires, plans, and a *preference function generator*. Beliefs, desires, and plans are generated by the *Belief*, *Desire*, and *Plan* functions, respectively. Beliefs and desires consist of an identifier (key) and a body (value). A belief body can be any valid JSON object or property (number, string, *null*, boolean, or array). A desire body is a function that processes the agent's current beliefs and returns the processing result. A plan has two functions; one as its *body* and one as its *head*. The head determines–based on an agent's beliefs–if the plan body should be executed. The body determines agent actions, as well as belief updates, taking the agent's beliefs as an optional input. *Intentions* are created by a preference function generator, a higher-order function that, based on the agents' current desires and beliefs, generates a function that reduces the agents' desires to intentions. Table 3a documents the *Agent* function signature, whereas Tables 3b, 3c, and 3d document the signatures for the *Belief*, *Desire*, and *Plan* functions, respectively.

Environment. The environment is generated by the *Environment* function that takes as its input an array of JS-son agents, an initial state definition (JSON object), and functions for updating the environment's state, visualizing it, and pre-processing (filtering or manipulating) it before exposing the state to the agents. The *update* function processes the agents' actions; for each agent, it determines how the environment's state should be updated, based on the

---

[7] In its current version, JS-son executes all steps *synchronously*. Supporting the asynchronous execution, in particular of agent plans is future work, as discussed in Sect. 8.

[8] Here, we only explain the core functionality for instantiating agents and environments. A comprehensive, continuously updated documentation of the JS-son API is available at https://js-son.readthedocs.io/en/latest/.

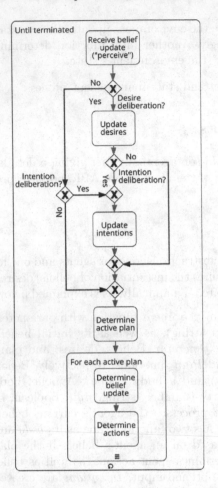
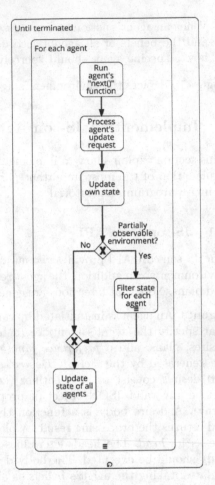

(a) JS-son reasoning loop. The *XOR* gateways allow for different reasoning loop approaches. The red sequence flows indicate the path of the belief-desire-intention-plan reasoning loop.

(b) JS-son environment: agent and state management process. The *XOR* gateway allows for partially and fully observable environments.

Fig. 1. JS-son reasoning and environment loop.

current state, the agent's actions, and the agent's identifier. The state update is then visualized as specified by the *render* function. In case a visualization is not necessary, the default *render* function makes the environment log each iteration's state to the console. The *stateFilter* function filters or manipulates the state as perceived by a particular agent, based on this agent's identifier and its current beliefs; by default (if no *stateFilter* function is specified), the state is returned unfiltered to the agent(s). Table 3 documents the environment's function signature.

Table 2. Function signature of the JS-son *Agent* and its components.

Name	Type	Description
(a) JS-son *Agent* function signature		
id	String	Unique identifier of the agent
beliefs	Object	Initial beliefs of the agents
desires	Object	The agent's desires
plans	Array	The agent's plans
preferenceFunctionGenerator	Array	Preference function generator; by default (if no function is provided), the preference function turns all desires into intentions
Returns	Object	JS-son Agent object
(b) JS-son *Belief* function signature		
Name	**Type**	**Description**
id	String	Unique identifier of the belief
value	Any (needs to be valid JSON object or JSON value)	The belief's initial value
Returns	Object	JS-son Belief object
(c) JS-son *Desire* function signature		
id	String	Unique identifier of the belief
body	Function	Function for computing the desires value based on current beliefs
Returns	Object	JS-son Desire object
(d) JS-son *Plan* function signature		
head	Function	Determines if plan is active
body	Function	Determines the execution of actions and update of beliefs
Returns	object	Plan object

Table 3. JS-son *Environment* function signature

Name	Type	Description
agents	Array of JS-son agents	Agents that the environment is managing
state	Object	Initial state of the environment
update	Function	Processes agent actions and updates the environment's state
render	Function	Visualizes the environment's current state
stateFilter	Function	Filters/manipulates the state that agents should perceive
Returns	Object	Plan object

4.2 Tutorial

The tutorial explains how to program *belief-plan* agents using a minimal example[9]. Running the example requires the creation of a new Node.js project (`npm init`), the installation of the `js-son-agent` dependency, and the import of the JS-son library.

```
const {
    Belief,
    Plan,
    Agent,
    Environment } = require('js-son-agent')
```

The tutorial implements the *Jason room example*[10] with JS-son. In the example, three agents are in a room:

1. A porter that locks and unlocks the room's door if requested;
2. A paranoid agent that prefers the door to be locked and asks the porter to lock the door if this is not the case;
3. A claustrophobe agent that prefers the door to be unlocked and asks the porter to unlock the door if this is not the case.

The simulation runs twenty iterations of the scenario. In an iteration, each agent acts once. All agents start with the same beliefs. The belief with the ID `door` is assigned the object {`locked`: **true**}; *i.e.*, the door is locked. Also, nobody has so far requested any change in door state (`requests`: **[]**).

```
const beliefs = {
    ...Belief('door', { locked: true }),
    ...Belief('requests', [])
}
```

---

[9] Tutorials that present more complex examples are available in the JS-son project documentation https://js-son.readthedocs.io.

[10] https://github.com/jason-lang/jason/tree/master/examples/room.

Now, we define the porter agent. The porter has the following plans:

1. If it does not believe the door is locked and it has received a request to lock the door (head), lock the door (body).
2. If it believes the door is locked and it has received a request to unlock the door (head), unlock the door (body).

```
const plansPorter = [
    Plan(
        beliefs =>
            !beliefs.door.locked &&
            beliefs.requests.includes('lock'),
        () => [{ door: 'lock' }]
    ),
    Plan(
        beliefs =>
            beliefs.door.locked &&
            beliefs.requests.includes('unlock'),
        () => [{ door: 'unlock' }]
    )
]
```

We instantiate a new agent with the belief set and plans. Because we are not making use of desires in this simple belief-plan scenario, we pass an empty object as the agent's desires.

```
const porter = new Agent('porter', beliefs, {}, plansPorter)
```

Next, we create the paranoid agent with the following plans:

1. If it does not belief the door is locked (head), it requests the door to be locked (body).
2. If it beliefs the door is locked (head), it broadcasts a thank you message for locking the door (body).

```
const plansParanoid = [
  Plan(
    beliefs => !beliefs.door.locked,
    () => [{ request: 'lock' }]
  ),
  Plan(
    beliefs => beliefs.door.locked,
    () => [{ announce: 'Thanks for locking the door!' }]
  )
]
```

```
const paranoid = new Agent('paranoid', beliefs, {}, plansParanoid)
```

The last agent we create is the paranoid one. It has these plans:

1. If it beliefs the door the door is locked (head), it requests the door to be unlocked (body).
2. If it does not belief the door is locked (head), it broadcasts a thank you message for unlocking the door (body).

```
const plansClaustrophobe = [
    Plan(
        beliefs => beliefs.door.locked,
        () => [{ request: 'unlock' }]
    ),
    Plan(
        beliefs => !beliefs.door.locked,
        () => [{ announce: 'Thanks for unlocking the door!' }]
    )
]

const claustrophobe = new Agent(
    'claustrophobe',
    beliefs,
    {},
    plansClaustrophobe
)
```

Now, as we have defined the agents, we need to specify the environment. First, we set the environments state, which is–in our case–consistent with the agents' beliefs.

```
const state = {
    door: { locked: true },
    requests: []
}
```

To define how the environment processes agent actions, we implement the updateState function. The function takes an agent's actions, as well as the agent's identifier and the current state to determine the environment's state update that is merged into the new state state = ...state, ...stateUpdate.

```
const updateState = (actions, agentId, currentState) => {
    const stateUpdate = {
        requests: currentState.requests
    }
    actions.forEach(action => {
        if (action.some(action => action.door === 'lock')) {
            stateUpdate.door = { locked: true }
            stateUpdate.requests = []
            console.log(`${agentId}: Lock door`)
        }
        if (action.some(action => action.door === 'unlock')) {
            stateUpdate.door = { locked: false }
            stateUpdate.requests = []
            console.log(`${agentId}: Unlock door`)
        }
        if (action.some(action => action.request === 'lock')) {
            stateUpdate.requests.push('lock')
            console.log(`${agentId}: Request: lock door`)
        }
        if (action.some(action => action.request === 'unlock')) {
            stateUpdate.requests.push('unlock')
            console.log(`${agentId}: Request: unlock door`)
        }
        if (action.some(action => action.announce)) {
            console.log(`${agentId}: ${
                action.find(
                    action => action.announce
                ).announce
            }`)
        }
    })
    return stateUpdate
}
```

To simulate a partially observable world, we can specify the environment's
stateFilter function, which determines how the state update should be shared
with the agents. However, in our case we simply communicate the whole state
update to all agents, which is also the default behavior of the environment, if no
stateFilter function is specified.

```
const stateFilter = state => state
```

We instantiate the environment with the specified agents, state, update function,
and filter function.

```
const environment = new Environment(
    [paranoid, claustrophobe, porter],
    state,
    updateState,
    stateFilter
)
```

Finally, we run 20 iterations of the scenario.

```
environment.run(20)
```

5   Potential Use Cases

We suggest that JS-son can be applied in the following use cases:

Data science. With the increasing relevance of large-scale and semi-automated statistical analysis ("data science") in industry and academia, a new set of technologies has emerged that focuses on pragmatic and flexible usage and treats traditional programming paradigms as second-class citizens. JS-son integrates well with Python- and Jupyter notebook[11]-based data science tools, as shown in Demonstration 1.

Web development. Web front ends implement functionality of growing complexity; often, large parts of the application are implemented by (browser-based) clients. As shown in Demonstration 2, JS-son allows embedding BDI agents in single-page web applications, using the tools and paradigms of web development.

Education. Programming courses are increasingly relevant for educating students who lack a computer science background. Such courses are typically taught in high-level languages that enable students to write working code without knowing all underlying concepts. In this context, JS-son can be used as a tool for teaching MAS programming.

Internet-of-Things (IoT) Frameworks like Node.js[12] enable the rapid development of IoT applications, as a large ecosystem of libraries leaves the application developer largely in the role of a system integrator. JS-son is available as a Node.js package.

Function-as-a-Service. The term *serverless* [1] computing refers to information technology that allows application developers to deploy their code via the infrastructure and software ecosystem of third-party providers without needing to worry about the technical details of the execution environment. The provision of *serverless* computing services is often referred to as *Function-as-a-Service* (FaaS). Most FaaS providers, like Heroku[13], Amazon Web Services Lamda[14], and Google Cloud Functions[15], provide Node.js support for their service offerings and allow for the deployment of JavaScript functions with little setup overhead. Consequently, JS-son can emerge as a convenient tool to develop agents and multi-agent systems that are then deployed as *serverless* functions. For a running example, see Subsection 6.4.

6   Examples

We provide four demonstrations that show how JS-son can be applied. The code of all demonstration is available in the JS-son project repository (https://github.com/TimKam/JS-son).

---

[11] https://jupyter.org/.
[12] https://nodejs.org/.
[13] https://devcenter.heroku.com/articles/getting-started-with-nodejs.
[14] https://docs.aws.amazon.com/lambda/latest/dg/nodejs-prog-model-handler.html.
[15] https://cloud.google.com/functions/docs/concepts/nodejs-8-runtime.

6.1 JS-son Meets Jupyter

The first demonstration shows how JS-son can be integrated with data science tools, *i.e.*, with Python libraries and Jupyter notebooks[16]. As a simple proof-of-concept example, we simulate opinion spread in an agent society and run an interactive data visualization. The example simulates the spread of a single boolean belief among 100 agents in environments with different *biases* regarding the facilitation of the different opinion values. Belief spread is simulated as follows:

1. The scenario starts with each agent announcing their beliefs.
2. In each iteration, the environment distributes two belief announcements to each agent. Based on these beliefs and possibly (depending on the agent type) the past announcements the agent was exposed to, each agent announces a new belief: either *true* or *false*.

The agents are of two different agent types (*volatile* and *introspective*):

Volatile. Volatile agents only consider their current belief and the latest belief set they received from the environment when deciding which belief to announce. Volatile agents are "louder", *i.e.*, the environment is more likely to spread beliefs of volatile agents. We also add bias to the announcement spread function to favor true announcements.

Introspective. In contrast to volatile agents, introspective agents consider the past five belief sets they have received, when deciding which belief they should announce. Introspective agents are "less loud", *i.e.*, the environment is less likely to spread beliefs of volatile agents.

The agent type distribution is 50, 50. However, 30 volatile and 20 introspective agents start with *true* as their belief, whereas 20 volatile and 30 introspective agents start with *false* as their belief. Figure 2a shows an excerpt of the Juypter notebook.

6.2 JS-son in the Browser

The second demonstration presents a JS-son port of *Conway's Game of Life*. It illustrates how JS-son can be used as part of a web frontend. In this example, JS-son is fully integrated into a JavaScript build and compilation pipeline that allows writing modern, idiomatic JavaScript code based on the latest ECMAScript specification, as it compiles this code into cross-browser compatible, *minified* JavaScript. The demonstration makes use of JS-son's simplified belief-plan approach[17]. Each Game of Life *cell* is represented by an agent that has two beliefs: its own state (active or inactive) and the number of its *active* neighbors. At each simulation tick, the agent decides based on its beliefs, if it

---

[16] The Jupyter notebook is available on GitHub at http://s.cs.umu.se/lmfd69 and on a Jupyter notebook service platform at http://s.cs.umu.se/girizr.

[17] The simulation is available at http://s.cs.umu.se/chfbk2.

should register a change in its status (from active to inactive or vice versa) with the environment. After all agents have registered their new status, the environment updates the global game state accordingly and passes the new number of active neighbors to each agent. Figure 2b depicts the *Game of Life* application.

6.3   Learning JS-son Agents

The third demonstration shows how *learning* JS-son agents can be implemented in a browser-based grid world[18]. The example instantiates agents in a 20×20 field grid world *arena* with the following field types:

- *Mountain* fields that the agents cannot pass.
- *Money* fields that provide a *coin* to an agent that approaches them (the agent needs to move onto the field, but the environment will return a coin and leave the agent at its current position).
- *Repair* fields that provide damaged agents with one additional health unit when approached (again, the agent needs to move onto the field, but the environment will return a health unit and leave the agent at its current position).
- *Plain* fields that can be traversed by an agent if no other agent is present on the field. If another agent is already present, the environment will reject the move, but decrease both agents' health by 10. When an agent's health reaches (or goes below) zero, it is punished by a withdrawal of 100 coins from its stash.

The agents are trained *online* (no model is loaded/persisted) using deep Q-learning through an experimental JS-son learning extension. Figure 2c shows the agents in the grid world arena.

6.4   Serverless JS-son Agents

The fourth demonstration shows how JS-son agents can be deployed to *Function-as-a-Service* providers. It is based on the belief spread simulation as introduced in the first demonstration (see Subsect. 6.1). The multi-agent simulation is wrapped in a request handler and provided as a Node.js project that is configured to run as a *Google Cloud Function*. The request handler accepts HTTP(S) requests against the `simulate` endpoint. The request *method* (*e.g.*, `GET`, `POST`, `PUT`) is ignored by the handler. Upon receiving the request, the handler runs the simulation for the specified number of *ticks*, configuring the *bias* in the agent society as specified by the corresponding request parameter (the higher the bias, the stronger the facilitation of *true* announcements). An example request against a fictional FaaS instance could be sent using the `curl` command line tool as specified in the code snippet below.

---

[18] This grid world is an adaptation of an environment in which learning JS-son agents are rewarded based on a specific, *fair* game-theoretical equilibrium in a given state, as presented by Kampik and Spieker [10].

```
curl -X GET 'https://instance.faas.net/simulation/simulate?ticks=20&bias=5'
```

Figure 2d depicts the simulation in the Google Cloud Functions management user interface.

7 Related Work

Over the past two decades, a multitude of agent-oriented software engineering frameworks emerged (see, *e.g.*, Kravari and Bassiliades [11]). However, most of these frameworks do not target higher-level programming languages like Python and JavaScript. In this section, we provide a brief overview of three agent proggraming frameworks–*osBrain*, *JAM*, and *Eve* that are indeed written in and for these two languages. We then highlight key differences to our library.

7.1 OsBrain

osBrain[19] is a Python library for developing multi-agent systems. Although osBrain is written in a different language than JS-son, it is still relevant for the comparison because it is *i)* written in a higher level programming language of a similar generation and *ii)* somewhat actively maintained[20]. Initially developed as an automated trading software backbone, the focus of osBrain lies on the provision of an agent-oriented communication framework. No framework for the agents internal reasoning loop is provided, *i.e.* osBrain does not provide BDI support. Also, osBrain dictates the use of a specific communication protocol and library, utilizing the message queue system *ZeroMQ* [9].

7.2 JavaScript Agent Machine (JAM)

Bosse introduces the *JavaScript Agent Machine* (JAM), which is a "mobile multi-agent system[...] for the Internet-of-Things and clouds" [5].

 Some of JAM's main features and properties are, according to its documentation[21]:

– Performance: through third-party libraries, JAM agents can be compiled to Bytecode that allows for performant execution in low-resource environments;
– Mobility and support for heterogenous environments: agent instances can be moved between physical and virtual nodes at run-time;

---

[19] https://osbrain.readthedocs.io/en/stable/about.html.
[20] As of March 2020, the last update to the source of *Eve* dates back more than 2.5 years to August 2017 (https://github.com/enmasseio/evejs/); the last update of the documentation of *JAM*–whose source code is not available–dates back more than 1.5 years to August 2018 (http://www.bsslab.de/?Software/jam). In contrast the last update of the osBrain source and documentation dates back roughly one year to April 2019 (https://github.com/opensistemas-hub/osbrain).
[21] http://www.bsslab.de/assets/agents.html.

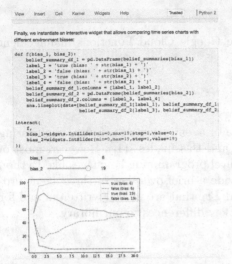

(a) Analysis of a JS-son multi-agent simulation in a Jupyter Notebook.

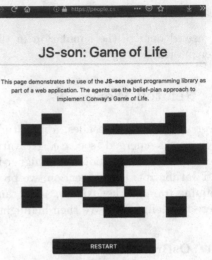

(b) JS-son: Conway's Game of Life, implemented as a web application.

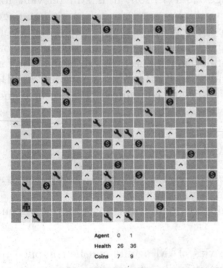

(c) JS-son agents in a grid world.

(d) JS-son multi-agent system, deployed as a Google Cloud Function.

Fig. 2. JS-son example applications.

- Machine learning capabilities, through integration with a machine learning service platform; however, no details on how this service can be accessed are provided in the documentation.

In its initial version, JAM agents required the use of a JavaScript-like language that is syntactically not fully compliant with any standard

JavaScript/ECMAScript version [4]. However, in its latest version, it is possible to implement agent in syntactically valid JavaScript. With its focus on agent orchestration, deployment, and communications, JAM's agent internals are based on *activity-transition graphs*, which implies that its functionality overlaps little with JS-son. Another point of distinction is that the JAM source code is not openly available; instead, the JAM website[22] provides a set of installers and libraries and software development kits for different platforms that can be used as black-box dependencies.

7.3   Eve

De Jong *et al.* [7] present *Eve*, a multi-agent platform for agent discovery and communications. It is available as both a Java and a JavaScript implementation. Similar to osBrain, Eve's core functionality is an agent-oriented, unified abstraction on different communication protocols; it does not define agent internals like reasoning loops and consequently does not follow a belief-desire-intention approach. Eve is provided as Node.js package[23], but as of March 2020, the installation fails and the Node Package Manager (npm) reports 11 known security vulnerabilities upon attempted installation. Still, Eve is in regard to its technological basis similar to JS-son. With its difference in focus–on agent discovery and communications in contrast to JS-son's reasoning loops–Eve could be, if maintenance issues will be addressed, a potential integration option that a JS-son extension can provide.

7.4   Comparison - Unique JS-son Features

To summarize the comparison, we list three unique features that distinguish JS-son from the aforementioned frameworks.

Reasoning loop focus with belief-desire-intention support. Of the three frameworks, only JAM provides a dedicated way to frame the reasoning loop of implemented agents, using activity-transition graphs. Still, the core focus of *all three* libraries is on communication and orchestration, which contrasts the focus of JS-son as a library that has a reasoning loop framework at its core and aims to be largely agnostic to specific messaging and orchestration approaches.

Full integration with the modern JavaScript ecosystem. As shown in Sect. 6, JS-son fully integrates with the JavaScript ecosystem across runtime environments. This is in particular a contrast to JAM, which provides installers that obfuscate the proprietary source code and require a nonstandard installation process. This can potentially hinder integration into existing software ecosystems that rely on *industry standard* approaches to dependency management for continuous integration and delivery purposes.

---

[22] http://www.bsslab.de/?Software/jam.
[23] https://www.npmjs.com/package/evejs.

While Eve attempts to provide an integration that allows for a convenient deployment in different environments, for example through continuous integration pipelines, it does in fact not provide a working, stable, and secure installation package.

Dependency-free and open source code. JS-son is a light-weight, open source library that does not ship any dependencies in its core version, but rather provides modules that require dependencies as *extensions*. In contrast, adopting JAM requires reliance on closed/obfuscated source code, whereas osBrain and Eve require a set of dependencies, which are in the case of Eve– as explained before–not properly managed.

8   Conclusions and Future Work

This chapter presents a lean, extensible library that provides simple abstractions for JavaScript-based agent programming, with a focus on reasoning loop specification. To further increase the library's relevance for researchers, teachers, and practitioners alike, we propose the following work:

Support a distributed environment and interfaces to other MAS frameworks. It makes sense to enable JS-son agents and environments to act in distributed systems and communicate with agents of other types, without requiring extensive customization by the library user. A possible way to achieve this is supporting the open standard agent communication language FIPA ACL[24]. However, as highlighted in a previous publication [14], FIPA ACL does not support communication approaches that have emerged as best practices for real-time distributed systems like *publish-subscribe*. Also, the application of JS-son in a distributed context can benefit from the enhancement of agent-internal behavior, for example through a feature that supports the asynchronous execution of plans.

Implement a reasoning extension. To facilitate JS-son's reasoning abilities, additional JS-son extensions can be developed. From an applied perspective, integrations with business rules engines can bridge the gap to traditional enterprise software, whereas a JS-son extension for *formal argumentation* (see, *e.g.*, Bench-Capon and Dunne [2]) can be of value for the academic community.

Move towards real-world usage. To demonstrate the feasibility of JS-son, it is important to apply the library in advanced scenarios. Considering the relatively small technical overhead JS-son agents imply, the entry hurdle for a development team to adopt JS-son is low, which can facilitate real-world adoption. Still, future work needs to evaluate how useful the abstractions JS-son provides are for industry software engineers.

Implement a Python port. While JS-son can be integrated with the Python ecosystem, for example via Jupyter notebooks, doing so implies technical overhead and requires knowledge of two programming languages[25]. To facilitate

---

[24] http://www.fipa.org/specs/fipa00061/index.html.
[25] Also, the module that allows for Node.js-Python interoperability (https://github.com/pixiedust/pixiedust_node) has some limitations, *i.e.* it lacks Python 3 support.

the use of agents in a data science and machine learning context, we propose the implementation of *Py_son*, a Python port of JS-son.

Acknowledgements. The authors thank the anonymous reviewers, as well as Cleber Jorge Amaral, Jomi Fred Hübner, Esteban Guerrero, Yazan Mualla, Amro Najjar, Helge Spieker, Michael Winikoff, and many others for useful feedback and discussions. This work was partially supported by the Wallenberg AI, Autonomous Systems and Software Program (WASP) funded by the Knut and Alice Wallenberg Foundation.

References

1. Baldini, I., et al.: Serverless computing: current trends and open problems. In: Chaudhary, S., Somani, G., Buyya, R. (eds.) Research Advances in Cloud Computing, pp. 1–20. Springer, Singapore (2017). https://doi.org/10.1007/978-981-10-5026-8_1
2. Bench-Capon, T.J., Dunne, P.E.: Argumentation in artificial intelligence. Artif. Intell. **171**(10–15), 619–641 (2007)
3. Bordini, R.H., Hübner, J.F., Wooldridge, M.: Programming Multi-Agent Systems in AgentSpeak Using Jason. Wiley Series in Agent Technology. Wiley, Chichester (2007)
4. Bosse, S.: Unified distributed computing and co-ordination in pervasive/ubiquitous networks with mobile multi-agent systems using a modular and portable agent code processing platform. Procedia Comput. Sci. **63**, 56–64 (2015)
5. Bosse, S.: Mobile multi-agent systems for the Internet-of-Things and clouds using the Javascript agent machine platform and machine learning as a service. In: 2016 IEEE 4th International Conference on Future Internet of Things and Cloud (FiCloud), pp. 244–253. IEEE (2016)
6. Chollet, F.: Deep Learning with Python, 1st edn. Manning Publications Co., Greenwich (2017)
7. De Jong, J., Stellingwerff, L., Pazienza, G.E.: Eve: a novel open-source web-based agent platform. In: 2013 IEEE International Conference on Systems, Man, and Cybernetics, pp. 1537–1541. IEEE (2013)
8. Hindriks, K.V.: Programming rational agents in GOAL. In: El Fallah Seghrouchni, A., Dix, J., Dastani, M., Bordini, R.H. (eds.) Multi-Agent Programming, pp. 119–157. Springer, Boston, MA (2009). https://doi.org/10.1007/978-0-387-89299-3_4
9. Hintjens, P.: ZeroMQ: Messaging for Many Applications. O'Reilly Media Inc., Sebastopol (2013)
10. Kampik, T., Spieker, H.: Learning agents of bounded rationality: rewards based on fair equilibria. In: 2019 The 31st Annual Workshop of the Swedish Artificial Intelligence Society (SAIS) (2019)
11. Kravari, K., Bassiliades, N.: A survey of agent platforms. J. Artif. Soc. Soc. Simul. **18**(1), 11 (2015)
12. Logan, B.: An agent programming manifesto. Int. J. Agent-Oriented Softw. Eng. **6**(2), 187–210 (2018)
13. Mascardi, V., et al.: Engineering multi-agent systems: state of affairs and the road ahead. SIGSOFT Eng. Notes (SEN) **44**(1), 18–28 (2019)
14. Nieves, J.C., Espinoza, A., Penya, Y.K., De Mues, M.O., Pena, A.: Intelligence distribution for data processing in smart grids: a semantic approach. Eng. Appl. Artif. Intell. **26**(8), 1841–1853 (2013)

15. Rao, A.S., Georgeff, M.P.: Modeling rational agents within a BDI-architecture. In: Allen, J., Fikes, R., Sandewall, E. (eds.) Proceedings of the 2nd International Conference on Principles of Knowledge Representation and Reasoning, pp. 473–484. Morgan Kaufmann Publishers Inc., San Mateo (1991)
16. Smilkov, D., et al.: TensorFlow.js: machine learning for the web and beyond. arXiv preprint arXiv:1901.05350 (2019)

SAT for Epistemic Logic Using Belief Bases

Emiliano Lorini$^{(\boxtimes)}$ and Fabián Romero

IRIT-CNRS, Toulouse University, Toulouse, France
emiliano.lorini@irit.fr

Abstract. In [4] a new epistemic logic LDA of explicit and implicit belief was introduced, and in [5] we presented a tableau-based satisfability checking procedure as well as a dynamic extension for it. Based on such procedure, we created a portable software implementation that works for the family of multi-agent epistemic logics, as well as for the proposed dynamic extension. This software implementation runs as a library for the most common operative systems, also runs in popular IoT and robot hardware, as well as cloud environments and in server-less configurations.

1 Introduction

We believe that semantics based on explicit representation of agents' epistemic states expressed as knowledge or belief bases, are a more natural paradigm for the description of intelligent systems such as robotic and conversational agents than the Kripkean semantics commonly used for epistemic logics [2]. In order to have a tool to experiment with such semantics and explore its use, we used the logic LDA (Logic of Doxastic Attitudes) given in [5] and implemented a tableau-based satisfability procedure for it.

2 Language, Semantics and Syntax

2.1 Language of Doxastic Alternatives

The language $\mathcal{L}_{\mathsf{LDA}}$ for the logic LDA is constructed in the following way. Assume a countably infinite set of atomic propositions $Atm = \{p, q, \ldots\}$ and a finite set of agents $Agt = \{1, \ldots, n\}$.

The language $\mathcal{L}_0$ is the language of explicit beliefs defined by the following grammar:

$$\alpha ::= \bot \mid p \mid \neg\alpha \mid \alpha_1 \wedge \alpha_2 \mid \triangle_i \alpha$$

where p ranges over Atm.

The multi-modal operator $\triangle_i \alpha$ has to be read "α is a formula in agent's i belief base".

The language of implicit beliefs $\mathcal{L}_{\mathsf{LDA}}$ is defined by the grammar:

© Springer Nature Switzerland AG 2020
L. A. Dennis et al. (Eds.): EMAS 2019, LNAI 12058, pp. 235–245, 2020.
https://doi.org/10.1007/978-3-030-51417-4_12

$$\phi ::= \alpha \mid \neg\phi \mid \phi_1 \wedge \phi_2 \mid \Box_i\phi \mid \Diamond_i\phi$$

where $\alpha \in \mathcal{L}_0$, the modal formula $\Box_i\phi$ has to read "agent i can deduce ϕ from its belief base" and the modal dual $\Diamond_i\phi$ has to be read "ϕ is consistent with agent i's belief base".

The semantics for this language is based on multi-agent belief bases according to the following definition.

Definition 1 (Multi-agent belief base). *A multi-agent belief base is a tuple $B = (B_1, \ldots, B_n, S)$ where $B_i \subseteq \mathcal{L}_0$, for every $i \in Agt$, and $S \subseteq Atm$.*

Formulas of $\mathcal{L}_0$ are interpreted relative to multi-agent belief bases.

Definition 2 (Satisfaction Relation). *Let $B = (B_1, \ldots, B_n, S)$ be a multi-agent belief base. Then, the satisfaction relation $\models$ for formulas in $\mathcal{L}_0$ is defined as follows:*

$$B \not\models \bot$$
$$B \models p \iff p \in S$$
$$B \models \neg\alpha \iff B \not\models \alpha$$
$$B \models \alpha_1 \wedge \alpha_2 \iff B \models \alpha_1 \text{ and } B \models \alpha_2$$
$$B \models \triangle_i\alpha \iff \alpha \in B_i$$

In order to interpret implicit belief operators, the following notion of doxastic alternative is required.

Definition 3 (Doxastic Alternative). *Let $B = (B_1, \ldots, B_n, S)$ and $B' = (B'_1, \ldots, B'_n, S')$ be two multi-agent belief bases. Then, $B\mathcal{R}_iB'$ if and only if, for every $\alpha \in B_i$, $B' \models \alpha$.*

So, B' is a doxastic alternative for agent i at B, if everything i explicitly believes at B is true at B'.

The notion of multi-agent belief model (MAB) is used for the interpretation of formulas in $\mathcal{L}_{\mathsf{LDA}}$.

Definition 4 (Multi-agent belief model). *A multi-agent belief model (MAB) is a pair (B, Cxt) where B is a multi-agent belief base and Cxt is a set of multi-agent belief bases, also called context.*

The following definition extends the satisfaction relation defined above to the full logical language. (Boolean cases are omitted as they are defined in the usual way.)

Definition 5 (Satisfaction Relation (cont.)). *Let (B, Cxt) be a MAB. Then:*

$$(B, Cxt) \models \alpha \iff B \models \alpha$$
$$(B, Cxt) \models \Box_i\varphi \iff \forall B' \in Cxt : \text{if } B\mathcal{R}_iB' \text{ then } (B', Cxt) \models \varphi$$
$$(B, Cxt) \models \Diamond_i\varphi \iff \exists B' \in Cxt : B\mathcal{R}_iB' \text{ and } (B', Cxt) \models \varphi$$

Therefore, the $\Box_i$-modality, relates a belief base B with every belief base B' which is a doxastic alternative from the point of view of the agent i at B.

2.2   Dynamic Extension

The dynamic extension of LDA we present in our companion paper allows us to describe actions of agents under observability conditions. This perceptive context, where the dynamic actions take place, is defined by the following grammar $\mathcal{L}_{\mathsf{OBS}}$:

$$\omega ::= \mathsf{see}_{i,j} \mid \mathsf{see}_i\omega$$

The expression $\mathsf{see}_{i,j}$ has to read "agent i sees what agent j does" and $\mathsf{see}_i\omega$ represents the fact that "agent i sees that ω".

The language $\mathcal{L}_{\mathsf{DLDA}}$ for DLDA (Dynamic LDA) is defined by the following grammar:

$$\phi ::= \alpha \mid \neg\phi \mid \phi_1 \wedge \phi_2 \mid \Box_i\phi \mid \Diamond_i\phi \mid [(p,\tau,i,\Omega)]\chi$$

where $\alpha \in \mathcal{L}_0$, p ranges over Atm, i ranges over Agt, τ ranges over $\{+,-\}$ and Ω is a finite set of formulas of $\mathcal{L}_{\mathsf{OBS}}$.

The action $+p$ consists in setting the value of the atomic variable p to true, whereas the action $-p$ consists in setting the value of the atomic variable p to false. The formula $[(p,\tau,i,\Omega)]\phi$ has to be read "ϕ holds after the action τp has been performed by agent i under the perceptive context Ω".

2.3   Input Syntax

The syntax used for the library is the following. Operations and precedence order for unparenthesized expressions in $\mathcal{L}_{\mathsf{LDA}}$ are (operators are separated by commas):

$$false := false, F, \bot$$
$$true := true, T, \top$$
$$box\ operator\ agent\ j := [j], \Box j$$
$$diamond\ operator\ agent\ j := <j>, \Diamond j$$
$$triangle\ operator\ agent\ j := \{j\}, \triangle j$$
$$negation := -, \sim, \neg$$
$$conjunction := \&, \wedge, /\backslash, \widehat{\ }$$
$$disjunction := \vee, \backslash/, |$$
$$implication := ->, \rightarrow$$
$$double\ implication := <->, \leftrightarrow$$
$$\cdot\ conjunction := \quad ;$$

Propositions are strings of lowercase letters of length greater than zero, followed by zero or more digits, agents are non-empty strings of digits.

We represent $\mathsf{see}_{i,j}$ in $\mathcal{L}_{\mathsf{OBS}}$ as "$i < j$" with infix right associative operator "$<$". We use ";" to separate observations in a perceptive context, and for the dynamic operator introduced as $[(p, \tau, i, \Omega)]$ we will use $i + p$ or $i - p$ to represent the Boolean value of the variable p for the agent i. Finally, "[(", ")]" will be used to open and close the definition of the operator. For example, if $\Omega = \{\mathsf{see}_{i,i}, \mathsf{see}_{j,i}, \mathsf{see}_i \mathsf{see}_{j,i}\}$, then the $\mathcal{L}_{\mathsf{DLDA}}$ operator $[(p, +, i, \Omega)]$ is written as:

```
[(i+p;i<i;j<i;i<j<i)]
```

For readability, we allow comments starting from a character '#' to the end of the line, and all contiguous white space characters including new lines are interpreted as a single space.

3 Tableaux

Definition 6 (Tableau Rules). *A tableau rule consists of a set Γ above a line called the numerator, and a list of distinct sets $\Gamma_1, .., \Gamma_n$ separated by $|$, called the denominators:*

$$\frac{\Gamma}{\Gamma_1 \mid \ldots \mid \Gamma_n}$$

The following definition specifies the conditions under which a rule is applicable.

Definition 7 (Applicable Rule and Saturated Set). *A tableau rule is applicable to a set Γ if Γ is an instance of its numerator and Γ is not an instance of one of its denominators. We say that a set Γ is saturated if there is no rule applicable to it.*

The condition requiring that for a tableau rule to be applicable to a set Γ, Γ does not have to be an instance of one of its denominators, guarantees that when constructing a tableau we do not loop indefinitely by applying the same rule infinitely often. In the following definition, we introduce the static rules for our tableau method.

Definition 8 (Static Rules). *Let X be a finite set of formulas from $\mathcal{L}_{\mathsf{LDA}}$, then:*

$$\bot\text{-}rule\text{:}\ \frac{\psi; \neg\psi; X}{\bot} \qquad\qquad \wedge\text{-}rule\text{:}\ \frac{\psi \wedge \phi; X}{\psi; \phi; \psi \wedge \phi; X}$$

$$\neg\text{-}rule\text{:}\ \frac{\neg\neg\psi; X}{\psi; \neg\neg\psi; X} \qquad\qquad \triangle_i\text{-}rule\text{:}\ \frac{\triangle_i \alpha; X}{\Box_i \alpha; \triangle_i \alpha; X}$$

$$\vee\text{-}rule\text{:}\ \frac{\neg(\psi \wedge \phi); X}{\neg\psi; \neg(\psi \wedge \phi); X \mid \neg\phi; \neg(\psi \wedge \phi); X}$$

The following extra rules are used for the KD and KT variants of the logic.

Definition 9 (T-rule and D-rule). *Let X be a finite set of formulas from $\mathcal{L}_{LDA}$, then:*

$$T\text{-rule: } \frac{\Box_i\psi; X}{\psi; \Box_i\psi; X} \qquad D\text{-rule: } \frac{\Box_i\psi; X}{\Diamond_i\psi; \Box_i\psi; X}$$

The D-rule corresponds to the property of global consistency (GC) on multi-agent belief models, while the T-rule corresponds to the property of belief correctness (BC). This correspondence is captured by the function cf such that:

$$cf(\text{D-rule}) = GC$$
$$cf(\text{T-rule}) = BC$$

Lemma 1 (Monotonicity). *For all static rules distinct from $\bot$-rule, if Γ_k is a denominator of Γ then $\Gamma \subset \Gamma_k$.*

The transitional rule allows to generate a new successor for a certain agent i.

Definition 10 (Transitional Rule). *Let X be a finite set of formulas from $\mathcal{L}_{LDA}$, then:*

$$\Diamond_i: \frac{\Diamond_i\psi; X}{\psi; \{\phi | \Box_i\phi \in X\}}$$

Observe that the transitional rule preserves the subsets relation, i.e. if we have two sets Γ, Δ such that $\Gamma \subseteq \Delta$ and the transtional rule applies to Γ (and therefore to Δ) then, the denominators Γ', Δ' of applying the $\Diamond_i - rule$ for an agent i to Γ and Δ respectively also have the subset relation $\Gamma' \subseteq \Delta'$.

The following definition introduces the concept of tableau.

Definition 11 (Tableau). *Let $X \subseteq \{T\text{-rule}, D\text{-rule}\}$. A tableau for Γ is a tree such that each vertex v carries a pair (Γ', ρ), where Γ' is a set of formulas and ρ is either an instance of a static rule applicable to Γ', an instance of a rule from X applicable to Γ', a transitional rule applicable to Γ' or the empty rule nihil, the root carries a pair (Γ, ρ) for some tableau rule ρ and for every vertex v, if v carries the pair (Γ', ρ), then the following conditions hold:*

- *if Γ' is not saturated then $\rho \neq$ nihil, and*
- *if ρ has k denominators $\Gamma_1, \dots, \Gamma_k$ then v has exactly k children $v_1, \dots, v_k$ such that, for every $1 \leq h \leq k$, v_h carrics (Γ_h, ρ') for some tableau rule ρ'.*

Observe that any sub-tree of a tableau is also a tableau.
The following definition introduces the concept of closed tableau.

Definition 12 (Closed Tableau). *A branch in a tableau is a path from the root of the tableau to an end vertex, where an end vertex is a vertex carrying a pair (Γ', nihil). A branch in a tableau is closed if its end node is of the form $(\{\bot\}, \text{nihil})$. A tableau is closed if all its branches are closed, otherwise it is open.*

From this definition and the tableau definition follows that any sub-tree of a closed tableau is also a closed tableau.

The proof of the following theorem is provided in the article.

Theorem 1. *Let $\varphi \in \mathcal{L}_{LDA}$ and let $X \subseteq \{T\text{-rule}, D\text{-rule}\}$. Then, if φ is satisfiable for the class $\mathbf{M}_{\{cf(x):x\in X\}}$ then all tableaux for $\{\varphi\}$ are open.*

The algorithm that our proof induces, has to check if there is any closed-tableaux, and for that has to check every possible configuration. In order to reduce the search space, we introduce the concept of strategy.

Definition 13 (Strategy). *Let $<_\sigma$ be an order for the tableau rules. We say that a tableau follows the strategy $<_\sigma$ if for every vertex (Γ, ρ) in the tableau, if $\rho' <_\sigma \rho$ then ρ' doesn't apply to Γ.*

We introduce the concept of weakening which will be used on the next theorem.

Lemma 2 (Weakening). *Let $\Gamma, \Gamma' \subseteq \mathcal{L}_{LDA}$. If there is a closed tableau for Γ, then there is a closed tableau for $\Gamma \cup \Gamma'$.*

Proof. If τ is a tableau for Γ then, we can create a tree τ' isomorphic to τ by mapping every node $(\Delta, \rho) \to (\Delta \cup \Gamma', \rho)$, since ρ applies to Δ then ρ applies to $\Delta \cup \Gamma'$ therefore τ' is also a tableau which applies the same rules in the same order than τ, and because τ closes, τ' also closes. $\qquad\square$

Theorem 2. *Let $<_\sigma$ be the following total order of the tableau rules:*

$$\perp - rule < \triangle_i - rule < \wedge - rule < \vee - rule < T - rule < D - rule < \Diamond_i - rule$$

If there is a closed tableau, then there exists a closed tableau that follows the strategy $<_\sigma$.

Proof. Let τ be a closed tableau, for each edge $((\Gamma, \rho), (\Gamma', \rho')) \in \tau$ if ρ' applies to Γ and $\rho' <_\sigma \rho$ then, we will create a closed tableau τ' that replaces the sub-tree with root (Γ, ρ) with another closed tableau with root (Γ, ρ').

The intuition is, by using this operation repeatedly, we can "bubble sort" the tableau by "pushing upwards" the lesser operators whenever they apply to upper nodes.

For each pair of rules ρ, ρ', we need to prove that if there is a closed tableau τ having an edge $((\Gamma, \rho), (\Gamma', \rho')) \in \tau$, $\rho' <_\sigma \rho$ and ρ' applies to Γ, then there is a closed tableau with (Γ, ρ') as its root.

$(\Gamma, \perp - rule)$ There is an edge $((\Gamma, \rho), (\Gamma', \perp - rule)) \in \tau$ and $\perp - rule$ applies to Γ, then, by applying the $\perp - rule$ we have a closed tableau.

$(\Gamma, \Diamond_i - rule)$ There is an edge $(\Gamma, \Diamond_i - rule), (\Gamma', \rho)) \in \tau$ and ρ applies to Γ. As the rule ρ applies to Γ, consider Γ_2 the denominator of applying ρ to Γ, as ρ is a transitional rule distinct from $\perp - rule$, by monotonocity $\Gamma' \subseteq \Gamma_2$ let Γ'_2 the denominator of applying the $\Diamond_i - rule$ on Γ_2, as the transitional rule preserves subsets $\Gamma'' \subseteq \Gamma'_2$ since there is a closed tableau for $(\Gamma, \Diamond_i - rule)$ by weakening there is a closed tableau for Γ_2.

$(*, *)$ The rest of the cases are proven by induction on the number of rules that apply to elements of Γ, as we can assume all $\triangle_i$ rules have been applied and all applicable $\Diamond_i - rule$ have been applied. The well known proof by invertibility of rules for tableau in modal logic [3] will apply with no modifications.

$\square$

4 Algorithm

We assume all formulas in B have been translated in negated normal form (NNF).

```
 1: procedure IsSatisfiable(B,s,i)              ▷ under the semantics s, i is Nullable
 2:     Parallel r ← SAT(B) [wait = false] do
 3:         if (¬r) then
 4:             return |cancel, ⊥|
 5:         end if
 6:     end Parallel
 7:     Parallel r ← SAT(B) do
 8:         if matches((ψ ∧ ¬ψ, X), B) then
 9:             return |cancel, ⊥|
10:         end if
11:         if matches((△_iψ; X), B, i) then
12:             return |current, IsSatisfiable(ψ; △_iψ; □_iψ; X, s, i)|
13:         end if
14:         if matches((ψ ∧ ξ; X), B) then
15:             return |current, IsSatisfiable(ψ; ξ; X, s)|
16:         end if
17:         if matches((ψ ∨ ξ; X), B) then
18:             return |wait, IsSatisfiable(ξ; X, s) ∨ IsSatisfiable(ψ; X, s)|
19:         end if
20:         if matches(◊_iψ; X, B, i) then
21:             for i ← 1, n do
22:                 spawn IsSatisfiable(next(i, ◊ψ; X, B), s, i)
23:             end for
24:         end if
25:         return |wait, ⊤|
26:     end Parallel
27: end procedure
```

5 Example

In this section, we use the logic $\mathcal{L}_{LDA}$ to formalize a simple scenario of human-robot interaction in a dynamic domain inspired the famous Sally-Anne false belief's task from the psychological literature on Theory of Mind [1].

We assume that $Agt = \{h, r\}$ where h denotes the human and r denotes the robot. The scenario is depicted in Fig. 1. The human and the robot are standing in front of each other on the opposite sides of a table. The robot has two boxes and two balls in front of him: box 1, box 2, a black ball and a gray ball. In the initial situation the black ball is inside box 1 and the grey ball is inside box 2. The human can perfectly observe her actions as well as the robot's actions. Similarly, the robot can perfectly observe its actions as well as the human's actions. Moreover, the robot can see that the human can see its actions and the human can see that the robot can see her actions. Therefore, the perceptive context is described by the following set of formula from the language $\mathcal{L}_{OBS}$:

$$\Omega_1 = \{s_{r,r}, s_{h,h}, s_{r,h}, s_{h,r}, s_r s_{h,r}, s_h s_{r,h}\}.$$

Let the atomic proposition *blackIn1* denote the fact that the black ball is inside box 1 and let *blackIn2* denote the fact that the black ball is inside box 2. Similarly, let *greyIn1* and *greyIn2* denote, respectively, the fact that the grey ball is inside box 1 and the fact that the grey ball is inside box 2.

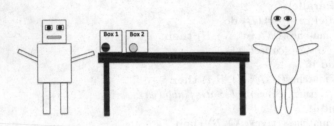

Fig. 1. Balls in the boxes scenario

We assume that in the initial situation the human does not explicitly believe that the black ball is inside box 1 and the human does not explicitly believe that the black ball is inside box 2, as she cannot see the box's content. Similarly, the human does not explicitly believe that the grey ball is inside box 1 and the human does not explicitly believe that the grey ball is inside box 2. We also assume that the robot does not explicitly believe that the human explicitly believes that the black ball is inside box 1 (resp. box 2) and that the robot does not explicitly believe that the human explicitly believes that the grey ball is inside box 1 (resp. box 2):

$$Hyp_1 \stackrel{\text{def}}{=} \neg\triangle_h \text{blackIn1} \wedge \neg\triangle_h \text{blackIn2} \wedge \neg\triangle_h \text{greyIn1} \wedge$$
$$\neg\triangle_h \text{greyIn2} \wedge \neg\triangle_r\triangle_h \text{blackIn1} \wedge \neg\triangle_r\triangle_h \text{blackIn2} \wedge$$
$$\neg\triangle_r\triangle_h \text{greyIn1} \wedge \neg\triangle_r\triangle_h \text{greyIn2}$$

Moreover, we assume that the robot explicitly believes that if the human explicitly believes that one ball is inside one box then she explicitly believes that the ball cannot be inside the other box:

$$Hyp_2 \stackrel{\text{def}}{=} \triangle_r((\triangle_h blackIn1 \rightarrow \triangle_h \neg blackIn2) \wedge$$
$$(\triangle_h blackIn2 \rightarrow \triangle_h \neg blackIn1) \wedge$$
$$(\triangle_h greyIn1 \rightarrow \triangle_h \neg greyIn2) \wedge$$
$$(\triangle_h greyIn2 \rightarrow \triangle_h \neg greyIn1))$$

We can use the logic $\mathcal{L}_{LDA}$ to infer that, in the perceptive context Ω_1, if the robot moves the black ball from box 1 to box 2 then, after the occurrence of the action, both the human and the robot will explicitly believe that the black ball is inside box 2, the robot will explicitly believe that the human explicitly believes that the black ball is inside box 2, and the robot will implicitly believe that the human explicitly believes that the black ball is outside box 1:

$$(Hyp1 \wedge Hyp2) \rightarrow [(r, + blackIn2, \Omega_1)](\triangle_r blackIn2 \wedge$$
$$\triangle_h blackIn2 \wedge$$
$$\triangle_r \triangle_h blackIn2 \wedge$$
$$\square_r \triangle_h \neg blackIn1)$$

Now, suppose the human moves away so that she cannot see anymore what the robot does and the robot knows this. In other words, let us suppose that the situation has changed into the following perceptive context Ω_2 in which the robot and the human can see their own actions but cannot see the actions of the other:

$$\Omega_2 = \{\mathsf{s}_{r,r}, \mathsf{s}_{h,h}\}.$$

In the new perceptive context Ω_2, if the robot moves the grey ball from box 2 to box 1 then, after the occurrence of the robot's action, the human will continue to believe that the black ball is inside box 2, without believing that the grey ball is inside box 1. Moreover, the robot still does not believe that the human believes that the grey ball is inside box 1:

$$(Hyp1 \wedge Hyp2) \rightarrow [(r, + blackIn2, \Omega_1)]$$
$$[(r, + greyIn1, \Omega_2)](\triangle_h blackIn2 \wedge$$
$$\neg \triangle_h greyIn1 \wedge \neg \triangle_r \triangle_h greyIn1)$$

Here it is the same example encoded for the tool's syntax, notice we encode the agent h as 1, and the agent r as 2, as numerical indexcs are required.

```
# Observe the semicolon ';' means conjunction (with the least precedence)
#Hypothesis 1
-{1}b1 & -{1}b2;        # Human doesn't explicitly believe either ball
-{1}g1 & -{1}g2;        # is in either box
-{2}{1}b1 & -{2}{1}b2;  # Robot doesn't explicitly believe the human believe
-{2}{1}g1 & -{2}{1}g2;  # if either ball is in either box
#Hypothesis 2
{2}({1}b1->{1}-b2;      # Robot explicitly believes that
    {1}b2->{1}-b1;      # if human believes any ball is in either box
    {1}g1->{1}-g2;      # then it also believes that such ball is not
    {1}g1->{1}-g2);     # in the other box (here enumerated the 4 options)

# The observation context is both observing each other
# and simultaneously aware of this fact and of themselves
-[( 2+b2; 1<1; 2<2; 1<2; 2<1; 1<2<1; 2<1<2 )](   # We set b2 true for the robot
   ({2}b2) & ({1}b2) & ({2}{1}b2);# All aware that black ball is in box 2
   \cite{ch12Fag87}{1}-b1              # Robot can conclude that human believes ...
)                          # ... that the black ball is not in box 1
```

As expected, after evaluating the translation, it returns that it is unsatisfiable. The tool is available for testing at https://tableau.irit.fr.

6   Implementation

6.1   Software, Architecture and Algorithms

We created a tool in the $F\sharp$ programming language (an open source, cross platform ML language for the Common Language Infrastructure (CLI)), that follows closely the paper as reference implementation, with the following speed improvements.

There are two separated API methods, one for the reduction of the dynamic extension, and the second for the evaluation of the satisfability given by the tableau procedure.

For the reduction of the dynamic extension, we implement the exact rewriting as specified in the paper, with no further optimization.

For the propositional case, we added a modern yet simple DPLL SAT solver, we focused more in having a clean and solid functional architecture for this rather than adding all possible heuristics, it is slower (2x–50x) than other modern SAT solver (we benchmark against Z3 [6]), and also is much simpler (the current implementation of the SAT solver has less than 1k lines of code). However, is written in $F\sharp$, so it is exactly as portable as the library itself, which simplifies enormously the development/testing and integration as compared as using a $C++$ library which is the language most modern SAT solvers are implemented. This solver is used to discard processes, but the solution when available, is given by the tableau itself. So this is only used to help speed up execution, and it can be disabled when calling the library.

We use a reactive asynchronous execution workflow that allows us to aggressively benefit from hardware parallelism when available.

We create a process tree which is the contraction of the tableau tree on the root node and all nodes created by applying a transitional rule. Each process runs a "SAT solver" for the propositional interpretation of the set of variables, and spawns one process for each transitional rule that would apply to the contracted tableau node. If the "SAT solver" is not satisfiable or any of the children sends a message saying it is unsatisfiable, it kills all remaining children and returns with the same message to its father. In other case, when all transitional children return a satisfactory configuration, it returns itself with the appropriate message to its father.

As we use immutable data structures, we can use shared memory between processes, in a safe and fast manner.

It is written entirely for the .net core platform, which runs in an array of architectures and operative systems, that include RaspberyPi, Linux, MacOs, Windows and the Windows 10 IoT which is rapidly increasing the array of hosts.

A trade off for the current version, is that we use a full in-memory approach. So, it runs well with models having few thousands of "modal" tableau nodes and few million propositional variables among them, but fails in much larger models, which we consider is acceptable for the kind of environments/problems the tool is designed for.

References

1. Baron-Cohen, S., Leslie, A.M., Frith, U.: Does the autistic child have a "theory of mind"? Cognition **21**(1), 37–46 (1985)
2. Fagin, R., Halpern, J.Y.: Belief, awareness, and limited reasoning. Artif. Intell. **34**(1), 39–76 (1987)
3. Goré, R.: Tableau methods for modal and temporal logics. In: D'Agostino, M., Gabbay, D.M., Hähnle, R., Posegga, J. (eds.) pp. 297–396. Springer, Dordrecht (1999). https://doi.org/10.1007/978-94-017-1754-0_6
4. Lorini, E.: In praise of belief bases: doing epistemic logic without possible worlds. In: Proceedings of the Thirty-Second AAAI Conference on Artificial Intelligence (AAAI 2018), pp. 1915–1922. AAAI Press (2018)
5. Lorini, E., Romero, F.: Decision procedures for epistemic logic exploiting belief bases. In: Proceedings of the 18th International Conference on Autonomous Agents and MultiAgent Systems (AAMAS 2019), IFAAMAS, pp. 944–952 (2019)
6. de Moura, L., Bjørner, N.: Z3: an efficient SMT solver. In: Ramakrishnan, C.R., Rehof, J. (eds.) TACAS 2008. LNCS, vol. 4963, pp. 337–340. Springer, Heidelberg (2008). https://doi.org/10.1007/978-3-540-78800-3_24

Jacamo-Web is on the Fly: An Interactive Multi-Agent System IDE

Cleber Jorge Amaral[1,2](✉) (iD) and Jomi Fred Hübner[2](✉) (iD)

[1] Federal Institute of Santa Catarina (IFSC), São José, SC, Brazil
cleber.amaral@ifsc.edu.br
http://www.ifsc.edu.br/
[2] Federal University of Santa Catarina (UFSC), Florianópolis, SC, Brazil
jomi.hubner@ufsc.br
http://pgeas.ufsc.br/en/

Abstract. This paper presents *jacamo-web*, an interactive programming IDE for developing Multi-Agent Systems (MAS). The standard programming method usually follows the sequence of compile, link and execute the application. Alternatively, the so-called interactive programming provides a way to modify a system while it is running. Besides saving developing time, it maintains the system's availability since the application is kept running while it is being changed. To illustrate *jacamo-web* interactive functions, we have developed a MAS for the financial market. It checks data of companies and applies known formulae to suggest whether to buy assets or not.

Keywords: Interactive programming · Just-in-time programming · Multi-agent oriented programming · On-the-fly programming · Incremental compiler

1 Introduction

Interactive programming is a way to develop a program while it is running, without stopping or restarting, acting directly over its instances [13]. It allows rapid prototyping, debugging and learning, as well as facilities for incremental development [7,12]. On the interactive approach, the programmer can enter a program or a fragment directly into an already running system. It reduces system development time since the usual compile-link-execute process is done in a single step [12]. This approach is also useful in cases where there is no precise specification of the problem at the design phase, and adaptations are required at run-time.

We can illustrate the interactive programming comparing a surgery with fixing a car. In the car case, we can stop it, lift the vehicle, proceed changes to fix some problem, and restart the engine. However, to treat an injured person

Supported by Petrobras project AG-BR, IFSC and UFSC.

by a surgery, we cannot interrupt the organism, it must be kept running. The interactive programming is like a surgery for computational systems. It also differs from standard programming because it generally acts on instances, i.e., it provides ways to fix the code of running entities. Usually, standard programming does not offer this facility. Standard programming focuses on providing tools to develop templates or classes which are the basis for generating static code instances.

Indeed, with this dynamic method, the software is "hot-swapped", allowing immediate execution making use of the existing instantiated data [6,8]. Among applications, the interactive programming is applied for algorithm development and data analysis in environments such as MATLAB®, R and SciLab, since it provides conductivity and convenience [4].

It is also useful for programming long term running systems, such as some open systems. Interactive programming gives tools to improve a part or the whole system at run-time [9]. For example, imagine stock market autonomous agents buying and selling all sorts of assets. It is usual that one needs to enhance some functions of the agents, for instance, their prediction models and decision-making rules. Interactive programming allows instantly applying such changes without stopping the agents.

This paper presents *jacamo-web* an Integrated Development Environment (IDE)[1], which uses the concept of interactive programming for the development of Multi-Agent Systems. It extends JaCaMo platform [5] adding facilities to create, modify and destroy agents, artifacts, and organisations at running time. This IDE is being shown by demonstrating an application of financial market consultants.

2   Jacamo-Web

JaCaMo is a Multi-Agent Oriented Programming (MAOP) platform that splits programming concerns of a MAS by the parts responsible for autonomous decisions: (i) the agents which are developed in Jason; (ii) their shared environment, programmed in CArtAgO; and (iii) the coordination of global behaviour, which is developed in MOISE [5]. *jacamo-web* implements RESTful endpoints to access JaCaMo functions, and adds a web interface for consuming such data allowing *users* to create, modify, interact with, and destroy agents, artifacts, and organisations. Although we have MAS IDEs where the agents themselves can modify the running system (by dynamically adding plans, changing beliefs of others, changing its organisation and environment). *jacamo-web* brings these features for the user (developer) using a web interface.

jacamo-web provides interactive functions of Read-Eval-Print Loop [11], in short REPL, paradigm. The acronym REPL refers to: Read user insertions, Evaluates them, Print the result for the user, all of this, repeatedly in a Loop [14]. This technology allows the user to send commands to agents, to insert new

---

[1] A demo application is running at http://jacamo-web.herokuapp.com/.

instructions or full blocks of code. Jason's API is equipped with REPL functions which are processed by Jason's internal interpreter.

In case of environmental artifacts, *jacamo-web* brings a built-in Java compiler. It allows the development of new artifacts by coding Java files which are compiled automatically. These new or changed artifacts can be used in the running system.

In the case of the organisation, *jacamo-web* allows the user to create new organisations and change those that are already running. For instance, the user can create, modify and remove roles, shared goals, coordination schemes, and norms.

3 Demonstration

The facilities provided by *jacamo-web* for users are demonstrated by the implementation of a MAS for the financial market. The organisation of the MAS has two roles: consultants, which read assets data to apply a particular formulae to suggest whether to buy it or not; and, assistants, which receive the user's requests, asking consultants about their opinions, compiling a final suggestion and replying to the user. The interface with final users is implemented using the Telegram cell phone application, which is being integrated through the Apache Camel framework [1,2].

Figure 1 shows the architecture of our application. *jacamo-web* extends JaCaMo which is a Java-based framework. *jacamo-web* implements RESTful endpoints for accessing JaCaMo facilities such as creating agents, send commands to them, and so on. For the financial agents application, we add another communication infrastructure based on an Apache Camel component called camel-jason. This infrastructure simplifies the integration of agents with external entities, the Telegram application, in our case.

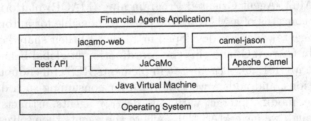

Fig. 1. Financial agents and *jacamo-web* architecture

In the financial market, there are some known investors that have shared the way they decide to buy an asset or not. For this demo, we adapt *Benjamin Graham*'s, *Decio Bazin*'s and *Joel Greenblatt*'s formulas [3,10][2]. Each of these

---

[2] Buying conditions: Graham: $Price < \sqrt{(22.5 * EPS * BVPS)}$; Greenblatt: $EBIT/(MarketCap + NetDebt) < 0.1$ and $ROIC < 0.1$; Bazin: $DY >= 0.06$ and $Debt/EV <= 1$.

decision rules is coded into agents with the same name as the original authors' formulae. These agents are connected to an artifact that gets financial data of assets from an external web-site. The assistant agent sends to the user consultant opinions as well as a summarised recommendation. The final recommendation is to *buy* the asset if at least two of the consultants are suggesting to buy.

To illustrate interactive functions *jacamo-web* is launching the *Financial Agents* project from JaCaMo project file definitions. This project has three consultant agents, one assistant agent, the artifact *fundamentus* and the organisation *financialorg*. The MAS is illustrated by the *jacamo-web* generated system's overview in Fig. 2. The diagram presents the organisation on the top where we have the group *financialteam* and the scheme *financialsch*. Below the organisation, the illustration presents the agents' dimension with the four created agents which play roles in the group and are committed with missions in the scheme. The bottom of the figure shows the environment dimension with the *workspace financialagents* and the artifact *fundamentus* in which some agents are focusing.

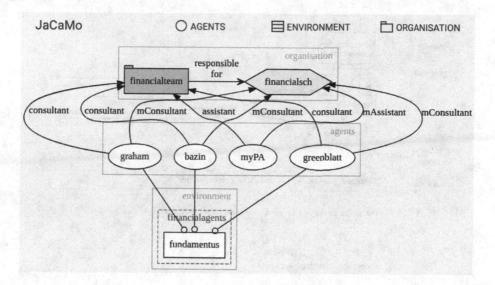

Fig. 2. Application overview showing runtime organisation, agents and environment

3.1 Agents' Interface

The agents' interface provides functions for creating, inspecting, editing and killing agents. Figure 3 is displaying the consultant *bazin*. The generated diagram illustrates *bazin*'s mind having two *namespaces*, *default* and *fundamentals*, in which its belief base is settled. This agent is focusing on the artifact *fundamentus*, it is playing the role *consultant* on the group *financialteam*, and it is committed to the mission *mConsultant* of the scheme *financialsch*.

One of the most important interactive facilities in MAS programming is plans library edition. *jacamo-web* provides two ways to interactively change agent's plans: (i) sending new plans using the `.send` internal action with the *tellHow* performative; and (ii) using the *jacamo-web* plans editor. In both ways, the agent keeps running without downtime. Old intentions that the agent is executing are not affected. However, the updated plans library will be used by new intentions of the agent. The main difference between these ways to edit plans regards to the persistence of the data. Plans added by *tellHow* are only added to the running instance of the agent. They are not persistent, i.e., if the agent is killed these plans are lost. In contrast, changes performed using the plans editor overwrites agent's model, i.e., they do not only affect the instance but they also modify the source code of the agent that is used when the agent is being launched.

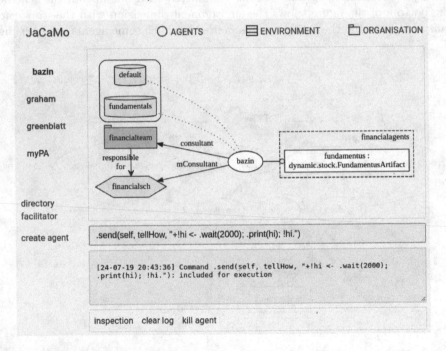

Fig. 3. Example of sending a plan by *tellHow* from command box on agent's interface

The first way to change an agent's plans library is shown in Fig. 3. We are sending a plan using the command box. In the figure, this box is shown just below the agent's diagram. The illustrated command uses the *tellHow* performative that adds a new know how knowledge in the agent's library, in this case, a plan which repeatedly prints the greeting "hi" every 2 s. After sending this command, a log box just below the command box displays a debug message saying that the command was included for execution. After being added to the plans library of the running instance of the agent, the new plan is ready to be executed. In other words, the agent has a new capability, in this example, the ability to say "hi" repeatedly.

The other way to change agent plans interactively is using *jacamo-web* plans editor as shown in Fig. 5. This interface is available from the inspection window by selecting an agent module to edit. The agent continues running normally while the user is coding. After editing and clicking on *Save & Reload* the plan library of the running agent is updated and its model is overwritten.

Using the plans editor interface, it is possible to make several changes in different plans at once as illustrated in Fig. 4. On the left side of the figure, there are two running intentions (*i1.1* and *i2.1*). They are respectively based on the plans *p1* and *p2*. The right side of the figure represents the new state of the agent's instance and model after an edition of its plans library. In this example, the user removed the plan *p1*, edited the plan *p2* and added a new plan called *p3*. It is shown that the old intentions *i1.1* and *i2.1* are kept without changes. Let us say that the agent generates a new intention from the plan it knows as *p2*. In this case, we are showing that this new intention will be based in the new version of this plan, here represented as *p2'*. In such situation, old and new intentions of a modified plan may coexist. Finally, in case of adding a plan, as exemplified, the plan *p3* could be used to generate the intention *i3.1*.

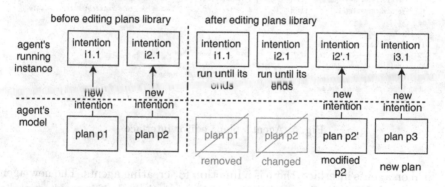

Fig. 4. The hot-swap function keeps old intentions while updates plans of the model.

In addition to agent's plans inspection, *jacamo-web* allows to inspect the agent's rules and belief base at running time as well as add, remove or change beliefs. A belief may be added just typing "+" followed by the belief in the command box of the agent. For instance, the command +divYield("itsa4",7.9), adds a belief that *dividend yield* of the *itsa4* asset is 7.9. The belief base can be inspected by the belief base inspection interface or by Jason test goals. In this case, the log box can be used to quickly show a piece of retrieved information using a test goal, e.g., typing in the command box ?divYield("itsa4",X); .print(X) the log prints the value 7.9.

The code completion function aids typing commands through the command box. This function provides suggestions of frequently used commands as the user types. It is based on a dictionary that is filled with all available internal actions this agent can perform, all available plans of this agent, and all external operations provided by any artifact this agent is focusing on. This facility improves the productivity during the system development and help users to learn available operations.

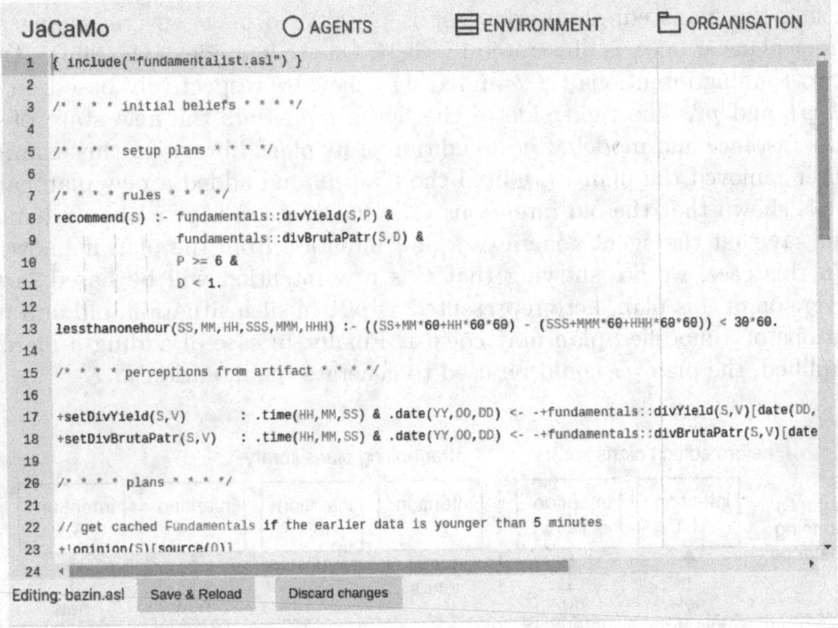

Fig. 5. Agent's plans editor interface

Still on agents interface, there is a function for creating agents. The new agent starts with a default code or with an existing agent's code if its name matches with an existing Jason's model (from an asl file). Alternatively, an agent can be created using the internal action `.create_agent` that can be executed by the command box of an existing agent. The interface also provides a function for killing the selected agent.

Finally, agents can also interactively be registered or deregistered from the *directory facilitator*. Again, using the command box it is possible to send commands to the running agent. For instance, from the agent graham we can call the command `.df_register(consultant)` to inform that this agent may perform the *consultant* service. The interface of *directory facilitator* shows a table with all the agents and the services they can provide.

3.2   Environment's Interface

For the environment programming, *jacamo-web* provides interface for inspecting *workspaces* and artifacts. Figure 6 shows the inspection of the artifact *fundamentus* which is in the workspace *financialagents*. The diagram shows that this instance is based on the template *dynamic.stock.FundamentusArtifact* and it is being focused by three agents. The artifact has no observable property since the box bellow its name is blank and it has two operations that agents can act on: `observeProperty` and `getFundamentals`.

In JaCaMo artifacts are created and destroyed by agents using the external actions `makeArtifact` and `disposeArtifact` respectively. In other words, JaCaMo already provides facilities to dynamically change the elements of the environment. *jacamo-web* introduces a way to create templates at running time which makes agents able to create artifacts based on templates that did not exist at the time the system was launched. The templates creation function opens a Java editor allowing the user to fill the new template with an artifact's model. After created, *jacamo-web* compiles the code and loads the model. An agent can build instances based on this new template.

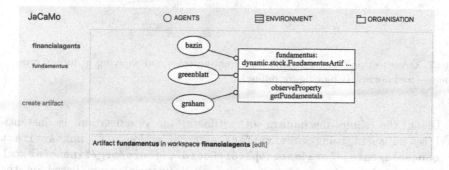

Fig. 6. Inspecting an artifact with *edit* template option.

jacamo-web also allows to *edit* an artifact template. In the same way of template creation, when editing an artifact template the user is changing the model which do not impact in the running instances of artifacts. In this sense, although *jacamo-web* is providing a built-in Java compiler making possible to add and edit templates while the system is running, it is still not possible to make changes on instances code in a REPL way. When it is desired to update an existing artifact instance, an agent has to dispose the running artifact and, after that, create a new one which will use the most updated template.

3.3   Organisation's Interface

In the organisation dimension, *jacamo-web* has functionalities to inspect them in different perspectives as shown in Fig. 7 in which *financialagents* organisation is being examined. The interface allows to show or hide groups, schemes and norms. It can be exploited by the user for consulting aspects such as the composition of groups, check whether the goals of a given scheme were already achieved or not, and so on. In the illustration, the schemes are shown on the top; the green text is the goal that is being achieved at the moment. The scheme is linked with the groups by norms which inform the commitment of the agents with the goals. The scheme and the group are shown in dark yellow colour which represents that they are well-formed since cardinalities were respected.

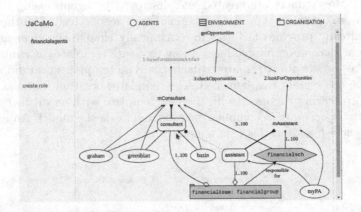

Fig. 7. Organisation's interface allowing creating roles and showing or hiding groups, schemes and norms. (Color figure online)

Using the same mechanism of artifacts, an organisation is instantiated by an agent using `makeArtifact` external action, e.g., `makeArtifact (financialagents, "ora4mas.nopl.OrgBoard", ["src/org/financial.xml"], OrgArtId)` creates an organisation called financialagents based on the descriptive model presented in the file financial.xml. JaCaMo supports creating and changing organisations in many aspects through commands executed by agents, which can also be executed by the user using the command box of a running agent. In addition to these inherited facilities, *jacamo-web* allows users to change the organisation's structure by creating non-persistent roles which can later be adopted by agents.

4   Conclusions

We have presented *jacamo-web*, an extension of JaCaMo a framework for the development of MAS. *jacamo-web* has shown that it can shorten the project life cycle. We could take advantage of instantiated contexts and quickly get responses from new code insertions. While developing a system like this financial application, we are often faced by common situations that need changes on agents, environment and organisations. *jacamo-web* allows applying such changes at running time, and the results are shown instantly. In case of open systems, they are supposed to be available for new entrants where IDE like *jacamo-web* are useful to help maintain the system's availability. In addition, we think it also facilitates to understand programming aspects, being an important tool for didactic purposes. As far as we know, *jacamo-web* is the first interactive MAOP IDE where the user can interact with the system while it is running.

References

1. Amaral, C.J., et al.: Finding new routes for integrating multi-agent systems using apache camel (2019)
2. Amaral, C.J., Cranefield, S., Hübner, J.F., Roloff, M.L.: Giving camel to artifacts for Industry 4.0 integration challenges. In: Demazeau, Y., Matson, E., Corchado, J.M., De la Prieta, F. (eds.) PAAMS 2019. LNCS (LNAI), vol. 11523, pp. 232–236. Springer, Cham (2019). https://doi.org/10.1007/978-3-030-24209-1_20
3. Bazin, D.: Faça Fortuna com Ações, Antes que seja Tarde, 6a edn. CLA Cultural (2006)
4. Bezanson, J., Karpinski, S., Shah, V.B., Edelman, A.: Julia: a fast dynamic language for technical computing. MIT, pp. 1–27 (2012). http://arxiv.org/abs/1209.5145
5. Boissier, O., Bordini, R.H., Hübner, J.F., Ricci, A.: Dimensions in programming multi-agent systems. Knowl. Eng. Rev. **34**, e2 (2019). https://doi.org/10.1017/S026988891800005X
6. Cascaval, C., Duesterwald, E., Sweeney, P.F., Wisniewski, R.W.: Performance and environment monitoring for continuous program optimization. IBM J. Res. Dev. **50**(2.3), 239–248 (2010). https://doi.org/10.1147/rd.502.0239
7. Choi, W.: Rehearse: coding interactively while prototyping. In: Extended Abstracts of UIST 2008, vol. 8, pp. 1–3 (2008)
8. Kistler, T., Franz, M.: Continuous program optimization: design and evaluation. IEEE Trans. Comput. **50**(6), 549–567 (2001). https://doi.org/10.1109/12.931893
9. Lattner, C., Vikram, A.: LLVM: a compilation framework for lifelong program analysis & transformation. In: Lattner, C., Adve, V. (eds.) International Symposium on Code Generation and Optimization, CGO, vol. 1, no. 4, pp. 75–86 (2004). https://doi.org/10.1109/CGO.2004.1281665
10. Reese, J., Forehand, J.: The Guru Investor: How to Beat the Market Using History's Best Investment Strategies. Wiley, Hoboken (2009)
11. Seibel, P.: Practical Common Lisp. The Expert's Voice in Programming Languages, 1st edn. Apress, New York (2005)
12. Tung, S.H.S.: Interactive modular programming in scheme. ACM SIGPLAN Lisp Point. **V**(1), 86–95 (1992). https://doi.org/10.1145/141478.141512
13. Wang, G., Cook, P.R.: On-the-fly programming: using code as an expressive musical instrument. In: NIME 2004 Proceedings of the 2004 Conference on New Interfaces for Musical Expression (2004). https://doi.org/10.1017/S1092852916000900
14. Wenzel, M.: READ-EVAL-PRINT in parallel and asynchronous proof-checking. In: Electronic Proceedings in Theoretical Computer Science, vol. 118, pp. 57–71 (2013). https://doi.org/10.4204/EPTCS.118.4. http://arxiv.org/abs/1307.1944v1

Author Index

Printed in the United States
By Bookmasters